Law, Society, Policy series

Series Editor: **Rosie Harding**,
University of Birmingham

Law, Society, Policy seeks to offer a new outlet for high
quality, socio-legal research monographs and edited
collections with the potential for policy impact.

Also available in the series:

Pandemic Legalities:
Legal Responses to COVID-19 – Justice and Social
Responsibility
Edited by **Dave Cowan** and **Ann Mumford**

Women, Precarious Work and Care:
The Failure of Family-friendly Rights

By **Emily Grabham**

D1613189

Find out more at

bristoluniversitypress.co.uk/law-society-policy

Law, Society, Policy series

Series Editor: **Rosie Harding**,
University of Birmingham

Find out more at
bristoluniversitypress.co.uk/law-society-policy

DEPRIVATION OF LIBERTY IN THE SHADOWS OF THE INSTITUTION

Lucy Series

BRISTOL
UNIVERSITY
PRESS

First published in Great Britain in 2022 by

Bristol University Press
University of Bristol
1–9 Old Park Hill
Bristol
BS2 8BB
UK
t: +44 (0)117 954 5940
e: bup-info@bristol.ac.uk

Details of international sales and distribution partners are available at
bristoluniversitypress.co.uk

British Library Cataloguing in Publication Data
A catalogue record for this book is available from the British Library

ISBN 978-1-5292-1199-3 paperback
ISBN 978-1-5292-1200-6 OA PDF
ISBN 978-1-5292-1201-3 OA ePub

Cover design: Andrew Corbett
Front cover image: The Time Chamber
Bristol University Press uses environmentally responsible print partners
Printed and bound in Great Britain by CMP, Poole

For Chris, Megan and Jamie

Contents

Cover Description

The book cover is black, with the title and author's name in white writing at the top, and the publisher's logo at the bottom. Below the title is an image of room with light coming in through windows and a large pair of glass doors, which are thrown open, on the right-hand side. On the left is a short flight of stairs leading to another room. The warm colour and low angle of the light suggest it is early morning or evening. The room inside is lit up but the small square frames on the doors and windows cast long shadows. You can glimpse trees outside the window. The room is unfurnished, with a brown carpet, white ceiling tiles and long strip lights, which are turned off. The photograph is of a large room – possibly a day room – in the West Sussex County Asylum, later known as Graylingwell Hospital, which closed in 2003. The photographs were taken in 2017 by two (anonymous) brothers, whose website, *The Time Chamber* (https://thetimechamber.co.uk/), documents empty and derelict buildings, including many former asylums.

List of Abbreviations

ADASS	Association of Directors of Adult Social Services
AMCP	Approved Mental Capacity Professional
AMHP	Approved Mental Health Professional
ATU	assessment and treatment unit
BIA	best interests assessor
CCG	clinical commissioning group
CIW	Care Inspectorate Wales
CMH	Campaign for the Mentally Handicapped (subsequently Values into Action)
CPT	European Committee on the Prevention of Torture and Inhuman and Degrading Treatment
CSA	Care Standards Act 2000
CQC	Care Quality Commission
CRPD	Convention on the Rights of Persons with Disabilities
CRPD Committee	Committee on the Rights of Persons with Disabilities
CSCI	Commission for Social Care Inspection
CTO	Community Treatment Order
DoLS	Deprivation of Liberty Safeguards scheme contained in Schedules A1 and 1A Mental Capacity Act 2005
DPM	disabled people's movement
ECHR	European Convention on Human Rights
ECPT	European Convention for the Prevention of Torture and Inhuman or Degrading Treatment or Punishment
ECtHR	European Court of Human Rights
EHRC	Equality and Human Rights Commission
EWCA	England and Wales Court of Appeal
HIW	Healthcare Inspectorate Wales
HRA	Human Rights Act 1998
HSCA	Health and Social Care Act 2008

ICCPR	International Covenant on Civil and Political Rights
ICU	intensive care unit
IMCA	independent mental capacity advocate
JCHR	Parliamentary Joint Committee on Human Rights
LPS	Liberty Protection Safeguards
MCA	Mental Capacity Act 2005
MHA	Mental Health Act (referring to the 1983 Act unless otherwise specified)
MHAC	Mental Health Act Commission
MWCS	Mental Welfare Commission for Scotland
NAA	National Assistance Act 1948
NCSC	National Care Standards Commission
NDT	National Development Team
NHS	National Health Service
NPM	National Preventive Mechanism
OPCAT	United Nations Optional Protocol on the Convention Against Torture
RPR	relevant person's representative
RTRS	*Registering the Right Support*
UDHR	Universal Declaration of Human Rights
UKSC	United Kingdom Supreme Court
VIA	Values into Action (formerly the Campaign for the Mentally Handicapped)

Acknowledgements

I have many people to thank, without whom this book would either not exist or would be measurably poorer.

This work would not have happened at all without a Wellcome Society and Ethics Research Fellowship, which I was fortunate enough to be awarded to study problems of empowerment under mental capacity law (grant reference number 200381/Z/15/Z). I regret I cannot thank him in person, but Paul Woodgate was immensely supportive before and during my fellowship and his loss is keenly felt.

Thanks to my colleagues at the School of Law and Politics, Cardiff University, which has been a wonderful home for this research. Particular thanks go to Phil Fennell, an early mentor and inspiration for this work, and to John Harrington for his kind critical feedback on draft chapters. Deep thanks also to Mary Donnelly, John Coggon and Alex Ruck Keene for their generosity and kindness in commenting on drafts. I regret I could not do justice to all their valuable insights and any mistakes are my own.

I would like to thank my publishers at Bristol University Press, particularly Helen Davis and the series editor Rosie Harding, who encouraged me to write this monograph, and Freya Trand for her assistance.

During the course of this research, I have had many valuable conversations and exchanges with people far more knowledgeable than I am about deinstitutionalization, legislation, regulation, philosophy and sociology. For the Oñati workshop on the legacies of institutionalization, which prompted me to write this book, I would like to thank Linda Steele, Claire Spivakovsky, Penny Weller and Sheila Wildeman. For other important conversations and exchanges of information and ideas I would like to thank Alison Tarrant, Andrew Holman, Camilla Parker, Dario Castiglioni, Dave Cowan, David Ferleger, Dawn Booker, Dawn Wallace, Diana Rose, Emily Kakoullis, Jane Meadus, Jean Collins, John Chesterman, Julie Doughty, Kevin Stone, Lorraine Currie, Luke Clements, Mervyn Eastman, Michael Bach, Nan Carle Beauregard, Neil Crowther, Nik Rose, Peter Bartlett, Rachel Griffiths, Rachel Hubbard, Rob Greig, Rosemary Hunter, Simon Jarrett, Steve Dowson, Theresa Joyce and Tom O'Shea.

I would also like to thank – although I shall not name them here – those I have interviewed for the 'other' book, next to be written, on the history of the MCA and its contested legacies of empowerment. These interviews provided valuable contextual information on the history of social care detention.

Finally, I should like to thank those people who have kept me (relatively) sane, fed, supported, and loved during the rather arduous journey this book has taken through a pandemic, maternity leave, and various illnesses and crises: my beloved family, Chris, Megan and Jamie, and my extended family and friends.

A Note on Terminology

This book is fraught with terminological challenges. It concerns populations and care settings without nationally or internationally agreed upon descriptors, and where terms used in law or policy can be laden with stigma and problematic implications; some historical frameworks use language considered insulting or offensive today (and likely also at the time).

For present-day terminology, when discussing matters *in general*, I use the terms commonly found in contemporary disability rights literature: 'psychosocial disabilities' (not mental illness or 'mentally ill'); 'cognitive disabilities' meaning disabilities linked to cognitive impairments such as dementia, brain injury or developmental disability; and 'people with intellectual disabilities' referring specifically to *developmental* cognitive impairments. When referring collectively to people with cognitive, psychosocial, developmental and similar disabilities I use the term 'mental disabilities'. While this is far from ideal I have yet to find a satisfactory alternative (suggestions warmly welcomed). I apologize for any offence given for not using alternative preferred terms within different communities.

When writing about specific legislation or policy, I have adopted the original terms therein because they often carried specific technical and socio-cultural meanings, and substituted terms risk inaccuracy. This means that at times I have had to write about 'mad' people, 'lunatics', 'idiots', 'subnormality' and 'mental defectives', because this was the terminology of the day. When introducing these terms I place them within quotes to stress this is not my preferred term but is the term used in the legislation or policy.

For the same reason, when discussing Anglo-Welsh law and policy I use 'learning disability' (to refer to people with intellectual disabilities, often defined clinically as an IQ below 70) and 'mental disorder'. 'Patients' usually refer to hospital inpatients, and 'service users' to people using formal health and social care services.

Occasionally I use 'P', a technical term connected to the Mental Capacity Act 2005, which is defined in the Court of Protection Rules as a person who lacks, or is alleged to lack, the mental capacity to make a particular decision.

When pinpointing a quotation, page numbers are given in rounded brackets and paragraph numbers in square brackets.

In several places I have quoted legal sources (cases or statutes) that refer to the masculine gender (that is, to 'he' or 'his' etc); the legal convention codified under s6 Interpretation Act 1978 is that 'words importing the masculine gender include the feminine'.

Series Editor's Preface

The Law, Society, Policy series publishes high-quality, socio-legal research monographs and edited collections with the potential for policy impact. Cutting across the traditional divides of legal scholarship, Law, Society, Policy offers an interdisciplinary, policy engaged approach to socio-legal research which explores law in its social and political contexts with a particular focus on the place of law in everyday life.

The series seeks to take an explicitly society-first view of socio-legal studies, with a focus on the ways that law shapes social life, and the constitutive nature of law and society. International in scope, engaging with domestic, international and global legal and regulatory frameworks, texts in the Law, Society, Policy series engage with the full range of socio-legal topics and themes.

1

Introduction

The socio-legal landscape of care is haunted by its carceral past. The asylums, workhouses, 'mental deficiency colonies' and large psychiatric hospitals that once warehoused thousands of men, women and children in England and Wales have almost all have been demolished, or repurposed as flats, prisons, schools, wedding venues even. People who might once have been incarcerated in those large Victorian buildings now live in a mythical space called 'the community', whose identity within the contemporary landscape of care derives from it being other than 'an institution'. The current prevailing ideology of care in countries like the United Kingdom is post-carceral (Unsworth, 1991), a succession of policies and initiatives promoting 'ordinary' or 'normal' lives in homes in the community, elevating autonomy, independence, 'person-centred' care, and choice and control. Post-carceral ideology takes aim not only at the carceral era's buildings, but at its institutionalizing core.

The community is a complicated place, easier to define by what it is not (a hospital) than what it is. Successive waves of post-carceral policy have deposited different care structures and settings on its shores. There are the first-wave quasi-institutions, which still predominate in the care of older people: residential care homes and nursing homes. Then there are second-wave quasi-domestic services, aspiring to break free of our institutional heritage: 'supported living', 'independent living', sheltered housing, and other kinds of 'housing with support'. Some families open their homes to receive strangers into their lives and care for them there ('shared lives'). There are respite services, day services, specialist educational services. Then there are ordinary domestic homes, the flats and houses that most UK citizens live in, where people might live alone or with family or friends. There, they might be cared for by loved ones, supported by homecare agencies or directly employed personal assistants, or by nobody at all.

The inhabitants of the post-carceral landscape of care make different journeys through it. Some are cared for where they have lived most of their life. Some move from places they call home into places they (or others) hope will become a home. Some move into services and settings intended to be temporary or transitional but could remain there for many years. Some move back and forth between 'the community' and hospital care, or through different community services. These moves, or support to stay put, might be arranged by the person themselves if they have both funds and the 'mental capacity' to make decisions for themselves. If they 'lack capacity' but have sufficient funds to pay for care, then private arrangements might be made by family members or others with formal authority to manage their property and affairs. Or, if a person lacks sufficient funds, or nobody else makes the necessary arrangements for them, their care might be arranged and funded by local authority social services. If their health needs are sufficiently severe, care might be funded and arranged by the National Health Service (NHS).

More than half a century into the post-carceral era, a new legal question settled over this landscape: *are some people deprived of their liberty by care arrangements in the community?* This question shakes the existential and socio-legal foundations of the post-carceral era. Care in the community signified freedom, liberation from the institution's carceral structures. Deprivation of liberty by community care arrangements – which I will refer to throughout this book as 'social care detention' – sounds like an oxymoron, a contradiction in terms. In the wake of this question, public and private spheres fold into one another, regulatory frontiers between institutional and domestic spaces dissolve.

To some, it sounds like a philosophers' question, answerable from an armchair, beckoning further questions: must you be a particular kind of subject to possess liberty in order to be deprived of it? What kind of liberty is at stake? The answer to the question is important, but equally important is why it has been posed at all. Questions of liberty are potent with tactics and tools, arguments and activism. Liberty is a powerful rallying cry in liberal democracies, and the conclusion that people are detained in post-carceral care settings has powerful consequences. This book tells the story of how and why we have come to ask whether some older and disabled people are deprived of their liberty by care arrangements in the community, and with what consequences.

Social care detention: a post-carceral socio-legal phenomenon

The socio-legal phenomenon at the heart of this book, social care detention, is currently under-examined and under-theorized within legal and critical disability scholarship. This may reflect the low status of 'social care' itself, associated with gendered reproductive labour, bodywork, 'chronic care' of 'unproductive' bodies, in contrast with the 'science based and cure-oriented' high status of medicine (Twigg, 2000: 112). Or this may reflect a historically produced sense that social care exists 'outside the law'; a major theme of this book.

I approach social care detention as a particular regulatory framing – safeguards for individual liberty – imposed over an underlying material reality of 'institutional', restrictive, supervisory and sometimes coercive practices in post-carceral community care settings. It is more closely entangled with the rationalities, administrative apparatus and personnel of social care than its near relation, mental health detention, whose centre of gravity remains the hospital and whose lead profession remains psychiatry. Social care detention also targets different populations than mental health detention; primarily older adults, people with intellectual disabilities and those with neurological or 'brain' based disease. It operates under different legal machinery – the Mental Capacity Act 2005 (MCA) – whereas the Mental Health Act 1983 (MHA) remains the main vehicle for mental health detention. The MCA is closely tied to the workings and norms of the post-carceral era (outlined in Chapters 4, 5 and 7), whereas the MHA is a direct descendant of our carceral past. I explore the characteristics of social care detention in Chapter 2, and stress the importance of not conflating its logics, workings or critiques with mental health detention: this is a distinct phenomenon, posing different (but no less challenging) critical questions.

This book examines the emergence of social care detention in England and Wales during the 21st century, and its roots in our carceral past. However, deprivation of liberty in community care settings is also recognized and regulated in a number of other countries. Some of these have close ties to the Anglo-Welsh legal system, such as Northern Ireland (Mental Capacity Act (Northern Ireland) 2016) and the islands of Jersey (Jersey Capacity and Self-Determination Law 2016), Guernsey (Capacity (Bailiwick of Guernsey) Law, 2020) and Gibraltar (Lasting Power of Attorney and Capacity Act 2018 (Gibraltar)). Social care detention is also recognized and regulated in several European countries with different legal traditions, such as Germany, Austria, Switzerland, the Czech Republic and Poland (Boente, 2017; Public Defender of Rights, 2017; Polish Commissioner for Human Rights, 2018). Some jurisdictions, such as Scotland and the Republic of Ireland, are currently consulting upon or developing new legislation to regulate social care detention (Scottish Law Commission, 2014; Scottish Government, 2016, 2018b; Department of Health (Ireland), 2017, 2019).

In several other Western jurisdictions, social care detention is not currently recognized by governments or within domestic law, but there are growing calls from activists, advocates and others concerned with the rights of older and disabled people for states to do so. For example, in Australia (Williams et al, 2014; Chandler et al, 2016, 2018a, 2018b; Grenfell, 2019), Canada (Law Commission of Ontario, 2017; Canadian Centre for Elder

Law, 2019), the USA (Kazin, 1989; Kapp, 1998; see discussion of ADAPT leaflet in Ben-Moshe, 2020: 255), Slovenia (Human Rights Ombudsman of the Republic of Slovenia, 2018), Croatia (Ombudsman of the Republic of Croatia, 2017), and Cyprus (Commissioner for the Administration and Protection of Human Rights (Cyprus, 2019). Several countries have seen recent litigation concerning 'deprivation of liberty' in community care services, including France (Conseil d'État, Juge des référés No 439822 8 avril 2020), Ireland (*AC v Patricia Hickey General Solicitor and Ors & AC v Fitzpatrick and Ors* [2019] IESC 73), and Australia (*Skyllas v Retirement Care Australia (Preston) Pty Ltd* [2006] VSC 409; *Sarah White v Local Health Authority & Anor* [2015] NSWSC 417). In Peru, litigation identified deprivation of liberty of a disabled man by his family in their home (*José Antonio Guillén Tejada* TRIBUNAL CONSTITUCIONAL. 2019. Sentencia recaída en el Exp. 0019-2014-PHC/TC (Peru)). International human rights bodies and human rights litigation have played a pivotal role in developing and disseminating the concept of social care detention, discussed in Chapter 5.

The form that social care detention safeguards take, and what is considered to be a deprivation of liberty in social care and community settings, can differ significantly between jurisdictions. In 2014 the UK Supreme Court ruled on the 'acid test' of deprivation of liberty in community care settings in *P v Cheshire West and Chester Council and another; P and Q v Surrey County Council* [2014] United Kingdom Supreme Court (UKSC) 19. Following *Cheshire West* it is likely that England and Wales have the most far-reaching system of recognition and regulation of social care detention globally. The Supreme Court was asked to consider whether three people with intellectual disabilities living in a small group home, a 'supported living' setting, and with a foster parent, were deprived of their liberty. Giving the leading judgment, Lady Hale held that a person who 'lacks capacity' to consent to their care arrangements, who is subject to 'continuous supervision and control' and is 'not free to leave', is deprived of their liberty irrespective of whether they are cared for in an 'institutional', community or even 'domestic' setting, whether they appear content, and whether their care is in their 'best interests' and the 'least restrictive' possible (*Cheshire West*, UKSC, [48–50], [71]–[72]).

This acid test of deprivation of liberty was adopted by a majority of Supreme Court justices. The dissenting justices expressed consternation that benign-seeming care arrangements in 'domestic' settings for people with intellectual disabilities could be construed as a 'deprivation of liberty'. For the majority, the ruling applied the logic of universal human rights to the liberty of disabled people: if these circumstances would amount to a deprivation of liberty for a non-disabled person, then so they must for a disabled person. Yet for the dissenting justices, the outcome of the acid test defied 'ordinary language' (*Cheshire West*, UKSC, [99], [108]). They pointed out that by dissolving the traditional distinction between 'institution' and 'home',

Cheshire West extends the machinery of deprivation of liberty safeguards into 'private' spheres of care, including – potentially – into family life itself. They questioned whether people once 'liberated' from institutions by landmark deprivation of liberty rulings were now likely to be considered 'deprived of their liberty' back in their homes in the community. In Chapter 8, I map the discursive contours of the deprivation of liberty litigation leading up to and including the Supreme Court's ruling, calling attention to the ways in which the common sense invoked by the dissenting justices was historically and culturally produced during carceral and early post-carceral eras. I examine how the deprivation of liberty framing was advanced and resisted inside and outside the courts.

The outcome in *Cheshire West* has a transgressive quality, identifying care arrangements for older and disabled people that are widely accepted and relied upon throughout Western societies, as forms of detention. This does not sit easily alongside popular understandings of care homes as benign spaces, nor of supported accommodation as the apotheosis of deinstitutionalization. Instead, it calls to understandings that lurk deeper in our cultural unconsciousness, of new carceral spaces and practices in 'the community'. *Cheshire West*, and social care detention more generally, challenge a cherished sense of ourselves as a post-carceral society.

Following the *Cheshire West* ruling, it was estimated that over 300,000 older and disabled people might require 'safeguards' for individual liberty in England and Wales. In Chapter 9, I examine how this threw existing systems for regulating social care detention into disarray and produced some deeply paradoxical outcomes. *Cheshire West* catapulted the UK to the forefront of global trends in recognizing and regulating social care detention. The searching questions it poses over the meaning of liberty in the post-carceral era, and the regulatory dilemmas faced in England and Wales in responding to it, will be of interest in other jurisdictions grappling with similar questions.

This book explores how and why social care detention has come to be so widely defined and extensively regulated in England and Wales. Part of the answer lies in the emergence of liminal, contested spaces of care in 'the community'; places that were intended – at least by some – to provide homes and respite from our carceral past, yet which share more than a passing resemblance to the characteristics of 'institutions'. Alex Fox (2018) and Simon Jarrett (2020) refer to this as an 'invisible asylum', where integration into community is partial, conditional on assessments of risk, capacity, and resources.

Regulating the 'invisible asylum'

These liminal spaces, where the logics of 'home' and 'institution' collide, are well documented within critical disability studies and related disciplines of sociology, carceral studies and geographies of care. Community care has been described as part of a broader 'institutional archipelago' (Ben-Moshe et al, 2014: 14), echoing Foucault's (1977a) disciplinary 'carceral archipelago'. In the post-carceral era the monolithic carceral institution, with its visible walls and clearly delineated spatial and regulatory boundaries, has been replaced by a carceral 'continuum' or 'matrix' (Ben-Moshe, 2013) extending from traditional sites of detention – prisons and hospitals – out into community settings of residential and nursing homes (for example, Spivakovsky, 2017), supported accommodation (for example, Drinkwater, 2005), and – some argue – even family homes (for example, Ben-Moshe, 2020: 22).

This is not a simplistic account of 'transcarceration' from one location to another, as if the experiences of a person living in a 1,000-bedded hospital at the height of the carceral era were identical to that of an older person in a 30-bedded care home, or a person with an intellectual disability in a small group home. Rather, it challenges us to engage in a deeper understanding of the dynamics of the carceral institution, to explore how its logics have (and have not) diffused across diverse loci in the community, and its entanglements with law. In Chapter 6, I argue that one way of distinguishing 'home' from 'institution' is the kind of 'decision spaces' they afford. Drawing from rich scholarship on 'total institutions' (Goffman, 1961) and the meanings of home (Fox O'Mahony, 2006), I argue that in their idealized senses, 'homes' are associated with critical opportunities for decision making – central to the development and expression of identity, whereas 'institutions' are associated with constrained decision spaces, where even remaining 'choices' are invigilated by others, leading to harmful effects for self, identity and well-being.

Determining the spatial and legal boundaries of 'the institution' is not straightforward in the post-carceral era. In Chapter 4, I describe how policymakers, activists and pioneers in community living sought to close down carceral institutions and replace them with non-institutional alternatives – *homes* in the community. However, 'institutional' dynamics emerged even in these new spaces, a phenomenon I call the 'institutional treadmill'. In Chapters 4 and 6, I explain how the economics of care, and the logics of legal incapacity, can imperil even those decision spaces that are intended or described as 'homes', creating what some call 'mini-institutions' in the community. These liminal spaces create considerable dilemmas for courts and regulators tasked with categorizing them as either 'institutions' or 'homes', considered in Chapter 7.

Why, then, have questions of liberty taken root in these liminal spaces of care? I borrow Ben-Moshe's (2020) distinction between abolitionist and reformist approaches to disability incarceration, to explain how deprivation of liberty framings are used both by those seeking to eradicate *all* carceral care arrangements (abolitionists) and those seeking to reform them via regulation (reformers). In legal terms, abolitionist advocacy is often connected to the UN Convention on the Rights of Persons with Disabilities (CRPD; United Nations, 2006a), explored in Chapter 5. The universalist ethos of *Cheshire West* reflects the CRPD's strong affirmation of full and equal legal personhood of disabled people sometimes described as a new 'paradigm' of human rights. The right to liberty contained within article 14 CRPD is understood by many as requiring the abolition of *all* forms of deprivation of liberty connected with disability (Doyle Guilloud, 2019). However, the *Cheshire West* acid test of deprivation of liberty poses unique challenges to abolitionists, picked up in Chapters 5 and 11.

Meanwhile many reformers have hoped that recognizing certain 'community' care arrangements as a deprivation of liberty will secure for their inhabitants certain regulatory advantages. These advantages are linked to a bundle of substantive and procedural rights connected to article 5 of the European Convention on Human Rights (ECHR; Council of Europe, 1950), the right to liberty and security of the person. Article 5 expresses an intrinsically reformist paradigm of the right to liberty, in contrast with abolitionist readings of the CRPD. For these reformers, social care detention is not so much a power to detain, as a system of safeguards imposed over already occurring disciplinary and carceral practices in community care settings. The safeguards potentially 'shine a light' on carceral practices, requiring accountability and – ideally – limiting their use.

In Chapter 10, I argue that reformers hoped deprivation of liberty safeguards might tackle problems of domination within social care, whereby people's choices over where they lived and within their living arrangements can be arbitrarily interfered with by those responsible for arranging and providing their care, including both a powerful welfare–incapacity complex and the person's own family. I argue that social care detention became an important weapon in an intra-professional culture war for those driving forward an 'empowering' post-carceral agenda against the forces of institutionalization and paternalism. However, I explain why it is increasingly unlikely the safeguards as currently construed can serve this purpose, and discuss possible alternative regulatory strategies.

To understand how and why some have come to view frameworks for detention as – paradoxically – 'empowering' (for example, HM Government, 2014: [7.5]), I look to the origins of what I call the 'law of institutions'. The law of institutions is a bifurcated regulatory framework, with two branches: licensing and regulatory monitoring of 'institutions', and 'safeguards' for the liberty of the individual. It was originally developed during the carceral era to regulate early carceral institutions, 'madhouses', to prevent wrongful confinement and improve conditions within. Yet, as I explore in Chapters 3 and 7, the history of the law of institutions is beset with regulatory paradoxes. History tells us that what begins as 'safeguards' for individual liberty can become the cutting edge of new forms of power.

At this point I will briefly insert myself into this narrative. I worked in a range of 'post-carceral' care settings throughout the 2000s before starting a PhD in law in 2009. Working primarily within community services for people with intellectual disabilities and autism, I saw people regularly physically, mechanically and chemically restrained, secluded in their rooms. Everyday choices that I took for granted – owning a mobile phone, seeing friends (having friends), deciding how to spend my day, what to eat, where to go, when to get up or go to bed – were significantly curtailed in these services. I 'turned to law' because I hoped the MCA could tackle problems which I came to call 'institutional domination' (Series, 2013). When I came across the DoLS scheme, I was drawn to describing some of the living arrangements I had encountered as a 'deprivation of liberty'; it seemed an accurate description of places where people were undeniably confined, coerced, supervised and controlled. I hoped the DoLS could call out these troubling practices, rendering providers and others accountable, establishing new tools for others to challenge them. Yet, in the years I have since spent examining how the DoLS operate in practice, I have some doubts as to whether they can reliably achieve these goals, and concerns that in the longer run they could have unintended consequences.

For those seeking to reform social care through the detention safeguards, the root of the problem is that the advantages we hope to secure are mired in a binary understanding of both the nature of institutions and liberty itself, when the problems we hope to address today are non-binary, multifaceted, and have a complex aetiology that the law of institutions often cannot penetrate. If the post-carceral era has extended the institutional archipelago into potentially all and any spaces of care, it is difficult for a legal apparatus anchored in a clearly defined spatial binary to make sense of what we mean by 'liberty'. Meanwhile there are risks that the DoLS will repeat the regulatory paradoxes seen throughout the history of the law of institutions, as Neil Allen (2015: 46) puts it of 'legitimising rather than preventing the problem', paradoxically 'cementing the care relationship to a prison paradigm'. Rather than liberate, the DoLS could create what Ben-Moshe (2020: 245) calls a 'governable cage'.

The central thesis of this book is that contemporary structures for regulating social care detention have deep roots in carceral-era legal machinery, but these became increasingly detached from its symbolic and conceptual foundations during the post-carceral era, giving rise to numerous seemingly paradoxical outcomes and practical difficulties. These problems are compounded by the way the *Cheshire West* judgment treats the subjective experience of the individual, as irrelevant to whether they are 'deprived of liberty' or not. The danger is that for some 'incapacitated' people there is no longer any possible outcome that looks like 'liberty'.

To put it simply: we are no longer clear about what problem(s) we are trying to solve, what positive goals we are striving for, and whether this carceral-era legal framework rooted in the law of institutions is the best means to effect these changes. For abolitionist and reformist projects alike, we need a clearer sense of what we mean by 'liberty' for these specific populations and what a positive outcome looks like. Posing questions of liberty may bring us toward a better understanding of our present-day problems, but we must go further to understand how we can fulfil the incomplete promise of the post-carceral era, alert to the danger that the machinery of liberty safeguards ties us into our carceral past.

About this book

How can we make sense of these contemporary questions of liberty, and unpick the thorny dilemmas they raise? The strategy adopted here is a critical genealogy – or 'history of the present' – an approach influenced by Foucault (1977a) which seeks to diagnose our contemporary problems by tracing their emergence and descent. Genealogists seek to delineate the norms, knowledges, power relations and practices we call upon when constructing and experiencing our present-day problems, to remind us of the forgotten struggles and repurposings that produced our present-day problems (Garland, 2014). Critical genealogies aim to loosen the hold of present-day ways of conceptualizing a problem in order to clear a space for the possibility of thinking otherwise, reshaping and expanding the terms of debate, and enlarging the space for contestations from different participants (Rose, 1999).

Echoing Scott (2004: 4), we can ask what kind of 'problem-space' has produced the questions, tactics and interventions associated with social care detention? As Scott observes, problem-spaces have temporal dimensions, which shape not only the context but also the terms of the debate. Questions posed out of their time under new historical conditions can 'appear lifeless, quaint, not so much wrong as irrelevant', leading us into 'dead ends' (Scott, 2004: 4).

Has our carceral-era heritage led us to pose the wrong questions, leading us into a regulatory dead end for the problems we face today? 'Deprivation of liberty' is one of several potential ways of characterizing the material realities of post-carceral care arrangements, rendering them amenable to a particular regulatory response: safeguards for individual liberty. Why has this seemingly paradoxical 'deprivation of liberty' framing for post-carceral care arrangements become attractive, and for whom?

This book follows in a tradition of historical studies of the 'tutelary relationship' – legally enshrined relations of paternalism directed toward adults with mental disabilities (Unsworth, 1987, 1991, 1993; Castel, 1988; Fennell, 1996), and histories of the care of people with mental disabilities (Bartlett, 1999a; Wright and Digby, 1996; Jarrett, 2020). Social care detention represents a recent, and in many ways surprising, development in the history of tutelary relationships: the resurrection and dramatic expansion of carceral law at the height of the post-carceral era.

I hope this book will be of interest to those developing or implementing social care detention safeguards, to activists, human rights advocates and litigators arguing for its recognition, regulation or abolition, and scholars trying to understand or critique these developments in the UK or elsewhere. I hope to raise the profile of social care detention as a unique and important phenomenon in our times; more than a mere footnote to mental health law.

This book also joins an ongoing conversation in critical legal and disability studies concerning the legacies of deinstitutionalization, the abolition of all carceral practices (including 'deprivation of liberty' and other 'restrictive practices'), and the promise of the CRPD. It began as an article about *Cheshire West* which rapidly outgrew its scope, lay dormant for several years, and was resurrected for a workshop at the Oñati International Institute for the Sociology of Law on the legacies of deinstitutionalization organized by Spivakovsky, Steele and Weller (2020). I am grateful to the organizers and other workshop delegates for the conversations and encouragement which eventually led to this book.

A note on the COVID-19 pandemic

I began this book long before the novel coronavirus COVID-19 was first identified in China. It was mainly written, however, during the lockdowns. While I wrote it from the comfortable confines of my home, millions of older and disabled people living in congregate care settings around the world were subject to more restrictive 'community' care than we have witnessed in living memory. Reflecting government guidance or institutional policy, but rarely underwritten by law, excursions from and visits to care homes largely ceased during this time. Many people were confined to their bedrooms – in conditions that would usually be described as seclusion or 'solitary confinement' – for weeks on end. While the rest of us were locked down, many care home residents were literally locked in. The pandemic amplified already existing forms of 'disability-specific lawful violence', drawing from the kinds of already existing practices and discourses embedded within guardianship, mental health and mental capacity legislation explored in this book, intensified through the 'emergency' (Spivakovsky and Steele, 2021).

Regulatory visits were suspended or dramatically reduced to limit the spread of COVID-19. Care homes became hyper-closed institutions.

Appalling reports surfaced of residents being neglected, or even of lying dead in their beds with nobody noticing, of residents giving up hope of seeing their loved ones again, turning their faces to the wall and literally dying of loneliness. And still, despite all these efforts to keep COVID-19 out, care home residents died on a scale unparalleled by any other group in society.

COVID-19 gave the lie to the idea that care homes and other congregate settings bring safety. Is it possible that COVID-19 may, in the long run, spell the end of congregate care settings in a post-pandemic world? The pandemic exposed the carceral realities of care homes through media coverage of isolated residents and relatives unable to visit. Yet it also exposed the limited penetration of law and liberty into this sphere of care. Few (if any) queried the legal basis for preventing residents from freely coming and going from care homes, or banning visitors (although see John's Campaign, 2021). COVID-19 confirmed that the world of care operates within a different legal space; once one becomes a care recipient in an institutional environment, one's legal status undergoes a radical transformation. One becomes a legal ghost: half there, half not.

There is a great deal more that can and must be said about the COVID-19 pandemic, the law and the spaces and politics of care. However, regrettably, I do not attempt to do this in this book. There is simply *too* much to say and insufficient space here. For practical reasons, then, I take 31 December 2019 as the end point of any statistical data I present concerning DoLS and social care detention, since after this the data quality declines and becomes directly affected by the pandemic. I make some reference to the COVID-19 pandemic but am not offering an analysis of the specific problems posed by it.

2

Distinguishing Social
Care Detention

Social care detention, and its growing reach into the lives of older and disabled citizens and their caregivers, is one of the most striking socio-legal phenomena of the 21st century. Following the Supreme Court's ruling in *Cheshire West*, the ambit of legal machinery designed to regulate institutional carceral care has broken free of its conceptual moorings and stands poised to regulate care arrangements far removed from formal 'institutions', producing paradoxical outcomes and practical dilemmas explored throughout this book.

By naming this socio-legal phenomenon 'social care detention' I intend to distinguish it from other forms of detention more familiar to legal scholars, and identify some of its unique characteristics. I want to bring social care detention out of the shadows of its near neighbour, mental health detention, challenging often implicit assumptions within mental health law, policy, scholarship and activism that social care detention (or detention under the MCA) is a form of mental health detention 'lite', pointing toward ways that this sense has been historically produced.

In England and Wales, 'social care' refers to non-medical care arrangements in 'community' settings. It has a separate statutory and administrative basis to healthcare. One important difference is that whereas NHS healthcare is generally provided free of charge, social care services are often arranged privately or else funded by local authority social services subject to a means test (for further details see Clements et al, 2019). The history of 'social care', which I describe in Chapter 4, is linked to the closure of older institutional provision, including workhouses and long-stay hospitals, with new services framed as meeting 'social' rather than 'medical' care needs. Two thirds of local authority-funded social care service users are older adults, aged over 65, and over half are female. The most common 'primary support reason' for local authority social care is physical support for older adults, but local authorities also support significant numbers of working-age adults with intellectual disabilities, and older adults needing 'support for memory and cognition' (NHS Digital, 2020a). Social care services are often relied upon by those with long-term disabilities and health conditions. In other countries it might go by different names – for example, 'long-term care', 'aged care', 'disability services' – and may be more closely linked to healthcare, insurance systems, religious organizations or social security.

Social care detention is very different from the 'paradigmatic' example of detention: the prisoner in his cell (Stark, 2019; *MIG & MEG* [2010] EWHC 785 (Fam), [136], [165], [235]). Its locus is 'the community', its trappings and intentions apparently benign, and its relationships with law more complicated. Social care detention could be viewed as a form of 'transcarceration', the spatial spread of carceral practices from institutions into the community (for example, Lowman et al, 1987) or, more fundamentally, as redefining the carceral as an embodied experience rather than a physical space (Moran, 2014). It is part of a family of 'non-paradigmatic' carceral practices that may take no 'institutional' centre at all; they are dispersed, mobile and can extend into domestic and 'private' spaces. Other examples of non-paradigmatic detention may include house arrest and curfews, control orders, community treatment orders in mental health (CTOs) and (Stark argues) the kettling of protestors. Yet social care detention differs from these because of the *social care* orientation of its logics, rationales and administrative apparatus, outlined in this chapter.

Locus

In a literal spatial sense, social care detention embodies law's 'expanding empire' (Sumption, 2019: 9), extending the legal machinery of detention safeguards well beyond traditional institutional loci into, potentially, any spaces of care. It exceeds medical law's 'inexorable expansion', documented by Veitch (2007: 1), into locations where predominantly non-medical care is delivered. Social care detention's near relation, mental health detention, also shows signs of outward expansion into 'the community' through existing and new legal regimes,[1] yet its primary locus and organizational centre remains the hospital, and its orientation remains medical.

In England and Wales, social care detention is regulated via the MCA. Since 2009 this has been under a framework known as the Deprivation

---

[1] Strictly speaking, only s17 MHA (leave of absence) may presently authorize detention in the community; community detention cannot be imposed via CTOs or conditional discharge (*Re MM* [2018] UKSC 60; *Welsh Ministers v PJ* [2018] UKSC 66). However, this may change in future reforms of the MHA (Department of Health and Social Care and Ministry of Justice, 2021a).

of Liberty Safeguards (DoLS, MCA Schedules A1 and 1A). From 2022 onward, this will be under the DoLS' successor, the Liberty Protection Safeguards (LPS, MCA Schedule AA1).[2] The DoLS extend only to more traditional institutional loci: hospitals (22 per cent) and care homes (72 per cent, NHS Digital, 2019b).[3] Although the use of DoLS in hospitals (general and psychiatric) raises important and interesting questions, the focus of this book is the role of detention safeguards in community settings.

Following *Cheshire West*, many other settings were implicated as potentially depriving residents of their liberty, including: supported living type services, schools, children's homes, publicly or privately arranged care provided in a person's own home by homecare staff or personal assistants, and even care provided by families (Chapter 9). These settings will be regulated via the LPS. The *Cheshire West* acid test of deprivation of liberty dissolves traditional regulatory distinctions between the domestic and institutional, the 'public' and 'private' spheres. This gives social care detention some of its most transgressive and paradoxical qualities, and poses searching existential questions for the post-carceral era.

Regulatory form

The MCA was widely presented as modern, progressive and 'empowering' legislation (for example, Department for Constitutional Affairs, 2007). The current scale of deprivation of liberty under the MCA would have astonished its creators. I explain more fully in Chapter 7 how they intended to establish 'informal' mechanisms for substitute decisions about health, care and welfare in the 'best interests' of people considered to lack the 'mental capacity' to make decisions for themselves.

In contrast, the MHA is widely viewed as coercive, even authoritarian. Whereas the DoLS and LPS – as the names suggest – are positioned as *safeguards* for individual liberty, mental health law commentators portray the MHA as a formal 'compulsory power', better avoided if possible. Their implication is often that the DoLS are not 'formal' detention, are not a 'compulsory power', and therefore their use is in some way less serious and less restrictive than the MHA, even if applied in identical contexts for the same purpose (for example, Fanning, 2016, 2018; Wessely et al, 2018b: 123).

---

[2] At the time of writing, the projected date for the implementation of the LPS was April 2022, but this date may be revised in light of the ongoing pandemic and the need to consult upon the new Code of Practice and regulations.

[3] The unaccounted for 6 per cent appear to have been erroneous applications from settings where DoLS do not apply.

Yet, when stripped down to their bare essentials, both instruments achieve very similar ends: they render lawful practices connected with care and treatment that would ordinarily be unlawful without the person's consent, including deprivation of liberty. An elemental analysis using Wesley Hohfeld's 'fundamental legal conceptions' (Campbell and Thomas, 2016) reveals both instruments to provide an immunity (protection against liability) for those responsible for certain acts of care or treatment without consent; they modify the person's own power to give or refuse consent, and place them under a legal disability. Given that their legal fundamentals are almost indistinguishable, why are the stories we tell about these two statutes so very different? This cannot be traced to what they are doing in a doctrinal sense, but rather their historical and social contexts, and the ways their target populations, problematics, rationalities and conceptual machinery have been discursively produced.

In contrast with the MHA's explicitly public law coercive character, the MCA was originally presented as a private law instrument enabling third parties to merely stand 'in the shoes of the person' to make decisions that they could not (legally speaking) make for themselves (Law Commission, 1995: [8.19]; see also *N v ACCG and others* [2017] UKSC 22, [1]); doing things *on behalf of*, not *to* a person. It is descended from a more ancient form of tutelary relationship, preceding the carceral era and not tied to carceral institutions: guardianship (Unsworth, 1991).

As mainly private law instruments, empowering mainly private actors, guardianship laws tend to involve less tightly defined jurisdictional parameters and regulatory controls than public law regimes such as the MHA (Rees, 2010), reflecting a traditional view that the state should limit the regulation of private personal relationships (Horwitz, 1982). Yet mental capacity, substitute decision making and guardianship laws are closely entwined with social care detention. Connections recur through recent international human rights litigation explored in Chapter 5. Other countries that regulate care home admissions or confinement often do so through guardianship or substitute decision making laws; I discuss some of these in Chapter 10. Social care detention fuses these two branches of the tutelary relationship distinguished by Unsworth, regulating relationships and matters that have hitherto been constructed as 'private' with public law style machinery.

The DoLS were inserted into the MCA in response to the *Bournewood* case, in which the European Court of Human Rights (ECtHR) ruled that an autistic man who had been informally admitted to Bournewood hospital in his 'best interests' had been unlawfully deprived of his liberty (*HL v UK* [2004] ECHR 720). I discuss this case, and the development of the DoLS, in Chapters 5 and 7. From *Bournewood* until *Cheshire West* the DoLS were relatively little used, owing to very narrow judicial definitions of deprivation of liberty, however DoLS applications increased dramatically in the aftermath of the Supreme Court's ruling (Care and Social Services Inspectorate Wales and Health Inspectorate Wales, 2015; Health and Social Care Information Centre, 2015b).

The story of social care detention in England and Wales has not, therefore, been one of a government deciding to create an instrument of mass detention with new and far-reaching coercive powers in the community. In this sense it differs from the story of CTOs, which are generally understood to establish *new* compulsory powers in community settings (for example, Fennell, 2010b; Spivakovsky, 2014). Rather, the story of social care detention in the 21st century is of a litigation and advocacy strategy that sought to frame already occurring social care practices connected to substitute decision making as a deprivation of liberty, in order to elicit new public law style 'safeguards' to regulate these. It is a paradoxical story positioning powers of detention as a 'positive tool that shines a light' on a person's care to determine whether restrictions are necessary, or even to 'empower' them (HM Government, 2014: [7.14], [7.15]).

This origin story embodies the spirit of 'legalism', expressed by one of its leading contemporary proponents, Larry Gostin (1986: v), as using the law 'to wrap the patient in a network of substantive and procedural protections against unjustified loss of liberty and compulsory treatment'. In contrast, the recent history of CTOs reflects 'medicalism' (Fanning, 2018), using the law to extend or consolidate medical power, granting clinicians or other welfare professionals greater discretion to define, interpret and respond to human needs. The history of mental health law is sometimes described as a pendulum swinging between poles of 'legalism' and 'medicalism'. Legalism's critics argue its 'formalities' are not only unnecessary but positively obstructive to clinical and welfare aims (Jones, 1980).

However, social care detention's primary target is not medical power; what began as reaction to 'doctor knows best' with *Bournewood* (Fennell, 1998) is today more concerned with regulating the disciplinary power of care providers and local authority social services, and stands poised to regulate even family-based care. And although the DoLS (and LPS) are notoriously complex, even among mental health law specialists, they embody a weaker form of legalism from the perspective of the procedural safeguards available in authorizing, reviewing and challenging detention than equivalent measures under the MHA (Series, 2019). Yet as I will discuss in the next chapter when reviewing the history of the law of institutions, legalism and medicalism/'welfarism' cannot be so neatly distinguished and counterposed; each contains the seeds of new forms of power and social control. Our task as critical socio-legal scholars is to examine the forms this takes and outline its possible future trajectories.

Target populations

The main populations whose care is now regulated as social care detention are older adults, often with degenerative neurological conditions such as dementia; people with developmental disabilities including intellectual disability and autism; and people with acquired brain injury or neurological illness. Over half of DoLS applications concern people with a primary diagnosis of dementia, and 13 per cent with learning disability (NHS Digital, 2019d).[4] Almost three quarters of DoLS applications relate to adults aged over 75; during 2017–18 one in every 16 adults aged over 85 was subject to a DoLS application (NHS Digital, 2018). In contrast, rates of detention under the MHA tend to decline with age, although there is a small increase for adults over 65 (NHS Digital, 2019c).

These disparate categories of persons are united by being recipients of 'social care' in community settings, but also as populations regarded as unsuitable or not intended for regulation via mental health law. In a 'law on the books' sense, both those detained under the MHA and those subject to MCA DoLS/LPS must have a diagnosed 'mental disorder' (MCA Sch A1 s 14 (DoLS); MCA Sch AA1 s13(b) (LPS)), defined by s1 MHA as 'any disorder or disability of the mind'. This reflects the exigencies of article 5(1) ECHR – discussed in Chapter 5 – which only permits 'deprivation of liberty' on limited grounds, including 'unsoundness of mind'. English law glosses this dated term 'mental disorder', reflecting requirements for 'objective medical evidence' of a 'true mental disorder' established in *Winterwerp v the Netherlands* [1979] ECHR 4. However, in practice 'mental disorder' is interpreted differently in relation to the MHA and MCA.

The MHA partially excludes people with learning disabilities from its scope 'unless that disability is associated with abnormally aggressive or seriously irresponsible conduct on his part' (s1(2A) MHA); an exclusion that does not apply to the MCA DoLS/LPS. Meanwhile the Law Commission proposed removing the 'mental disorder' test entirely from the MCA, on the grounds that it excluded people with a 'pure brain injury' (Law Commission, 2015: [6.13]). On the face of things, it is not obvious why a 'pure brain injury' resulting in impairments to mental capacity would not constitute a 'disorder or disability of the mind' – there is no case law or guidance to that effect. Their proposal to use 'unsoundness of mind' instead was not adopted by government. However, these distinctions reflect a deeply embedded cultural

---

[4]   Unfortunately the remaining categories are difficult to interpret, as it is unclear how conditions such as brain injury, stroke or neurogenerative disease would be categorized.

sense of the MHA as about certain populations – the 'mentally ill' – but not properly about those with long-term cognitive disabilities.

In the next chapters I will show that this partitioning of (in broad terms) those with psychosocial disabilities and those with long-term 'cognitive' impairments is rooted in longstanding historical distinctions between those with temporary or permanent conditions. By the late carceral era, the key operative distinction was between those considered 'treatable' and 'curable' and those in need of 'permanent' care, destined for different legal and institutional controls. Ben-Moshe (2020: 107) argues that this parsing out of the 'incurable' was essential 'for psychiatry to become a legitimate profession, let alone a science'. Social care – and its forerunners in the workhouses, 'idiots' asylums', and 'mental deficiency colonies' – became a parallel domain to the main asylums, taking charge of the lives of those largely excluded from the realm of psychiatry, 'mental illness', treatment and cure.

Connected with this institutional partitioning of detainable populations, a view took hold in the late 19th century, gathering pace in the mid-20th century, that 'formal' legal measures were unsuitable, unnecessary and undesirable for people with dementia or intellectual disabilities. In Chapters 3 and 7, I will show how this produced a 'common sense' that these populations were not proper subjects of the law of institutions. They were 'non-volitional'; possessing neither a 'will' nor 'liberty', and therefore in no need of legal safeguards. This pervasive sense of older and disabled adults with cognitive impairments as 'non-volitional' has exerted a profound influence on modern mental health and capacity law, including a backlash against *Cheshire West*. One important function of social care detention is re-crystallizing a sense of older and disabled adults as (almost) fully fledged legal persons, and their care as a matter of legal concern.

The legacy of this partition continues today over the contested role of the MHA in detaining adults with intellectual disabilities or autism, and some older people with dementia, in psychiatric settings. Although the DoLS are mainly used for authorizing deprivation of liberty in care homes (72 per cent) and general hospitals (20 per cent), a small proportion of applications (2 per cent) concern detention in 'mental health establishments' (NHS Digital, 2019b). A highly complex legal interface governs whether psychiatric patients are detained under the MHA or MCA (Allen, 2010). In very broad terms, patients 'within scope' of the MHA who are objecting to admission or treatment, are 'ineligible' for detention under the MCA. This reflects the distinction forged in the early post-carceral era, discussed in Chapter 7, between 'resistant' patients (for whom the MHA was intended) and 'non-volitional' populations – people with intellectual disabilities and older 'senile' adults – for whom legal 'formalities' were considered unnecessary, but whose care is now mainly managed under the MCA.

It has been a longstanding advocacy position of organizations like Mencap that people with intellectual disabilities, not having a 'mental illness', should be removed from the scope of the MHA altogether (for example, Lord Renton, 1980). A recent review of the MHA considered 'removing' people with autism as well (Wessely et al, 2018b). However, even advocates of this position acknowledge that these groups could then be detained in psychiatric hospitals under the MCA instead (Hollins et al, 2019; Joint Committee on Human Rights, 2019). The Law Commission (2017b) had concluded that the safeguards available under the MCA DoLS/LPS were inadequate to the task of regulating mental health detention; they would lose layers of legal protection from the MHA's more rigorous machinery yet remain detained in the same places subject to the same regimes. The government has committed only to 'consider' the matter further (Department of Health and Social Care and Ministry of Justice, 2021b: 83).

At stake in this apparently arcane argument over which legal framework is more appropriate for detaining different populations are the different cultural constructions and stigmas of these groups. 'Mental illness' – and thereby the MHA – has become associated with dangerousness, whereas the populations targeted within social care detention are viewed as harmless innocents, childlike and 'incapable' persons in need of care (Ben-Moshe, 2020). This partitioning of detainable populations means that opportunities for collaborative activism may be missed, and different stigmas could inadvertently be reinforced for each group by the other's concern to avoid being labelled as 'mentally ill' (and dangerous) or, conversely, 'disabled' (and 'incapable') (for example, Spandler et al, 2015). For those who are increasingly parsed out of mental health law into (in)capacity legislation, there is a danger that advocacy opposing the MHA inadvertently implicitly positions the MCA as less controversial, less problematic and less stigmatizing simply because those directly affected tend to be less politically organized and vocal about its effects.

Problems, rationalities and legal technologies

What contemporary problems are the interventions gathered under the legal umbrella of social care detention directed toward? What political rationalities – the 'changing discursive fields within which the exercise of power is conceptualised' – produce and guide these problems and interventions, and what 'moral justifications' and 'governmental technologies' do they engage (Rose and Miller, 1992: 175)? By bringing the distinctive rationalities, justifications and legal technologies of social care detention out of the shadows of mental health detention, we can analyse it as a socio-legal phenomenon that is both more important and more interesting than merely mental health detention 'lite'.

Mental health detention's overarching rationality is that (compulsory) treatment can cure – or at least improve – 'mental disorder', thereby managing putative associated risks to the person themselves and/or others. Social care detention's overarching rationalities cannot be so neatly encapsulated. Its expansive remit is regulating 'living arrangements' (*Cheshire West*, UKSC, [1]), encompassing many varied interventions and problems. For example: to deliver everyday care, ensuring basic needs such as nutrition, medication and personal hygiene are met; 'safeguarding' interventions to address neglect (including self-neglect) or abuse; close supervision to manage everyday risks such as road traffic, cooking, falls, or putting inedible objects in their mouth; managing dietary concerns, or drug and alcohol addictions;[5] managing 'challenging behaviour' including self-injury or 'aggression'; managing concerns about sexual relationships, including 'incapacity' to make decisions around sex, abusive/exploitative sexual relations, or 'inappropriate' sexual behaviours; managing concerns about personal relationships more generally, for example alleged 'undue influence'; preventing exploitation or harm by strangers; and so on. I will consider which overarching rationalities could unify these diverse activities shortly.

Elongated temporality

Social care detention's problems and interventions embody a different temporality to mental health detention. These are semi-permanent states of affairs, in contrast with mental health detention's intensive but comparatively short-lived punctuation points in a person's life. Half of mental health inpatients in England and Wales spend under four weeks in hospital, a third are discharged in two weeks, and it is rare for inpatient stays to exceed six months (Wyatt et al, 2019) (although hospital stays lasting for years are common for people with intellectual disabilities (NHS Digital, 2021)). In contrast, social care detention's timescales are long term, measured in months, years or, indeed, lifetimes. This has implications for social care detention's form of legalism, which under DoLS and LPS favours longer authorization and review periods than the MHA (Series, 2019).

Whereas mental health detention interrupts 'normal time', social care detention often secures adherence to 'normal' temporal lifecourse patterns, for example of leaving home and attaining 'independence' upon reaching adulthood, or the normal (for our culture) progression of older adults into residential care. Its elongated temporality reflects its target populations,

---

5   The MCA's provisions for deprivation of liberty do not (presently) encompass addiction itself, but can be engaged where addiction is said to be linked to 'incapacity' caused by a mental disorder (for example, *RB v Brighton and Hove City Council* [2014] EWCA 561).

whose relatively unchanging (or declining) conditions place them, as Steele (2017: 378) puts it, 'in a permanent state of mental incapacity' in contrast with those constructed as 'temporarily mentally incapacitated from their usual state of autonomy, thus only requiring minimal medical and care interventions to return them to their prior state'.

This means that the potential for violence within social care detention is visible only over longer timescales. Not the punctuated assault (although we might also see that) but the potential damage done to relationships, sexualities, the making of homes, selves, lives and deaths, through the management of 'living arrangements' over many months and years. The potential stifling of possibilities-for-being through the long-term erosion of everyday choices, freedoms and privacy is slowly done, like 'water dripping on stone' (Vincent, 2010: 47).

Legal technologies

The legal technologies of social care detention and mental capacity law are sometimes favourably contrasted with mental health law as less coercive, less dated, less stigmatizing, less *carceral*. To understand this appeal, we must first understand contemporary assaults on the core rationality of mental health detention. Critics of mainstream psychiatry question the validity of the concept of 'mental disorder', and whether psychiatry's mainly pharmacological interventions are effective or appropriate in addressing the forms of human suffering or difference clustered under this label. This critical assault comes from within psychiatry, from rival professions (for example, British Psychological Society, 2013), critical scholars and movements of users and survivors of psychiatry (Morrison, 2005; Rose, 2018).

Critics also challenge mental health detention's claim to manage risk, querying whether mental disorder *is* associated with greater risks to self and others than general risks within the population (Jones and Shattell, 2014); whether those risks are sufficiently well defined (Fanning, 2018); whether psychiatry can accurately predict and effectively manage those risks, and whether risk-focused interventions ultimately cause greater harm than good (Szmukler and Rose, 2013). Meanwhile detention premised on the 'risk' + 'mental disorder' formula is considered discriminatory, singling out those so labelled for coercive interventions not practised on other 'risky' members of society (for example, Campbell and Heginbotham, 1991; Minkowitz, 2006–7).

While these fundamental elements of Anglo-Welsh mental health law remain intact, some critics look toward alternative rationalities, moral justifications and legal technologies to underpin coercive psychiatric interventions. From this vantage point, the (in)capacity and substitute decision making formula of the MCA appears promising. There are growing calls for 'fusion law', or capacity-based mental health law (Dawson and Szmukler, 2006; see also: Richardson, 1999; Law Commission, 2017b: 150–1; Wessely et al, 2018b: 231–9). Some jurisdictions have taken this path (Callaghan and Ryan, 2016; Sheridan Rains et al, 2019), and the Mental Capacity Act (Northern Ireland) 2016 is fully 'fused' capacity and mental health detention legislation. However, abolitionists, citing the CRPD, view capacitarian mental health law as still ultimately (indirectly) discriminatory, falling short of the abolition of all forms of disability-specific detention and compulsory treatment (Flynn, 2013; Minkowitz, 2006–7).

In contrast, the MCA enshrines some important post-carceral rationalities and values in law, discussed in Chapters 4 and 7. It codifies a rebuttable 'presumption of capacity' (MCA s1(2)) and employs a 'decision-specific' and 'functional' (or 'cognitive') test of mental capacity, favoured by a growing number of jurisdictions (Then, 2013). The Law Commission (1991, 1993a, 1995) intended this to preserve greater autonomy in decision making than so-called 'status' based approaches removing legal capacity across all areas, and greater 'value neutrality' than 'outcome' approaches, such as 'reasonableness' or risk. It later came to include elements of 'supported decision making' (MCA s1(3)), echoing – but not mirroring – approaches to legal capacity under the CRPD (Series, 2015a).

The MCA's 'best interests' standard for substitute decision making requires consideration of the person's own past and present wishes, feelings, values and beliefs (MCA s4(6)). However, this 'substituted judgement' element holds no statutory priority over other considerations: 'The purpose of the best interests test is to consider matters from the patient's point of view. That is not to say that his wishes must prevail' (*Aintree University Hospitals NHS Foundation Trust v James* [2013] UKSC 67, [45]). The MCA's principles also require consideration of 'less restrictive' interventions (MCA s1(6)), a key post-carceral concept discussed in Chapters 4, 5 and 7. I will not analyse the MCA's principles in greater detail here, but call attention to the greater flexibility of 'substitute decision making' than the binary questions of detention and compulsory treatment under mental health law, facilitating more flexible responses to the diverse problems and interventions subsumed under social care detention.

Capacity approaches can be more risk-tolerant than the MHA, as for example in the landmark case of Mr C, a mental health patient found to have capacity to refuse the amputation of his gangrenous leg, notwithstanding his schizophrenia diagnosis and extremely poor prognosis without surgery (*Re C (Adult: Refusal of Medical Treatment)* [1994] 1 W.L.R. 290). Similarly, 'best interests' decisions can prioritize the person's own wishes and feelings over risks to health or life (Ruck Keene and Friedman, 2021), as in the more recent case of Mr B, who also had a diagnosis of schizophrenia and declined a proposed amputation of a gangrenous leg (*Wye Valley NHS Trust v Mr B* [2015] EWHC 60 (COP). Psychiatrists increasingly turn to the MCA to justify *non*-treatment under the MHA (for example, *Nottinghamshire Healthcare NHS Trust v RC* [2014] EWHCOP 1317). Yet, as I argued in a commentary on Mr B's case (Series, 2016), these outcomes are highly contingent on the views and values of those assessing capacity and making best interests decisions. Claims to value neutrality might be better understood as value pluralism (Coggon, 2008). Both capacity and best interests, are to a large degree, 'in the eye of the beholder' (Ruck Keene, 2017b). Those deploying the MCA's legal technologies must wrestle often incommensurable values in deciding outcomes (Kong et al, 2020), the inherent instability of its underlying principles and their 'radical under-specificity' (Coggon and Kong, 2021: 1).

Empowerment and vulnerability

Consequently, outcomes under the MCA are heterogeneous, hard to predict, and absorb many different rationalities. One much-vaunted rationality is 'empowerment'. The MCA boasts many celebrated examples of judges prioritizing the person's own wishes over risks to life or health, including several cases discussed later in this book. However, it is important not to simplistically equate 'empowerment' with non-coercion; the rationality of 'empowerment' can justify and structure some of the MCA's most coercive interventions. This embodies what Rose (1999) calls governing through 'powers of freedom', that is 'freedom as a governmental rationality' as opposed to a 'powerful slogan of resistance' (Rose in Carvalho and Lima, 2016: 801).

The case of ML (*Northamptonshire Healthcare NHS Foundation Trust v ML (Rev 1)* [2014] EWCOP 2) offers a striking example. ML, an autistic young man, had been living with his parents until he was detained under the MHA. In hospital he was repeatedly secluded for long periods in unsafe conditions, and was traumatized by the experience. He was eventually discharged from detention by a mental health tribunal. Back home, his 'challenging behaviours' were slowly improving, with input from a National Autistic Society day centre. However, his healthcare team felt this fell short of his full 'potential'; it did not sufficiently challenge his rigid routines, limited diet and 'aggressive' behaviour when he felt overwhelmed. They asked the Court of Protection to declare that it was in ML's best interests to spend 12–24 months in a specialist unit for 'extinction' behavioural therapy, exposing him to stimuli that triggered his 'challenging behaviours' and potentially temporarily making them much worse. ML's parents worried he would find this very distressing, that it could damage their relationship with him, and in consequence his stay would be extended. Mr Justice

Hayden concluded that while there was no guarantee this treatment would work, ML had 'greater potential' than his current arrangements realized. Holding that '[t]he objectives of any regime of care ought to aspire to the goal of achieving independent living', but that this 'may not always mean that ML's personal happiness is given priority' [44], Hayden J made the declaration that the intervention was in ML's best interests. However, because of the rules governing the interface between the statutes, the MHA would still need to be used. Concerned that ML's family might discharge him, Hayden J reserved to himself the county court power to displace ML's nearest relatives, and wrote a letter to any tribunal hearing a future appeal explaining why he – a High Court judge – considered detention in ML's best interests.

The decision endorsed a controversial treatment criticized as abusive by autistic people (Dawson, 2004), the efficacy of which is doubted by researchers (Sandbank et al, 2020). It eroded the MHA's safeguards and ran counter to national policies to keep autistic people out of inpatient units (discussed in Chapter 7). However, my critical point is that the MCA's absorbent and expansive best interests standard more readily accommodated the progressive-sounding rationalities of 'fulfilling potential' and 'independence' than the MHA's risk formula. In other words, by accommodating other considerations than 'risk' the MCA can sometimes facilitate coercion where the MHA might not. Paradoxically, 'empowerment' oriented rationalities such as independence can sometimes result in more – not less – coercive outcomes than risk alone.

The second major overarching rationality animating the MCA and social care detention is 'vulnerability'. This theme recurs through contemporary mental capacity law scholarship, often invoked to justify specific interventions or to expand its reach outward to new situations and populations (for example, Dunn et al, 2008; Herring, 2016; Lindsey, 2016; Clough, 2017; Kong, 2017). Vulnerability's appeal lies in grounding claims that the state should intervene to increase citizens' resilience to harms to which they might otherwise be exposed (for example, Fineman, 2010). Typically, scholars maintain that vulnerability is *universal*, an inherent part of the human condition, linked to the realities of our embodiment, our mutual interdependence and (often unacknowledged) reliance on the care of others. Yet vulnerability theorists also often highlight particularly 'inherently' vulnerable populations, for example children, older adults and disabled people, for targeted interventions (for example, Wilson, 2019). 'Vulnerability' can ground interventions that work with a person to increase their resilience, but they can also target 'vulnerable' populations for interventions that they do not want. For this reason, critics of the vulnerability 'zeitgeist' argue that this rationality can potentially damage the pursuit of social justice (Brown, 2011). The 'vulnerability' label is often resisted by writers within a disability rights tradition (for example, Scully, 2014; Yeo, 2020). Abolitionist approaches to legal capacity and disability-specific detention eschew it, opposing protective interventions not anchored in the 'will and preferences' of the person, often highlighting counter-productive outcomes of these interventions (Keeling, 2018).

Herring (2016: 25) defines a person as vulnerable if they face 'a risk of harm', they do not 'have the resources to be able to avoid the risk of harm materializing' and they 'would not be able to adequately respond to the harm if the risk materialized'. 'Vulnerability' is, therefore, implicitly linked to 'risk', but its characterization differs from the risks associated with mental health law. Fanning (2016) positions interventions under the MCA at a 'lower' end of a risk spectrum than the MHA, but many risks managed by the MCA are serious. Some are more predictably harmful than the notoriously difficult-to-predict risks of suicide or violence in mental health. To borrow two examples from *Cheshire West*: a person without a sense of road safety being unsupervised near a busy road, or a person at risk of choking because they frequently place inedible items in their mouth. Both DoLS and the LPS require assessment of whether deprivation of liberty is both 'necessary' and 'proportionate' to the risk of harm that would befall a person otherwise (MCA Schedule A1 s16; Schedule AA1 s13), reflecting the requirements of articles 5 and 8 ECHR. The MCA's formula, therefore, offers no way out of the risk conundrum, but rather adopts an even more open ended approach to risk management than the MHA.

Like 'empowerment', the vulnerability rationality is expansive, establishing new frontiers for intervention at the fringes of the MCA. I noted earlier how the MCA's mechanisms for social care detention are still coupled to the 'mental disorder' diagnostic criterion, and a functional test of 'mental capacity'. However, at the fringes of the MCA an 'inherent jurisdiction' of the High Court is expanding the reach of social care detention and protective interventions to include situations where the person concerned may be found to have mental capacity – and thereby fall outside the structures of the MCA – and even their status as of 'unsound mind' is contested (*Mazhar v The Lord Chancellor* [2017] EWFC 65; *Mazhar v Birmingham Community Healthcare Foundation NHS Trust & Ors (Rev 1)* [2020] England and Wales Court of Appeal (EWCA) Civ 1377). These interventions are grounded almost exclusively in the vulnerability of the person as a result of their social and relational context rather than any mental disability per se. For example, Mr Meyers lived with his son, having promised his wife when she died that he would take care of him. The son had serious drug and alcohol problems, and his aggressive behaviour prevented care workers from meeting Mr Meyers' physical care needs, leaving him in a dire state of squalor and physical neglect. The local authority removed Meyers to a care home while they cleaned the property, and sought an order authorizing them to prevent him returning until his son had been removed. Mr Meyer had no mental disorder, although a social worker described his relationship to his son as 'co-dependent'. He was held to have mental capacity to decline this intervention, however it was granted by the court under its inherent jurisdiction (*Southend-on-Sea Borough Council v Meyers* [2019] EWHC 399 (Fam)).

Herring (2016: 63) suggests that removing diagnostic criteria from the MCA altogether would not only satisfy CRPD-influenced criticisms of disability discrimination, but could also ensure that more vulnerable adults 'benefit' from protective interventions, regardless of disability status. *Meyers* highlights that while the MCA and social care detention are currently tied to medical 'mental disorder' and 'mental capacity' formulae because of the restraining influence of article 5(1)(e), they are increasingly straining at the leash. Vulnerability – and potentially empowerment – take aim at predominantly *social* not medical problems; it is possible to imagine a future in which social care detention breaks free of its basis in mental disability and impairment altogether, perhaps even free of 'mental incapacity', and becomes a fully fledged vulnerability jurisdiction. Whether this would represent progress and equality, or a worrying expansion of interventionist governmental rationalities, is debatable.

Professionals and expertise

Social care detention inverts the traditional professional hierarchies and recognized expertise associated with mental health detention. Since its inception in the late 18th century, the law of institutions located doctors at the centre of its administrative apparatus. More recently non-medical professionals, predominantly social workers, have held the role of Approved Mental Health Professional (AMHP, formerly 'approved social worker') to hold medical power in check: 'a kind of Anti-Psychiatric translation of the checks and balances of Whig constitutionalism' (Unsworth, 1987: 9). Yet social care detention under the MCA has begun to reverse this psychiatric professional hegemony.

Doubtless psychiatrists are still vested with special status in determining questions of mental capacity in the Court of Protection (Case, 2016; Lindsey, 2019; Gurbai et al, 2020). Yet the days of automatic deference to psychiatric expert opinion on this are numbered (Ruck Keene et al, 2019b). In some cases, judges have rejected unanimous psychiatric evidence of 'incapacity' after having interviewed the person directly (for example, *CC v KK and STCC* [2012] EWHC 2136 (COP)), and in others have preferred the evidence of social workers employing 'tangible techniques' to support a person's ability to make a decision where psychiatrists failed to do so (*LBX v K, L, M* [2013] EWHC 3230 (Fam)). A greater judicial emphasis on supported decision making may further empower social care and advocacy professionals. Meanwhile, although the DoLS require a psychiatrist to conduct the 'mental health assessment' to confirm a diagnosed 'mental disorder', the LPS contains no specific role for psychiatrists. There must be evidence of 'mental disorder', but this could be obtained from a person's GP or – the Law Commission (2017b: [9.60]) suggested – a psychologist or psychotherapist (Series, 2019).

It is in the realm of 'best interests', however, that psychiatric hegemony has been almost entirely displaced by increasing receptiveness to a wider range of expertise, particular that of social care professionals. Best interests originally reflected the *Bolam* standard of whatever a 'body of responsible medical opinion' thought best (*Re F (Mental Patient: Sterilisation)* [1990] 2 AC 1; [1991] UKHL 1; citing *Bolam v Friern Hospital Management Committee* [1957] 1 WLR 582). Yet this was subsequently revised to encompass non-medical emotional, social and welfare considerations (*Re A (Male Sterilisation)* [2000] 1 FLR 549). Case law places a growing emphasis on the wishes and feelings of the person themselves, especially since the Supreme Court decision in *Aintree University Hospitals NHS Foundation Trust v James*, although there are some striking departures from this approach (Ruck Keene and Friedman, 2021). In some cases, the testimony of friends, family, or even the person themselves, may displace professional opinion in best interests decisions (for example, *London Borough of Hillingdon v Neary* [2011] EWHC 1377 (COP)). This reflects the inherent open-endedness of the 'best interests' standard, and its permeability to a range of values, perspectives and claims to knowledge and expertise.

The best interests assessment is considered the 'cornerstone' of the DoLS (Law Commission, 2017b: [9.23]), performed by a specialist Best Interests Assessor (BIA). BIAs may come from a range of professional backgrounds (The Mental Capacity (Deprivation of Liberty: Standard Authorisations, Assessments and Ordinary Residence) Regulations 2008 SI 2008/1858), but the majority tend to be social workers. Others are nurses, psychologists or other (non-medical) professions. A significant proportion are dual qualified as AMHPs (Goodall and Wilkins, 2015). The LPS replaces the BIA role with Approved Mental Capacity Professionals (AMCPs), who have even greater powers than their predecessors to review the basis for social care detention and potentially decline to authorize it, to make recommendations or require changes to arrangements, or take other steps necessary to resolve concerns or disputes relating to social care detention. The core assessment under the LPS is no longer 'best interests', but rather whether arrangements giving rise to a deprivation of liberty are 'necessary' and 'proportionate', although best interests will remain in 'formulating' the arrangements (Series, 2019). BIAs and their successors, AMCPs, are required to undergo specialist training on the MCA and human rights.

Typically, BIAs – as well as specialist Independent Mental Capacity Advocates (IMCAs) who may support and represent people subject to the DoLS/LPS – are champions of social care detention, viewing its conceptual and regulatory machinery as tools to challenge, rather than promote, restrictive practices (for example, Graham and Cowley, 2015; James et al, 2019). In a BIA practice handbook Hubbard and Stone (2020: 2) describe the role as follows:

> Best Interests Assessors (BIAs) are experienced, knowledgeable health and social care professionals who investigate and explore people's lives and care and provide a snapshot of how their care is, or could be, the least restrictive possible. The independent, yet critical, observer role they play can be invaluable in bringing insight into ways to increase a person's ability to make choices about their life. Their ability to notice restrictive aspects of care that have been forgotten, or to identify paths for decision making that have not yet been explored, is a vital element of their value.

The core expertise valued here is *governing carcerality*: techniques of *reducing* restrictions to the greatest extent possible within the constraints of the contemporary landscape of care. They are reformers, 'empowerment entrepreneurs' (to paraphrase Becker, 1963/2018) working to effect changes within the system using the new tools and legal technologies of social care detention to prod, interrogate and sometimes loosen the grip of carceral practices in the community. These post-carceral reformers daily perform an impossible calculus, of reconciling the MCA's often irreconcilable imperatives, striving to effect small (but often significant) changes within large and complex systems which they remain a part of.

A third category of expertise is increasingly prominent and valued within social care detention's machinery and ideologies: the 'street level' human rights lawyers (to paraphrase Lipsky, 2010/1980) who take up claims on behalf of detained persons and their families, and defend public bodies. Lawyers, and in particular human rights lawyers, played an instrumental role in the litigation that led to the creation of DoLS. DoLS, crucially, widened access to legal aid to litigate new questions enveloped by social care detention, creating (and profiting) industries of legal experts – including academics like myself – staking our own jurisdiction to pronounce upon socially and politically charged and legal-technocratic questions (Veitch, 2007). There are important interplays between these street level human rights lawyers and the empowerment entrepreneurs working within social care detention's administrative structures. Lawyers provide training and resources, equipping them with often detailed knowledge of the technical details and human rights stories that sharpen their deployment of these legal tools.

The role of families

Social care detention envelops families within its 'legal complex' (Rose and Valverde, 1998) in different ways. It overlays shifting power relations, struggles and alliances between care recipients, their families and friends, and health and social care professionals and agencies, offering each new tools, tactics, practices of power and forms of resistance to act on the other. It constructs families as custodians, liberators, cogs and squeaky wheels. Those ensnared within this legal complex may find themselves bewildered, surveilled, trapped in a dead end, or may happen upon a lever on this blinking legal-bureaucratic dashboard that radically transforms their situation.

Classically, the law of institutions figured families as 'custodians' of the person (Yeates, 2007), those with 'natural' authority to enter into private arrangements with an institution, or to 'petition' for a relative's entry into a public asylum. Families may now encounter social care detention as 'custodians' when privately arranged care home placements trigger the DoLS/LPS application process. In this role, families may be surprised – perhaps appalled – that care arrangements in the 'best interests' of their relatives are now described as a 'deprivation of liberty', requiring 'authorization' from a 'supervisory body' (under DoLS) or 'responsible body' (under LPS). They may find the succession of assessments intrusive.

Friends or relatives may be appointed as a 'relevant person's representative' (RPR) under DoLS, or an 'appropriate person' under the LPS; roles that figure them less as custodians of the person than champions of their *rights*. Where the wishes of the care recipient coincide with their relative this may seem so much needless bureaucracy. However, if the person objects to the care arrangements their relatives have put in place, the law expects the RPR/ 'appropriate person' to actively assist them in exercising rights of challenge. Relatives are expected to assist a person in challenging care arrangements they may have endorsed, or be passed over for these roles (*AJ v A Local Authority* [2015] EWCOP 5). Both the DoLS and the LPS also insert IMCAs into the authorization process, to assist the person in exercising rights of challenge. However, pathways to advocacy are not straightforward and, under the LPS, 'appropriate persons' can effectively block their relation's access to advocacy (Series, 2019). Social care detention thereby inserts layers of surveillance and state control over private care arrangements, and new (albeit tenuous) paths of resistance for older and disabled people to family-arranged care.

Where care is arranged and funded by local authorities or the NHS, families may find themselves as mere cogs in a bewildering welfare–incapacity complex. However, if they actively oppose the arrangements then they may need to act as 'liberators' (Unsworth, 1987: 9). In comparison with the MHA's analogous role of 'nearest relative', families have fewer avenues for resistance under the DoLS/LPS: they may be passed over for the key roles of RPR/'appropriate person' altogether if the supervisory/responsible body deems it not in the person's 'best interests', and they have no right to 'object' to admission or 'discharge' by merely giving written notice. Statistical studies of DoLS appeals reveal that families very rarely initiate court challenges to detention (Series et al, 2017b). One octogenarian RPR, attempting to liberate a friend from a care home, described feeling 'the full force of the state was battling against her', a 'complex and harrowing' experience (House of Lords Select Committee on the MCA, 2014: [287]). In one celebrated case of liberation via the DoLS, discussed in Chapter 8, Mark Neary successfully challenged the detention of his autistic son, Steven Neary, in a 'positive behaviour unit', but the process took almost a year (*London Borough of Hillingdon v Neary* [2011] EWHC 1377 (COP)).

Families might also be positioned in this legal-bureaucratic web as squeaky wheels, sources of friction against social care's overarching rationalities of 'empowerment' and managing 'vulnerability'. Social care detention processes can be connected with 'safeguarding' matters; in some cases DoLS may serve as a post-hoc safeguard on poorly conducted investigations or unfair procedures. Meanwhile families may also come into conflict with professionals acting to 'empower' their relatives by removing them from family-based care, on grounds that this will foster their independence and autonomy, sometimes with the result that the 'empowered' person is deprived of their liberty. I discuss examples of this paradoxical phenomenon in later chapters.

And finally, following *Cheshire West*, families will increasingly find themselves drawn into this legal web through surveillance and management of care which they provide within their own homes. As I explain in Chapter 8 the acid test means that some 'informal' care arrangements are now legally categorized as a 'deprivation of liberty' requiring 'authorization' and management via the courts (at present) or LPS (in future). 'Domestic DoLS', as this is colloquially known, extends the law of institutions into wholly new territory, not even reached at its most extensive during the carceral era (Chapter 3). This possibly unintended by-product of *Cheshire West* holds considerable potential for a toxic political backlash against not only social care detention's primary legal structures (MCA DoLS/LPS) but human rights law itself. Yet it is not wholly clear what problem a legal framework classically directed toward managing the threat of institutional carceral care is addressing in family care environments, nor what new problems and politically charged socio-legal relations it will engender here.

★★★

Social care detention harnesses a varied range of problems met by 'social care' interventions to the carceral-era legal machinery of safeguards for individual liberty, doing so under the paradoxical and often irreconcilable banners of empowerment and vulnerability. A number of interlocking legal technologies shaped by post-carceral ideologies make up this machine: 'decision-specific' substitute decision making; a functional/cognitive test of mental capacity; 'best interests' with elements of substituted judgement; human rights standards of 'necessity', 'proportionality' and 'least restriction'; new techniques of 'supported decision making'. Together these technologies enable highly flexible legal responses, capable of encompassing almost any question posed regarding the care, treatment and general welfare of its target populations in surprisingly granular detail. Yet this machine is also enormously complicated. Despite initial intentions for a simple, principled and informal capacity jurisdiction, it resembles an expensive new car requiring a specialist garage when a dashboard warning light shows. Its outcomes can be hard to predict, being highly permeable to a wide range of often-conflicting rationalities, values and considerations, contested knowledge and expertise; a great deal depends on the end users. Coupled to the expansive and transgressive acid test of deprivation of liberty, it has the potential to reshape the landscape of care.

Social care detention poses politically charged questions about the limits of what law can do to ameliorate serious problems in post-carceral community care settings, and the potential dangers of seeking to do so. These questions and dilemmas cannot be clearly understood so long as social care detention – and detention under the MCA more generally – is approached as merely a variant of mental health detention, a sub-section in healthcare law textbooks, as 'informal', non-compulsory, as mental health detention 'lite'. Social care detention is not less coercive than mental health detention, it is a different phenomenon, addressing different kinds of problems, different populations, with different interventions and different legal machinery.

However, social care detention can appear less coercive than mental health detention for a number of reasons: because its locus is 'the community', which is symbolically associated with liberation from the institution (although carceral-institutional practices exist there too); because it is seen as a system of *safeguards* on what is already happening and not a new compulsory power (although what is already happening can be very coercive); because its overarching rationalities appear emancipatory and benevolent (although this can result in lower thresholds to intervene, rather than less coercive interventions); because its legal technologies are closely aligned to the values and norms of the post-carceral era (although their fundamental elements achieve the same ends as compulsory powers, but with weaker tools for would-be liberators); because they are operated by reformers with a strong allegiance to post-carceral projects, destabilizing medical hegemony (facilitating expansion into new categories of 'the vulnerable'); and because history has taught us to consider its target populations as not really in possession of 'liberty' in the first place, consigned to a realm beyond the law, of legal ghosts.

3

The Law of Institutions

During what Unsworth (1991) and Castel (1988) called the carceral era, a period dating from the late 18th century through to the middle of the 20th century, the landscape of care became increasingly dominated by institutional confinement. A bifurcated legal framework developed to regulate the institutional confinement of people with mental disabilities, which I call the 'law of institutions'. One branch of the law of institutions conferred safeguards for individual liberty; the second branch deployed licensing and inspection to regulate the conditions within. I address these frameworks together, referring to them as the 'law of institutions', to highlight that they were directed toward governing institutions and their operators as much as acting upon their target populations.

These classical carceral-era legal structures have endured for almost 250 years. In England and Wales today, the liberty safeguards branch is performed by the MHA and the MCA DoLS/LPS, and regulatory functions are performed by the Care Quality Commission (CQC) in England, and the Healthcare Inspectorate Wales (HIW) and Care Inspectorate Wales (CIW). Similar structures exist across most Global North and some Global South countries (Pathare and Sagad, 2013; World Health Organization, 2017). Similar principles and logics are also encoded into international human rights law, explored in Chapter 5.

The first half of this chapter considers how carceral care came to be problematized, and the turn to law to manage these problems. Just as social care detention is imbued with reformist rationalities, the law of institutions was an important tool for 19th-century reformers driving through a new 'humane' vision of care, premised on the curative asylum. It established medical hegemony over the management of 'lunacy' and became a key weapon in intra-professional culture wars. Yet despite its original purpose in restraining carceral institutions, I show how the law of institutions provided a scaffolding for carceral expansion during the 19th century under new rationalities, making inroads into the management of 'lunacy' by families and within the home. Like social care detention, 19th-century legalism encountered resistance formulated in terms of the privacy of patients and families, and the economic interests, benevolent intentions and clinical expertise of institutional operators. Yet these were not simply opposing forces, but rather a mutually 'enabling relay between law and disciplinary power' (Golder and Fitzpatrick, 2009: 27). What can we learn today from the paradoxes and struggles of 19th-century legalism?

In the second half of this chapter, I examine the rationalities and forms of 'expertise' that increasingly partitioned the main target populations of social care detention – people with intellectual disabilities and older adults with dementia – from the main 'lunacy' institutions and regulatory structures. New specialist institutions, surrounded by less thoroughgoing forms of legalism, enfolded the increasingly diverse problematizations and extended temporalities characterizing social care detention today. I show how these distinctive rationalities and carceral systems both laid the foundations for contemporary social care, including different kinds of professional expertise and administrative structures, and produced a sense of populations that do not belong within lunacy administration, and whose liberty is less worthy of salvaging.

The law of institutions: a landscape sketch

The law of institutions overlays a particular picture of the landscape of care. Within this landscape there are certain enclosed and isolated locations – 'institutions' – that are spatially, legally and socially separate from the 'community' and distinguished from private homes. Symbolically, and legally, the carceral institution came to be synonymous with 'detention' and public law regulatory structures; home and community represented freedom and the private sphere.

A key tenet of the law of institutions is that some people belong in 'institutions' (at least some of the time), and others do not. Contemporary mental health law parses these populations through the concept of 'mental disorder', replacing earlier medico-legal categories of 'lunacy', 'insanity', 'idiocy' and 'mental deficiency' discussed in this chapter. A key function of the law of institutions is to sort populations into the locations (institution or community) where they correctly belong through processes governing admission and discharge. This sorting mechanism serves several protective functions: first, to protect those living in 'the community' from 'dangerous' persons who properly belong in the institution; second, to protect those who belong in the institution from the hazards of life in the community; and third, to protect those who belong in the community from inappropriate institutional incarceration. A fourth function is legitimation and protection from liability for institutionalized carceral care.

The law of institutions' regulatory branch seeks to ensure that institutional conditions do not fall below a standard that would be tolerated by society (albeit not necessarily standards that most of society would wish to live in). Like the sorting function, this regulation and monitoring function rests on an imaginary landscape of care where institutions are clearly identifiable spatial locations that can be registered and visited. Institutions are distinguished within this regulatory landscape from homes and other private dwellings in the community; locations that are inapt for regulatory monitoring and visitation. Whereas homes are construed as private, institutions are construed as hidden, closed settings, separated from the community, but rendered publicly accountable by this regulatory apparatus.

In later chapters I will show how both branches of the law of institutions struggled to manage the increasingly blurred boundary between homes and institutions during the post-carceral era. Here, I focus on beginnings, how the conceptual, legal and social foundations of these remarkably durable regulatory structures were laid.

Regulating the 'trade in lunacy'

Institutional care predates the carceral era (for example, almshouses), while forms of 'community care' – including kinship care, domestic assistance and 'boarding out' with other households – continued throughout it. However, historians of the period concur that unprecedented numbers of older and disabled people came to be confined to increasingly large institutions during the carceral era (Horden and Smith, 1998; Bartlett and Wright, 1999; Suzuki, 2006). In Britain this 'great confinement' gathered momentum during the 19th century (contra Foucault (2001/1961), who dated this earlier), reaching its high-water mark in the mid-20th century. Porter (1987: 111) reports an official count of 2,590 'lunatics' in licensed houses for the 'mad' in the 1810s; by 1899 nearly 100,000 'lunatics' were detained in public asylums, workhouses and licensed houses (Commissioners in Lunacy, 1899), and by 1955 there would be over 153,500 NHS hospital beds for 'mental treatment' and 'lunacy', 58,400 for 'mental deficiency', and 1,500 'chronically sick' in long-stay psychiatric annexes (Lord Percy, 1957).

The beginnings of this carceral trend were not, however, the result of a coordinated exercise of central authority, but rather the product of an emerging capitalist culture (Porter, 1987, 1994). Formal powers to detain the 'furiously mad and dangerous' did exist – codified in the Vagrancy Acts of 1714 and 1744 (Blackstone, 2016: 16). They were directed toward maintaining public order rather than securing care or treatment, authorizing detention in any 'secure place'; potentially a madhouse, but also possibly a workhouse, lock-up, bridewell or gaol (Jones, 1972; Porter, 1987). However, most people confined in madhouses in the 18th century would have been placed there by families, perhaps wanting to draw a 'discreet veil' (Scull, 1993: 20) over the existence of mad relatives. Others would be placed by public bodies – parishes discharging obligations toward the 'impotent poor' under the old Poor Law, or by the naval or war offices. Most of those confined as mad in the 18th century were not subject to formal compulsory powers (Jones, 1972), but received into madhouses on the non-juridical authority of those willing to pay the keepers' fees. As Foucault (2006: 95) observed of parallel developments in France, practices of confinement in private madhouses did not originate in a legal power, but rather came to be 'surrounded' by legal procedures, mirroring the contemporary narrative of social care detention as a system of safeguards on practices that were already occurring.

Why did the madhouses come to be clothed in the law of institutions? What problems led 18th-century England to turn to law? The law of institutions developed in response to pressure exerted by 'claims makers' (Butler and Drakeford, 2005: 2) – journalists, campaigners, committees of inquiry and regulatory commissions – calling attention to threats to society posed by this private carceral industry. Skilfully deploying litigation and scandal they narrated two key concerns: the danger of wrongful confinement, and appalling conditions within private madhouses.

Owing to the secrecy surrounding the industry, relatively little is known about conditions within 18th-century private madhouses. Madhouse keepers were entrepreneurs in an increasingly lucrative 'trade in lunacy' (Parry-Jones, 1972; Porter, 1987, 1994). They were not necessarily medical men; only a handful made promises of treatment or cure. They might be people providing small-scale 'boarding out' services for parishes, specializing in the care and management of 'lunatics' or, at the other end of the market, medical men or clergy might care for a 'single patient' within their own home, offering 'privacy' for wealthy or powerful families. Large madhouses, like the notorious Hoxton madhouse which held 486 patients by 1815, were 'highly exceptional' during the 18th century. Most were very small, holding perhaps four to ten patients (Porter, 1987: 141). Parry-Jones (1972) and Porter (1987) consider that at least some private madhouses and early charitable asylums treated their inmates with kindness, although Scull (1993: 20–1) contends that those catering to the 'pauper lunatics' market offered 'confinement of a meaner sort'. Within the public imagination, the 'gothic madhouse run by scheming ruffians' was associated with scandalously poor treatment (Scull, 1993: 24), while the first hospital for the 'mad' – Bethlem – 'became a byword for man's inhumanity to man' (Porter, 1987: 123).

In the late 18th century, the problem of wrongful confinement and the appeal to individual liberty were more effective drivers of reform than the conditions of confinement. This way of narrating the problem was non-abolitionist; implicit in 'wrongful confinement' is the sense that some people are rightly confined, and what is needed are juridical mechanisms and some form of expertise to sort those populations.

Daniel Defoe (1728) called for the 'suppression' of madhouses, railing against the 'vile Practice now so much in vogue among the better Sort' of husbands confining wives to 'these cursed houses' thereby burying 'his vertuous Wife alive, that he may have the greater Freedom with his Mistresses'. An influential article in the *Gentleman's Magazine* called for redress 'in a land of liberty' (Urban, 1763). Habeas applications on behalf of those claiming to be wrongfully confined in madhouses at the behest of spouses or parents came before the courts. In *Rex v Turlington* (1761) 97 ER 741 Lord Mansfield despatched a physician to a private Chelsea madhouse kept by Turlington to determine whether Mrs Deborah D'Vebre was indeed 'mad'. Upon the doctor's sworn affidavit that she was not, the writ was granted and D'Vebre was released. In *Rex v William Clarke* (1762) 97 ER 875, the court was satisfied by an affidavit from the physician who had sent a Mrs Hunt to a madhouse that she 'was not in a condition fit to be taken out of the care and custody of those to whom her person was intrusted'. Medical men began to cement their hegemonic role within the law, professing expertise in who should – and should not – be confined.

In response to growing public pressure, a parliamentary committee was established, chaired by the Whig MP Thomas Townshend (1763: 8), to report on the 'State of the Private Madhouses in This Kingdom'. Townshend's Committee heard evidence from witnesses claiming to have been wrongfully confined in madhouses, and from Turlington – the keeper of the Chelsea madhouse. Turlington told the Committee that it was his practice to admit all persons brought to him, that no physicians visited the house and no register of persons was kept. His agent, King, told the Committee that during his six years as Turlington's superintendent, he had 'never admitted [a person] as a Lunatic', and that he would not refuse any person brought, provided someone could pay their board.

Following this rather startling evidence, the Committee was persuaded that the state of private madhouses in the kingdom did indeed require legislation. Townshend's (1763: 4) report encapsulated the basic twofold reformist problematization of institutional carceral care:

1. The manner of admitting persons into houses now kept for the reception of lunatics; and,
2. The treatment of them, during their confinement.

It took Townshend 11 years to pass legislation regulating madhouses. The Madhouses Act 1774 established, for the first time, the two basic elements of the law of institutions: a regulatory system for licensing and visitation, and mechanisms to protect against wrongful confinement.

Lunacy (law) reform

By most accounts, the 1774 Act embodied an 'ineffectual' form of legalism (Jones, 1972: 31). Its licensing technology made it a criminal offence to 'conceal, harbour, entertain, or confine, in any house or place kept for the reception of lunatics, more than one lunatic at any time' without a licence, punishable by a substantial fine. A similar offence of running an unregulated care service underpins care regulation today. However, despite the criminal sanction, regulatory supervision was weak. Licensing and visitation were overseen by a Physician Commission in metropolitan London, elected from members of the Royal College of Physicians, and Justices of the Peace elsewhere. The Commission held periodical meetings to consider licence applications and visited all licensed institutions annually. However, they had no powers to revoke or refuse licences, visits were announced and perfunctory (Jones, 1972; Porter, 1987; Scull, 1993), and the Commission chose not to use the one remaining weapon potentially at their disposal – public censure – for fear of libel actions (Roberts, 1981). The 1774 Act introduced a minimal admissions procedure – a madhouse keeper could only admit a paying patient if there was a signed 'lunacy' certificate by a medical man (who could himself be the keeper, or in his pay). Habeas applications remained the only means of challenging confinement. Its tendency was 'to *license* the abuses of the status quo, rather than eradicate them' (Porter, 1987: 152).

The 1774 Act did, however, place institutional regulation firmly 'on the agenda of public concern' (Porter, 1987: 153), creating a platform for reformers to lobby for a more expansive and thoroughgoing form of legalism, and for new rationalities of institutional confinement. Early 19th-century madhouses and charitable asylums supplied a ready stock of scandalous conditions and dubious practices for reformers to stoke public outrage and call for stronger regulation and improved institutions (Butler and Drakeford, 2005; Wise, 2012). The 19th century was regularly punctuated by lunacy reform legislation driven by these scandals, building ever more elaborate safeguards against conflicts of interest in institutional admissions processes, and more expansive and thoroughgoing institutional regulation.

The next major juncture in lunacy reform was the 1828 Madhouses Act, the eventual fruits of a campaign by the chair of the Parliamentary Select Committee on Madhouses (1815, 1816), George Rose, arguing for the 'indispensable necessity of legislative interference' (HC Deb 11 July 1815 vol 31 cc 1145). Rose's committee raised concerns about the conditions of those incarcerated in charitable hospitals and workhouses – which lay outside the scope of the 1774 Act – as well as private madhouses. It highlighted the case of Bethlem inmate William Norris, who had been chained for nine years in an iron collar so restrictive he could not stand, yet who appeared perfectly sane to visitors, who found him reading a book. Filthy and overcrowded conditions were reported at Bethlem, the York Asylum and elsewhere, as well as the suspicious deaths of inmates.

The 1828 Act replaced the Physician Commission with the Metropolitan Commission, who conducted a national survey of 'public and private asylums' across England and Wales (Metropolitan Commissioners in Lunacy, 1844). The Lunacy Act 1845 expanded their role into a new national licensing body and inspectorate – the Lunacy Commission – which remained the ultimate authority in lunacy regulation for an impressive seven decades.

Like social care detention, 19th-century legalism was expansive; regulators and reformers sought jurisdiction over new locations and populations. The Commissions' supervision eventually extended over private licensed houses, public asylums, charitable hospitals, workhouses and gaols where 'lunatics' were 'kept'. Its regulatory powers and duties were extensive by today's lights. The Metropolitan Commission was required to send three commissioners (including one doctor), and the Lunacy Commission a doctor and a barrister, to every licensed house at least four times a year (increased to six by the Lunacy Act 1890). They were empowered to 'examine the Persons confined' in such manner as they saw fit, and to summon witnesses to give evidence on oath.

Their duties included inspecting every part of the house or hospital, lunacy certificates, making enquiries about the number of patients, their diet, any occupation and amusements, inquiring whether any patient was 'under Restraint, and why', and whether 'there has been adopted any System of Non-coercion' and its results (Lunacy Act 1845, ss 61, 64). The Commissions were also empowered to discharge patients if after several successive visits they concluded that a person was detained without 'sufficient cause'; a power they exercised infrequently, however, preferring to informally 'suggest' to the patient's friends or Parish Officers that they were ready for 'liberation' (Commissioners in Lunacy, 1847: 471). In parallel, 'asylum visitors' were required to 'inspect' all patients on regular visits. The Commissions reported annually to the Lord Chancellor on the state and conditions of those places they visited.

Nineteenth-century legalism was preoccupied with managing the financial conflicts of interests of institutional operators and medical men through safeguards to secure the 'liberty of the subject'. Legislative reforms often followed widely publicized scandals of 'wrongful confinement' in private madhouses involving wealthy or powerful families; their stories are eloquently told by Wise (2012). The 1828 Act added a requirement for a second medical opinion for admission; later legislation required that these doctors not be in partnership (Lunacy Act 1845, s45), nor receiving 'a percentage' or otherwise interested in payments by the patient to the establishment (Lunacy Acts (Amendment) Act 1862, s24), nor be related to the patient, nor have their care as a single patient, nor be on the managing committee of the hospital or be a commissioner (Lunacy Act 1890, ss 30–3). The Lunacy Act 1890, dubbed the 'triumph of legalism' by Kathleen Jones (1972), required judicial authorization for any non-urgent 'reception orders' for admission to an institution (usually by a Justice of the Peace). The 1890 Act remained in force until it was repealed in 1960.

Nineteenth-century reformers espoused a positive vision of humane and curative institutional confinement, of *asylum*, carefully counterposed to the 18th-century madhouse's associations with manacles and whips, cruelty and fear (Porter, 1987). These 'moral entrepreneurs' (Becker, 1963/2018; Scull, 1993) took as their inspiration the 'moral treatment' practised by Samuel Tuke (1813) at the Quaker-run York Retreat. This system of care espoused 'humane' treatment combined with moral discipline, an inspiration for the 'non-restraint' movement later championed by the psychiatrists John Conolly and James Bucknill. The idea of a humane, scientific, moral and – critically – *curative* model of institutional confinement heavily influenced the work of the Lunacy Commission (Fennell, 1996). It was the guiding rationality for a national scheme of constructing county asylums (Scull, 1993), eventually mandated by the County Asylums Act 1845.

The asylums firmly established the hegemony of the medical profession in the management of 'lunacy' (Unsworth, 1993). They enabled the development of the 'science of mental disease' by containing populations for observation and classification, for pioneering and practising new treatments (Foucault, 2001/1961). By today's lights many of these treatments were brutal and ineffective: surgical interventions, including clitoridectomies and other gynaecological surgeries, paving the way for widespread use of subsequently discredited psychosurgeries such as lobotomy and prefrontal leucotomies in the 1940s; and reliance on often lethal narcotic agents to sedate patients: belladonna, hyoscyamine, paraldehyde, strychnine. The legality of surgical procedures without the patients' consent was a source of institutional anxiety; some doctors sought not only the consent of the nearest relative but also the sanction of the Lunacy Commission, who were 'not only now being seen as the arbiter in cases where surgical treatment had to be given without the patient's consent, but also as a form of insurance against possible liability' (Fennell, 1996: 72).

Meanwhile, as the 19th century wore on, the asylums became increasingly overcrowded, and conditions deteriorated (Scull, 1993). The massive growth in the institutionalized population has been attributed (variously) to the new wealth and commercial opportunities for managing 'mad' family members among the emerging middle classes, changing social circumstances with industrialization that made it harder for working class families to care for 'lunatic' or 'idiot' relatives, the Poor Law shift toward institutional 'indoor relief' in the mid-19th century, the changing face of the 'curative' asylum which made it less socially unacceptable to seek an institutional solution to familial difficulties, and perhaps also growing intolerance of 'mad' or disabled persons within the wider community (Porter, 1987; Scull, 1993; Wright, 1997; Jarrett, 2020).

What was the role of law in this expansion and intensification of institutional confinement? In the late 18th century, reformers' aimed to restrain a private 'trade in lunacy', to ensure only the 'truly mad' were incarcerated, and to ameliorate the worst conditions in madhouses. The Lunacy Commission has been praised for removing the most 'overtly custodial' features of lunacy institutions; the use of whips, chains and other 'mechanical restraints' to manage the mad was virtually eliminated (Hervey, 1987: 277). Yet, over the next two centuries, carceral institutions grew in number and in size, and new forms of violence proliferated – including lethal medications, brutal surgeries, 'water' cures and other harmful measures under the dubious guise of 'treatment'.

The law of institutions did not act as a mere brake, but also served as a scaffold supporting the construction of these carceral edifices. It conferred legitimacy on carceral practices that was lacking in the eyes of the 18th-century public, partly by establishing the hegemony of doctors as experts in the management of lunacy, adopting a seductive 'enlightened' carceral rationality – of 'humane', scientific and curative treatment, and by appearing to act as a restraint on more dubious exercises of disciplinary power.

The paradox at the heart of the law of institutions – or law and disciplinary power more generally – is described by Golder and Fitzpatrick (2009: 64) in the following terms:

> By purporting to exercise its supervisory jurisdiction only over the more egregious aberrations, abuses and excesses of disciplinary power, law confirms the basic claim at the heart of disciplinary power to adjudicate on questions of normality and social cohesion. In so doing, it inscribes the disciplinary project in the very nature of things.

The law of institutions did not merely restrain psychiatric power, but also constituted its authority (Fennell, 1986; Foucault, 2003). Medical men were aware of this. Although some resisted the necessity for 'medical certification', an editorial (1861) in the *Journal of Mental Science* (now the *British Journal of Psychiatry*) asked what else prevented the authority to confine being bestowed on rival professions, such as lawyers or the clergy?

Reflecting on this history, the question we must ask ourselves today is what existing and new forms of power might we be confirming through the machinery of social care detention? What are the dangers of uncritically embracing its expansive rationalities? This history warns us of the regulatory paradoxes that legalism can license and normalize a problematic status quo – as Porter argued the 1774 Act did – and create platforms for the expansion of new carceral rationalities, practices, structures and populations.

Frontiers of resistance

Domestic psychiatry

What resistance did carceral-era reformers meet in championing the law of institution and its increasingly aggressive legalism? Townshend battled opposition to madhouses legislation in the House of Lords. Scull (1993) and Porter (1987) attribute this to physicians and clergy, many of whose members profited from the care and confinement of 'single patients' from wealthier families, and the wealthy and powerful families who might use their services. Hervey (1987: 210) describes how 'an extensive and cohesive network' of private licensed houses, lunacy practitioners and the Asylum Officers Association provided opposition to the Lunacy Commission. Meanwhile, working uneasily alongside reformers, former lunacy institution inmates formed the first 'survivor' group – the Alleged Lunatics Friend Society – which, while it failed to mobilize public support and was 'constantly treated with disdain' by lunacy authorities, managed to make a 'substantial contribution to patients' rights', thereby strengthening reformist legalism (Hervey, 1986: 245).

I wish to dwell on two particular frontiers of resistance in the 19th century that we can also discern in the struggles and skirmishes of social care detention today: contested frontiers between families, 'lunacy' management and the law of institutions, including what Suzuki (2006) calls the sphere of 'domestic psychiatry', and the role of the law of institutions as a weapon in intra-professional culture wars.

During the carceral era the authority of families to incarcerate and decarcerate their relatives as they saw fit was slowly eroded and authority to confine and liberate was gradually transferred to medico-welfare institutions, adjudicated over by the Commission. At the beginning of the carceral era, families featured mainly as 'custodians' of the person, exercising the 'natural' authority to confine their relations. In regulating the private madhouse trade via safeguards for individual liberty, the law of institutions inserted a mediating role of law and medical expertise into private arrangements between families and 'keepers'. Families were gradually refashioned from the 'Person by whose Authority such Person was sent' to a madhouse (Madhouses Act 1828, s37) to 'petitioners' (Lunacy Act 1890 s5), 'requesting' the lunacy authorities to confine their relations (Lunacy Act 1845, Schedule B). The management of mad relatives was no longer a private family matter, but subject to higher authorities.

As these higher authorities consolidated powers to confine, the law began to feature families as 'liberators'. The Madhouses Act 1828 makes no reference to how families might discharge their relatives from private madhouses – presumably this 'power' was implicit in their role as the 'authority' for sending the person. However, from the Lunacy Act 1845 onward, families could be 'barred' from exercising powers of discharge by doctors certifying that the patient was 'dangerous and unfit to be at large'. Then, as today, liberation was harder for those relying on state authorities to provide alternative means of support to institutional confinement. From the County Asylums Act 1828 onward, 'pauper lunatics' could only be discharged by a relative or friend if they satisfied parish overseers that they would 'no longer be chargeable to the Parish'.

For wealthy and powerful families, a more powerful inspectorate threatened their 'private' interests in managing mad relations, risking their exposure (Jones, 1972; Roberts, 1981). This played out in skirmishes over the boundaries of the law of institutions, particularly concerning 'single patients' who were likely to have been placed in a 'single house' precisely to preserve secrecy. From the 1774 Act until the close of the carceral era, the minimalist definition of a 'lunacy institution', subject to licensing and visitation by a Commission, required the presence of 'two or more' lunatics kept for profit (Lushington, 1895). This definition was designed to exclude single patients with wealthy relations from licensing and regulation requirements (Hervey, 1987; Jones, 1972: 181). However, the 1828 Act eventually imposed certification requirements on single patients, and this remained the case until the Lunacy Act 1890 was repealed in the 1960s. We should note, therefore, that *Cheshire West* did not break new ground by including even those living in individual quasi-domestic arrangements within the ambit of liberty safeguards.

A 'register' of all lunatics was a key safeguard against mysterious disappearances into lunacy institutions; yet wealthy families objected to the names of their relatives appearing on a document open to all commissioners (Wise, 2012). Duties to notify the Commission of single patients were widely resisted and ignored (Commissioners in Lunacy, 1858: 77–8; Hervey, 1987). Eventually the Commission established a 'private register' of single patients, which could only be viewed by a 'private committee' within the Commission. Although the Commission did not license 'single houses', members of this private committee were eventually empowered to visit single patients received for profit (Lunacy Act 1845, s89, s91), and were later granted powers to discharge them (Lunacy Amendment Act 1853, s17).

The Commission also sought to expand its oversight to include 'lunatics' being cared for in their own homes or the family home; those Jones (1972: 181) calls 'Mrs Rochesters', after the 'mad' wife confined to an attic by her husband and a nurse/keeper in Charlotte Brontë's 1847 novel *Jane Eyre*. These most intimate sites of 'domestic psychiatry' (Suzuki, 2006), single patients and 'hidden lunatics' in private dwellings, were narrated by the Commissioners in Lunacy (1858: 78) as the 'most helpless and neglected class of the Insane', detailing shocking accounts of severe neglect in their reports. The Commission called for powers to remove single patients, and to visit and require medical reports on those cared for by their families (Select Committee on Lunacy Law, 1877, 1878). The Commission also prosecuted alleged 'false imprisonment', neglect and abuse of those confined within domestic settings, with mixed success. One judge found that the law did not permit a man to 'take upon himself the custody of a lunatic', another concluded there was no imprisonment as 'the lunatic was a prisoner by nature' (Suzuki, 2006; Wise, 2012: 189, 193). This discursive trope of 'the prison within' (Ben-Moshe, 2020: 261) is deployed by courts to neutralize claims to liberty where they are unwelcome – here in the domestic sphere. We will encounter it again in the deprivation of liberty litigation discussed in Chapter 8.

Although powers existed for removal of lunatics 'wandering at large', the Commission's powers to forcibly remove patients from private dwellings to the asylum were unclear. Within the domestic sphere they were mainly limited to issuing warnings or advice to families, applying 'invisible pressure' through the intervention of other relatives, friends or neighbours (Suzuki, 2006: 173). By highlighting, publicizing and prosecuting cases of neglect and abuse of 'hidden lunatics', domestic confinement began to lose its social legitimacy and arouse public anxiety (Suzuki, 2006; Wise, 2012). A new rationality of protecting adults against domestic abuse or neglect was enfolded into lunacy law, and is central to social care detention today. Local Justices of the Peace were empowered to visit persons 'deemed to be a lunatic' who were 'not under proper care and control' or were 'cruelly treated' and make directions for their removal to an asylum (Lunacy Act 1890, s59(3)). The Lunacy Commission was empowered to visit and require medical reports on any person 'detained or treated as a lunatic or alleged lunatic', even within private families, where such persons came to their knowledge, and to request that the Lord Chancellor may make directions for their removal for care elsewhere (Lunacy Act 1890, s206). The commissioners did not, however, subsequently report on using this power, suggesting it was little used.

As the carceral era wore on, regimes of domestic psychiatry were increasingly subjected to external supervision and intervention: 'the existence of a lunatic in a family itself destabilized the boundary between the public and private spheres and invited forceful intervention from the outside world', constantly threatening 'to transform the domestic sphere of the family into an open field of contention' (Suzuki, 2006: 117, 131). Yet, at the same time, the Commission was cautious: 'public opinion was still not ripe for state officials routinely to enter domestic spaces unless there were grave allegations of wrongdoing' (Hervey, 1987; Wise, 2012: 194).

Non-restraint

The law of institutions did not so much restrain carceral practices, as transform, legitimate and expand their reach by absorbing new reformist rationalities. Yet these rationalities were not passively absorbed, but rather the law itself – through the Lunacy Commission in this case – was an active agent in selecting between competing claims to expertise and authority. The non-restraint philosophy that inspired many reformers and infused the work of the Commission was not uncontroversial within psychiatry. Debates raged in the newly established *Asylum Journal* and elsewhere, with critics highlighting concerns about the alternatives proposed (primarily seclusion, sedation, 'blistering' and purgatives), calling the growing use of narcotics to manage confined populations 'chemical restraint' (Fennell, 1996).

Yet there were limits to how far the Commission, as a regulator, could impose its views on the appropriate treatment of patients, lest it stray into the protected territory of clinical expertise. The Commission 'denied itself a role in decisions about medical treatment', yet the 'conundrum of where treatment ends and restraint or punishment begins' was almost insoluble (Fennell, 1996: 27). In a notable example, the Commission prosecuted medical superintendent Charles Snape for manslaughter after directing a 'shower bath' to 'calm' a patient who had hit him, that was so forceful the patient suffocated. The prosecution failed and Snape was reinstated in his role after the court and asylum authorities considered this a question of 'treatment', falling within his clinical discretion (Fennell, 1996). During its lifetime, the Commission sought to closely regulate practices of concern that it could not outright prohibit, such as bathing, seclusion and restraint, because they straddled the boundary between regulatory jurisdiction and clinical expertise. The 'paradoxical result' was that 'whilst intended to limit their use it also legitimised them as medical interventions' (Fennell, 1996: 35).

In later chapters I will show how today's 'empowerment entrepreneurs' aim to use regulation and social care detention safeguards to limit practices of concern, yet similar paradoxical results can ensue. This is partly because certain terrain is protected – for example, funding allocations by public bodies. But it is also because even when 'black boxes' are prised open, becoming open fields of contestation in law – as, for example, 'best interests' is today (Harrington, 2017) – they can never be wholly and irrevocably colonized by a particular rationality, reformist or otherwise. Law's 'very lack of perduring and determinate content' renders it 'inherently amenable to appropriation and instrumentalization by external powers' (Golder and Fitzpatrick, 2009: 83). As a weapon in intra-professional culture wars, today's reformers would do well to note Foucault's (1977b: 151) point, that law is always open to a 'resurgence of new forces', and 'can be bent to any purpose' – not always the purpose reformers would read into it.

Partitioning populations

In Chapter 2, I explained that one of the key differences between social care detention and mental health detention is their main target populations.

Social care detention is oriented toward the confinement of older adults, particularly those with dementia, and people with developmental disabilities. These populations are also widely viewed as properly 'outside' of mental health law. This section explains how social care detention's target populations were gradually separated out from the main legal and institutional structures of the asylums and lunacy legislation during the 19th and 20th centuries. Different rationalities for confinement came to enfold new social 'problems' now managed via social care detention. Traces of these problematizations can still be discerned in contemporary rationalities of 'empowerment' and 'vulnerability' today. The elongated temporality of social care detention was fundamental to partitioning these populations, the sense that here were people in a state of 'perpetual infirmity' (Brydall, 1700; cited in Jarrett, 2020: 26), presenting a social, familial, economic, national and legal burden.

'Idiots' and 'senile dements' within lunacy law

Legal distinctions between developmental and psychosocial disability are not new. Pre-carceral legal structures distinguished between guardianship of the estates and wealth of 'idiots' – those born into a state of 'incapacity' for whom a lifetime solution was required, and 'lunatics' in a temporary state of incapacity, for whom only a temporary solution was needed (Neugebauer, 1996; Jarrett, 2020). Yet these distinctions applied only to the very wealthy, linked to the Crown's interest in protecting land and bloodlines.

During the carceral era, when the tutelary relationship expanded to include the poor and unlanded, different impairments were tumbled together into an expansive definition of 'lunatic', which explicitly included 'idiots' (for example, Lunacy Act 1845, s114; Lunacy Act 1890, s341). The law of institutions only gradually distinguished 'idiocy' and 'imbecility' (a less severe 'grade' of 'idiocy') from the more general category of 'lunacy' (Digby, 1996: 131).

During the 19th century, families remained the primary caregivers for people with intellectual disabilities (Wright, 1998, 2001) and dementia (Andrews, 2014; Andrews, 2017), although growing numbers 'drifted' into the workhouse (Bartlett, 1998, 1999a; Andrews, 2014; Andrews, 2017; Jarrett, 2020: 218). Some, however, ended up in the asylums. There, as 'chronic' and 'incurable' cases, they presented dilemmas for the rationalities of mental health detention, 'silting up' the asylum and frustrating its therapeutic claims (Select Committee on Lunatics, 1860; Digby, 1996: 5; Andrews, 2014). Analysis of historical asylum records suggest 'chronics' and 'incurables' were indeed swelling the asylum population. Although for most the asylum was a 'temporary' measure, the statistical outcome of even a relatively small proportion of admissions remaining in the asylums for a long time is that eventually they became a large proportion of the overall inmate population (Wright, 1997).

Older people with dementia – known as 'senile dements' or 'senile imbeciles' – also represented a 'perpetual classificatory residuum' for the lunacy system (Andrews, 2014: 241). They represented a small proportion (3.9 per cent) of overall asylum admissions, but were still regarded as a strain on the overcrowded asylum system (Commissioners in Lunacy, 1883) and as 'too challenging' to conform to workhouse regimes (Andrews, 2017: 244). Dementia was often construed by psychiatrists as a natural rather than pathological phenomenon, deploying certification strategically as a mechanism to resist asylum admission (on grounds of lack of lunacy) (Andrews, 2017). We might draw connections with the Law Commission's (2017: [9.13]) belief that 'pure' brain disorders do not constitute 'mental disorders' as defined by s1 MHA.

These populations were problematic for other aspects of the asylum's therapeutic rationalities. The detention of 'harmless chronics', not 'dangerous' to themselves or others, brought common law libertarianism into conflict with psychiatric expansionism (Unsworth, 1993). By the late 19th century, the asylum was considered to have 'failed' in its curative aspirations, in part because of the problem of 'chronics'. Psychiatrists like Henry Maudsley wanted to wrestle psychiatric treatment free of its connection with detention, rebranding 'asylums' as hospitals, focusing on the treatment of curable patients, positioning psychiatry as a 'normal' branch of medicine.

This aspiration relied upon the legalization of *voluntary* treatment – breaking the connection between inpatient status and detention (Unsworth, 1993). Voluntary status was opposed by those concerned about the lack of protection for the liberty of patients (Select Committee on Lunacy Law, 1877). Advocates of voluntarism viewed 'liberty' as a 'popular bugbear' standing in the way of progress (Haynes, 1870: 564). The 1890 Act only permitted 'voluntary' treatment with the written consent of two Lunacy Commissioners or Justices of the Peace (s229). Eventually, the Mental Treatment Act 1930 introduced a 'power to receive voluntary patients', requiring a formal application by the patient. Where patients were 'incapable' of making an application, it could be countersigned by two doctors. This provision was little used (Unsworth, 1987), but established the notion of a patient who was simultaneously inapt for certification under lunacy laws yet 'incapable' of voluntarily seeking treatment (or even 'unwilling' to). They would later become known as the 'non-volitional'.

The difficulties presented by 'chronic' and 'incurable' patients signalled a need for new rationalities for their confinement, not linked to 'cure'. Ideally, they would be confined in new spaces, separate from the main asylums, presided over by different experts, professing expertise not in cure but in the management of this problem population. This, I argue, is the space where we will find more direct antecedents and rationalities of social care itself, and social care detention.

Workhouse 'care'

The workhouse was the second monolithic institution of the carceral era, established by the Poor Law Amendment Act 1834 (known as the 'new Poor Law'). Workhouse provision was based on the principle of 'least eligibility': nothing but 'extreme necessity' should induce any person to surrender their 'free agency' and accept this accommodation (Poor Law Commissioners, 1834: 271). Although the workhouse's main rationality was discouraging pauperism by making even the worst labour more attractive than 'indoor relief', it also provided care for the 'impotent' poor without alternative means of support (Bartlett, 1999a). A substantial proportion of 'pauper lunatics' were in workhouse care in the 19th century; it was not a mere 'sideshow' to the asylum (Bartlett, 1998). Many 'idiots' lived in the workhouses (Wright and Digby, 1996; Jarrett, 2020) and although fewer people survived into old age in the 19th century, significant numbers of 'aged paupers' were also 'relieved' there (Andrews, 2014; Boyer, 2016).

The workhouses were eventually enveloped in the law of institutions, subject to both centralized control and inspection and safeguards for individual liberty. Statutory powers to confine 'harmless' persons 'not in a proper State to leave the Workhouse without Danger to himself or other', also required medical certification (Poor Law Amendment Act 1867). Those considered 'dangerous' to themselves or others were to be removed to the asylum; a route for many 'idiots', 'lunatics' and people with senile dementia (Bartlett, 1998, 1999b; Andrews, 2017). Within this system, professional Poor Law officers played a role analogous to family 'petitioners' seeking to place someone in the asylum.

In 1870, specialist Poor Law institutions – 'imbecile asylums' – were built at Leavesden and Caterham to house London's 'chronics and incurables'. These were distinct from the charitable 'idiots asylums', discussed shortly, housing more than 1,000 inmates each (Jarrett, 2020). The Caterham asylum also received a significant proportion of older adults and 'senile imbeciles', provoking resistance from its managers and doctors who viewed these as 'the *wrong type* of patients', disrupting institutional aspirations to be 'orderly places filled with healthy, obedient, industrious patient-inmates' (Andrews, 2014: 131, 133).

In several respects then, workhouse care and confinement was an important antecedent of social care detention. Many people with intellectual disabilities, dementia and other 'incurable' cognitive impairments were detained in these settings, where they were categorized as 'harmless' and distinguished from the 'dangerous' patients in asylums. Their care and confinement was mediated and overseen by professionals specializing in the administration of the poor. The continuity with social care detention is also reflected in the transfer of the Poor Law Union's responsibilities to local authorities in the 1920s, which would be reconfigured as 'social services' in the mid-20th century (Means and Smith, 1983). Meanwhile, workhouses became 'public assistance institutions' and, as I will discuss in the next chapter, many were still operating as 'care homes' in the 1960s (Townsend, 1962).

Idiots asylums

The institutional separation of 'idiots' from the main asylum population required new rationalities, a new expertise and interventions that could claim to resolve a social problem. In the early carceral era doctors showed little interest in 'idiocy'; there seemed little to say and no hope of cure (Jarrett, 2020). However, in the late 19th century, a French psychiatrist – Dr Itard – reported a celebrated case of a 'wild boy'. He claimed that 'incurables' could be made useful – or at least less burdensome to others – through training. Specialist institutions for the education and training of 'idiots' were established in France, Switzerland and Germany (Jones, 1972; Rose, 1985a; Gladstone, 1996). The first 'School for Idiots' in England opened in Bath in 1846 (Carpenter, 2000), and the first charitable 'idiots asylum' opened in 1847, eventually becoming the Earlswood Asylum, holding 561 inmates by 1881. A handful of others followed (Jones, 1972).

Idiots institutions and their inmates presented a dilemma for the Lunacy Commission: should these be regulated as lunacy institutions, engaging the lunacy certification processes, or were these something else? Their founders petitioned the Commission for an exemption from lunacy legislation (Carpenter, 2000; Wright, 2001). While sympathetic, the Commission ultimately erred on including idiot asylums within lunacy law, lest this set a dangerous precedent to other kinds of institution (Wright, 2001). They reasoned that Earlswood fell within their jurisdiction because 'for the purposes of discipline and instruction, an absolute right is necessarily asserted over the personal liberty of all its pupils' (cited in Carpenter, 2000: 174; Commissioners in Lunacy, 1850: 291). The logic is strikingly similar to the *Cheshire West* decision in disregarding the purpose of the institution and the nature of its inmates, and pressing home the 'absolute right' exercised over them.

Idiots asylums housed only 3 per cent of idiots reported to a national census by 1881 (Tuke, 1882: 310). In the late 19th century, idiocy became a focus of activity for the Charity Organisation Society. Its founder, Octavia Hill, is considered an early forerunner of modern social work. The Society aimed to address the problems of poverty through self-help and reducing dependency on charity. Picking up the theme of the 'idiot' as an economic and social 'burden', which could be improved by training, they called for more specialist idiots asylums (Rose, 1985a). The campaign was supported by the Lunacy Commission.

The campaign led to the Idiots Act 1886, which established a separate regulatory regime for idiots asylums. The Act failed in its stated purpose of encouraging more idiots asylums (Jones, 1972), but it established two important principles for our purposes: that separate legal structures for the confinement of people with intellectual disabilities is desirable, and that these can be attended by a weaker form of legalism. Although the Lunacy Commission retained responsibility for licensing and visiting idiots asylums, the certification procedure was less onerous, requiring only one medical certificate certifying that the idiot or imbecile was 'capable of receiving benefit from the institution', no judicial order and only annual visitation from the Commission. The logic was that further safeguards were 'unnecessary for this population (Lushington, 1895: 812). These principles appear to have been uncontroversial; the Act attracted virtually no parliamentary debate (Rose, 1985a). This reflects the declining emphasis on the liberty of 'harmless incurables' during the carceral era (Unsworth, 1993). Meanwhile 'the idiotic person had come to be perceived as a creature of the institution, a fit object for medical care, treatment and control' (Jarrett, 2020: 245).

Mental deficiency colonies

Institutional confinement of people with intellectual disabilities accelerated during the 20th century, when they came to symbolize 'racial decline in an era of national degeneration' (Wright, 2001: 194). This nexus of race and disability – 'race-ability' (Ben-Moshe, 2020) – was central to British colonial nationalism, constructing colonized peoples as 'incapable' and requiring guardianship by a 'rational race' (Jarrett, 2020: 106). In Britain, people with intellectual disabilities were construed as a racial and national threat, passing on hereditary impairment, a source of criminality, poverty and moral decay, a deviant burden on societies and economy. Unlike earlier discourses of burden, the family of the 'mental defective' was also problematized, a target to act upon and – if necessary – to overcome (Welshman and Walmsley, 2006).

A new conceptualization of 'the feeble-minded' solidified, expanding powers of intervention into populations that hitherto were considered unsuitable for certification under existing lunacy laws, through new categories of 'moral imbeciles' and 'mental defectives' (Rose, 1985a). Mary Dendy, a member of the Manchester School Board and the Eugenic Education Society who had close links to the Charity Organisation Society, became a powerful advocate for the permanent segregation of the 'feeble-minded' in specialist institutions and 'colonies', holding this as a new 'principle of public right-doing' (Dendy, cited in Jackson, 1996: 161). This new 'scientific morality'

(Dendy, cited in Jackson, 1996: 161) fused together multiple diffuse threats to society with the vulnerability of the 'feeble-minded' to exploitation (physical, sexual, criminal) to justify their confinement (Welshman and Walmsley, 2006; Sandland, 2013).

Dendy and others persuaded the Royal Commission on the Care and Control of the Feeble-Minded (1908: [9]) that there were growing numbers of 'mentally defective' persons, 'whose training is neglected, over whom no sufficient control is exercised', posing a significant threat to themselves and society: producing 'crime and misery', 'injury and mischief', 'much continuous expenditure wasteful to the community and to individual families', and transmitting such defects to future generations. The Commission mainly eschewed eugenic arguments in favour of economic considerations, but accepted the basic problematization of the 'feeble-minded' as socially dangerous and individually vulnerable (Rose, 1985a).

The Commission's recommendations led to the Mental Deficiency Act 1913, which established 'mental deficiency colonies' for the confinement of 'defectives'. It extended this supervision beyond the institution's walls, placing local authorities under statutory duties to 'ascertain' 'defectives' in their areas, and ensure they were 'dealt with' by being placed either in an institution or under statutory guardianship or supervision. An important purpose of these arrangements was to manage their sexuality and, in particular, to prevent 'procreation' (Fennell, 1996). The Act was later expanded to include 'moral imbeciles' whose 'defect' resulted from accident and was not present at birth (Mental Deficiency Act 1927), bringing brain injury within this stigmatized population.

The 1913 Act's 'certification' procedures were similar to the 1890 Lunacy Act, requiring an application by a petitioner (usually a parent or guardian) or local authority officer, and two medical certificates. The 'judicial' safeguard, however, was reserved for the newer (and more controversial) categories of 'defective' other than idiots or imbeciles, reinforcing the sense that developmental disability warranted a diluted legalism. A new central Board of Control replaced the Lunacy Commission and assumed new responsibilities as 'a comprehensive service for the insane, the senile and epileptic as well as the idiot, imbecile or feeble-minded' (Jones, 1972: 194).

There was strong support for the Bill from Dendy, the Commission, and public bodies including councils, education committees and boards of guardians and it achieved remarkable cross-party consensus. Its sole opposition was self-styled 'radical' Liberal MPs Josiah Wedgwood and Handel Booth (Jones, 1972; Jarrett, 2020). Wedgwood, who filibustered the Bill, described it as a 'monstrous' cruelty, injustice and threat to individual liberty (*Hansard* HC 28 May 1913 vol 53 col 284). The legislation prompted debate about the value – or otherwise – of individual liberty for 'mental defectives'. A joint committee in support of the Bill circulated a leaflet headed 'LIBERTY – Some examples of what is done in its name', including case-histories of 'feeble-minded' children abandoned and starving, abused, exploited and violent to others (Jones, 1972: 196–7). In their guide to the new legislation, Wormald and Wormald (1914: 6) defended the Bill against criticism that it might be used as an instrument of 'capricious detention' without 'satisfactory cause' on the grounds that:

> The liberty of the subject does not consist in allowing persons who are not responsible nor accountable for their actions to commit crime, to drift into intemperance and immorality, to be cruelly treated or neglected or to injure the community by reason of the uncontrolled reproduction of their type, but rather by an organization that is humane and adaptable to mould their lives and conduct so as to secure for them a maximum of comfort and happiness conformable with social order. ... The mentally defective almost more than any other class of afflicted persons need care and protection rather than liberty.

The 1913 Act operated in parallel with the Lunacy Act 1890 until both were dismantled in the mid-20th century (Chapter 7). Although its community supervision and guardianship provisions were not as widely used as its proponents hoped (Fennell, 1992), its 'relentless' drive to incarcerate increased the number of people with intellectual disabilities detained in specialist institutions from around 5,000 in 1905 to almost 60,000 fifty years later (Jarrett, 2020: 269). Institutionalization of people with intellectual disabilities had become a normal, and socially and politically sanctioned response, the culmination of a journey from 'being accepted members of society, whatever difficulties that might entail, to state-defined outcasts and objects of fear, loathing and pity'. They were consigned to a medically dominated system which had nothing to offer them but exclusion, pervasive regulation and dull monotony interspersed with cruel and ferocious punishment, dehumanization and neglect (Jarrett, 2020: 268).

★★★

By the mid-20th century, huge numbers of people with mental disabilities were confined across different institutions purporting to provide care. We have not yet encountered the dispersed, quasi-domestic and mobile arrangements characterizing contemporary social care detention – we will meet these in the next chapter – but we have encountered several key threads from which it is woven. First, the very *idea* of the institutional panacea as a solution to increasingly diverse national 'problems' paved the way for interventions to manage these far beyond the institution's walls. We see the beginnings of this outward expansion in the regulation of 'domestic psychiatry' and community supervision of 'mental defectives'.

Second, a heterogeneous population united in being set apart from the therapeutic claims of mental health detention by dint of the 'permanence' of their incapacity and their 'harmless' (not dangerous) nature. Different rationalities, sites of confinement and legal frameworks, linked to discourses of 'vulnerability' and 'burden', developed in response, within forerunners of social care. Third the emergence of organized systems of state provided non-medical care, and new professions concerned with the management and alleviation of poverty and related social problems, coupled to the Poor Law's harsh principle of 'less eligibility' and the ideal of 'self-help'. And finally, the law of institutions: initially conceived of as a *restraint* on institutional confinement, progressively stretched like elastic across a steadily growing carceral complex, expanding to encompass new populations and problems. A carceral system and its legal container stretched to its limits. Something had to give.

4

The Post-carceral Landscape
of Care

Between the town where I grew up and the nearest city lay Powick Hospital – one of the large Victorian county asylums, built in 1852. English composer Edward Elgar sometimes conducted the asylum orchestra. In 1968, *World in Action* filmed the first of a new genre of documentaries, exposing on national television its shocking inner workings and appalling treatment of elderly female patients (*Ward F13*; Nairn, 1968). It was not even filmed undercover; the hospital superintendent felt the public should be outraged over conditions in hospitals like his. Yet Powick was still operational when I was born in the early 1980s. It closed in 1989; its patients dispersed into 'the community', its buildings and vast grounds redeveloped as high-end residential accommodation. As teenagers we wondered who would wish to live there, among the ghosts.

The story of Powick Hospital mirrors that of almost the entire network of Victorian asylums,[1] and symbolizes the post-carceral narrative of transition from hospitals to *homes*. As Figure 4.1 shows, the post-carceral era saw a dramatic decline in hospital beds for 'mental illness', 'geriatric' patients and people with intellectual disabilities: over 200,000 in 1955 dwindled to fewer than 20,000 in 2020.

The tide turned against large institutional accommodation in a series of overlapping waves of scandals, policies, closures, new post-carceral ideologies and configurations of care. People with psychosocial and developmental disabilities, and older adults, were carried out on different currents. I focus here on the 'deinstitutionalization' of social care detention's main target populations – older people and those with dementia, and people with

---

[1] A complete list of the fates of all asylums in England and Wales, with links to past and contemporary photographs, is available here: www.thetimechamber.co.uk/beta/sites/asylums/asylum-history/the-asylums-list

Figure 4.1: NHS hospital beds 1955–2020

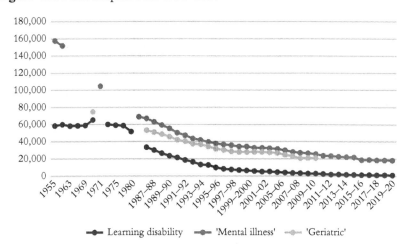

─●─ Learning disability ─●─ 'Mental illness' ─●─ 'Geriatric'

Source: Lord Percy (1957: 311); National Health Service (1962); Department for Health and Social Security (1971, 1975); Jay (1979); House of Commons Social Services Committee (1985); Wright et al. (1994); Johnson et al. (2010); NHS Digital (2020b).

Note: Gaps in this chart are because data on NHS beds were not routinely gathered or published until relatively recently. Also note that this includes only NHS bed data and not beds in the independent sector that may be commissioned by the NHS.

developmental disabilities – but theirs is a complicated story to tell, at times intersecting and rebounding, at times diverging.

I begin by focusing on the growing opposition to institutions after the Second World War and the emergence of countervailing philosophies of care. I then turn to examine the policies and initiatives of 'first-wave deinstitutionalization': establishing local authority 'social care' and 'residential care' homes, closing the workhouses and long-stay hospitals. I then consider 'second-wave deinstitutionalization', aiming to eradicate lingering 'institutional' practices in the community through new models of 'housing with support'.

Although we can date the beginnings of the post-carceral era earlier (Unsworth, 1991), the Second World War was, as William Beveridge (1942: 6) put it, a 'revolutionary moment' in the deinstitutionalization of people with mental disabilities for several reasons. The revelations of the Nazi Holocaust in pursuit of 'racial hygiene', including the genocide of disabled people, helped discredit the eugenic 'science' justifying the mass incarceration of 'mental defectives' (Jarrett, 2020). The doctors' trial at Nuremberg catalysed the development of modern medical ethics and medical law during the late 20th century, which increasingly focused on consent (Miola, 2007). The horrors of war and totalitarian regimes led to the creation of new international human rights instruments. These were critical preconditions for the recognition of social care detention in European and domestic law, the subject of later chapters.

Meanwhile the far-reaching traumas of war softened public attitudes toward 'mental illness' (no longer 'lunacy'). Psychiatry's claim to be a scientific and effective branch of medicine was boosted by the discovery of new antipsychotic treatments holding hopes of cure in the 1950s. A gathering sense that large hospitals were no longer necessary for most people with psychosocial disabilities led to deinstitutionalization programmes across the Western world (Kritsotaki et al, 2016).

In the mid-century a new generation of civil society reformers challenged carceral care arrangements, negative attitudes, and the medical and legal establishment, leading to major changes in law and policy. These included Age Concern (founded 1940), Mencap (founded in 1946 as the National Association of Parents of Backward Children), Mind (founded 1946 as the National Association for Mental Health) and Liberty (founded in 1934 as the National Council of Civil Liberties).[2] The post-war period also saw the establishment of the UK welfare state, based on Beveridge's (1942) proposals for the NHS and a scheme of 'national assistance' to replace the Poor Law, laying the foundations of modern 'social care'.

Ideologies and reformers

Despite the growing repudiation of eugenic ideology and carceral care, it was several decades before the hospital system released its grip on people with intellectual disabilities; this required a 'countervailing thrust of advocacy and new ideas' (Jarrett, 2020: 281–2). Post-carceral ideology accrued gradually, beginning with critiques of the existing system, bolstered by hospital scandals, then the development of new normative and practical models for care and support by grass-roots reformers. Over the decades these ideologies would become new orthodoxies for social care policy and practice, new forms of 'expertise' for new kinds of care professionals, and new rationalities for the kinds of interventions associated with social care detention outlined in Chapter 2.

Scandals

Scandal was a key driver of reform in the post-carceral era (Butler and Drakeford, 2005). Just as 19th-century reformers used appalling conditions in

---

[2] Because these organizations changed their names several times, I use their contemporary names when discussing them unless I am referencing a specific publication under an earlier name.

madhouses to build support for asylums, 20th-century hospital abuse scandals were framed as evidence not of a few rotten apples but of fundamentally the *wrong system of care* (Townsend, in Morris, 1969).

When campaigner Barbara Robb (1967) published a dossier of evidence alleging serious abuses of older patients with dementia in seven hospitals, her allegations were rejected by a House of Commons inquiry, which discredited both Robb and her witnesses. However, her campaign brought the enclosed world of psychiatric institutions under a spotlight, inspiring other whistleblowers to step forward, priming government and public 'to the possibility that the NHS had flaws' (Hilton, 2019: 188). When the *News of the World* subsequently published a staff nurse's allegations of abuse and neglect of patients with intellectual disabilities at Ely Hospital, near Cardiff, they were upheld in a government inquiry by Geoffrey Howe (1969). The Ely Hospital scandal proved pivotal in shifting policy and public opinion away from long-stay hospital provision for people with intellectual disabilities. Following Ely, further scandals exposed abusive and neglectful treatment in 'mental handicap' and mental hospitals, including South Ockendon, Normansfield, St Augustine's Hospital, and the Whittingham Hospital (Butler and Drakeford, 2005). Meanwhile television documentaries – such as Nairn's (1968) film of Powick Hospital, and Evans' (1981) *Silent Minority* about 'mental handicap' hospitals – shocked the general public with grim scenes of everyday life inside these closed institutions.

Over 40 years after Ely the argument was still having to be made by reformers that hospitals were 'the wrong model of care' for people with intellectual disabilities (Mansell, 2011; Greig and other signatories, 2011). The numbers of people with intellectual disabilities in psychiatric hospitals had fallen from over 60,000 in the 1970s to around 3,000 in 2010, although a growing proportion of these were private sector hospitals rather than NHS-run. In 2011, BBC *Panorama* aired undercover footage of appalling physical and emotional abuse of adults with intellectual disabilities and autism at Winterbourne View hospital near Bristol (Kenyon, 2011). Winterbourne View was operated by Castlebeck, a large private equity-owned hospital and care home operator. The abuse scandal received considerable coverage in the national media.

In response, a new national policy, *Transforming Care*, aimed to rapidly reduce hospital placements and develop alternative community support (Department of Health, 2012). Yet by 2014 the numbers had barely reduced (Health and Social Care Information Centre, 2015a). A subsequent policy, *Building the Right Support* (NHS England et al, 2015), focused on developing community services and infrastructure to enable inpatient facilities to close. We will revisit this initiative in Chapter 7, as it shaped an interesting counter-institutional regulatory strategy.

At the time of writing, over 3,300 people with intellectual disabilities or autism remain in hospital; more than half have been there for over two years (NHS Digital, 2021). Solidifying this sense of failure, in 2019 BBC *Panorama* exposed abuse of adults with intellectual disabilities and autism at another independent sector hospital, Whorlton Hall (Plomin, 2019), and further scandals have ensued since then. For our purposes – understanding social care detention – an important legacy of these hospital abuse scandals has been reinforcing a sense that the 'community' is a locus of freedom, with a lower risk of abuse, in contrast with hospital accommodation.

As we will see in this and later chapters, 'community' services certainly can be less restrictive than hospitals, but they can also be highly coercive. Regulatory audits of specialist hospital and residential services for people with intellectual disabilities found physical, chemical, mechanical restraint and seclusion in community settings, albeit somewhat less frequently than in hospitals. However, in the community restrictive practices are less tightly regulated (CQC, 2012, 2020b).

Meanwhile institutional abuse still occurs in 'community' settings, although it tends not to command the same level of media and public interest as hospital scandals, possibly because it is rarely aired on national television. To select a few examples, staff at Mendip House, a care home run by the National Autistic Society taunted, humiliated and physically assaulted residents, making them crawl on all fours and eat chillies and raw onions (Flynn, 2018). Residents in a Devon care service were neglected, physically assaulted, routinely secluded for lengthy periods without food, drink, heating or access to toilets, and made to perform housework and gardening tasks as compliance 'tests' (Flynn, 2019). Staff at a day centre in Doncaster used service users for 'target practice', knelt on them, and locked one woman in a cupboard (Poole, 2014). A similarly awful catalogue of abuses exists for people with dementia in residential care services. In Peterborough, for example, four staff in a dementia care home were convicted of abuse for telling confused residents they were in a brothel and they were going to be killed (Brown, 2014). A coroner raised concerns about the deaths of five dementia care home residents from neglect (Georgiou, 2014). The CQC (2020c) has documented cases of sexual abuse of people with dementia by care staff.

The point of this harrowing (and heavily abridged) litany is not to argue that community services are any more or less risky than hospitals, but to highlight that these cases have not been deployed as scandals by reformers proposing an alternative vision of care. It is not obvious – once one has got service users 'into the community' – where else there is to go. Whatever is creating the risk of abuse, it is not simply the location or registration status of a service, but something harder to define (and therefore harder to close down or abolish) about the quality of its inner dynamics. The CQC (2021) lists 'inherent risks' for 'closed cultures' of care where there is an elevated risk of abuse, including: 'services where people are unable to leave of their own accord', 'live-in' services including supported living and shared lives, one-to-one support, people being 'highly dependent on staff for their basic needs' and less able to 'speak up' for themselves. These factors have a considerable overlap with the *Cheshire West* acid test and they extend far beyond the confines of 'institutions' as traditionally understood.

Sociological critique

From the 1960s, institutions became prime targets of sociological critique. Erving Goffman's (1961) *Asylums* provided a rich yet grim description of inmates' everyday lives in a large American mental hospital, based on his own undercover observations while working there. Goffman's core argument was that institutional life damaged inmates through processes he termed 'mortification of the self', which became known as 'institutionalization'. Michel Foucault's (2001/1961) *Madness and Civilization* was the first of several critiques of psychiatric and disciplinary power exercised within institutions of various kinds. Closer to home, Seebohm Rowntree's (1947/1980) study of workhouse care exposed it as exploitative and scandalous. Subsequently, Peter Townsend's (1962) *The Last Refuge* offered a powerful indictment of residential care provision for older people, with strikingly similar observations to Goffman's: regimentation, isolation, loss of self-determination, and a phenomenon he termed 'depersonalisation'. Pauline Morris's (1969) *Put Away*, with a lengthy foreword by Peter Townsend, reported on a Mencap-funded study of 'institutions for the mentally retarded'. Meanwhile American sociologist Robert Edgerton (1967: 205) studied the lives of those released from institutions, struggling to 'pass' in the community and conceal the 'shattering stigma' of 'mental retardation' with a 'cloak of competence'.

Sociological interest in 'total institutions' lent scholarly expertise to the growing sense that they did more harm than good. *Asylums* was a central text for post-carceral reformers and abolitionists alike, even influencing key figures in English mental health law (Gostin, 2007). I return to consider Goffman's characterization and critique of institutions in more detail in Chapter 6. Goffman himself – along with anti-psychiatrist Thomas Szasz (1971) – formed the American Association for the Abolition of Involuntary Mental Hospitalization. However, this 'expertise' on institutions derived from observation, not subjective experience.

'Independent living' and disability rights

During the 1970s, groups of younger physically disabled people self-organized, creating a new political force – the Disabled People's Movement (DPM). Central to the British DPM was a new understanding of disability as *social oppression* rather than an inevitable consequence of individual impairment – known as the social model of disability (The Union of the Physically Impaired Against Segregation and The Disability Alliance, 1976; Oliver, 1990). Some younger physically disabled people living in residential care homes (including homes for older people) demanded alternatives. They explored an alternative model to 'care', developing in the USA, known as 'independent living' (Evans, 2003). Central to the independent living model is exercising control over one's own support and living arrangements – a reversal of the disempowering dynamics of institutionalization and – some disabled people would argue – 'care' itself (Shakespeare, 2000; Kelly, 2016).

This word – 'independence' – is a keystone of post-carceral discourse, recurring through social care policy as early as the 1940s. Yet its meaning is at times dangerously unclear. For a century, disabled people were narrated as 'burdens' – to family, economy, society and state. 'Dependency' is a keyword of post-war Western welfare, with pejorative and moralizing overtones, connected with this historic sense of burden (Fraser and Gordon, 1994). In this cultural context, 'independence' evokes the 'self-help' philosophy of Octavia Hill and the Charity Organisation Society, the doctrine of 'self-reliance' under the New Poor Law. So understood, 'independence' embodies the 'will to empower' within welfare democracies, governmental strategies of 'self-help' targeting the poor and 'problem' populations (Cruikshank, 1999). For example, Edgerton (1967: 193–5) cites mid-century scholarship on 'independence' and intellectual disability, defining it as 'living without the need for assistance from others'. 'Independence' understood as living with less support, as alleviating *burden*, invites corrective interventions. We can trace a direct line of descent from the 'training' provided by idiots asylums and mental deficiency colonies and the kinds of independence-promoting coercive interventions endorsed in cases like ML's (*Northamptonshire Healthcare NHS Foundation Trust v ML*), discussed in Chapter 2.

Yet this is not what the DPM meant by 'independent living', for whom it is a manifesto for the kinds of self-determination imperilled by institutionalization, social marginalization and inaccessible communities. A commonly cited definition of independent living, developed by the Disability Rights Commission (2002), is:

> all disabled people having the same choice, control and freedom as any other citizen—at home, at work, and as members of the community. This does not necessarily mean disabled people 'doing everything for themselves', but it does mean that any practical assistance people need should be based on their own choices and aspirations.

Despite the strong and clear expression of independent living in the writings of the DPM, and its articulation as a new legal right under article 19

CRPD – discussed in the next chapter – it is frequently misunderstood and mistranslated into policy and law (Yang, 2013; Tarrant, 2019).

The DPM experimented with different ways to exercise direct control over their support and living arrangements (Evans, 2003). During the 1980s they campaigned for 'direct payments' from local authorities – cash in lieu of services –which disabled people could use to pay a care provider, or even directly employ 'personal assistants'. The term 'personal assistant', rather than carer, implied someone who was directly employed by and took direction from a disabled person, assisting them in their everyday lives; deliberately evoking the relationship between a business executive and their PA (Barnes, 1992). The Community Care (Direct Payments) Act 1996 eventually granted this right, and the Health and Social Care Act 2008 (HSCA) later enabled payments to a third party on a person's behalf, where the person in receipt of support lacked the capacity to manage a direct payment.

Opposition to psychiatry

During the post-carceral era, mental health patients (and ex-patients) began to self-organize as political campaigning organizations with renewed vigour, known today as the 'user and survivor movement' (Campbell, 2005). One such organization, the Mental Patients' Union (founded 1973), demanded the abolition of involuntary treatment, irreversible treatments and seclusion, and access to patients' preferred treatments (Spandler, 2006). During this period, radical psychiatrists such as Szasz (1961) also opposed mental health detention and compulsory treatment, contending 'mental illness' was a myth; a stance dubbed 'antipsychiatry'. In Trieste, Italy, psychiatrist Franco Basaglia successfully campaigned for a law that closed the entire network of psychiatric hospitals in the region, a hugely influential moment in Western deinstitutionalization (Kritsotaki et al, 2016).

The user/survivor movement remained relatively distinct from the DPM until quite recently, although there was some recognition of common cause (Spandler et al, 2015). Meanwhile, the main target populations of social care detention – people with developmental disabilities and older people with dementia – remained outside both movements until recently. In 1980, the UK's first user-led intellectual disability self-advocacy organization, People First, was established by people with learning difficulties,[3] but remained outside of the mainstream DPM until the 1990s (Campbell and Oliver, 1996). The activist politics of mental health often distinguishes between 'psychosocial' conditions and 'brain based' disabilities such as intellectual disabilities or dementia (Spandler and Poursanidou, 2019).

---

[3]   People First prefer the term 'learning difficulty' to 'learning disability' or 'intellectual disability'.

Today, user-led organizations for people with intellectual disabilities often struggle to secure funding and to make their voice heard over the larger and better resourced charities, which are often carer or professional led. Organizations led by people living with dementia have developed only relatively recently,[4] and have yet to assume the same visibility and political force as the DPM and user and survivor movements. This means that campaign groups of people with direct lived experience of social care detention – as opposed to mental health detention – are thin on the ground, if they exist at all. This can make social care detention appear less contentious than mental health detention for want of organized opposition.

Normalization

During the 1970s, a new approach to 'mental handicap' commanded growing interest and influence within civil society and the social care professional world: normalization. This creed would guide a new progressive movement seeking to close the long-stay hospitals and support people with intellectual disabilities in the community, often pitting these late 20th-century 'reformers' against a medical-paternalist establishment. This would become a new intra-professional culture war whose rationalities, discourses and normative principles we can still discern in social care detention today.

Niels Erik Bank-Mikkelsen, a Danish resistance fighter, social worker, policy reformer and advocate for the rights of disabled people, is often credited with inventing normalization. He developed legislation and services to get people with intellectual disabilities out of institutions, which he felt resembled the concentration camps he experienced during the war. Defined by an early proponent as 'making available to the mentally retarded patterns and conditions of everyday life which are as close as possible to the norms and patterns of the mainstream of society' (Nirje, 1969: 181), normalization was brought to international attention by Wolf Wolfensberger (Wolfensberger et al, 1972). A charismatic German-American psychologist, Wolfensberger identified and rejected othering narratives of deviance that justified the institutional segregation of people with intellectual disabilities as 'subhuman', 'a menace', an 'object of pity', a 'holy innocent', a 'diseased organism' or an 'eternal child'. For Wolfensberger, normalization was 'self-evidently valid as well as "right"' (p41), premised on a powerful rhetorical appeal to shared humanity.

Normalization is built from concepts with a strong affinity to the MCA's principles, and was referred to by the Law Commission (1991: [2.1]) in their preparatory work on the MCA. It rejected 'presumptions' of incapacity

---

[4]   See, for example, the DEEP network: www.dementiavoices.org.uk/

of people with intellectual disabilities, resonating with the 'assumption' of mental capacity unless established otherwise (s1(2) MCA). It sought to maximise capabilities and competencies, resonating with the 'support principle' (s1(3) MCA) and 'decision-specific' capacity. It stressed allowing disabled people the 'dignity of risk' (see Perske in Wolfensberger et al, 1972), resonating with the requirement that a person must not be treated as lacking capacity merely because they make an 'unwise' decision (s1(4) MCA). It is easy to see how the MCA appealed to progressive social care professionals raised on these principles.

The principle of 'least restriction' (s1(6) MCA) also indirectly derives from normalization. Its proponents – including Wolfensberger et al. (1972: 143, 185) – envisaged a 'continuum' of living arrangements and a 'continuum of supervision', including boarding with families, and 'homelike' cottage-like residences with 'small groupings' of residents, 'providing an evolution toward decreased dependence'. It conjured an image of a 'straight line running from the least to the most restrictive environment' with all people with intellectual disabilities located somewhere along this continuum (Taylor, 2005: 96). At first, the 'continuum concept' facilitated arguments for new services in the community. Litigation and legislation in the USA eventually won a 'right' to be cared for in the 'least restrictive' environment along this continuum. Yet critics argue that it still implicitly sanctions segregation and restriction – the question is only to what extent – and 'conditional' acceptance into the community (Taylor, 2005). More recently 'least restriction' has paradoxically become a means to defend the idea that some people require *more* restrictive environments (Ben-Moshe, 2020). The idea of a 'continuum' of services and restriction was central to domestic litigation over the meaning of deprivation of liberty – explored in Chapter 8 – premised on the idea that there is a cut-off point along this continuum below which deprivation of liberty does not occur.

Normalization galvanized a generation of professionals working in social work, social care, advocacy, psychology and civil society, becoming an orthodoxy among progressives defining themselves against 'paternalists' still adhering to institutional confinement (Deeley, 2002). Many attended Wolfensberger's Programme Analysis Service System (PASS) training programmes, spending time living alongside people with intellectual disabilities in services and institutions, to see it from their perspective and assess it against these new norms (Welshman and Walmsley, 2006). Normalization influenced newly formed organizations, such as the Campaign for the Mentally Handicapped (CMH, later Values into Action), who campaigned to support people with intellectual disabilities to live outside of institutions, to tackle 'service culture', and instigated early developments in self-advocacy (Shearer, 1972; Williams and Salamon, 1979). An influential paper by The King's Fund (1980, reprinted 1982), *An Ordinary Life*, became a touchstone expression of this new philosophy, blending ideas of deinstitutionalization and normalization with a new emphasis on 'choice and control', echoing the ideas and language developing within the independent living movement. Yet not all civil society groups concerned with intellectual disability were convinced by normalization. The chairman of Mencap, George Lee, viewed it as a 'denial of handicap' that had been taken too far (National Society for Mentally Handicapped Children and Adults (Mencap), 1980).

Undoubtedly normalization was central to the closure of the long-stay hospitals and inspired a generation of professionals and reformers who built alternative services in the community and opposed deeply damaging carceral-era discourses. Yet normalization sought to 'enhance' people's 'social images' and 'personal competencies' (Wolfensberger, 1983) by changing the person themselves to better fit within society. In this sense, normalization (or 'social role valorization', as Wolfensberger later relabelled it) is fundamentally *assimilationist* (Ben-Moshe, 2020), demanding conformity as the price of social acceptance (Yates et al, 2008), and reflecting the concerns 'of professionals rather than of people with learning difficulties' (Chappell, 1992: 35). This directly contrasts with the social model of disability, and its understanding that *society* should change to accommodate disabled people (Welshman and Walmsley, 2006), and the radical abolitionist paradigm connected with the CRPD.

Normalization is linked to interventionist rationalities aiming to make a person more 'normal', whether they wish to be acted upon in this way or not. For example, Wolfensberger et al. (1972) proposed that professionals should seek to normalize the weight, gait, haircut and clothes of people with intellectual disabilities, even suggesting cosmetic surgery for people with Down syndrome. He evan advocated controversial behaviourist techniques involving physical punishments ('aversives') to normalize behaviour. Returning to our example of ML, encountered in Chapter 2, we can see how 'normalization' can be woven together with progressive-sounding rationalities of 'independence' and historical discourses of 'burden', into a potentially highly coercive corrective rationality to make a person more *normal*: to leave home in the 'normal' way, to live and behave more 'normally', to achieve levels of 'potential' and self-reliance as measured against a 'normal' person. When interventions are woven from these progressive-sounding rationalities, perhaps espoused by professionals proud of adhering to new progressive orthodoxies of normalization and independence, we risk losing sight of how coercive they may in fact be.

Normalization as a philosophy had little to say about other institutionalized groups, particularly older people. Indeed, Wolfensberger et al. (1972: 86) himself considered older age 'a great leveller' for people with intellectual disabilities as they might be placed in nursing homes alongside older people, implying that certain forms of institutionalization are in fact 'normal'. The 'normalization' of institutional care of older adults pervaded parallel initiatives directed toward older adults. The King's Fund (1986: 14, 21) produced a subsequent paper to *An Ordinary Life*, addressing the care needs of older people. Unlike its counterpart it accepted the need for residential care provision, focusing instead on making sure accommodation was comfortable, attractive, 'normal in appearance' and 'as small and ordinary as possible', aiming to soften institutional features of residential care for older adults, rather than eradicate it entirely.

Person-centred care

A later generation of progressive reformers, many of them galvanized by Wolfensberger's writings and PASS training, pioneered new techniques to support people with intellectual disabilities living in the community, known as 'person-centred planning' (Lyle O'Brien and O'Brien, 2000). Pioneered in North America by John O'Brien and others (O'Brien and Lovett, 1993), person-centred planning stressed *individuality* and redesigning services and supports to fit the specific person and their own 'personal image of a desirable future'. This was acknowledged to be disruptive to service cultures, and deliberately so; person-centred planning aimed to unpick the 'depersonalization' associated with institutionalization.

Person-centred planning techniques emphasized getting to know a person through relationship rather than assessment, with attention to their personal history, values and aspirations. O'Brien and colleagues (O'Brien and Lovett, 1993: 1) considered the person themselves 'and those who love the person' as 'the primary authorities on the person's life direction'. This group surrounding a person was sometimes called their 'circle of support'. This approach implicitly rejected hierarchies of knowledge privileging disciplinary expertise based on generalizable knowledge of populations (most pertinently, medicalized models).

Early models of person-centred planning have strong parallels with radical approaches to supported and facilitated decision making associated with article 12 CRPD, explored in the next chapter. This post-carceral emphasis on individual subjectivity is legally expressed in diluted form in the MCA's duties to support decision making and consider the wishes and feelings of the person. It has led to new claims to professional expertise in discerning or determining a person's own 'true' or 'authentic' preferences, their individual desirable future, by advocacy workers, BIAs or independent social workers. Sometimes this can pit them against others – particularly the person's family – who might also claim expertise in knowing the wishes, feelings, and perhaps hidden communications of a particular individual. For example, in *LBX v K, L, M* [2013] EWHC 3230 (Fam), a court-appointed social worker spent several days with a young man with intellectual disabilities exploring his preferred living and family contact arrangements, in which he expressed a different view to that expressed in the presence of his father.

In parallel to developments in the intellectual disability world, pioneers such as Tom Kitwood (1997) were developing 'person-centred' approaches for people living with dementia. Remarkably, there is no apparent cross-referencing between Kitwood's work and that of O'Brien or his UK counterparts, but there are clear overlaps in approach: tackling the devaluation and depersonalization of institutions and traditional service cultures, building relationships and engaging with the values and wishes of the person. Analogous to Wolfensberger's PASS programme, Kitwood developed Dementia Care Mapping™, to enable care staff 'to take the perspective of people with dementia in assessing the quality of care they provide' (Downs, 2015). Kitwood considered this a 'paradigm shift' in approach. Yet, reflecting the deeply embedded 'normalization' of institutionalization of older adults, Kitwood did not reject the residential care model outright. He considered it a 'darker possibility' that people might remain living in their own homes 'beyond the point when it is consistent either with their well-being or that of their carers' (Kitwood and Booker, 2019: 48, 50).

First-wave deinstitutionalization: from medical to social care

Having outlined the key ideologies and movements opposing institutionalization and medical paternalism, I turn to the altogether messier business of explaining how the carceral legacy of workhouses and long-stay hospitals was gradually transformed into today's landscape of social care. This is necessarily an abridged summary of a long and complicated history, of evolving bureaucracies, policies and service models (Welshman and Walmsley, 2006; Means et al, 2008; Johnson et al, 2010). I approach it thematically rather than chronologically.

A labyrinthine legal framework accrued piecemeal, placing local authorities under duties to assess and meet 'eligible' social care needs (as distinguished from 'healthcare' needs), and (unlike the NHS) to *charge* for social care services subject to financial eligibility assessments. These powers and duties were eventually consolidated and 'modernized' by the Care Act 2014 (in England) and the Social Services and Well-being (Wales) Act 2014 (see Clements, 2019).[5] The 2014 Acts form the basis of present-day local authority social care functions, in providing or commissioning services for those unable to arrange or pay for their own care.

---

[5] No textbooks exist for social care law in Wales, but see: www.lukeclements.co.uk/rhydian-social-welfare-law-in-wales/ and https://socialcare.wales/hub/sswbact

From workhouses to 'sunshine hotels'

The National Assistance Act 1948 (NAA) abolished the Poor Law. It was one of a raft of statutes establishing the 'welfare state' after the war, based on Beveridge's proposals. Its architect was Nye Bevan, the Labour Minister for Health, whose exposure to poverty in the Welsh valleys engendered a sense of burning injustice about the 'inhumanity' of the Poor Law and that 'evil institution' – the workhouse (Hansard HC Deb 24 November 1947 vol 444 col 1608).

The NAA transferred 'care' functions from Poor Law relieving officers to welfare departments of councils (Clements et al, 2019). Local authorities were empowered to provide services in private homes or in what the statute called 'homes for disabled persons and the aged'. Bevan envisaged these as places affording residents 'dignity', and 'the maximum of privacy and independence'. They would be smaller – 25–30 persons – as Bevan contended that 'Bigness is the enemy of humanity' (col 1609). The *Daily Mail* dubbed them 'sunshine hotels' (Means and Smith, 1983).

In a theme that recurs with wearying regularity in the history of social care, reality did not reflect the vision. A little over a decade later, Peter Townsend (1962) conducted a major study of English residential care homes. He found many were former workhouses, barely changed since becoming 'homes', still accommodating hundreds of people: bare unplastered walls, 'wards' of up to 50 beds, scant furniture, iron bedsteads, straw mattresses and coarse institutional clothing. Workhouse culture persisted; residents lived regimented and isolated lives, denied meaningful occupations, privacy and freedoms. Townsend found voluntary and private homes aesthetically superior and smaller, yet little better in terms of activities, isolation, privacy and self-determination. Most residents did not wish to live in these 'homes', remaining only for want of alternatives. He found that 1 per cent had been placed there under a new compulsory power to secure 'necessary care' (s47 NAA), others were threatened with its use. Residents sank into apathy and misery. Townsend reasoned this 'depersonalization' sprang from the very nature of communal life, arguing they should be supported to remain living in their own homes with better housing and welfare services.

In a remarkable study, Johnson, Rolph and Smith (2010) tracked down what happened to the 173 homes studied by Townsend, visiting those still operational. Most former workhouses had closed by the 1970s, and many local authority care homes closed when national standards were introduced in the 1980s. More residents had cognitive impairments such as dementia. Conditions were improved, but they echoed Townsend's findings of 'institutional' environments and regimes, and residents living there 'with more or less resignation' owing to a lack of alternatives (p94).

Residential care homes and nursing homes still dominate the landscape of social care today, particularly for older people. Townsend estimated that only 1.5 per cent of retirement age adults lived in residential care accommodation in 1962. Today, the Office for National Statistics (2020) estimates that 1 per cent of all adults in England and Wales live in residential care homes, rising to 3 per cent aged over 64, and 15 per cent aged over 85. Meanwhile, the prevalence of people with dementia living in care homes today may be as high as 70 per cent (Prince et al, 2014). For older adults at least, we live in an increasingly institutionalized society.

Marketization and 'personalization'

Following concerns that local authority welfare functions were poorly coordinated and ineffective, they were obliged in 1970 to form unified 'local authority social services' departments. The NAA had not used the term 'social care', but administratively it came to distinguish those care functions apportioned to local authorities from the 'health' related functions of the NHS (Clements et al, 2019). Rose (1998: 55) tracks the evolution of the term 'social' from Beveridge's time – signifying individuals standing together, shoulder to shoulder, pooling risk – to indicating dependence, 'an underclass, the marginalised, the excluded', echoing carceral-era discourses of burden and deficiency. This sense of 'social care' as concerned with the management of a national and economic burden, of a group that society (and politicians) would rather forget about, a demographic 'problem' caused by an 'ageing society' and increasing numbers of people living with significant impairments, lurks beneath policy in this area.

Local authority residential accommodation developed slowly, but private and voluntary sector residential care grew dramatically between the 1970s and 1990, stimulated by a centrally funded 'supplementary benefit' that could cover care costs (Johnson et al, 2010). The Thatcher government viewed this increasing and uncapped expenditure as unsustainable, determining that '[c]are in the community must increasingly mean by the community' (Department of Health and Social Security, 1981: 3). The director of the supermarket chain Sainsbury's, Roy Griffiths (1988), was asked to make recommendations for reform. The government accepted his recommendations to limit local authority social care budgets and transform local authorities from providers to commissioners of care (Department of Health, 1989). From the 1990s onward, community care was transformed from a 'bricks and mortar' place to a market (Welshman and Walmsley, 2006: 39), with local authorities assessing service users' needs then securing 'best value' in meeting them through competitive tendering.

By 2019, 76.7 per cent of all care home 'beds' in England were provided by for-profit providers, 12.6 per cent by voluntary sector providers and only

9.6 per cent directly by local authorities (Naylor and Magnusson, 2019). Most local authority expenditure is on commissioned services; however, care assessment, support planning, commissioning and safeguarding remain mainly 'in house' (NHS Digital, 2019a). Roughly half of residential care service users are 'self-funding' and half are funded by local authorities or the NHS. The market for older people's care was estimated at £15.7bn in 2016 (Laing, 2018a). Meanwhile, pay and employment rights for the social care workforce steadily eroded (Hayes, 2017).

A central rationality for the marketization of social care was facilitating consumer 'choice'. Yet the reality was (and is) that local authorities – not care recipients – are the customers, and their motivations and concerns are not necessarily the same. Far from delivering 'a plethora of small-scale, responsive, customer-focused services', the market tendency was toward monopoly, standardization, and achieving economies of scale (Drakeford, 2006: 936). A recent analysis by Grant Thornton (2018) suggests newer care homes tend to be more profitable because they tend to be larger.

Health and social care policy in the new millennium increasingly emphasized 'choice', 'independence' and 'person-centred' care (Department of Health, 2005b; 2006a; Department of Health and Others, 2007). Different rationalities became entangled in a single policy that has dominated adult social care ever since: personalization. Although personalization borrowed language and ideas from the DPM and the person-centred philosophies discussed earlier, critics describe this as 'appropriation' while 'promoting a wholly distinct agenda of public sector marketisation' (Beresford, 2014; Tarrant, 2020: 281).

'Personalization' was coined by an 'innovation consultant', Charles Leadbeater, proposing that public services could be improved through 'self-directed support', giving service users a greater role and responsibilities for 'designing solutions' to meet their own needs and having a more direct say over how public money was spent on their care (Leadbeater, 2004: 20; Leadbeater et al, 2008). Some care professionals and voluntary sector figures developed a new model of 'self-directed support', based on the idea that service users could direct local authorities to spend a notional 'personal budget' on how they would like their assessed care needs to be met (Duffy, 2005; Dowson, 2007). In fact, the law bestows no such rights on service users (Tarrant, 2020). Self-directed support introduced new jargon, semi-automated and opaque systems to allocate increasingly scarce resources (Series and Clements, 2013), and new bureaucracy and intermediaries – brokerages – to manage budgets and payments. Studies of its efficacy report mixed results. Some groups report benefits, but older people and those with multiple and complex impairments are particularly likely to have 'notional' budgets managed by the local authority, and may not necessarily experience greater choice and control (Beresford, 2014; Needham and Glasby, 2014).

Meanwhile, those directly managing budgets (through direct payments) can find this onerous and stressful; one parent carer asking 'Why have I found myself as a director of a small company just so Steven can go swimming?' (Neary, 2015).

In one sense, personalization aims to uproot 'service culture' and the 'depersonalization' historically associated with institutionalization. Echoes of the 'person-centred' approaches advocated by O'Brien, Kitwood and others infuse the 2014 legislation, exhorting professionals to 'involve' the person in assessments and care planning, placing them under 'supported decision making' duties that are arguably more powerful than the MCA's meagre 'support principle'. The Care Act's 'principles' (s1) stress 'control by the individual over day-to-day life'. The English statutory guidance claims that the Act's overarching 'well-being' principle in fact subsumes the concept of 'independent living' (Department of Health and Social Care, 2020a: [1.18]–[1.19]), a claim dismantled by Collingbourne (2014), and betrayed by the guidance's own (mis)interpretation of this as 'Supporting people to live as independently as possible, for as long as possible'.

The grim reality of the dream of personalization is that whatever fine words are enshrined in legislation, unless the 'market' offers the service and the local authority will fund it, 'choice and control' can be extremely limited. For those seeking control over *who* supports them, when and how, 'personal assistance' via a direct payment may be the only way. Yet, even here, local authorities may not release sufficient funds to secure staff for enough hours, to pay a decent wage and discharge employers' responsibilities (Hayes, 2017). Here, the burden-inflected rationality of promoting 'independence' can work against service users. They might be told – as Luke Davey was – that reducing direct payments and personal assistance will enhance their independence by improving their self-reliance (R (Davey) v Oxfordshire County Council [2017] EWHC 354 (Admin); R (Davey) v Oxfordshire County Council & Ors [2017] EWCA Civ 1308). 'Developing independence' is a legitimate need, the Court of Appeal reiterated [122], and needs – not wishes – are paramount [121].

'Homes not hospitals'

People with intellectual disabilities took a different journey through this history. The NAA explicitly excluded 'lunatics' and 'mental defectives' from new local authority care functions. During the 1950s, civil society groups – led by Liberty – campaigned to close mental deficiency colonies and abolish the legislation. Liberty brought a series of successful habeas actions on behalf of people confined in the colonies. Following a conference attended by Mencap, Mind and like-minded progressives, the National Council for Civil Liberties (1951) argued in *50,000 Outside the Law* that the colonies themselves, and their legal underpinning, were unfit for purpose. Liberty ensured the issue was kept in the headlines, and eventually the minister caved to pressure – establishing the Royal Commission on the Law Relating to Mental Illness and Mental Deficiency, chaired by Lord Percy (1957). Percy mainly dismissed their complaints, and those of other aggrieved 'lunatics' and 'defectives', but concluded the system needed wholesale reform. Liberty would hail this as one of their 'great successes' (Lilly, 1984: 74).

For Percy, the issue was less that the older system was corrupt and failed to protect liberty, and more that public attitudes had undergone a fundamental shift since the war. Mental illness should now be seen as an illness like any other, treated in general hospitals, and not ensnared in abhorrent and unnecessary Victorian legislation, conferring stigma for detained patients and excessive 'formalities' for doctors. We will pick up the thread of Percy's recommendations for law in Chapter 7. Noting that around half the beds in the NHS estate were given over to inpatient treatment for 'lunacy' and 'mental deficiency', Percy proposed a shift toward 'community care' where possible, and a 'general division of functions' between hospitals – who would provide specialist medical and nursing care – and local authorities, who would provide 'social' care [47]. Percy envisaged, however, that 'helpless patients' – people with intellectual disabilities and 'senile dements' needing 'continual nursing' – would remain in hospital, others would receive 'training' to 'make the patient fit to live in the general community' [47].

Care in the community was slow to materialize. By 1960, hospital beds for mental illness had fallen slightly but those for 'mental subnormality' had increased (National Health Service, 1962). At the Mind annual conference, Conservative Health Minister Enoch Powell (1961) announced his intention to close the 'great isolated institutions', 'rising unmistakeable and daunting out of the countryside' and 'brooded over by the gigantic water tower'. This 'colossal undertaking' would require overcoming 'sheer inertia of mind and matter' and 'resistance to our assault', including from the hospital staff themselves. Powell's *Hospital Plan* relied upon increased local authority residential accommodation, particularly for older people, but like Percy he assumed that people with intellectual disabilities would still require hospital care (National Health Service, 1962).

The abuse scandal at Ely Hospital and subsequent hospital scandals reported in the 1960s and 1970s stimulated initiatives to close the 'mental handicap' hospitals, and heralded the adoption of 'normalization' as a key policy for people with intellectual disabilities. A new national policy, *Better Services for the Mentally Handicapped* (Department for Health and Social Security, 1971), lamented the lack of local authority residential care accommodation for people with intellectual disabilities. Echoing the 'normalization' mantra, it stressed that 'mentally handicapped' people should not be unnecessarily segregated from the 'general life of the community', needing simulation, training, education and purposeful occupation or employment to 'develop to his maximum capacity' and be given 'as nearly normal a life as his handicap or handicaps permit' [40]. *Better Services* adopted 'home' as a normative anchor for these new residential services [161], even for those remaining in hospital: the 'hospital becomes in effect his home' and should be as 'homelike' as possible [184].

Normalization received further policy backing from Peggy Jay's (1979) report on mental handicap nursing. Jay's recommendations flowed 'from our belief in the primacy of a "normal" lifestyle for mentally handicapped people'. The mantra of 'as normal a lifestyle as possible' was to encompass even those with the most profound and complex disabilities [22], [34]. Mentally handicapped people 'have a right to enjoy normal patterns of life within the community', 'a right to be treated as individuals' but required 'additional help' from communities and services to develop their 'maximum potential' [86]. Jay endorsed the principle that people should live, learn and work 'in the least restrictive environment appropriate to that particular person' [92]. People should have opportunities to live in small groups, close to their social and geographical community, and their accommodation should be 'as much like the accommodation we ourselves would wish to live in' [133], [136]. The report acknowledged the risk that 'institutional approaches' could also emerge 'in the community' [138], visualizing a future where people might live in rented flats or houses with support, as individuals, couples or small groups, describing such accommodation as 'truly independent living' [137].

Despite these shifts in official policy, by the mid-1970s community services for people with intellectual disabilities were still 'a comparative rarity' (Department of Health and Social Security, 1975). A National Development Group and National Development Team (NDT) were established to advise the government, local authorities and health authorities on resettling people from the long-stay hospitals in the community. The difficulties were partly financial: it cost nearly as much to run a half-empty hospital as a full one, so health authorities had little financial incentive to move patients out, while local authorities received no additional funding for discharged patients (Welshman and Walmsley, 2006). In the early 1980s, however, some used supplementary benefits to secure private residential care accommodation.

In the 1990s, there was renewed focus on hospital closures, spurred by campaigners like Jim Mansell and groups such as Values into Action (VIA, former CMH). Mansell had established one of the earliest group homes, supporting patients from Ely Hospital. His review of services for people with 'learning disabilities' and 'challenging behaviour' established the policy principle that even this population could live in the community with the right support (Mansell, 1993; see also Mansell, 2007, 2010).

The NDT continued to visit learning disability hospitals, encouraging, persuading and supporting health authorities to develop closure plans (Greig 1995/2001).

The hospital numbers steadily declined, mainly attributable to 'death rather than discharge' and slowing admissions (House of Commons Social Services Committee, 1985: [37], [50]). By 2000 there were around 10,000 NHS hospital beds for people with learning disabilities, and over 53,000 specialist residential care placements (Department of Health, 2001).

The New Labour government adopted a national learning disability strategy, *Valuing People* (Department of Health, 2001), describing this as the first government policy prepared with direct input from disabled people themselves. It was based on four key principles, reflecting key elements of post-carceral discourse: 'rights', 'independence', 'choice' and 'inclusion'. In a foreword, Tony Blair emphasized that '[p]eople with learning disabilities often have little choice or control over many aspects of their lives', and the document went on to say that:

> Like other people, people with learning disabilities want a real say in where they live, what work they should do and who looks after them. But for too many people with learning disabilities, these are currently unattainable goals. We believe that everyone should be able to make choices. This includes people with severe and profound disabilities who, with the right help and support, can make important choices and express preferences about their day to day lives. (Department of Health, 2001: 24)

Yet, given this emphasis on choice, *Valuing People* had surprisingly little to say about legal capacity – which constrained the parameters of choice for many people with intellectual disabilities, making only passing reference to the parallel development of the MCA [4.29], a story I pick up in Chapter 7. Progress toward the aspirations of *Valuing People* was patchy, missing targets to close learning disability hospitals in 2004 (Department of Health, 2005c). The policy was 'reaffirmed' (HM Government, 2010: foreword) but the implementation team was later disbanded by the Coalition government.

By 2010 only 2,465 NHS hospital beds for 'learning disability' remained (Figure 4.1). However, new specialist independent sector providers of assessment and treatment units (ATUs) flooded into this marketized field of healthcare. The specialist hospital market for learning disability and autism is valued at over £200m, mainly commissioned and funded through the NHS (LaingBuisson, 2019). Despite scandals like Winterbourne and Whorlton, the sector enjoys 'robust demand' (LaingBuisson, 2018) because of a lack of adequate community alternatives, festering like a small but painful and seemingly ineradicable pressure sore beneath social care.

Second-wave deinstitutionalization

By the 1980s, reformers intent on assisting people with intellectual disabilities and older adults to move out of institutions were growing disillusioned with the realities of community care. Studies of resettled learning disability hospital residents found 'institutional' lives in group homes (Collins, 1993). Even the term 'homes' had acquired 'negative connotations' (The King's Fund, 1980, reprinted 1982: 11). Practitioners influenced by the *Ordinary Life* philosophy began to experiment with new models of care based around *housing* with support. This model became known as 'supported living', or sometimes 'independent living'. The aim was to enable people with intellectual disabilities 'to live in real homes of their own' (Kinsella, 1993: 14), with meaningful choices over where and with whom they lived, how they lived their lives and how they were supported. Similar ideas developed relating to older adults, building on Townsend's call for 'sheltered housing', or support to enable a person to 'age in place' in their own home.

The underlying assumption of 'second-wave' deinstitutionalization was that by 're-classify[ing] the person as a private citizen living in their own home … service agencies have to treat them as they would treat other members of the public' (Mansell's foreword to Clement and Bigby, 2010). In Chapter 6, I will explore why the social and cultural norms of home were invoked as a counterweight to the forces of institutionalization, and how the reality is often a more complicated weaving together – or distortion – of the norms of both, producing liminal spaces whose status as 'home' or 'institution' can be contested.

These new models of 'housing with support' also transformed the legal fabric of care, from regulated institutional settings to 'private dwellings', domestic homes, with important implications for their regulation and monitoring. In Chapter 7, I consider how the law of institutions has struggled to cope with liminal places that blur the dynamics of home and institution.

Supported living and supported decision making

Darenth Park was the first of the long-stay mental handicap hospitals to close, raising questions of where its residents should be resettled. A group of reformers, inspired by the *Ordinary Life* philosophy, opposed local plans for a campus-based service. At a conference they conceived a radical vision: to find ordinary housing for the residents to occupy as tenants and support for their new lives. The Southwark Consortium, established in 1983, brought together the voluntary and public sectors, employing housing and support coordinators (Rochester, 1989). By 1992 there were 40 similar organizations around the country (Brend, 2008: 24). This new model of housing with support received policy backing in *Valuing People*, and access to new public funds unavailable for traditional residential care, such as Supporting People and the Independent Living Fund.

The pioneers of supported living based it on a philosophy that centred a person's right to make decisions or choices about their living arrangements. Decision making was considered central to enabling people 'to live in real homes of their own' rather than 'mini-institutions in the community' (Kinsella, 1993: 6, 14). We will revisit this idea that 'real homes' and institutions can be distinguished by the extent to which they afford their inhabitants a genuine 'decision space' in Chapter 6.

One pioneer, Peter Kinsella, published the 'Reach Standards for Supported Living' in 2002 to guide providers, commissioners, regulators and others as to its underlying philosophy (Warren and Giles, 2019); they read as follows:

1. I choose who I live with;
2. I choose where I live;
3. I have my own home;
4. I choose how I am supported;
5. I choose who supports me;
6. I get good support;
7. I choose my friends and relationships;
8. I choose how to be healthy and safe;
9. I choose how I am part of the community;
10. I have the same rights and responsibilities as other citizens;
11. I get help to make changes in my life.

The Reach Standards have been endorsed and used by many organizations, including the National Development Team for Inclusion, who propose this as a test for whether there is a 'true tenancy' (Wood and Greig, 2010; Wood et al, 2010), guidance for commissioners (Welsh Local Government Association, 2019), third-sector providers, voluntary organizations, professional bodies (Changing Our Lives, 2014) and care regulators (Commission for Social Care Inspection and Healthcare Commission, 2006; CQC, 2017b). In Chapter 7, I will show how this has given The Reach Standards a quasi-legal status in the regulation of supported living, which is often difficult to reconcile to its realities.

Because supported living relied on tenancies and – often – direct payments, it ran into difficulties around 'mental capacity'. As I will explain in Chapter 7, it is possible under Anglo-Welsh capacity law to make life-changing health and welfare decisions in the 'best interests' of a person lacking 'mental capacity' – such as placing them in residential care – with a minimum of legal formality, but the same is not true for managing money and entering into binding contracts.

Organizations arranging tenancies and direct payments faced questions as to whether people 'had capacity' for this. VIA published a series of guides entitled *Funding Freedom*, outlining how people with intellectual disabilities could be supported to manage a direct payment through practices they would come to refer to as 'supported decision making' (Dowson, 1990; Holman and Collins, 1997; Beamer and Brookes, 2001; Edge, 2001). For service users unable to manage a payment even with support, they set up 'independent living trusts', extending the idea of a 'circle of support' to a small board that could manage the payment to support the person in line with their wishes (Leece and Bornat, 2006). These grass-roots approaches generated an ethos of supported decision making and legal capacity with strong parallels to the radical abolitionist model of legal capacity associated with article 12 CRPD, discussed in the next chapter. VIA's members criticized the MCA for inadequate provision for supported decision making, and handing too much power to those acting in the 'best interests' of disabled people (Collins, 2003).

Deinstitutionalizing older people?

More radical deinstitutionalization initiatives often passed older adults by. The underlying assumption, even expressed by progressive reformers, has been that moving into residential care is normal, natural and sometimes unavoidable in older age. From as early as Powell's 'community care plan' (Ministry of Health, 1963: 285, [47]), through to today's statutory guidance on the Care Act (Department of Health and Social Care, 2020a: [1.15]), social care has characterized remaining in one's existing home as 'living independently' – an endeavour that is supported only 'as long as possible'. Beyond this point, a move into residential care is treated as almost inevitable.

In comparison with working-age adults (including those with intellectual disabilities) older people often get less funding for their care, even if their 'needs' are similar (Series and Clements, 2013). They are less likely to receive direct payments, and more likely to have a 'managed personal budget' (NHS Digital, 2019a). Residential services for older adults tend to be larger. Data from the CQC's (2020a) directory of registered services show that care homes for older people have, on average, 38 beds, whereas those for working-age adults have 28. Homes for people with dementia have, on average, 43 beds, whereas those for people with intellectual disabilities, on average, have 12. In Chapter 7, I describe policies aiming to eradicate larger institutional residential provision for people with intellectual disabilities; no equivalent policies exist for older adults.

Models of 'housing with support' do exist for older adults, however. In the 1980s, action projects experimented with supporting 'highly dependent old people' in 'non-institutional settings' (The King's Fund et al, 1986; Skeet, 1986), inspired by Scandinavian approaches (The King's Fund,

1979). Specialist housing schemes for older people developed, known as sheltered housing, extra care housing or 'retirement villages'. These schemes potentially offered greater privacy than residential care and may enable couples to remain living together (Means et al, 2008). However, Clough, Leamy, Miller and Bright (2005: 163) found that space restrictions put off some potential residents, one describing them as 'rabbit hutches'. Recent initiatives emphasize alternative support structures, including mutual support, cooperatives, homesharing and telecare (Branfield and Beresford, 2010). These schemes are currently fairly small-scale but can achieve positive outcomes, even for people with high support needs (Branfield and Beresford, 2010; Bowers et al, 2013).

However, many older adults have strong bonds to their existing home and community (Clough et al, 2005; Levenson and Joule, 2005). The issue is less getting people *out* of institutions than preventing admission, enabling people to 'age in place'. 'Ageing in place' informs care policy across Europe, North America and Australasia (Milligan, 2009), although the phrase is rarely used in Anglo-Welsh care policy. However, problems can ensue when people's functional capacities decline, or their housing is insecure or inadequate to their needs (Means, 2007; Sixsmith and Sixsmith, 2008; Milligan, 2009). 'Ageing in place' can also be problematic for relatives if a person's needs or behaviour greatly exceed what they can support or live alongside. Sixsmith and Sixsmith (2008: 222) described some 'very old' people becoming so housebound that their homes became like 'prisons', yet the respondents themselves preferred this to the alternative of moving into residential care.

Another major policy limitation is cost. In England and Wales, some local authorities have introduced 'maximum expenditure policies', capping the value of a 'personal budget' at the cost of a residential care placement (*R (D) v Worcestershire County Council* [2013] EWHC 2490 (Admin)). This means that a person may not be supported to remain living at home if a move into a care home would be cheaper. When I worked for a homecare provider in the late 2000s, the local authority would not fund more than four homecare visits per day for older adults before turning to residential provision (although younger adults could often secure more homecare support). Revenue streams for working-age adults in supported accommodation are often not available past the age of 65. Community care means testing and charging policies can also create perverse incentives to move homeowners into residential care (Dilnot et al, 2011).

The institutional treadmill

The story of the post-carceral era is, in some respects, one of success – the large carceral-era institutions are now almost all gone. Yet in other ways it is marked by tragedy, in the sense meant by Scott (2004: 13), where the 'future is never a Romantic one in which history rides a triumphant and seamlessly progressive rhythm, but a broken series of paradoxes and reversals in which human action is ever open to unaccountable contingencies – and luck'. The tragedy of the post-carceral era is that 'institutional' and carceral practices can be found even within the most progressive new models of care, as if we are coupled to an institutional treadmill, pulling us back into the very past we are trying to leave behind us.

Even within supported living, empirical studies – discussed in more detail in Chapter 6 – have observed institutional practices, staff imposing rules and regimes, controlling space as if it were their employer's and not somebody else's home that they were working in (Drinkwater, 2005; Fyson et al, 2007; Family Mosaic, 2012). Institutional abuse scandals do not seem to emerge with the same frequency in supported living services as in hospitals and care homes. However, in 2004 the Commission for Social Care Inspection (CSCI) and Healthcare Commission (2006) investigated NHS-run Cornish hospitals and supported living services for people with intellectual disabilities. Investigators concluded the supported living services did not reflect *Valuing People*'s values or the Reach standards and that 'institutional abuse was widespread' (p5). One person was tied to a bed or wheelchair for 16 hours a day, residents were locked in their houses or their rooms by staff, taps and light fittings were removed, CCTV monitored residents within their own homes, restraint and sedation were used excessively, and police investigated allegations of physical abuse by staff, including use of cold showers to punish residents (Devon and Cornwall Constabulary, 2009). As Duffy (2012: 7) put it, 'We'd knocked down the walls, we'd moved people into the community, but we'd taken the institution with us'.

These trends are not only found in the UK. A recent major study of independent living across Europe concluded that 'rather than ending institutional care, many countries are re-imagining it instead', concluding 'we face a proliferation of "hidden" or "mini" institutions' (Crowther, 2019a: 6, 23). Altermark (2017: 1319) draws analogies between this 'history of deinstitutionalisation, liberation, and disappointment' and postcolonialism; narratives of liberation and progress can too easily mask new forms of oppression, power is 'transformed' – it does not disappear – after deinstitutionalization.

However, this does not mean that these new models of support have not improved things. Researchers revisiting Townsend's research sites in the 2000s did find some improvements (Johnson et al, 2010). Supported living service users report an improved quality of life compared with previous hospital or residential care accommodation (Sines et al, 2012; Bigby et al, 2018). A meta-analysis of studies on community care found that it was 'consistently associated with greater patient satisfaction and quality of life across specialties' (Killaspy, 2007: 79). The realities of post-carceral care are a long way from post-carceral ideology, but for most people it is a significant improvement on what came before.

Why do institutional practices continue to emerge even in the most progressive and aspirational settings? In Cornwall, staff from long-stay hospitals moved to work in supported living without adequate training, bringing with them the same culture and learned patterns of interaction. But most services today do not employ staff from the old long-stay hospitals, so answers must lie elsewhere. One supported living provider asked anthropologists to study its own services, where there had been reports of 'institutional' practices. They identified an 'outdated and inappropriate culture' that had emerged among staff, shaped by 'apathy and lack of concern', 'ignorance' and 'individual cruelty'. A 'culture of fear, blame and punishment' meant other staff were afraid to speak up (Family Mosaic, 2012: 3, 18). Other factors may relate to the dire working conditions of the social care workforce and structural factors in the management of services (Hayes, 2020). But what is patterning and guiding these 'inappropriate' models of care in the first place? Staff may fall back on existing culturally entrenched models of care – for example, the care of children (Tipper, 2003) – or be guided by dominant discourses of 'incapacity', 'normalization' and the 'duty of care' which position staff as powerful and residents as persons to be acted upon by them (Jingree, 2014). Historical narratives of 'deficiency', danger, burden and othering discussed in this book likely also shape institutional practices and abuses.

However, cultural explanations only get us so far. Even the most progressive workforce would struggle to deliver support in line with the vision of reformers, because economic forces themselves produce institutionalizing-carceral tendencies, a phenomenon Ben-Moshe (2020) refers to as 'Dis. Inc' – 'Disability Incarcerated, Disability Incorporated'. To put it simply, it is much more efficient in terms of staff time (and therefore cost) to deliver care in a way that minimizes travelling between service users (the ideal distance being a walk between beds not a traipse across city traffic). This logic configures care as specific tasks to be completed rather than individual relationships, favouring routinization and efficient timetabling over the needs or preferences of the care recipients. A story symbolizing this dynamic, told to me by several people familiar with the old hospitals, is ward staff serving residents a tureen of tea and coffee mixed together instead of taking the time to ask what drink each patient preferred.

In today's post-carceral landscape of care, the dynamic is less visible but no less present. When I worked for a homecare provider, my employer's goal was an 'efficient' rota with minimum 'slack' – that is, minimizing staff travel time between visits to homes, or waits between visits. Staff would be put on specific routes, minimizing the distance between visits. This meant it was rarely possible to cater to service users' preferences for particular staff members, or even times when they would prefer to be woken up (ranging from 7 am to 11 am) or put to bed (ranging from 7 pm to 10 pm). Some service users would receive care from staff they did not like, or from dozens of different staff in a month; small wonder that there were those who were confused, hesitant to let strangers into their house, or simply fed up with repeatedly explaining how they needed to be supported. Understandably, some would 'refuse care'. All this before you have even got to the problem of 15-minute visits, and a sector with very high workforce turnover (Skills for Care, 2020). An inquiry by the Equality and Human Rights Commission (EHRC) reveals these problems are endemic across the sector, no doubt made worse by deminishing local authority funding for commissioned services. Where people's needs are greater, residential provision can achieve economies of scale by congregating people together in cheaper properties outside of highly populated or desirable locations. The institutional treadmill is partly powered by care economics' tendencies toward congregated and segregated models, often far from home communities.

This dynamic means that supported living can end up emulating 'institutional' residential provision. As 'housing with support' models became attractive to care market investors, drawn by new funding streams unavailable in residential care, existing residential care homes began to re-register as supported living services. Sometimes this was actively supported by service users, seeking greater rights, choice and control over their care and accommodation (National Development Team for Inclusion, 2011). But in other cases, greater rights, choice and control did not materialize, leading Kinsella (2008) to lament that '[t]oo much of what goes today as Supported Living is relabelled Residential Care'. New 'supported living' services were built as 'clusters' of 'living units'; a far cry from 'ordinary homes, on ordinary streets'. Care market investment analysts recommend a 'clustered client base allowing staff to be employed full time at a single location' (Laing, 2018b: 72), replicating similar economies of scale to larger residential care provision, to ensure profitability or even mere survival in an increasingly unstable care marketplace. Purpose built 'supported living' is now so normal that regulations define it as property intended for occupation by people needing support, specifically excluding the person's existing home as a chosen location for support (The Care and Support and After-care (Choice of Accommodation) Regulations 2014 SI 2014/2670).

A central tenet of the supported living philosophy is choice and control over *who* provides support. This is – to an extent – reflected in the regulatory distinction between this and residential care (discussed in Chapter 7). Yet 'supported living' providers increasingly link support services to housing to ensure profitability and longer-term security (Voluntary Organisations Disability Group and Anthony Collins Solicitors, 2011). This means that service users cannot simply hire and fire their preferred providers or personal assistants. The 'longevity and "stickiness" of service users' are viewed by market analysts as strengths of successful supported living business models, in which 'synergies with adult specialist care home operation' are advantageous (Laing, 2018b: 75). Meanwhile, creative experiments with alternative living arrangements and forms of support are often overlooked by public bodies preferring to commission block contracts with larger providers (Fox, 2018). 'Choice and control' over one's living arrangements in line with post-carceral philosophies of independent living and the Reach Standards run counter to profitability and survival in today's care markets.

Family-based care

The NAA 1948 marked a 'turning point' in relations between families, the state and those needing care or support. Whereas the Poor Laws had – since 1601 – placed families under legal duties to care for their relations, with creation of the welfare state 'the ultimate responsibility for the needs of elderly ill, disabled and poor people rested with the state and not with families or charities' (Clements et al, 2019: 1.24). For families living in England and Wales today, there is no longer any legal expectation that they provide care for older or disabled adults, or that adults needing care or support should be forced to depend upon family.

Nevertheless, a large proportion of people needing care and support live in 'private' domestic accommodation, often with support from friends or relatives – known as 'informal carers' in social care parlance. Of working-age people with intellectual disabilities, 37 per cent live with family or friends (Hatton, 2020). One third of people with dementia live in their own homes, many supported by informal carers (Lewis et al, 2014). Many receive additional support from local authorities: homecare visits, day centres, or direct payments to purchase alternative 'community' services. Some people are also placed with families, who receive payments to support them, known as 'shared lives' (or sometimes, more paternalistically, 'adult fostering') (Fox, 2018). Family-like living arrangements by non-kin carers were enjoyed by HL in *Bournewood*, and MIG in *Cheshire West*.

Family-based care holds an ambivalent status within post-carceral ideologies, particularly for working-age adults with intellectual disabilities. Whereas for older adults it is considered 'normal' and often desirable to live with one's family, living with one's parents after 'coming of age' violates the norms of adulthood and independence stressed within the normalization literature. Wolfensberger et al. (1972: 47) considered the legal shift away from parental responsibility to support disabled adults an important rejection of their status as an 'eternally-dependent child'. The Jay (1979) report also stressed that establishing 'a life independent of the parental home' was 'the normal pattern within our society' and that families should no longer be 'regarded as the central agent in care' [128]. The MCA expresses this outlook by rejecting family as the default substitute decision maker for those lacking capacity – I explain this mechanism in more detail in Chapter 7. The Law Commission (1993a: [2.8]) viewed family substitute decision making as tantamount to 'extended minority'. Left unexpressed was that this often transfers de facto substitute decision making power to health and social care professionals.

For many disabled people, state support is potentially liberating for both themselves and informal carers; it is closely tied to the ethos of independent living (Campbell, 2008). Berggren and Trägårdh call the idea that the state confers freedom by liberating people from dependency on family, charity and church, 'statist individualism'; it finds particularly strong expression in the Swedish welfare state. They connect this to a 'Swedish theory of love', which posits that 'all forms of dependency corrupt true love' (Trägårdh, 2014: 27). Kulick and Rydström (2015: 231) argue that the 'catch' to this 'moral philosophy' is 'that relationships between individuals who depend on each other and/or who stand in unequal power relationships' are regarded as fundamentally undesirable, objectionable, inauthentic and incomprehensible. This presents difficulties for disabled people who choose to remain in relationships (sexual, familial or otherwise) perceived as unequal or dependent.

The problem is not the state enabling people who wish to do so to leave home, as for example in *ZK (Landau-Kleffner Syndrome: Best Interests)* [2021] EWCOP 12 and *K v LBX* [2012] EWCA Civ 79. Rather, it is that the combination of a statist individualist outlook (that the state's function is to liberate from private dependencies), with the corrective undertow of normalization (that the state's function is to produce 'normal' adults), and a burden-inflected discourse of independence as self-reliance, produces a viewpoint that cannot comprehend why a disabled adult might prefer to remain living with their family, and for whom 'independent living' is not a priority. This outlook can produce coercive aspects of social care detention's 'empowerment' rationality, embodied by the case of ML.

Research into care and disability often presents families as unreconstructed barriers to post-carceral imperatives of empowerment and independence (for example, Jingree and Finlay, 2011). This trope of the 'overbearing carer' looms large in welfare litigation under the MCA. Some people with intellectual disabilities do experience their parents as over-protective and barriers to self-determination (Haigh et al, 2013; Curryer et al, 2018); for them, a shift to state provision could indeed be emancipatory. However, Williams and Robinson (2001) found that when conflicts arose between professionals and family carers, professionals often stereotyped carers as over-protective or having a conflict of interest, without sufficiently exploring their concerns. Other studies argue that 'authoritative' and combative 'warrior hero' family carer identities emerge against a backdrop of a lifetime battling for services and against formal care systems that cannot be relied upon to deliver appropriate support (Lashewicz et al, 2014) and which blame carers as 'failing' when they ask for support (Clements and Aiello, 2021).

Family relationships are also recognized in research as an important source of happiness, care and support for many people with intellectual disabilities (Haigh et al, 2013), as reservoirs of deep knowledge about a person and champions of their rights, central to the person-centred planning ethos (Hillman et al, 2012). Empirical studies of supported decision making within families express 'cautious optimism' while noting some examples where it was 'difficult to disentangle the views of adults with disabilities as their voices can be diminished or negated in conversation' (Saaltink et al, 2012; Lashewicz et al, 2014: 31, 32). The structures of adult social care and the machinery of social care detention navigate complex and often competing imperatives to respectfully include families, to recognize them as (potentially) deep wells of personal knowledge and central relationships in a person's life, yet to police these insofar as they encroach on post-carceral imperatives to empower.

★★★

Let us assemble the threads identified in this chapter, and those from the last, to consider how they are woven together in the fabric of social care detention. The institutions as buildings are gone; targeted populations and institutional carceral practices are now dispersed across a complex landscape of care, a public/private hybrid in all senses – administrative, economic, legal, spatial and personal. This landscape presents particular problems for the law of institutions insofar as it is designed to regulate spatially localized phenomena. In Chapter 6, I consider the micro-dynamics of post-carceral care arrangements, the blurring of the domestic and institutional, before considering the difficulties this presents for the law of institutions in Chapter 7.

Generations of reformers sought to demolish not only the 'institutions' but institutionalization itself, through new ideologies emphasizing 'normal' or 'ordinary' lives, independence, choice and control, stressing the importance of '*real* homes' in the community. Yet the old narratives of deficit, burden, of lives in need of management and bodies and minds in need of correction have not disappeared, and can sometimes intertwine with post-carceral discourses to produce powerful corrective and sometimes coercive interventionist rationalities. For some disabled adults this is positively emancipatory, but these post-carceral discourses require careful unpicking as, for others, it can ground coercive interventions under the cloak of empowerment. For older people, particularly those with dementia, institutionalization *is* still normal – perhaps even more normal now than it was at the height of the carceral era; there has been no 'Trieste' moment for them.

Ideologies centring the person, their wishes and feelings – the DPM's understanding of 'independent living', early person-centred philosophies of care – resonate with the abolitionist human rights approaches discussed in the next chapter. Yet they operate in material environments of resource scarcity, and of themselves cannot combat the economic forces of institutionalization that significantly constrain 'choice and control'. In an era when *the decision* became the base unit of freedom, the options to decide between are often limited or undesirable.

New generations of reformers raised on these ideologies wage daily battles against carceral and institutional practices on the front lines of social care, becoming the 'empowerment entrepreneurs' who wield the MCA and social care detention itself as tools which they argue can amplify the person's 'voice', shine a light on institutional and restrictive practices, perhaps loosen their hold a little or even a lot (Whitaker, 2014; Currie, 2016; James et al, 2019; Hubbard and Stone, 2020). The question is not whether these anti-carceral aspirations are right – to me, it is self-evident that they are – the question is whether the law of institutions, applied in this material context, is a fickle friend in delivering reformist or abolitionist goals.

5

Social Care Detention in Human Rights Law

Social care detention is anchored in the right to liberty. Although, as I argued in Chapter 3, this has deep roots and antecedents in the carceral era, 21st-century social care detention is a global phenomenon, with close links to international human rights law. Indeed, it is plausible that without international human rights instruments, particularly the ECHR, Anglo-Welsh domestic legal frameworks regulating social care detention (the MCA DoLS/LPS) would not exist. The problems sheltering under the umbrella of social care detention might be understood as different kinds of legal problem, or perhaps not as legal problems at all. This chapter provides an overview of the international human rights settlement, from its development shortly after the Second World War through to the present day, with a view to understanding its pivotal role in developing and cross-fertilizing the concept of social care detention.

Human rights at the end of the carceral era

International human rights law was born in the aftermath of the Second World War, developed by politicians, activists and lawyers building a new world from the wreckage of the war. They were informed by the Nuremberg prosecutions of appalling 'crimes against humanity' perpetrated by the Nazis. This included the trial of Nazi doctors responsible for medical experiments and a euthanasia programme that murdered thousands of older and disabled people living in institutions. The initial draft of the ECHR was by British lawyer David Maxwell-Fyfe, a prosecutor at Nuremberg.

These new international human rights law instruments aimed to protect world citizens from their own governments, even from each other. They were drafted, adopted and monitored by new intergovernmental organizations – the United Nations (UN) and the Council of Europe. As the Preambles to the UN (1948) Universal Declaration of Human Rights (UDHR) and the

Council of Europe (1950) ECHR attest, they considered respect for human rights the foundation of freedom, peace and justice in the world.

As I will discuss in Chapter 8, some contemporary critics of social care detention argue that these instruments were not 'about' the kinds of situations considered in *Cheshire West*, but were directed toward the kinds of 'bestial abuses' perpetrated by the Nazis, or found in the Soviet gulags (*Rochdale Metropolitan Borough Council v KW & Ors* [2014] EWCOP 45, [11]). The suggestion is that social care detention is a corruption or misapplication of post-war human rights norms and values. So, we will take a moment to consider what world the 'right to liberty', as enshrined in the UDHR, the ECHR and their close relations, was born into, and what – if anything – their framers might have thought about the rights of disabled people.

Many commentators on the development of international disability human rights law argue that disabled people were 'invisible' to the framers of these post-war human rights instruments, despite the horrifying atrocities and Nazi genocide of institutionalized and disabled people (Dhanda, 2006–7; Kayess and French, 2008; Quinn, 2009; Kanter, 2015). They point to article 2 UDHR, emphasizing the universality of human rights. It lists groups with certain protected characteristics – 'race, colour, sex, language, religion, political or other opinion, national or social origin, property, birth or other status' – stressing their entitlement to all rights and freedoms, yet nowhere mentions disability. This silence on disability is replicated in article 19 of the International Covenant on Civil and Political Rights (ICCPR, UN, 1966), and the non-discrimination provisions of article 14 ECHR. One possible originalist reading is therefore that disabled people like MIG, MEG and P were entirely invisible to the framers of the UDHR and ECHR.

The reality is gloomier than mere invisibility. Many enthusiastic champions of the UDHR and ECHR were advocates of eugenic sterilization or segregation of 'mental defectives' before the war, including H.G. Wells (Partington, 2003) and Winston Churchill (Fennell, 1992). The *Travaux Préparatoires* for the ECHR (European Court of Human Rights, undated) record a UK proposal to explicitly prohibit involuntary sterilization and involuntary medical treatment under article 3 ECHR (prohibiting inhuman and degrading treatment and torture). This was rejected after the Danish representative highlighted that several European countries still had legislation permitting involuntary sterilization on eugenic grounds. Meanwhile, the framers of article 5 ECHR – the right to liberty – were keen to list those forms of detention considered acceptable within a democratic society, as an additional safeguard against political abuse. Therefore, article 5(1)(e) lists 'persons of unsound mind' as one of a few limited categories for lawful detention. The *travaux* records no debate for this provision; it seems to have been common ground that incarceration on grounds of 'unsoundness of mind' was legitimate.

We know, therefore, that disabled people were not quite *invisible* to the framers of the ECHR. They were deliberately excluded from some fundamental protections, and secured only procedural protections for their rights to liberty. I doubt we want to carry this carceral-era reading of human rights forward through originalist interpretations. Nevertheless, if we did pause to wonder what the ECHR's framers understood 'deprivation of liberty' to mean in relation to 'persons of unsound mind', it is instructive to note that this was drafted with high levels of input from British lawyers at a time when carceral-era lunacy and mental deficiency legislation still operated. Under these laws, even a 'single patient' received for profit in a domestic setting – 'boarded out' in the home of a clergyman, a doctor, or attended by a nurse, for example – would have required 'certification' and visitation. This is probably the closest historical analogy that we have to the situations of MIG or P in *Cheshire West*. We know, therefore, that neither the nature of a person's disability, nor their residing in a 'domestic' setting, nor these being 'private' arrangements between families and persons paid to care for them, were reasons to deny them procedural protections under the right to liberty at the time these instruments were drafted.

The post-carceral turn in international human rights law

Recognition of disabled people as positive rights-bearers under international human rights law crystallized slowly during the post-carceral era. Kanter (2015) provides a comprehensive history of this evolution. I highlight threads from our earlier narrative which were woven into international human rights law, paving the way for recognition and regulation of social care detention.

In December 1971, the UN adopted its first instrument formally and explicitly recognizing disabled people as rights-bearers – the (non-binding) 'Declaration on the Rights of Mentally Retarded Persons' (UN, 1971). The Declaration was based on a draft text developed by the International League of Societies for the Mentally Handicapped – an international network of mainly carer-led organizations (sometimes dubbed the 'parent movement') founded in 1961, concerned about the life circumstances of their sons and daughters with intellectual disabilities. The League was galvanized by a keynote speech by normalization's father, Bank-Mikkelsen (1969), who argued for a charter of rights enshrining core elements of its philosophy.

While the final text did not go quite as far as Bank-Mikkelsen would have liked (Herr, 1976), it elevated elements of normalization as human rights norms. The first clause of the Declaration states that '[t]he mentally retarded person has, to the maximum degree of feasibility, the same rights as other human beings', and goes on to enumerate rights to healthcare, education, 'training' and guidance to 'enable him to develop his ability and maximum potential'. Perhaps reflecting its origins in the parent movement, the Declaration does not reflect Wolfensberger's stress on adulthood, but instead states that '[w]henever possible, the mentally retarded person should live with his own family or with foster parents and participate in different forms of community life'. It goes on to state that '[t]he mentally retarded person has a right to a qualified guardian when this is required to protect his personal well-being and interests'. The final clause embodied the spirit of legalism, which increasingly imbued this first wave of disability human rights, stressing that any restriction or denial of rights for people with intellectual disabilities should be attended by 'proper legal safeguards against every form of abuse', subject to assessment of their 'social capability' by 'qualified experts', 'periodic review' and 'right of appeal to higher authorities'. The 1971 Declaration, and the subsequent UN (1975) 'Declaration on the Rights of Disabled Persons', both accepted that specialized institutions might sometimes be 'necessary' or 'indispensable', in which case they should mirror 'normal life' as closely as possible for a person of the same age.

Between 1983 and 1993, the UN declared a 'decade of disabled persons', appointing rapporteurs on conditions of disabled people worldwide. Daes (1986) and Despouy (1991) highlighted the appalling conditions found in mental disability institutions. The United Nations (1991) adopted a set of principles for '[t]he protection of persons with mental illness and the improvement of mental health care' (known as the MI Principles), directed toward psychiatric institutions and compulsory treatment. The MI Principles working group was chaired by a British government lawyer, Henry Steel (1991), with representatives from several states and organizations representing religious groups, lawyers, criminologists, psychiatrists, and one single organization of disabled people (Disabled Peoples' International).

The MI Principles reflected the basic tenets of the law of institutions: that there is a population – 'persons with mental illness' – who may sometimes need to be detained in 'mental health facilities' for their protection or that of others; that they should be identified through legal procedures involving qualified experts in mental illness; that they should be protected against arbitrary confinement by rights to review and appeal. Lengthy provisions detailed the substantive and procedural safeguards attending measures of confinement, compulsory treatment or restrictions on legal capacity reflected the legalism that increasingly characterized Western mental health laws, including the MHA 1983. They also reflected, to some extent, the language of normalization, for example in statements that 'to the extent possible' people with mental illness should be able to live in 'the community' (principles 3 and 7) and be treated in the 'least restrictive environment' (principle 9). The post-carceral shift toward community-based services is also reflected in references to 'social care' as well as health care.

Meanwhile, the Council of Europe Committee of Ministers (1999, 2004, 2009) busied themselves producing 'Recommendations' enshrining very similar principles concerning the 'legal capacity' and 'legal protection of incapable adults', and protecting the 'rights and dignity' of persons with 'mental disorder'. These informed the body of human rights law concerning 'deprivation of liberty', legal capacity and involuntary treatment developed by the ECtHR in the 21st century (Bartlett et al, 2007).

By the late 20th century, the legal and social situation of disabled people was increasingly visible within the international human rights community. The established approach was qualified rights to live 'normal' lives in the community, while enveloping psychiatric institutions in swathes of legal regulation. Seen in today's lights, none of this seems especially radical. Kanter (2015) and others close to the global DPM call this the 'old paradigm' of human rights, in contrast with the 'new paradigm' embodied by the CRPD – which I will discuss shortly. This 'old paradigm' is, as Kanter points out, built on a medical model of disability and mental illness. Rights to 'community' and 'normal life' exist but are heavily qualified by imperatives to 'protect' and 'rights to treatment' (whether wanted or not). The old paradigm expresses an increasingly ornate legalism, providing for 'an ever more perfect and safeguarded process of loss' (Quinn, 2013: 7): loss of legal capacity, loss of liberty, loss of ordinary rights to self-determination.

For reformers in many states, this represented significant progress. Post-carceral inflected legalism provided new tools to chip away at institutional confinement, advocate for better living conditions, less coercion, better treatment of those incarcerated, less restrictive alternatives (Rosenthal and Rubenstein, 1993; Lord, 2010). Yet, the reformers' dilemmas is that with each hammer blow against institutions that emancipates some clients or groups from particularly abhorrent circumstances, the basic tenets of the law of institutions – that confinement of some is sometimes necessary and acceptable, subject to legal safeguards and suitable conditions – is forged anew, and sometimes stronger for it.

Recognizing social care detention in human rights law

By the late 20th century, soft-law international human rights instruments positioned disabled people as rights-bearers. They particularly targeted psychiatric institutions, using human rights law to establish normative and procedural standards determining whether and when people with mental disabilities belong in institutions or community, and to regulate the conditions and treatment within psychiatric institutions.

Social care detention was not yet recognized; the community was the promised land. None of the instruments described earlier indicated that a person could be 'deprived of their liberty' in a care home, let alone their own home; the implicit locus of detention was psychiatric facilities. An early Human Rights Committee (1982: [1]) General Comment on the right to liberty under article 9 ICCPR stressed that deprivation of liberty did not only mean in criminal cases but also applied to 'mental illness, vagrancy, drug addiction, educational purposes, immigration control, etc.', but made no mention of social care settings. A more recent version calls upon states to provide 'community' facilities as less restrictive alternatives to mental health detention (United Nations Human Rights Committee, 2014: [19]), implying adherence to post-carceral mythology of community as the locus of liberty.

Since the new millennium, however, this began to change as different human rights bodies and rapporteurs stated that deprivation of liberty could exist in 'social care' and community settings. For example, the UN Working Group on Arbitrary Detention (WGAD, 2017: [55]) stated that it was 'increasingly aware' of people being detained in other 'institutional' settings such as 'social care homes for older persons, care facilities for those with dementia and private institutions for people with psychosocial disabilities'. The WGAD emphasizes that 'deprivation of liberty' is a question 'of fact'; if the 'person concerned is not at liberty to leave, then all appropriate safeguards' must be in place to protect against arbitrary detention [56]. It based this analysis on a 1964 working definition of detention as 'the act of confining a person to a certain place, whether or not in continuation of arrest, and under restraints which prevent him from living with his family or carrying out his normal occupational or social activities' (WGAD, 2012).

Social care detention under the ECHR

The most pronounced drive toward recognition of social care detention as a human rights concern has been under the ECHR. This development is particularly important for UK law because, unlike all the other human rights treaties discussed in this chapter (including the CRPD), only the ECHR has been 'incorporated' into domestic law, via the Human Rights Act 1998 (HRA). This means that the domestic courts can adjudicate violations of the ECHR, including unlawful deprivation of liberty; something they cannot do for violations of the CRPD, which holds only persuasive authority (Lawson and Series, 2018). Human rights litigation in the Strasbourg court paved the way for the insertion of the DoLS into Anglo-Welsh law – and similar provisions in many countries across Europe – providing the conceptual tools for the *Cheshire West* acid test.

Human rights litigation advancing recognition of social care detention under the ECHR has been brought or supported by activist and civil society groups concerned with the living conditions of people with mental disabilities living in institutions (psychiatric or otherwise) across Europe. These include the Mental Disability Advocacy Centre (now 'Validity'),

Interights, the European Disability Forum, the International Disability Alliance, the Centre for Disability Law and Policy at NUI Galway[1] and the World Network of Users and Survivors of Psychiatry. However, these organizations had different motivations in bringing, or intervening, in this litigation. For some organizations, the goal was explicitly abolitionist (for example, *Mihailovs v Latvia* [2013] ECHR 65); to highlight that deprivation of liberty occurred in social care facilities in order to argue for its abolition. For other organizations, the goal appears to have been reformist with an abolitionist end goal, to 'chip away' at the edifices of guardianship and social care detention, or as former director of the Mental Disability Advocacy Center Oliver Lewis (2011: 707) puts it, to 'bulldoze barriers to the life world'. Establishing certain kinds of social care institution as sites of detention helped ground arguments for 'true' community living, and by highlighting the connections between guardianship and unregulated detention to present guardianship itself as problematic.

For reformers, coupling social care placements to the machinery of article 5 ECHR potentially secures access to a bundle of procedural rights that can be used to challenge them. These rights have been established incrementally by the ECtHR in its jurisprudence on mental health detention, beginning with *Winterwerp v the Netherlands* in 1979 (Bartlett et al, 2007). I have described more fully elsewhere how these ECtHR rights have been interpreted and embedded in the MCA DoLS/LPS (Series, 2019). However, in outline they require that: any 'deprivation of liberty' be in accordance with a 'procedure prescribed by law' (article 5(1)); that the individual – or a representative acting on their behalf – be informed of the reasons for the detention and their rights (article 5(2), *Van Der Leer v The Netherlands* [1981] ECHR 6); and that those who are deprived of their liberty can bring proceedings to challenge it before a court, which is empowered to order their discharge from detention (article 5(4)).

In practice, this means formal, legally prescribed assessments by experts – predominantly psychiatrists (*Winterwerp*, [45]) but potentially psychologists or psychotherapists (Law Commission, 2015: [7.175]) – to provide 'objective' evidence of a 'true mental disorder' of 'a kind or degree warranting compulsory confinement' (*Winterwerp* [39]). These assessments must be sufficiently independent of the detaining authorities to 'counterbalance' the 'broad powers vested in health-care professionals' (*IN v Ukraine* [2016] ECHR 565, [81]).

The ECtHR has woven post-carceral human rights norms into article 5, echoing the principle of least restriction. Deprivation of liberty must be

---

[1] I helped to draft some of their intervention in *MS v Croatia (No 2)* [2015] ECHR 196 as a research fellow in Galway in 2013.

'necessary': 'less severe measures' must 'have been considered and found to be insufficient to safeguard the individual or public interest' (*Litwa v Poland* [2000] ECHR 141, [78]). It must also be 'proportionate' to the aims pursued. The Strasbourg court has recently asserted this means preserving 'the maximum freedom of movement', 'dignity' and 'right to self-determination' (*Hiller v Austria* [2016] ECHR 1028, [54]). Protective measures taken without prior consultation with the relevant person will 'require careful scrutiny' (*Stanev v Bulgaria* [2012] ECHR 46, [153]) and so far as is possible they should reflect 'the wishes of individuals capable of expressing their will' (*Mihailovs v Latvia*, [145]).

The Strasbourg court has also strengthened rights of challenge by reiterating that it is not enough to simply inform a person of this right if they are, in practice, incapable of exercising it without assistance; it must be communicated to somebody who can represent their interests (*ZH v Hungary* [2012] ECHR 1891). The court has repeatedly reiterated there must be 'special procedural safeguards' to facilitate appeals against detention, which may entail 'empowering or even requiring' a representative to act on their behalf (*MH v UK* [2013] ECHR 1008, [93]). A person should not be reliant on the discretion or goodwill of others to appeal against their detention (*Stanev v Bulgaria*, [174]). In Chapters 7 and 10 we will revisit why this rights–bundle may have seemed attractive to those acting on behalf of people with cognitive impairments in social care settings in England and Wales, but first let us consider how social care detention came to be recognized by the ECtHR.

The way the Strasbourg court approached questions of liberty held important consequences for strategic litigation. Deprivation of liberty under article 5 ECHR is conceptualized as having three elements (*Storck v Germany* [2005] ECHR 406). First, an 'objective element', of whether a person has in fact been confined to a place for a non-negligible period of time – sometimes known as their 'concrete situation' (*Guzzardi v Italy* [1980] 3 EHRR 333, [92]). Second, a 'subjective element', concerning whether the person has given a 'valid consent' to their confinement (*Storck* [74]). And third, whether these arrangements are 'imputable to the state'. Imputability is interpreted broadly, including both arrangements directly involving public authorities, but also where the state has 'positive obligations' to protect against interferences with liberty by private persons (*Storck* [89]).

The objective element distinguishes between mere restrictions on liberty and deprivation of liberty. The difference is 'one of degree or intensity, and not one of nature or substance', a question of fact which takes into account 'the type, duration, effects and manner of implementation of the measure in question' (*Guzzardi*, [93]). This 'particularist' framing is favoured by judges wary of establishing broad principles with 'automatic' legal consequences (Harrington, 2017: 150).

The Strasbourg court has not delineated equivalent substantive and procedural human rights protections under article 8 ECHR (the right to respect for home, family and private life). This means that mere 'restrictions on liberty' or even very serious interferences with home, family and private life, do not attract the well-elaborated substantive and procedural rights-bundle of article 5. The right to liberty is, as Clements (2011: 678) puts it, 'a cliff edge right': once secured, it brings the 'detainee' procedural and potentially other protections, yet 'on some fragment of context' these rights evaporate. This is compounded by the Strasbourg court's reluctance to analyse 'institutionalization' itself as a human rights concern under article 8 ECHR (Lewis, 2011, 2012, 2018). The pairing of a particularist framing of 'deprivation of liberty' and a 'cliff edge' in human rights protection, creates a field ripe for strategic litigation and resistance over the meaning of deprivation of liberty. This is what we have seen in both Strasbourg and the UK.

The *Bournewood* case applied this subjective/objective test of deprivation of liberty to the situation of HL, a British autistic man who had been 'informally' admitted to hospital, and who – according to the UK government at least – had neither 'objected' nor attempted to leave (*HL v UK* [2004] ECHR 720). The government argued that the regime he experienced was equivalent to a 'voluntary' patient who had validly consented, therefore he could not be said to be detained. There are reasons to doubt the veracity of these statements which I will discuss in Chapters 7 and 8, however, the ECtHR took the point at face value: could a person who was 'incapable' of consenting to confinement, who was not objecting and who had not attempted to leave, still be 'deprived of their liberty' in the meaning of article 5 ECHR? The court found they could be: the distinction relied upon by the UK government between *actual* restraint and restraint conditional on a person attempting to leave was of no consequence under the Convention [90]. The court identified as the 'key factor' that 'the concrete situation was that the applicant was under continuous supervision and control and was not free to leave' [91]. This formula would reverberate through subsequent Strasbourg rulings on social care detention, leading Lady Hale to conclude in *Cheshire West* that this was the acid test of deprivation of liberty under the ECHR (*Cheshire West*, UKSC, [48]–[49]).

The question of whether social care placements could amount to deprivation of liberty was first put to the court in *HM v Switzerland* (2002) 38 EHRR 314. HM, a Swiss pensioner, was placed in a nursing home by local authorities following concerns about self-neglect, relying on a Swiss civil code provision for 'Deprivation of Liberty on Grounds of Welfare Assistance' [18]. HM's expressed wishes were ambivalent: she appealed against the placement in the domestic courts, expressing a desire to 'get out' [21], yet recognized it was better for her to stay in the home and subsequently agreed to remain there. Before the ECtHR she alleged she was unlawfully deprived of her liberty, since 'neglect' was not a lawful ground of detention. The Swiss government contended that article 5 ECHR was not concerned with nursing home placements. The ECtHR concluded that HM was not deprived of her liberty within the meaning of article 5, emphasizing HM's freedom of movement and contact with the outside world, and that she herself later agreed to remain in the home. Judge Jorundsson dissented, however, stressing that she was not permitted to leave the institution to return home, and would have been brought back if she had.

It was Rusi Stanev's case – brought with the support of the Mental Disability Advocacy Centre – that saw the Grand Chamber of the Strasbourg court recognize social care detention for the first time. The facts of the case were so strong in framing Stanev's confinement as arbitrary, 'institutional' and deeply troubling that it is hard to see how the court could have avoided this conclusion. In *Stanev v Bulgaria* [2012] ECHR 46, Mr Stanev had been diagnosed with schizophrenia in the 1970s but a later psychiatric assessment found no symptoms of this. He had been placed under guardianship at the request of his relatives. His guardian, a local council officer, placed him in the Pastra Care Facility without consulting him.

The facility was in a remote mountain location, isolated from society, housing 92 male residents. The conditions were utterly deplorable – heavily criticized by the European Committee on the Prevention of Torture and Inhuman and Degrading Treatment (CPT) – whose role I consider below. The ECtHR considered they constituted inhuman and degrading treatment under article 3 ECHR, noting the poor condition of the living quarters, poor quality food, unhygienic toilets and scant washing facilities, absence of any meaningful activities and that the residents did not even possess their own clothes. The court stressed the long duration of Mr Stanev's stay – seven years – suggesting that the extended temporalities of social care detention may elevate what might not be considered 'inhuman or degrading' as a temporary measure into a fundamental human rights violation [209]. Stanev had tried to challenge his placement and restore his legal capacity, but as a person under guardianship he had no legal standing before the court and so could not initiate the proceedings himself. He had considerable freedom of movement within the facility, and some freedom to come and go, but this was at the discretion of the home's director and he was brought back by police if he absconded for too long. On these trips he would walk for miles, visiting a local monastery to talk to tourists, and providing assistance to local villagers (Flynn et al, 2018).

The ECtHR concluded Rusi Stanev was indeed deprived of his liberty, echoing the reasoning in *HL v UK*: 'he was under constant supervision and was not free to leave the home without permission whenever he wished' [128]. This detention was arbitrary and did not comply with the substantive and procedural protections of article 5 ECHR. However, the court declined to consider whether Stanev's institutionalization violated his article 8 rights to home, family and private life.

In short succession the ECtHR handed down three further judgments finding that applicants placed by guardians in social care facilities were deprived of their liberty (*D.D. v Lithuania* [2012] ECHR 254; *Kędzior v Poland* [2012] ECHR 1809; *Mihailovs v Latvia* [2013] ECHR 65). These cases were again supported by international disability and user/survivor NGOs. In each case, the ECtHR employed variations of the acid test formula (*D.D.*, [146]; *Kędzior*, [57]; *Mihailovs*, [129]). It bears noticing – and critics of *Cheshire West* would stress this point – that each of these cases originated in post-Soviet countries, which are still very reliant on large-scale, isolated and highly institutional social care facilities (Mladenov and Petri, 2019). Each country operated guardianship laws which typically deprive a person of 'legal capacity' (the ability to make legally valid decisions) across all areas of life, including even the ability to challenge one's placement or being put under guardianship. These 'concrete situations' were so very similar to mental health detention in large-scale institutions, and their legal situation so plainly problematic, it is not surprising the court ruled as it did.

For reformist civil society groups supporting these cases, this litigation was as much about 'chipping away' at guardianship as it was about highlighting 'deprivation of liberty' in social care facilities (Lewis, 2011). However, the outcomes fell short of abolitionist goals, of persuading the ECtHR to declare that these forms of disability-specific deprivation of liberty and deprivation of legal capacity should be abolished altogether and replaced with rights to live fully in the community (Lewis, 2012).

The cases secured greater substantive and procedural protection for those placed in social care facilities by their guardians, entrenching the 'law of institutions' in residential community settings. This pattern is now fanning out across Europe; several countries are embarking upon reforms to guardianship laws and developing deprivation of liberty safeguards for social care placements (Public Defender of Rights, 2017; Polish Commissioner for Human Rights, 2018; Commissioner for the Administration and Protection of Human Rights (Cyprus), 2019). In other countries, human rights organizations cite cases like *Stanev* to push for equivalent reforms (Ombudsman of the Republic of Croatia, 2017; Human Rights Ombudsman of the Republic of Slovenia, 2018). Some European states – including Germany, Austria and Switzerland – already operated public and private law systems for authorizing deprivation of liberty in 'social care' settings, but 'social care detention' is unrecognized and unregulated in both France and Spain (Boente, 2017). Recent litigation in France, brought by organizations representing autistic people confined to care homes during the COVID-19 pandemic, was unsuccessful. The Conseil d'État rejected the argument that these confinements amounted to a deprivation of liberty because they resulted from a mere Ministerial recommendation and did not have the character of an act of law (Conseil d'État, Juge des référés No 439822 8 avril 2020). The Strasbourg cases seem to have precipitated a growing movement across Europe advocating for recognition and regulation of social care detention, but this is not without resistance.

But to what extent does recognizing and regulating social care detention help secure the *actual* liberation of those confined? It is difficult to give any general answers to this. Progress across Europe toward 'community' living is slow, although may be enhanced by EU *ex ante* conditionality on structural funding, prohibiting it from being spent on repairing or replacing 'institutions' and encouraging the building of community services (Crowther, 2019a). For Mr Stanev himself, his celebrated landmark human rights story took him from imprisonment in (in his own words) 'the most terrible place' to being the first person deprived of legal capacity to attend their own hearing in Strasbourg. Following the ruling he was released from Pastra but placed in another 'home' and his guardianship was not lifted (Flynn et al, 2018: 199). Stanev never reached freedom; he died in 2017, at the age of 61. His story is a sad reminder that extending and entrenching the law of institutions to new locations will achieve only limited change unless we build better material alternatives.

Monitoring social care detention

Similar trends toward recognizing social care detentions can be seen in human rights bodies concerned with the second branch of the law of institutions – monitoring conditions in places of detention to ensure they do not fall below acceptable standards. Shortly after the new millennium, two new treaty bodies were established at the UN and the Council of Europe, concerned with preventing torture and inhuman and degrading treatment through systems of independent monitoring of places of detention. Both the European Convention for the Prevention of Torture and Inhuman or Degrading Treatment or Punishment (ECPT, Council of Europe, 2002) and the Optional Protocol on the Convention Against Torture (OPCAT, United Nations, 2006b) require states parties to allow independent monitoring bodies access to places of detention, in order to prevent abuse. The CPT achieves this through its own visitation system across Europe, however OPCAT requires states to establish their own independent National Preventive Mechanisms (NPMs) to visit places of detention and report on conditions therein. OPCAT monitoring of health and social care detention in the UK is performed by the bodies responsible for licensing and regulatory inspection: the CQC, CIW and HIW.

The question therefore arises – where are people deprived of their liberty, such that they require visiting by the CPT or NPMs? The OPCAT and ECPT initiatives derive from the work of a Swiss banker, Jean-Jacques Gautier, who was inspired by the International Committee of the Red Cross' prison visiting system during times of war (Murray et al, 2011). They were established around the 'paradigmatic' example of detention – the prisoner in his cell – but have adopted more expansive understandings of detention, including social care detention.

The ECPT adopts the article 5 ECHR definition of 'deprivation of liberty', and therefore reflects Strasbourg jurisprudence. It produced guidance for monitoring social care settings in 2015 (European Committee for the Prevention of Torture and Inhuman or Degrading Treatment or Punishment, 1998; Pirjola and Raškauskas, 2015).

Article 4 of the OPCAT defines 'deprivation of liberty' as 'any form of detention or imprisonment or the placement of a person in a public or private custodial setting which that person is not permitted to leave at will by order of any judicial, administrative or other authority'. Deprivation of liberty for 'medical reasons' and in psychiatric settings were discussed during the negotiations of OPCAT, but not social care (Nowak et al, 2019: 741–2). However, the Special Rapporteur on Torture, Manfred Nowak (2007), called for 'social care centres' to be included in monitoring visits because of the volume of individual communications he received concerning violence against women in these settings. The Association for the Prevention of Torture (2010: 29), a body founded by Gautier and instrumental in developing the ECPT and OPCAT, also states that 'social care homes' should be included within the SPT and NPM visiting mandate.

Some OPCAT signatories have, however, resisted including 'social care' settings within preventive detention monitoring. Some countries, relying on a Russian translation of article 4 of OPCAT as being held 'under (armed) guard' (содержания под стражей'), argued that orphanages and social care homes did not fall within its scope (Human Rights Implementation Centre, 2011). Most NPMs today, however, accept that social care institutions fall within their monitoring remit, and therefore many countries that have ratified OPCAT implicitly recognize social care detention even if they do not regulate it as such domestically. Almost all the most recent NPM reports to the SPT include social care settings such as nursing homes, residential care for older or disabled people, and children's homes.[2]

---

[2]   In 2020 I examined the most recent (English language) NPM reports on the SPT website and the following countries included references to monitoring of social care settings: Austria; Bulgaria; Croatia; the Czech Republic; Denmark; Finland; Germany; Greece; Hungary; Kyrgyz Republic; Lithuania; the Netherlands; Norway; Poland; Serbia; Slovenia; Sweden; United Kingdom.

Several countries have only recently included social care within their monitoring mandate. Some were influenced by seminars organized by the SPT or other NPMs on the topic, or scandals in social care services within their country (Greek Ombudsman, 2016; Commissioner for the Administration and Protection of Human Rights (Cyprus), 2019). Most NPMs focus on clearly defined social care 'institutions' such as 'disabled homes' or nursing homes. However, Finland includes, and Norway is considering including, supported housing services for people with intellectual disabilities (Norwegian Parliamentary Ombudsman, 2018: 3; Parliamentary Ombudsman of Finland, 2018: 74, 110). Some NPMs are adopting expansive interpretations of social care detention, not quite as extensive in reach as the acid test but including 'domestic' and 'non-institutional' services, at the further reaches of the post-carceral project.

Countries such as France and Australia, which do not currently include social care institutions within their NPM's preventive monitoring mandate, are outliers. However, their reasons for refusing to include these settings tells us something about governmental resistance to recognizing and regulating social care detention. In France, the Contrôleur Général des Lieux de Privation de Liberté (2012: 244) argued that its mandate should include retirement homes, citing the 'far from negligible' risks of fundamental rights violations, 'closely comparable' to that of prisons and psychiatric institutions before the NPM was established. However, there were 'serious obstacles' to this: social care placements were generally privately arranged by families rather than public authorities; comparing older people in residential care to the position of a 'captive' might be thought 'illogical' or even 'rather disrespectful'; and 'in theory' no formal legal obstacles prevented older people from leaving. Finally, the 'scale of the problem' would require a significant increase in resources. Subsequently, the Contrôleur Général des Lieux de Privation de Liberté (2014: 42) expressed regret that this proposal to extend its monitoring mandate to include retirement homes 'did not receive a favourable response'.

Australia recently ratified the OPCAT. The Australian government decided to exclude social care settings from the NPM mandate, on the basis that 'aged care facilities do not fit within the concept of 'places of detention' as set out in article 4 of OPCAT' (Senate Standing Committee on Legal and Constitutional Affairs, 2019). This has been met with concern by those arguing that aged care homes and community facilities for disabled people can be places of detention and that current monitoring is inadequate, citing a serious institutional abuse scandal in an aged care facility, Oakden (Lea et al, 2018; Grenfell, 2019; Weller, 2019). The Oakden scandal prompted a Royal Commission into Aged Care (2021), whose recent recommendations included an enhanced system of quality monitoring and vague references to rights to liberty, yet made no mention of OPCAT despite this being raised in multiple submissions. Perhaps arguments for enhanced 'quality' monitoring were culturally palatable, but the 'detention' framing was not. A parallel Royal Commission into Violence, Abuse, Neglect and Exploitation of People with Disability (2020) is ongoing, examining concerns about the use of 'restrictive practices', and has also received multiple submissions arguing that disability services should be included within the OPCAT mandate.

It is possible that, eventually, Australia will follow New Zealand, which ratified OPCAT in 2007 but only began monitoring social care facilities in 2019/20 (New Zealand Human Rights Commission, 2018; White, 2019). Currently, however, despite the clear inclusion of social care institutions within OPCAT guidance and the work of sister NPMs, both Australia and France resist the very *idea* that social care settings could be associated with deprivation of liberty, cleaving toward the traditional paradigm of the prisoner and understandings of deprivation of liberty as a question of formal legal authority rather than of fact. Only Finland has adopted the logics of social care detention to the extent it includes supported housing within its NPM monitoring mandate (even the UK has not done this, despite *Cheshire West*).

Abolitionist human rights

Over the past 20 years, 'social care detention' has been recognized as a significant human rights concern by major international human rights bodies. Their chief concerns were arbitrary detention – without adequate safeguards or means of challenge – and the conditions of confinement; mirroring those animating Thomas Townshend and the early reformers who created the law of institutions. The response has been to develop increasingly elaborate human rights norms and procedures for regulating social care placements amounting to detention, and independent monitoring systems to prevent abuse.

While reformist-influenced human rights law extended and thickened the law of institutions, a radical alternative paradigm of human rights has developed, connected with the UN CRPD. As Kanter (2015) and others have recounted, the UN CRPD resulted from decades of strategic campaigning by disabled people's organizations and their allies (Dhanda, 2006–7; Kayess and French, 2008). People with lived experience of disability (including psychosocial disability) and disabled people's organizations played a central role in drafting and negotiating the CRPD. Whereas earlier human rights instruments either ignored disabled people entirely or were drafted by people without lived experience of disability, the CRPD embodies the 'nothing about us without us' ethos of the DPM. It is therefore built on what Ben-Moshe (2020: 112) calls 'maroon abolitionist knowledge', the knowledge of those directly experiencing or at risk of incarceration. Consequently, it is imbued with a sense of *urgency*, impatient with reformist 'chipping away' at the legal and physical edifices of institutionalization. This abolitionist logic is directed toward institutionalization and its legal underpinnings – involuntary treatment (article 17 CRPD), disability-specific deprivation of liberty (article 14 CRPD), deprivation of legal capacity and substitute decision making (article 12 CRPD) – and the creation of alternatives, including a right to live independently and be included in the community (article 19 CRPD).

At first glance, the CRPD's roll call of rights resembles the core UN human rights instruments. However, on closer inspection it differs in important respects. Its description of disability reflects a social not medical model (article 1), and the themes of equality and non-discrimination are visible in almost all of its substantive rights. Its emphasis is on rights to self-determination, a limited emphasis on protection (article 16), with no mention of 'vulnerability' at all. This was deliberate choice by its drafters, who associated 'protection' measures such as guardianship and institutionalization as human rights abuses in themselves (Keeling, 2018).

The CRPD's provisions concerning mental health detention – articles 14 (on liberty), 15 (on whether involuntary treatment constituted torture or inhuman and degrading treatment) and 17 (integrity of the person) – were particularly contentious during the negotiations, as proponents of disabled people's organizations, particularly user/survivor groups, argued for norms that would outlaw all forms of non-consensual care, treatment and confinement (Bantekas et al, 2019). The final text is, in certain respects, ambiguous. Some – notably the Committee on the Rights of Persons with Disabilities (CRPD Committee) – interpret it as requiring the abolition of mental health detention and involuntary treatment, while others – including other UN human rights bodies – consider it as permitting mental health detention subject to safeguards (Doyle Guilloud, 2019). This has led to what Martin and Gurbai (2019) call the 'Geneva impasse'. The tension between old and new paradigms is particularly acute in relation to the right to liberty, where article 5 ECHR only permits deprivation of liberty on certain limited grounds – including 'unsoundness of mind' – and article 14 CRPD states that 'the existence of a disability shall in no case justify a deprivation of liberty'. The ECHR would appear to only permit something akin to mental health or social care detention on disability-related grounds; the CRPD appears to prohibit these altogether (Bartlett, 2009; Fennell and Khaliq, 2011).

It is not possible to do justice here to the flourishing scholarship, policy work and activism on the CRPD, particularly concerning mental health and disability-related detention and legal capacity. However, because social care detention is so closely linked to legal capacity, and because – as I will argue later on – the scope of the acid test is closely linked to what we mean by 'mental incapacity' – I will offer a few comments on the CRPD's notoriously contentious and sometimes difficult to interpret provisions on legal capacity. Article 12 CRPD is the 'right to equal recognition before the law'. It requires states to 'recognize that persons with disabilities enjoy legal capacity on an equal basis with others in all aspects of life' (article 12(2)), to provide access to the support that disabled people may require in exercising legal capacity (article 12(3)) and to ensure that there are 'appropriate and effective safeguards to prevent abuse' for all measures relating to the exercise of legal capacity, and these safeguards shall 'respect the rights, will and preferences of the person, are free of conflict of interest and undue influence' and include elaborate legalism-inflected requirements for regular review (article 12(4)).

Article 12's provisions were deliberately crafted to be ambiguous, to enable the treaty to be signed and adopted by states parties who wished to preserve substitute decision making, yet backed by disabled people's organizations who advocated for its abolition (Dhanda, 2006–7). However, in 2014 the CRPD Committee (2014a) adopted General Comment No. 1 on article 12. Their authoritative (but non-binding) interpretation is that it prohibits all forms of substitute decision making, including guardianship and other 'denials of legal capacity'; states must replace this with regimes of 'supported decision making'. This is perhaps an unfortunate expression, evoking arrangements whereby a person who can express clear choices receives support to make decisions, raising questions of what happens for those unable to express a clear choice at all. This challenge is often posed by critics of the CRPD as 'what about a person in a coma?' (Gooding, 2015).

However, by 'supported decision making' the Committee refers to a new paradigm of 'universal legal capacity'. This recognizes the choices of those capable of expressing them as legally valid (whatever their putative 'mental capacity'), but adopts an approach called 'facilitated decision making' in the literature for those unable to express clear choices (Bach and Kerzner, 2010; Flynn and Arstein-Kerslake, 2014). Where a person is unable to 'clearly' express a choice, trusted third parties may make decisions and act on their behalf in accordance with the 'best interpretation of their will and preferences', as opposed to an 'objective' best interests standards (CRPD Committee, 2014a: 21). On this understanding, even if a third party is making decisions on your behalf, provided you are thought not to object to that person making decisions for you or the outcome of the decisions they make, and they have made their best efforts to understand and reflect what they *think* you want (or would want), then this is a 'supported' and not 'substituted' decision in the ontological universe of the CRPD.

We will leave charged metaphysical debates as to whether this is really 'substitute decision making' by another name for someplace else (I offer my own thoughts on this elsewhere: Series, 2015a; Series and Nilsson, 2018). Strategically, positioning 'facilitated decision making' as something other than substitute decision making, as adhering as closely as possible to our best guess at what the person wants rather than what we think is best for them, tries to close off the dynamics of institutionalization, whereby a person ends up living in a place they do not want to be, with living arrangements that do not reflect their own (likely) preferences. This ethos is remarkably similar to early British philosophies of person-centred care, discussed in the last chapter. This is unsurprising, as work by a Canadian counterpart of British pioneers of community living – Michael Bach – has influenced this aspect of the 'new paradigm'.

This approach to supported or facilitated decision making could potentially resolve one of the more troubling paradoxical outcomes of the acid test: how a person who is positively happy in their living arrangements can be said to be detained. The 'universal legal capacity' paradigm contains the conceptual tools to understand how a person who 'lacks capacity' could give a 'valid consent' to care arrangements that could otherwise be a 'deprivation of liberty', so long as this is anchored in their will and preferences, with suitable safeguards to prevent abuse. I will revisit this approach in later chapters.

However, as Rusi Stanev's case demonstrates, securing 'legal capacity' and rights to liberty will not deliver freedom from institutionalization unless we also change the material realities of housing, support and communities. The CRPD fuses civil and political rights to liberty and legal capacity with social, economic and cultural rights (O'Cinneide, 2009), including a *sui generis* right to 'live independently and be included in the community'. Although article 19 CRPD borrows the problematic language of 'independence', which as I have shown in earlier chapters can easily be conflated with corrective and coercive discourses of burden and self-reliance, it is clear from the way this right is formulated that its goal is a holistic right to self-determination in one's living arrangements and inclusion in community:

> States Parties to the present Convention recognize the equal right of all persons with disabilities to live in the community, with choices equal to others, and shall take effective and appropriate measures to facilitate full enjoyment by persons with disabilities of this right and their full inclusion and participation in the community, including by ensuring that:
> a) Persons with disabilities have the opportunity to choose their place of residence and where and with whom they live on an equal basis with others and are not obliged to live in a particular living arrangement.
> b) Persons with disabilities have access to a range of in-home, residential and other community support services, including personal assistance necessary to support living and inclusion in the community, and to prevent isolation or segregation from the community.
> c) Community services and facilities for the general population are available on an equal basis to persons with disabilities and are responsive to their needs.

A General Comment on article 19 by the CRPD Committee (2017) describes institutionalization in all its forms as violating this right. Arguably, the CRPD – and article 19 in particular – gives legal expression to the full vision of the post-carceral era, of disabled people entitled and enabled to live in a place of their choosing on an equal basis with others, with access to personal assistance, included and participating in responsive, receptive and accessible communities. In her detailed examination of article 19 and its antecedents, Kanter (2015) suggests that it enshrines a right to *home*, and argues that this right – not the right to liberty – holds the greatest promise for deinstitutionalizing disabled people. I will revisit this thematic opposition between 'home' and 'institution' in the next chapter.

Social care detention and abolitionist human rights

To what extent, then, do the treaty bodies, rapporteurs and activists closely linked to the CRPD recognize social care detention? The answer, somewhat unexpectedly, is surprisingly little in comparison with the 'old paradigm' instruments considered above.

The General Comment on independent living recognizes that institutionalization can take many forms, and calls upon states to 'release all individuals who are being confined against their will in mental health services or other disability-specific forms of deprivation of liberty' (CRPD Committee, 2017: [48]), but does not elaborate what those other forms of deprivation of liberty might look like. Certainly, there is no recognition that deprivation of liberty can occur even in specialist services intended to promote independent living. Similarly, a 'statement' on article 14 by the CRPD Committee (2014b) (issued in response to the United Nations Human Rights Committee (2014) statement discussed earlier), affirms its position on the 'absolute prohibition of detention on the basis of impairment'. However, its force is directed toward involuntary confinement in 'mental health institutions'; again, there is no explicit mention of other forms of disability-specific detention, for example in residential social care facilities. Meanwhile, the CRPD Committee's (2014a) General Comment on article 12 discusses the connection between guardianship laws and involuntary institutional placement yet does not explicitly identify these practices as *detention*. The impression – rightly or wrongly – is that the CRPD Committee is strongly oriented toward the situation of people with psychosocial disabilities who are concerned about mental health detention, but are less attuned to those at risk of social care detention. This is unfortunate, because social care detention presents difficult dilemmas for abolitionists, and it would be helpful to have the CRPD Committee's leadership and guidance on this.

The CRPD Committee has had several potential opportunities to recognize deprivation of liberty in residential care and other social contexts through individual complaints submitted via the CRPD's Optional Protocol (UN, 2006c). In two cases complainants argued that refusals of planning permission to modify their homes to enable them greater opportunities for rehabilitation or access to the community constituted an unlawful deprivation of liberty (*HM v Sweden* (3/2011) 21 May 2012 CRPD/C/ 7/D/3/2011; *Simon Bacher v Austria* (26/2014) 6 April 2018 CRPD/C/ 19/D/26/2014). The Committee ruled these complaints inadmissible. In *Y v Tanzania* (23/2014) 30 October 2018 CRPD/C/20/D/23/2014 an albino man was unable to attend school because the state had not protected him against persecution and physical attacks on albino people and a black market in their body parts. The CRPD Committee upheld several aspects of his complaint but concluded that 'the author was never deprived of his liberty in the sense of article 14 which relates to any form of detention or institutionalization of persons with disability' [7.7]. These complaints tell us both that for some people living with disability 'deprivation of liberty' captures a sense that their living arrangements do not afford them full self-determination and freedom; they deploy liberty tactics to call attention to this injustice. Yet the Committee interprets the right to liberty as directed toward 'institutionalization', and something *done to* a person, rather than something *not done* to assist them.

A series of complaints against Australia alleged that the people living in community care facilities were deprived of their liberty because of the failure to provide adequate housing and support in the community. Two were subsequently withdrawn after support was provided (*Kendall v Australia* (15/ 2013) 29 April 2019 CRPD/C/21/D/15/2013; *MR v Australia* (16/2013) 5 July 2018 CRPD/C/18/D/16/2013), the third was ruled inadmissible because deprivation of liberty arguments had not been raised before the domestic courts (*DR v Australia* (14/2003) 19 May 2017, CRPD/C/17/ D/14/2013). Disappointingly, therefore, the Committee did not engage with arguments that DR was deprived of his liberty in a residential centre consisting of small 'pods' with four bedrooms and communal facilities because he could only leave with staff's permission, nor the Australian government's counter-argument that 'for a person to be deprived of liberty, he or she must be subject to "forceful detention" at a "certain narrowly bounded location"' [4.32], and that substitute decisions by guardians concerning residence do not amount to detention.

Social care detention has been recognized by the previous UN Special Rapporteur on Disability, Catalina Devandas Aguilar (2019: [14], [15], [17], [18], [22]), who commissioned thematic work on disability and deprivation of liberty. While identifying mental health detention as the most 'recognized' form of disability-specific detention, she also described 'placement in institutions' and 'home confinement' as 'common forms' of disability-specific deprivation of liberty. Devandas Aguilar does not define deprivation of liberty but does propose that: 'To the extent that persons with disabilities are placed in institutions without their free and informed consent or are not free to leave, they are deprived of their liberty' [18]. This encompassed 'social care institutions', 'supported housing' and even situations where older people with dementia might be 'impeded from leaving their own homes'.

A fuller definition is proposed by Flynn, Pinilla-Rocancio and Gómez-Carillo De Castro (2019: 27) in a study commissioned to inform the Special Rapporteur's report: 'an individual is deprived of their liberty when s/he is: confined to a restricted space or placed in an institution or setting; or under continuous supervision and control; not free to leave; and the person has not provided free and informed consent'.

The parallels to the *Cheshire West* acid test are remarkable. It is doubtful they are accidental; the report's lead authors are based at the Centre for Disability Law and Policy at NUI Galway, and likely familiar with the acid test because this informed recent Irish government proposals for a DoLS-like scheme.

A broad reading of 'deprivation of liberty' is useful for abolitionists conscious that institutionalization-like phenomena can occur in the community or even domestic settings. However, it also presents dilemmas insofar as the acid test includes people who are positively happy with their living arrangements and may not be in any kind of 'institution' at all. In their consultation response to the Department of Health (Ireland) (2019: 32, 41), the Centre for Disability Law and Policy expressed concerns about categorizing 'everyone who is suspected to lack capacity' as deprived of their liberty, arguing that recent capacity legislation in Ireland 'recognizes that even where a person is deemed to lack capacity, appointed supporters can interpret his or her will and preferences to form the basis of a decision'. Few other abolitionist commentators on disability-specific deprivation of liberty have directly engaged with the dilemmas of social care detention and the acid test; this suggests some may endorse facilitated decision making-inspired approaches to resolve these paradoxical situations.

★★★

The basic problematization of 'institutional' care and the legal response of the law of institutions are replicated under contemporary international human rights law. Since their development after the war – a time when disabled people were invisible, or worse, to the framers of these international human rights instruments – they have become imbued with post-carceral norms and the spirit of legalism. Several treaty bodies now recognize social care detention. Although resisted by some states, most international human rights bodies now recognize that a person may be deprived of their liberty in a care home, a nursing home or similar; the fact of being 'in the community', or lacking 'legal capacity' does not mean rights to liberty lose traction.

Those seeking recognition of social care detention under international human rights law have different goals. A broadly reformist strain of law, embodied by the ECHR, OPCAT and EPCAT, seeks to extend the law of institutions over social care institutions to ameliorate the worst abuses of institutional community care and secure individual rights of challenge. Others pursue abolitionist goals: by 'calling out' some living arrangements in the community as 'deprivation of liberty', they aim to eradicate institutionalization in all its diverse forms. Some pursue reformist means with abolitionist goals in mind, chipping away slowly at the edifices of guardianship, substitute decision making and legal incapacity. But the law of institutions will only get us so far if we do not build the alternatives we want to see.

It is surprising – and disappointing – to see such limited engagement between abolitionist readings of the CRPD and the dynamics and dilemmas of social care detention. As I argued in Chapter 2, social care detention is fundamentally different from mental health detention, affecting different populations, loci, interventions, targeting different 'problems' and guided by different rationalities, legal technologies and 'experts'. While there are certainly some cases where it is obvious what 'abolition' of social care detention would look like – closure of care facilities like Pastra, for example – there are many examples considered in this book where this is less clear cut. Some cases can be filtered out by constructing 'valid consent' from the tools of the CRPD's 'universal legal capacity' approach (Series, 2020). I will argue in later chapters that this would be a useful approach under the DoLS/LPS. However, it only takes us so far.

In particular, it is unclear what 'abolition' looks like for somebody like P in the *Cheshire West* case, who is living in so-called 'independent living' accommodation, with a purported tenancy, and 'support' enabling him to do things which at least his supporters believe he might enjoy. But as we will learn in more detail in Chapter 8, P's life is also characterized by supervision, control and physical restraint, which aims to stop him from choking on things he puts in his mouth. This is no theoretical risk; it had led to hospital admissions for choking in the past. The abolitionist emphasis on eradication of all restrictive practices might be read as implying there should be no such interventions, that staff should not physically intervene to prevent someone like P from choking, or likewise to prevent MIG or MEG from wandering in front of traffic, or others at risk from similar everyday hazards. This is a stark outcome, difficult to reconcile to the vision of disability rights. Yet the alternatives are also hazardous to the abolitionist intentions behind the CRPD. It is understandable why advocates of the CRPD's new paradigm are hesitant to engage with these hardest of hard cases, lest the old paradigm regrows through these cracks. Yet, while these situations might be hard, they are not at all unusual in social care. They demand our attention, not relegation to the shadows of the new paradigm.

Some abolitionists caution against any reading of the CRPD permissive of non-consensual interventions (Minkowitz, 2017), calling for the abolition of all 'restrictive practices' and 'disability-specific lawful violence' (Cadwallader et al, 2018). However, others argue that some limited protection measures might be permissible in situations of 'grave and imminent harm to life, health or safety' (Flynn and Arstein-Kerslake, 2017: 54), something that is 'disability neutral', akin to the doctrine of necessity (Gooding and Flynn, 2015). Yet as others have argued (Steele, 2017), and I will show in Chapter 7, these doctrines can expand to accommodate considerable coercion, with very limited substantive or procedural safeguards. Apparently 'neutral' doctrines can still disproportionately target people with cognitive disabilities. And they do not help us with the more fundamental question of what we *call* these situations, where a person may be subject to 'continuous supervision' and at least some degree of 'control' to prevent real, grave and imminent risks where these are ever-present. If this is not a deprivation of liberty, then what is it? And if it is, then how does this fit within the 'new paradigm', which calls for the abolition of all disability-specific forms of deprivation of liberty?

I do not have answers; and there may not be a single answer. Part of the reason I wrote this book was to pose the question.

Addressing those who ask about the 'dangerous few' in prison abolition circles, Ben-Moshe (2020: 124) argues that we need to learn from the 'successful deinstitutionalization closures' of disability institutions, which began with the resettlement of 'those labeled as having the most significant needs'. Yet this answer will not do here, because many of those labelled as having the most significant needs – those, for example, that Mansell helped resettle – are men and women like P, in the *Cheshire West* case, who we now recognize as deprived of their liberty in the community, even in 'supported living' and perhaps in their own homes.

Social care detention is uncomfortable from an abolitionist perspective because the answer is not merely 'closure' and relocation. By defining deprivation of liberty in relational terms, the acid test leaves nowhere to hide from these uncomfortable and often intractable dilemmas. Perhaps, then, questions of deprivation of liberty are not productive for our present predicament. Perhaps they are ghosts from our carceral past come knocking. In the next chapter I will consider other ways of conceptualizing both our positive goals (real homes, in the community) and the harms of institutions that we hope to avoid, and suggest this may be a more helpful orientation than the binary logics of the law of institution.

6

Institution/Home

In one of Connecticut's finest care homes, Ellen Langer and Judith Rodin (1976) conducted an experiment. They allocated the residents of one floor of the care home to a 'responsibility induced' experimental condition, and those on another floor (carefully matched for health, age, mobility and ability to communicate) to a 'comparison' group. The friendly nursing home administrator read each group a communication. The 'responsibility induced' group were 'reminded' of their responsibility and ability to decide whether 'you want to make this a home you can be proud of and happy in'. They were 'reminded' that they could decide how they wanted the furniture in their rooms arranged, how to spend their time, who to visit, and how they could influence how the home was run. Residents were offered a choice of which night they'd like to watch a movie and given the option to select a plant as a gift to 'take care of as you like'. The comparison group were given a similarly upbeat message, but this one stressed the staff's responsibility for their happiness, for arranging their furniture, and that they were 'permitted' to visit others. They were told which night they could watch a movie and were given a plant and told that staff would take care of it (p194). Three weeks later, residents in the responsibility induced group reported significantly greater levels of happiness after the intervention than the comparison group. Nurses reported they were significantly more active, alert and sociable. When they revisited the study 18 months later, Rodin and Langer (1977) found these results were sustained. Moreover, significantly fewer people in the experimental group had died in comparison with the control group.

At the time of their experiment it was well established that for 'normal' subjects (college students and schoolchildren), increased choice and control over even relatively minor aspects of one's life or activities was associated with reduced anxiety and increased well-being. Langer and Rodin's (1976: 191) intuition was that increasing choice and control for those living 'in a virtually decision free environment', as they put it, could measurably improve well-being. Their landmark study generated a new approach to gerontology. Further research confirmed the importance of 'control' over environment for older adults and other populations, including both objective control and a subjective sense of being able to influence outcomes. Moreover (and echoing the approach to independent living endorsed by disabled people's organizations) studies found enhanced well-being even for people who 'depended' on others, provided they exercised choices and their own goals were supported (Mallers et al, 2014). Functional independence was less critical than choice and control over support and outcomes.

Langer and Rodin's study, and further empirical research in this tradition, concluded that 'control' over one's living arrangements and environment is vital to health and well-being. Conversely, studies of 'institutionalization' report harmful consequences of living in what Langer and Rodin called a 'decision free' environment. Both Goffman (1961) and Townsend (1962) described institutionalized people sinking into apathy and misery; Townsend termed this 'depersonalization' and Goffman 'mortification of the self'. The finding, across the literature, is that 'decisions', 'responsibility', 'choice' and 'control' are fundamental to human flourishing, and that environments that deplete these opportunities are harmful, corroding the self.

These studies also show that even micro-choices – how one arranges one's furniture, which night you watch a movie, whether to water a houseplant or let it die – can improve well-being. Or, to put it another way, opportunities for the expression and flourishing of self do not wait for the 'big' decisions, but are tightly woven into our everyday lives and surroundings. In an analysis of Goffman's (1961) ethnography of 'total institutions' and Foucault's writings on subjectivity, philosopher Ian Hacking (2004: 282) explains the significance of even micro-choices like this:

> We push our lives through a thicket in which the stern trunks of determinism are entangled in the twisting vines of chance. Still, you can choose what you can do, under the circumstances. The choices that you make, situated in the thicket, are what formed you and continue to form you.

Where a person's circumstances are extremely constrained, all that may be left are 'little choices', but 'they are choices all the same' (p287). Hacking's analysis implies that the 'mortifying' effects of institutions result not only from geographical confinement, but confinement within a very limited *decision space*, where even the most mundane and everyday choices – micro-opportunities for the expression and cultivation of identity – are constrained. Far from being trivial or mundane, the erosion of everyday choices such as when to get up or what to eat betokens dire constraints upon possibilities-for-being and the flourishing of identity and self.

This belief lies at the heart of post-carceral ideology. As 'the decision' became the base unit of freedom, post-carceral laws like the MCA parcel out legal (in)capacity on a 'decision-specific' basis. As we saw in Chapter 4, it was not sufficient to simply close the large institutions and relocate their residents, because institution-like phenomena could emerge in the community as well. Decisions became a metric of how 'institutional' an environment was, and 'home' (or 'real homes', 'ordinary homes') came to signify decision-rich places where people could live and flourish in ways denied by institutions. In later chapters I will explore how both branches of the law of institutions are increasingly used to secure a larger decision space for social care users, albeit far from the radical clearing of the decision space envisioned in connection with rights to independent living and the CRPD.

But what kinds of decisions distinguish 'institutions' from 'homes' in their idealized forms? Who and what determines which decisions are offered or denied? Is it sufficient to offer someone a pot plant, help them rearrange the furniture (or, in the argot of contemporary social care, to 'personalize' their bedroom) to call a place a home? I turn to the vast multidisciplinary research literatures on 'total institutions' and 'homes' to map out their contrasting decision spaces, which are significantly more complex than simplistic accounts of 'personalization' imply.

To organize this unwieldy material I borrow a conceptual framework from socio-legal scholar Lorna Fox O'Mahony[1] (Fox, 2002, 2005; Fox O'Mahony, 2006; 2013). Her synthesis of research on the meanings of home identified three core clusters – *home as territory*, *home as a centre for self-identity* and *home as a social and cultural unit*. To these I add a fourth – the aesthetics of 'homes' and 'institutions' – because this is often used as a legal and cultural shorthand to identify somewhere as 'homelike' rather than 'institutional'. Drawing from Goffman's (1961) landmark ethnography of total institutions, *Asylums*, and work in that tradition, I show how for each cluster of characteristics and decisions associated with home, there is an opposing cluster of characteristics and decisions denied or restricted in institutions. In their idealized forms, 'home' and 'institution' are constructed in these research studies along opposing poles: 'Being homelike versus being institutional are used in opposition to one another. One cannot define what is homelike without defining what is institutional and vice versa' (Lundgren, 2000: 112).

The difficulty is that although 'homes' and 'institutions' are constructed in opposition to each other, these are not abstract concepts, but inextricably entwined with the subjectivity of those dwelling within these spaces. The realities of caregiving, disability and 'incapacity' complicate these polarities. In Chapter 4, I discussed economic and cultural factors that could drive

---

[1] Previously known as Lorna Fox, as in some references here.

institutionalization by constraining choices over where and with whom a person lives and how they are supported. In this chapter, I consider the problems posed by constrained abilities – factual or legal – to make 'decisions'. To put it simply, if a person is neither able nor allowed to make the kinds of decisions we associate with 'home', their living arrangements start to resemble the characteristics we associate with institutions. This produces liminal and contested spaces of caregiving, where characteristics of 'home' and 'institution' collide, and we can no longer draw clear or comfortable distinctions between these settings. I describe some examples in the literature of 'homes' that display institutional characteristics, and 'institutions' where a person has made a home.

These idealized and polarized accounts of home and institutions are historically and culturally specific to contemporary Western liberal societies, with class, gendered and – I suggest – ableist dimensions (Forty and Cameron, 1986; Chapman and Hockey, 2002; Shin, 2014). They are built upon a liberal caricature of the human condition, what Quinn and Arstein-Kerslake (2012: 37) call the 'masterless man', a 'rational, self-directing, wholly autonomous individual', choosing their own destiny in a void. For some people with cognitive impairments, reducing 'home' to 'decision making' – where this is understood in terms of decisions made with full 'mental capacity' – may consign them to permanent home-lessness. Yet as we saw in Chapter 5, there are other ways to conceptualize 'decisions' for people with significant cognitive impairments, based on the cultivation and preservation of relationships of trust, and attunement to what we can discern of their 'will and preferences'. This invites possibilities that we might conceptualize other – less ableist – ways of understanding what it is to make a place a home, which harness its potential for human flourishing yet avoid the harms of institutionalization.

Home as territory

> [T]he house of every one is to him as his castle and fortress, as well for his defence against injury and violence as for his repose.
> *Semayne's Case* (1 January 1604) 5 Coke Rep. 9

For lawyers, the dimension of *home as territory* holds great significance, signifying a locus of control and a level of autonomy, privacy and security unavailable elsewhere. This category, first suggested by Hayward (1975) and echoed throughout the literature on home (Moore, 2000; Easthope, 2004; Mallett, 2004) resonates with the widely quoted dictum derived from *Semayne's Case*, 'an Englishman's home is his castle'. Home is a place with unique jurisdictional properties, where the owner or tenant is quasi-sovereign and protected by law against certain unwelcome intrusions or interferences by others (Fox, 2002; Barros, 2004; Fox O'Mahony, 2006).

Choice and control over everyday life

A significant body of research indicates that older people[2] value home as territory. As a place where you can 'do what you want', enjoy privacy, and take *responsibility* for (Sixsmith, 1986: 287). A place where older people felt most in control of their lives (Dupuis and Thorns, 1996), or were 'beholden to no one', affording maximum autonomy and privacy (Stones and Gullifer, 2016: 458). For older adults contemplating a move into residential care, their home was regarded as a place where 'they had liberty in decision-making' (Leibing et al, 2016: 15).

In direct contrast, a defining feature of life in a 'total institution' is loss of control over even the most mundane features of everyday life – deciding whether to have sugar and milk in one's coffee, or whether to have a cigarette. Institutional inmates are not sovereign: the institution 'belongs to the staff' (Goffman, 1961: 20). Goffman emphasized the depth of penetration of institutional life into a person's locus of control: 'minute segments of a person's line of activity may be subjected to regulations and judgements by staff; the inmate's life is penetrated by constant sanctioning interaction from above. ... The autonomy of the act itself is violated' (p43).

The CRPD Committee (2017: [16(c)]) identifies this as the paramount feature of 'institutions': 'It is not "just" about living in a particular building or setting, it is, first and foremost, about losing personal choice and autonomy as a result of the imposition of certain life and living arrangements.'

The Committee goes on to note that '[i]nstitutional settings may offer persons with disabilities a certain degree of choice and control, however, these choices are limited to specific areas of life and do not change the segregating character of institutions'. Moreover, 'choices' can misfire and may reflect or embed disempowering dynamics. Care and support staff may not always possess the requisite skills and rapport with an individual to effectively offer choices and support decisions between those choices (Antaki et al, 2008). Staff may not readily accept refusals of 'choices' offered that pursue institutional agendas (Finlay et al, 2008). Some 'choices' – for example, giving permission to go to the toilet at a particular time – implicitly convey that staff exercise ultimate control (Antaki et al, 2009).

Disabled people who have experienced institutionalization in psychiatric or residential settings are especially attuned to the freedoms of 'home' (Duyvendak and Verplanke, 2016). Home can represent 'a secure base from which to launch efforts towards recovery' for people who have experienced mental health detention (Borg et al, 2005: 243). Ware et al (1992: 302–3)

---

[2]   In the research literature, this is generally people aged 65 and over. 'Very old' people are aged 85 and over.

interviewed previously homeless people who had moved into a housing scheme. They valued their new-found privacy and freedom of action. They did not consider homeless shelters 'real homes' because of the rules, regulations and control exercised by staff over residents' movements within the shelter. In their new homes, the tenants (not staff) determined the rules of shared spaces and they could 'sleep all day' if they wanted to.

Loss of privacy

Home as territory also implies privacy. This is considered integral to psychological well-being (Fox, 2002; citing Smith, 1994). For the tenants interviewed by Ware et al (1992: 303–4), privacy was an important difference between their new homes – where they could lock their door, secure their belongings and 'relax' out from under the gaze of staff – and the shelter, where 'all spaces are penetrable by staff'.

Surveillance by staff is a routine characteristic of institutional life. Inmates are constantly looking over their 'shoulder to see if criticism or other sanctions are coming' (Goffman, 1961: 43). And whereas in its positive idealization, home implies a space of physical security and refuge from others, a 'haven' from the world (Mallett, 2004), Goffman emphasized that life in an institution involves continued exposure to 'interpersonal contamination' through violations of bodily integrity and personal space – for example, through bodily or room searches, or confiscation of one's possessions (Goffman, 1961: 36).

Control of the threshold

Control of the threshold – over who is admitted and who may leave – is a key distinction between the characteristics of homes and institutions. Homes are associated with 'strong walls to ward off unwanted intruders', preserving 'chosen interactions with community', whereas institutions are associated with external walls that block out the outside and 'real life' (Leibing et al, 2016: 15).

Twigg (1999: 384) views the material and legal 'capacity to exclude' as central to protecting privacy and autonomy within the home, meaning that those who enter – friends, relations, even care workers – do so 'as guests' (see also Angus et al, 2005). Home-dwellers can thereby 'resist the dominance of care workers and professionals' because '[a]t the simplest level you can refuse them entry. You can tell staff to leave', unlike residential care homes 'where the space belongs not to the residents but the staff' (Twigg, 1999: 386). O'Brien (1994: 2) viewed 'control of the threshold' as essential to providing meaningful homes for people with intellectual disabilities.

In law, control of the threshold is embedded in a right known as 'exclusive possession' (*Street v Mountford* [1985] AC 809 (House of Lords)), defined by one housing law textbook as meaning the tenant 'can exclude the whole world, including the landlord' (Astin, 2018: [1.29]). Many supported living service users hold tenancies, meaning in theory they hold legal rights to 'exclusive possession' (National Development Team for Inclusion, 2015). However, as we will see, the reality is often more complicated than this. Powers to exclude may be conditioned by the realities of relying on others for assistance in everyday life (Milligan, 2009).

In contrast, institutions are 'symbolized by barriers to social intercourse with the outside and to departure' (Goffman, 1961: 4), in the form of walls, locked doors, or geographical remoteness. Even where doors are unlocked and institutions are 'open' staff may still exercise control over entry and departure through permission seeking, as, for example, in the case of Rusi Stanev. Another potential barrier is reliance on others for personal mobility, and some ordinary domestic homes may present physical barriers to mobility within and beyond the house (Angus et al, 2005). The control research implies we should focus on the extent to which the person's physical environment and support enables them to come and go in accordance with their preferences and goals, rather than people's freedom to move without assistance.

Within an institution, residents may not be able to exclude staff from 'private' spaces such as bedrooms, or staff will designate some spaces out of bounds to inmates, such as kitchens or offices. Some care homes aim to preserve some 'control of the threshold' by requiring staff to knock on residents' doors (Tipper, 2003; Green, 2020) but this is not always reliably observed (Malmedal, 2014). At law this is conditioned by the fact most care home residents occupy their rooms on licence rather than as tenants or owner occupiers, and so do not have exclusive possession.

Home as territory in liminal spaces of care

Studies of care settings tell us that when people lose choice and control over everyday life this erodes their feeling of being 'at home'. Nursing home residents interviewed by Groger (1995) insisted that a 'nursing home could never be a home'. Groger observes (with palpable frustration) that residents associated 'home' with autonomy and independence.

Even settings that aspire to offer people homelike and non-institutional living arrangements can replicate these institutional dynamics. Svanelöv (2019) found that small group homes for people with intellectual disabilities in Sweden imposed an 'institutional clock', dictating when residents must eat, sleep, wash or visit the bathroom. Staff controlled shared spaces, excluding residents from kitchens or staff toilets, granting only limited privacy in bedrooms. Roberts (2012) found that although residents in a small community housing scheme in Nova Scotia had considerably more freedom than in traditional care facilities, that freedom was still bounded; staff still felt obliged to ensure residents got up, ate healthy meals, and were protected from perceived risks. Residents perceived themselves as having limited freedoms and expressed ambivalence over whether the housing scheme was their home.

As we saw in Chapter 4, supported living services were developed in England and Wales to enable people with intellectual disabilities 'to live in real homes of their own' (Kinsella, 1993: 14). The Reach Standards embody the idea of home as a territory where a person enjoys a significant locus of control. Yet studies of supported living have found that residents often do not enjoy 'home as territory' in the same way as other citizens. Although tenants nominally hold rights of exclusive possession, support staff may hold keys and enter the property freely, they may exercise control over space within the property and even designate some spaces (such as spare bedrooms) 'staff offices' from which residents are excluded (Tipper, 2003; Fyson et al, 2007). They may impose rules and restrictions on residents (Fyson et al, 2007). The anthropological study commissioned by Family Mosaic (2012) even found staff imposing punishments on residents for breaking rules. Supported living residents may have limited privacy because of surveillance by staff, staff gossip and practices of record keeping (Drinkwater, 2005; Family Mosaic, 2012). Although supported living residents may enjoy greater freedoms than those in group homes, they may still have little control over *how* support is provided (Bigby et al, 2017). As we will see in the next chapter, supported living residents may in practice have limited choice over *who* provides support, and therefore who enters their home.

However, some care service users do report feeling 'at home' in formal care facilities. One resident in Groger's (1995) study considered the nursing home to be his home; he had chosen to move there after rejecting several alternative placements. Leith (2006: 323) found that older women moving into an assisted living facility 'voluntarily and independently', deliberately set out to create new routines and friendships, to shape their new environment, concluding: 'Home reflects the autonomous decision to find a home somewhere.' Thein, D'Souza and Sheehan (2011) found that people with dementia reported more positive experiences of a move into residential care if they felt in control of the decision to move. Therefore, even in more 'institutional' settings, some sense of 'home' is possible, but is linked to positive choices to make a place a home.

To complicate matters further, studies of informal and formal care within ordinary domestic homes have observed dynamics of caregiving associated with 'institutions'. As Twigg (1999: 381) puts it, 'The coming of disability … may impose a new social ordering' in the domestic sphere.

Observational research of family care of people with dementia living at home has identified elements of 'custodial care' associated with total institutions, including routines, surveillance and 'mortification of the self' (Redfern et al, 2002; Askham et al, 2007; Clarke et al, 2010). 'Contested territories' emerged over activities perceived by family carers to be risky, such as whether a person could go out alone, drive, manage their finances or smoke (Clarke et al, 2010). This dynamic was not only distressing to care recipients, but also sometimes for carers – one husband commented, 'It's horrible keeping your wife a prisoner in her own home' (Askham et al, 2007: 14).

Although these researchers drew analogies with the custodial care elements of total institutions, they stressed that '[h]omes are not total institutions, and people with dementia are not inmates' (Askham et al, 2007: 21). They argued that elements of 'routine' are necessary for the functioning of any household, and that surveillance was used to keep a person safe, ensure they were not scared or distressed, and to prevent disruption to the ordering of the household (Askham et al, 2007). The researchers' own ambivalence in describing what are clearly 'private' domestic dwellings, and family-based care as 'institutional' mirrors similar concerns over applying the 'deprivation of liberty' label in this context, which we will explore in later chapters.

Home as a centre for self-identity

Home is deeply connected to identity (Hayward, 1975; Sixsmith, 1986; Easthope, 2004; Mallett, 2004). Fox (2002: 599) calls it an 'identity shell': a product of our self-identity, and the place where we have freedom to express it. For people with cognitive impairments such as dementia, homes can provide 'the physical scaffolding that supports who we are' (Lindemann, 2009: 419). The protection human rights law affords home, family and private life is intimately connected to facilitating the expression and development of personality and personal identity (Marshall, 2014).

In contrast, the force of Goffman's critique of total institutions was that they *mortified* the self, or in Townsend's words they result in 'depersonalization'. Carboni (1990: 34) writes that nursing home residents face 'non-personhood; identity becomes murky because they no longer have a special bond with a place ... the roots that fed each informant's identity and provided nurturance were more than merely pulled up; it seemed that the roots were actually severed'. Autistic institution survivor Amanda Baggs (2012) described her own experiences in a blog post entitled 'What makes institutions bad':

> The cause of the problem is a certain exercise of power. Of person over unperson. And in order to survive it the inmates have to become as much of that unperson as they can manage. And that does violent damage deep inside the self, that can be incredibly hard to repair.

It's violent even when it comes with purported love and sweetness and light.

Whereas homes express the identity of the individual, institutions are 'forcing houses for changing persons; each is a natural experiment on what can be done to the self' (Goffman, 1961: 22). An important contrast between 'home' and 'institution', then, is whether a set of living arrangements reflect the person's own wishes and goals for themselves, or somebody else's goals imposed upon them (even if such goals are clad in the progressive language of normalization, independence or fulfilling potential).

For some people it may be relatively straightforward to determine whether their home reflects their identity, or an attempt to impose or correct their identity. However, in some cases this may require an exercise in interpretation. This is likely to be the case in the kinds of situations where 'facilitated decision making' is envisaged as being used to arrive at a 'best interpretation' of a person's 'will and preferences'. The difficulty, here, is that interpretations of a person's identity will vary with those doing the interpreting. An example is provided by Clement and Bigby's (2010) description of a man with intellectual disabilities whose living space was 'interpreted' by one care manager as a family home – bright, airy, tidy, well-decorated, with tables laid for every meal – and by a subsequent manager as a 'bachelor pad', with the house untidy and unkempt, and a pool table in the lounge. The point is not that we should abandon attempts at understanding a person and interpreting their identity as best we can, and simply impose upon them the living arrangements we think are best, but rather that interpretation is a complex exercise, often without clear answers, and it affords considerable power to those doing the interpreting (Skowron, 2019). This requires careful attention to the quality of relationship between interpreter(s) and interpreted, to the person's wider rights and social and cultural world, and to their historic and daily interactions with the 'micro' that makes up their world.

Home as a social and cultural unit

Home is associated with connection – to other people, and to place. In its positive idealization, home is a central 'locus for relationships with family and friends' (Fox, 2002: 590; see also Moore, 2000; Mallett, 2004), although its reality can also be associated with loneliness and isolation. For some, the 'social home' is more important than any other aspect of home (Tanner et al, 2008: 201–1). Homes are places where one can offer hospitality to chosen visitors, or invite people to stay; maintaining social bonds that are integral to sustaining identity and a sense of self (Sixsmith, 1986; O'Brien, 1994). In contrast, care services frequently impose limitations on visiting times, may also limit who may visit, and may even require 'safeguarding checks' for overnight stays if they are permitted at all (as in *A Local Authority v TZ (No. 2)* [2014] EWHC 973 (COP)). The institutional power of care homes to limit social contact became especially acute during the pandemic; in contrast supported living providers were reminded that residents lived in their own 'homes' and therefore visits could not be prohibited by staff unless subject to national lockdown rules (Department of Health and Social Care, 2021).

Most adult home-dwellers exercise a degree of choice over who they live with, however care home residents rarely do and supported living service users may not. Residents are, in the words of asylum inmate John Perceval in 1840, 'placed amongst strangers' (Mental Health Act Commission, 2003). The social world of the institution was characterized by Goffman (1961: 18–22) as a 'basic split between a large managed group ... and supervisory staff', with social mobility between these two strata 'grossly restricted'. The result is that '[t]wo different social worlds develop, jogging alongside each other with points of official contact but little mutual penetration'.

Home can provide a sense of rootedness and belonging, attachment to a specific place[3] (Easthope, 2004). As Fox O'Mahony and Sweeney (2010: 296–7) note, international definitions of homelessness describe it as 'a condition of detachment from society characterised by the lack of affiliative bonds ... carrying implications of belonging nowhere rather than having nowhere to sleep'. Some studies of nursing homes and other institutions report that residents experience a form of 'homelessness' (Carboni, 1990; Bitner, 2019).

For those who have dwelt in their homes a long time, it is familiar, associated with past critical and meaningful experiences (Sixsmith, 1986). For older adults this attachment to place can give a sense of purpose in life and preserve an enduring sense of self through 'a warehouse of memories' connecting past to present (Stones and Gullifer, 2016: 464, 465). This sense of rootedness informs the 'ageing in place' philosophies outlined in Chapter 4. Home is an anchor for the self.

Homes, institutions and families

Although by no means all home-dwellers live with their families, home is also associated with family life (Mallett, 2004). Goffman viewed family life as fundamentally different to the social world of the institution and indeed 'incompatible' with it: the very existence of the 'total institution' depended on the 'suppression of a whole circle of actual or potential households', whereas households provided 'a structural guarantee that total institutions

---

[3]   Albeit that 'place' might move, or even be mobile – as for traveller or nomadic peoples.

will not be without resistance' (Goffman, 1961: 22). This description of familial resistance to 'institutions' reflects some of the stories of families as 'liberators' in this book – for example, *Bournewood* and *Neary*. But families can also act as 'custodians', entering into arrangements with institutions to care for their relations (for example, *AJ v A Local Authority [2015] EWCOP 5*, as Goffman himself noted.

Goffman did not explore the distinction between 'institutions' and family life further in *Asylums*. Perhaps his perspective on family life was shaped by being a non-disabled, adult, American man, whose writings reflected his experiences of a post-war male breadwinner model of family life. Family relations can (and often do) operate hierarchies – the most obvious being parents and children (or 'breadwinners' and 'dependents'). Sometimes there may be a sense of distinct social worlds 'jogging alongside each other' within households. As discussed earlier, some researchers have identified 'custodial care' reminiscent of 'institutions' in family life (Askham et al, 2007; Clarke et al, 2010). Although these researchers hesitate to draw a direct analogy. Avni (1991), does describe family life as a 'total institution' in a study of women who had experienced domestic violence with similar elements of control, confinement and 'mortification of the self'.

Some 'institutions' and services draw from the symbolic ideology of family, presumably to soften 'institutional' impressions. For example, Camphill Communities operate group homes run by 'house-parents'. Care staff may draw 'on the model of parents and children' in making sense of their role (Tipper, 2003: 39). However, this analogy can consign a person to the minority status of a child (Wolfensberger et al, 1972). Goffman (1961: 47, 108) observed that institutional life 'disrupted' or 'defiled' a person's status as an 'adult'. In Foucault's (2001/1961: 239) critique of Tuke's York Retreat, which modelled itself on 'family' care, he wrote: 'Madness is childhood'. Wherever the difference between families and institutions is to be found, it is not – I suggest – that people are inevitably freer when living with families; many are not.

Noting that there are 'countless noninstitutional contexts', including many families, where 'people have no control over their lives', Ben-Moshe, Chapman and Carey (2014: 14) argue that there are still important differences between family life and carceral/institutional living arrangements. One possible distinction is that (some) families can provide better 'scaffolding' for the self than social care professionals because of their deeper and richer knowledge of the person's biography and personality. This is why families are often invoked in the person-centred planning and supported decision-making literature. Yet this research also indicates that this is not everyone's experience of family. Many of us can think of relatives who would be stifling as caregivers, or whose perception of our identity is positively at odds with our own, who understand or respect little of our 'will and preferences'.

Meanwhile, some care workers and professionals may have longstanding relationships with a person, providing essential scaffolding for the self.

Another intuitive distinction – but equally messy, elusive and difficult to define – is that family relationships are culturally associated with *love*, whereas formal care relationships generally are not. 'Love' is a significant consideration in many cases concerning rights to home within the capacity jurisdiction (for example, *Re PB* [2014] EWCOP 14; *Re GC* [2008] EWHC 3402 (Fam)). However, love can also be pathologized and problematized as 'co-dependence', and linked to abuse or neglect (for example, *Southend-On-Sea Borough Council v Meyers*; *PC and Anor v City of York Council* [2013] EWCA Civ 478). By contrast, care-professional cultures typically emphasize emotional detachment (Lynch et al, 2009). Love between staff and service users is taboo and 'unprofessional', perhaps even likely to 'trigger a safeguarding investigation' (Fox, 2018: 384).

These distinctions are admittedly messy. At a practical level, 'institutions' (including those aspiring to provide homes) have an administrative basis, that families simply lack, which the law of institutions can interface with. Families do not (generally) write 'care plans' or policies, record reams of notes about a person's daily life for the purpose of sharing knowledge with each other, they do not have formal chains of command, nor formal training in how to 'do' family life. They do not need to, because their individual and collective knowledge of a person comes from their ongoing relationships with them and each other. The law of institutions is designed to interface with a specific legal entity – a service provider – often with a specified point of contact (for example, a care manager), not a cluster of sometimes-related people muddling along with their own lives together under one roof. During the carceral era, an institution was defined by whether a person was kept for *profit*; a particularly important contrast given the economic drivers of institutionalization discussed in Chapter 4.

Meanwhile, 'institutions' can dominate both individuals *and* their families but the reverse is almost never true. Perhaps it is simpler to say that some of us – myself included – wish to draw a 'strategic' distinction between family life and institutions, a line that 'helps our analysis and activism' and informs our legal and political responses, while recognizing its 'imperfections, arbitrariness, and problems when that's most pressing' (Ben-Moshe et al, 2014: 15). I will revisit why it is undesirable and inappropriate to overlay family life with institutional models of care regulation in later chapters.

Batch living

By the end of the carceral era, institutions came to be associated with their vast size. The Washington hospital where Goffman (1961) conducted his ethnographic study housed 7,000 patients. For him 'batch living' was a central feature of total institutions, and a key point of contrast with family life: 'each phase of the member's daily activity is carried on in the immediate company of a large batch of others, all of whom are treated alike and required to do the same thing together', their lives coordinated together under an overarching rational plan.

Echoing this association between institutions and size, several contemporary de-institutionalization policies limit the size of congregate settings. A limit of ten or 12 is typical (for example, Working Group on Congregated Settings, 2011; Roberts, 2012; Crowther et al, 2017). In Chapter 7, I discuss a the CQC policy discouraging new services for people with intellectual disabilities or autism housing more than six people together. Size, or number of 'beds', is an attractive proxy for regulators, policymakers, and others who must make decisions in advance of a service being opened, or without any close proximity to its residents, as to whether it is (or will be) 'institutional' or not.

However today it is well recognized that 'institutional' dynamics can emerge in smaller community settings (Mansell and Beadle-Brown, 2010). None of the institutional characteristics outlined above – from surveillance and control to the quality of relationships within a setting – are inherently linked to the size of a setting or the number of inhabitants. Contemporary definitions of 'institutions' by disability rights advocates are careful to stress that '[a]n institution is not defined merely by its size' (People First Canada, cited in Mansell and Beadle-Brown, 2010: 106; World Health Organization and World Bank, 2011: 305). The CRPD Committee (2017: [16(c)]) recognizes that 'institutionalized settings can differ in size', and 'defining elements of institutions or institutionalization' can appear even in individual homes. More recent guidelines have turned to the 'culture' rather than 'size' to define institutions and community care for regulatory and policy purposes, stressing in particular control over decision making (European Expert Group on the Transition from Institutional to Community-based Care, 2012).

This is not to say that size is unimportant, however. As Nye Bevan put it, 'bigness is the enemy of humanity'. The greater the number of people cared for in one service the more likely it is that 'institutional' dynamics will emerge (Crowther et al, 2017). It can be much harder to adopt mitigating strategies fostering person-centred care and choice and control in larger settings. As a matter of logic, the more people living together, the less choice and control each person has over who else they live with and the less privacy they will have. Empirical studies of care services for people with intellectual disabilities have found that services with more than six people are associated with worse support outcomes (Bould et al, 2019; Bigby et al, 2020). Studies of older people's services recommend 'micro-services' with no more than five staff members (Glasby et al, 2018). Greater size increases the probability of 'institutional' dynamics emerging; smaller size does not guarantee their absence.

Access, inclusion and belonging in community

In the deinstitutionalization literature, the 'community' is the locus of freedom. Post-carceral discourses emphasize 'access to community' and 'social integration', as if the 'community' is a space to which ' "we", the non-intellectually disabled, belong, and which "they", the intellectually disabled, are given support to "access" ', Jarrett (2015: 107) writes. We forget that, before the asylums, people were 'natural members of the community embedded within social, economic and familial networks'. Communities were not places to which one had 'access' but were simply where people *belonged*.

Community, as a place of belonging and rootedness, is a potentially important dimension of home. Yet its significance varies for different people. Curiously, 'community' features infrequently in general scholarship on home – it does not emerge as a key theme in any of the major reviews of the literature (for example, Moore, 2000; Fox, 2002; Easthope, 2004; Mallett, 2004). This could reflect taken-for-granted aspects of access to community for academic researchers, or an individualized and geographically dislocated understanding of home.

Some studies have found group differences in whether 'community' or neighbourhood are considered important aspects of home. In Korea, there is no equivalent word for 'home' (only 'house'), but similar meanings around belonging are conveyed by *gohyang*, which roughly translates as 'hometown' (Shin, 2014). Saunders (1989) found respondents from Burnsley, in the north of England, more likely to equate 'home' with 'neighbourhood' than respondents from other (more southerly) English towns. Duyvendak and Verplanke (2016) found that for gay communities in the Netherlands their 'neighbourhood' was central to 'home', but this was not the case for 'deinstitutionalized' adults with intellectual disabilities. However, Strnadová, Johnson and Walmsley (2018) found that Australian adults with intellectual disabilities felt that neighbourhood was an important element of belonging, and particularly feeling safe.

Total institutions are associated with deep ruptures between a person and their community. 'Out of area' placements are considered a particulary problematic and risky form of institutionalization (Department of Health, 2012). Goffman (1961: 18) stressed inmates' restricted contact 'with the world outside the walls'. The CRPD Committee (2017: [16(c)]) includes as a 'defining element' of an institution, 'isolation and segregation from independent life within the community'.

However, the emphasis by the CRPD Committee on 'independent life within the community' betokens more than merely physically locating services within towns or residential areas. Rather, it concerns a mode of being 'within' one's surrounding neighbourhood. The supervisory reach of institutions can extend into 'the community', as for example under CTOs or leave of absence from hospital. Goffman described programmes of 'town parole' where some patients were given temporary leave from an institution, or discharged under conditions and supervision. Rusi Stanev was not living 'in the community', although he visited nearby towns. Autistic self-advocates stress that a person is not truly living 'in the community' unless 'free to come and go as we please' (Autistic Self-Advocacy Network et al, 2011). Even then, one might freely 'access' a community yet not feel fully 'of' it, included and participating in it, such that the community itself becomes one's home.

The aesthetics of home and institutions

When deciding whether a care arrangement constitutes an 'institution' or a home, detention or liberty, courts and regulators often appeal to its physical and aesthetic aspects (Chapters 7 and 8). The danger of this approach is that these proxies miss the underlying relational dynamics of institutions. However, our environments bear physical traces of the power negotiations of caregiving. Homes, as we saw earlier, are spaces where we 'perform' identity through even mundane decorative choices (Hurley, 2013). Meanwhile, the 'design semantics' of institutions tell us something about their creators' intentions and attitudes toward its inhabitants (Vihma, 2013). The bare walls of a prison cell or asylum reception centre, for example, deliberately signify an 'institutional' aesthetic, the erosion of individual identities, cultivating a feeling of non-home (van der Horst, 2004; Vihma, 2012).

The aesthetics of the late carceral era – Powell's (1961) 'gigantic water tower and chimney' brooding over the landscape – differ from contemporary health or social care institutions. Commercial social care has a readily recognizable aesthetic: larger (often pale brick) buildings with wings and gables (or modern looking blocks of 'living units' for supported living or new retirement villages), external signage displaying the provider's name, bulk bought furniture of a kind rarely seen in domestic homes (often in beige or dirty pastel shades), magnolia walls, laminated signs and notices, uniformed staff, fire doors, and so on. Mitigating these institutional features, 'homeyness' and 'homelike' aesthetics are pursued in the design of residential aged care facilities (Fay and Owen, 2012; Vihma, 2013; Bitner, 2019). Commercial studies explore which architectural features older people and their families – as potential consumers – consider 'homelike', 'homey' or 'institutional' (for example, Marsden, 1999). 'Artification', employing art and decorative objects in an environment (decorative plants, artificial flowers, tablecloths, vases, dressers, etc.), is a common strategy for projecting a pastiche of 'homeyness' in care facilities (Vihma, 2012).

Fay and Owen (2012: 40) regard this emphasis on decoration as 'trivializing' the idea of home at the neglect of more important issues – the protection of privacy, autonomy and respect for residents. Yet these 'mundane materialities' can provide critical insights into the discourses and power dynamics of care arrangements (Buse et al, 2018). Services seeking a 'homelike' aesthetic implicitly recognize the post-carceral imperative to provide 'homes'. Yet a 'homelike' decorative aesthetic can reveal less visible power dynamics of services. Institutional 'homey' décor is rarely chosen by the residents themselves but reflects the aesthetic projections – or paternalistic impositions – of staff or other 'experts' (Lundgren, 2000; Peace and Holland, 2001; Johnson et al, 2010; Vihma, 2012). This immediately recognizable 'homely' aesthetic speaks to generalizations and mass production, not the mess and idiosyncrasies of real homes. Co-design practices, where residents are involved in the architectural and decorative design of services, are rarely employed in elder care (Vihma, 2012). Even where an apparently 'homelike' aesthetic is projected to outsiders – including visitors, inspectors or service commissioners – to residents it may represent another arena in which their decision making and opportunities for self-expression are constrained.

In line with post-carceral trends toward 'person-centred care', most care services now invite residents to 'personalize' their living space, typically their bedroom. The CQC regard this as an indicator of good practice (Green, 2020: 227). Yet, the fact that the care sector even requires a word – 'personalization' – to describe supporting or permitting residents to decorate their own bedrooms (a word that is almost never used for the decoration of ordinary homes) speaks to background power asymmetries over control of space. This 'prescribed personalization' of bedrooms reconciles conflicting commercial imperatives with the codification of person-centred care (Nettleton et al, 2018). The focus on the personalization of bedrooms – as opposed to shared living spaces – reflects a sense that 'the joint spaces do not belong to the tenants' (Lundgren, 2000: 110). (Tipper, 2003) draws an analogy with children's control and responsibility over their bedrooms when living with their parents.

Twigg (1999: 387) suggests that when living at home and surrounded by your possessions – family photographs, pictures of yourself when young, holiday mementos, books – 'it is not possible to be wholly reduced to anonymity'. But our possessions do not, of themselves, create a sense of home. This requires more than merely surrounding a person with their possessions; it is achieved through 'practices, routines and interactions' with one's material surroundings (Lovatt, 2018: 367, 372). Acting on the physical environment – for example, creating gardens, home improvements, furnishings, decorations – can transform a dwelling place into a home (Tanner et al, 2008: 201–2). Care staff may rearrange furniture, introduce equipment, or render an environment scrupulously clean – like 'a hotel' – or conversely accumulate clutter and junk that the home occupier does not want to reflect on themselves (Angus et al, 2005: 161, 174), 'institutionalizing' the home (Milligan, 2000).

Liminal places, contested spaces

Social care detention feels transgressive because it collapses imaginary boundaries between 'home' and 'institution', yet in their idealized forms almost every positive dimension of 'home' has a negative opposite in 'institutions'. There should be no space where the polarized characteristics of home and institution collide; and yet there are. The landscape of social care is replete with liminal places that are designated or intended to be 'homes' yet whose inner dynamics can replicate some or many problematic aspects of institutions. Meanwhile, there are pockets of institutional life where residents have made for themselves a home. These liminal spaces present dilemmas for regulators and courts tasked with determining the boundaries of the law of institutions. In the next chapters I will explore how the discursive and cultural associations of 'home' and 'institution' explored in this chapter are appealed to by those seeking to draw and redraw these contested boundaries.

We can never definitely settle these arguments; wherever we draw a boundary there will be a degree of arbitrariness and contingency. Neither 'home' nor 'institution' carry an essential, or even generally agreed upon, meaning, and much turns on the subjective experience of their inhabitants. Both Goffman (1961: 17) and Fox O'Mahony (2002: 593) were clear that the characteristics of 'home' and 'institution' they identified were not found in all instances, nor were they peculiar to homes or institutions. They are better understood as 'family resemblance' terms. If the vast literature on the meanings of home converges on agreement anywhere, it is that home carries different meanings for different people; it is an essentially contested concept (Carr et al, 2018). Similarly, even today, there is no agreed upon definition of an 'institution' (Mansell and Beadle-Brown, 2010; European Union Agency for Fundamental Rights (FRA), 2012; Flynn and Gomez-Carrillo, 2019), creating problems for deinstitutionalization initiatives (European Expert Group on the Transition from Institutional to Community-based Care, 2012; Cojocariu and Kokic, 2018; Crowther, 2019a).

However, the absence of an essential core does not render 'home' empty of meaning, far from it; it speaks to humanity's sheer flexibility in adapting to diverse and complex environments and living arrangements. Nor does the lack of agreed clear definitions for 'home' or 'institution' render these concepts empty of utility; many fundamental concepts in our social, ethical, political and legal systems are difficult to define, contested and lack an essential (non-tautological) core. Their non-essential nature simply means we should take great care to explore *how* and when and why we use these terms in particular ways (a grammatical investigation, as Wittgenstein (2001) would have it), sensitive to cultural, social and historical differences in use, and carefully consider the socio-legal implications of different usages.

It is less helpful to ask for a definitive answer to the questions '*is this* an "institution"?' and '*is this* a "deprivation of liberty"?' than 'in what ways would it be helpful and it what ways could it be harmful, to regulate this living arrangement as an institution, or as a deprivation of liberty?' And then perhaps, 'are there other ways that we could conceptualize this living arrangement, that afford different and better suited regulatory responses?'

One way of reconceptualizing our dilemma is by recognizing home as a particular kind of *decision space*; a specific geographical locus pregnant with fluid possibilities for making certain kinds of decisions that are important for people to flourish. These include macro-decisions over *where* one lives (and often, by implication, who one lives with) as well as micro-decisions over *how* one lives, including taken-for-granted choices such as who to admit or who to exclude from one's living space (including carers), and how one imprints upon, moves within and interacts with one's immediate environment and neighbourhood, and the temporal patterns of one's everyday life. By identifying some decisions considered especially central to home in law, for example exclusive possession (or 'control of the threshold'), we also make visible the important role that law and legal capacity plays in establishing and protecting 'home'.

Clearly the decision space one inhabits is heavily conditioned by life circumstances. Choices over where and with whom one lives, for example, are heavily conditioned by economic, cultural, family and social constraints. Choices over *how* one lives may be heavily shaped by who one lives with, and so on. In Chapter 4, I identified the significant constraints imposed by the market economy of care; similar constraints exist concerning appropriate accessible housing in 'ordinary streets' or suitable for a person's full life course. Attentiveness to such constraints, and the ways in which the decision spaces embodied by 'home' are made precarious, is important. Yet even within those constraints, homes are potentially made and identities formed by – as Hacking puts it – pushing our way through this thicket, through the everyday and mundane choices that pass barely noticed by most.

The 'decision space' conceptualization of home uncovers a thorny problem for post-carceral ideology. As Mansell put it in his foreword to Clement and Bigby's (2010: 14) book, for many people with cognitive impairments the reality is that 'other people – family members, advocates, service agency staff – have to make decisions about these things on behalf of the person'. Questions of mental and legal incapacity are hazardous for supported living and post-carceral ideology, creating all kinds of legal dilemmas which I explore in the next chapter.

Yet this need not necessarily mean that all is lost, that we should abandon the pursuit of home and describe anyone with significant difficulties 'making decisions' about their living arrangements as living in 'institutional' environments. Plainly many people with significant cognitive impairments *do* enjoy living in their own homes – there are examples throughout this book – so the real question is how can we make sense of this? As Fox O'Mahoney's category of home as a social and cultural unit tells us, home is far from an individualistic endeavour, even if we live alone. Meanwhile, the control literature tells us that a subjective sense of influencing outcomes is more important than functional independence.

The CRPD's 'new paradigm' of legal capacity and supported decision making potentially offers a way forward: when we make decisions with or on behalf of that person about where and how they live, based on a close and trusting relationship with them and deep (often intuitive) knowledge of their history and responses to their environment, and these decisions are our best interpretation of where and how they would wish to live, then we are helping them to make a home. Conversely, when we select and order living arrangements that impose other people's goals and decisions on them, including to 'correct' a perceived problem with their identity, and these do not reflect our best interpretation of their wishes and preferences, then we replicate the dynamics of the institution.

Regulating the micro?

When Rampton high security hospital introduced a smoking ban to promote the physical and mental health of patients, the patients decided to sue. They argued that the hospital had become their *home*, and that consequently the ban violated their article 8 ECHR rights to respect for home and private life. Regulations for a national smoking ban in public places had a specific exemption for 'any premises where a person has his home', including places 'where a person may be detained', however an exemption for mental health units was only temporary and the patients argued this was unlawful. Their barrister, Paul Bowen, argued that rights to private life were not lost upon incarceration, but indeed the 'loss of other rights makes the remaining ones commensurately more important'. Furthermore, smoking was 'capable of being of fundamental importance to a person', thereby engaging their right to private life *(R (G) v Nottinghamshire Healthcare NHS Trust* [2008] EWHC 1096 (Admin) [51], [72]). At stake in the patients' claim was the extent to which the law protects the kinds of micro-decisions which I have argued distinguish 'institutional' from 'home' environments. Goffman, Hacking and others argue that far from being trivial, these micro-decisions are where opportunities for the everyday expression and development of self reside. As Langer and Rodin so convincingly showed, their loss can be positively harmful.

In the administrative court, Pill LJ felt there was 'some justification' in the patients' argument that Rampton was their home, noting an average length of stay of eight years [10], yet ultimately 'a distinction is to be drawn' between 'a private home in which a person freely resides … and an institution' [102]. Failure to provide smoking facilities did not come within the ambit of article 8 [105]. On appeal, Lord Clarke MR and Moses LJ concurred: 'Rampton is not the same as a private home and the distinction is of significance. It is a public institution' (*Re (E) v Nottinghamshire Healthcare NHS Trust* [2009] EWCA Civ 795[40]). While it would be 'offensive' [44] for the state to intrude into the 'inner circle' of a person's own home, for example dictating 'what a person eats or drinks' [42], 'it does not follow that the same activities within a public hospital where patients are detained are similarly protected' [41]. In such an environment, patients' rights to privacy are 'seriously restricted and always overlooked', they cannot 'choose freely' what to eat or drink 'not simply because restrictions can be justified, but more fundamentally because of the nature of the institution' [44]. The implication was clear: a person's rights are radically transformed when they move across the imaginary divide bisecting the law of institutions; they enter a new jurisdiction where the institutional authorities – not they – are sovereign.

In his dissenting judgment, Keene LJ accepted that the ECHR was 'not intended to protect trivial aspects of day-to-day life' [98], but 'for many people [smoking] forms an important part of their personal lives and possesses a value which reaches a level which qualifies for protection under article 8 as part of their personal autonomy' [100]. North of the border, a Scottish patient brought a similar case, challenging a state hospital ban on visitors bringing, or patients purchasing, unhealthy food (*Lyons v Board of the State Hospital* [2011] ScotCS CSOH_21). Unlike her English brother judges, Lady Dorrian recognized that the case

> does not simply deal with a trivial aspect of everyday life. For the detained inmates of the state hospital, the freedom to receive food parcels from visitors and to make purchases from an external source are some of the few areas in which they may exercise some sort of personal autonomy or choice. [25]

While article 8 ECHR did not mean that detained patients were entitled to eat whatever they chose, it meant interferences with this right must be justified as necessary and proportionate, north of the border at least.

The law struggles with the micro, with the compound, clustered, cumulative and incremental (Clements, 2011, 2020). From the perspective of closing the floodgates to a raft of potential claims concerning 'micro'-details of the lives of institutionalized people, it is preferable to consign these matters to a legal 'black box', delegating jurisdiction over the micro to institutional authorities.

However, the MCA is explicitly attentive to the 'micro'; the Code of Practice states: 'The same rules apply whether the decisions are life-changing events or everyday matters' (Department for Constitutional Affairs, 2007: [1.1]). Its post-carceral logics entail preserving even the smallest decisions visible to law. In the Court of Protection, the 'micro' is increasingly litigated – including cases concerning a person's diet (*A Local Authority v M & Ors* [2014] EWCOP 33), shaving pubic hair (*A Local Authority v ED & Ors* [2013] EWCOP 3069; *IH (Observance of Muslim Practice)* [2017] EWCOP 9), or – increasingly – access to the internet and social media (*Re A (Capacity: Social Media and Internet Use: Best Interests)* [2019] EWCOP 2). These cases reveal that while the courts can recognize 'everyday' matters as raising fundamental questions of personal and religious freedoms under the capacity jurisdiction, resolving these disputes through litigation is time consuming and expensive.

★★★

Post-carceral ideology aims to secure 'real' or 'authentic' homes for people at risk of institutionalization – in large-scale visibly 'carceral' accommodation, or in liminal spaces where the characteristics of 'home' and 'institution' collide. I have argued that one way to parse what we mean by 'home' in contradistinction to 'institutions', and to clarify the ultimate goals of the post-carceral era, is in terms of whether they offer an expansive decision space, where a person has control over macro-decisions of where and with whom they live, and micro-decisions of how they inhabit that space, who enters it, the temporal rhythms of their day, how they express their identity and achieve their goals. A space to flourish.

These spaces are made precarious by the economic forces of institutionalization: economies of scale that tend toward congregate living at some distance from 'home' communities, minimal choice over who provides care, and often insufficient support to facilitate one's goals and preferences. Yet they are also made precarious by institutional dynamics that seek to correct, change or fundamentally alter – rather than support, cultivate and enable – a person's identity. This can play out through substitute decision making; the imposition of living arrangements in a person's 'best interests'. The abolitionist universal legal capacity paradigm offers an alternative way to conceptualize how people with more significant cognitive impairments might still enjoy an expansive and responsive decision space, cultivating rather than stifling or correcting their identity.

The question for the post-carceral era is how (if at all) can law assist in achieving this aim? Is the law of institutions the best machinery we have? The kinds of decision spaces we are seeking are complex and multidimensional, calling for attention to macro-economic and relational questions, yet also sensitive to the subjective and the micro. These are not questions that courts and regulators cope well with. For the most part they prefer binary and abstract questions: is this an institution? Is this person deprived of their liberty? Answering in the affirmative can delegate jurisdiction over the everyday to institutional, regulatory or administrative authorities. Yet in the post-carceral landscape of care, where the boundaries between 'home' and institution' are increasingly murky, these questions are hard to answer.

7

Regulatory Tremors

As the tide turned against institutionalization during the mid-20th century, the law of institutions fell into crisis. Its associations with a Victorian custodial mindset and increasingly discredited eugenic outlook were problematic for those wanting to put psychiatry on a new footing – as a science of 'mental illness', medical treatment like any other, a modern, humane and expert discipline (Unsworth, 1987, 1991). Critics of 19th-century legalism argued that the law of institutions prevented timely treatment and fettered clinical discretion. Certification conferred no discernible benefits to patients, only stigma (Jones, 1972). Similar arguments were made about the role of judges in penal matters and sentencing (Wootton, 1963). Disciplinary professionals and administrative bodies, as the true experts, should be afforded maximum therapeutic discretion to deal with deviant populations.

Meanwhile, newly established civil society organizations questioned whether these legal frameworks really did protect individual rights to liberty and secure appropriate institutional conditions. Through policy interventions like Liberty's *50,000 Outside the Law* (National Council for Civil Liberties, 1951) and test cases, they depicted the entire system (and especially mental deficiency laws) as an over-broad authority to incarcerate, a system riddled with economic and other conflicts of interest, presided over by the apathetic Board of Control. The 'safeguards' conferred few benefits and therefore needed strengthening; it was diagnosis, confinement and public perception – not the legal process itself – that conferred stigma.

In the face of this two-pronged legitimacy crisis, and a desire to reduce the number of NHS hospital beds reserved for 'lunacy', 'mental treatment' and 'mental deficiency', the government established the Royal Commission on the Law Relating to Mental Illness and Mental Deficiency, chaired by Lord Percy (1957). Percy fell firmly into the anti-legalism camp. He considered certification stigmatizing and 'objectionable' to modern sensibilities [211], hampering doctors' ability to treat patients without interference from non-experts. 'Formal' detention procedures were necessary only to overcome active resistance by patients or families. For those patients considered incapable of seeking voluntary admission yet not actively resistant – the 'non-volitional' – a policy of 'informality' was preferred.

As to the regulatory branch of the law of institutions, Percy considered an independent national inspectorate with authority over a Minister of the Crown's domain an unconstitutional endeavour [738]. He recommended that this outdated experiment, bearing a 'stamp of origin' from the early 19th century [729], be abolished altogether. The Minister for Health would 'consult' with hospitals and drive any necessary improvements.

Percy's recommendations led to the MHA 1959, which is generally considered a victory for medicalism over legalism. It encoded into mental health law a rationality of 'informality', which was 'just as liberating for the psychiatrists as it was for their patients' (Hale, 2011: 1). In this new era, where 'legalism' was a 'dirty word' (Hale, 2014: 140), the law of institutions was fundamentally recast as a compulsory power for overcoming resistance, rather than a safeguard for the liberty of the individual.

I examined the policy impacts of Percy's recommendations in Chapter 4, of flows of people gradually washing out of the large institutions and into the 'community', different populations carried out on different currents. In this chapter I outline the legal transformations of the post-carceral era, which can be considered in distinct phases, before turning to consider the paradoxical consequences for each branch of the law of institutions.

To 'informality' and back again

Initially at least, as the tide turned against custodial institutions, both branches of the law of institutions were radically cut back. This period of de-juridification and 'informal' care and treatment, from the late 1950s until the mid-1970s, coincided with a Keynesian economic phase, establishing a strong welfare state and relatively closed national markets (Jessop, 1997). It was characterized by strong medical-welfare paternalism, where professionals exercised considerable discretion, reflected in medical law during this period (Harrington, 2017). This phase is embodied by the case *Bolam v Friern Hospital Management Committee* [1957] 1 WLR 583, which held that a doctor is not negligent if an imputed practice was 'accepted as proper by a responsible body of medical men'. I revisit this period of medicalism (or 'professionalism'; Montgomery, 1989), de-juridification and 'informality' in more detail below. These rationalities paved the way for a particularly powerful welfare–incapacity assemblage, which helps explain how social care detention assumed such a far-reaching form in England and Wales in comparison with other countries, as a counterweight to professional dominance.

By the late 1960s, following scandals at Ely and other hospitals, this deregulated landscape fell into crisis (Butler and Drakeford, 2005). A new generation of reformers – activist lawyers and jurists such as Ian Kennedy, Andrew Grubb and Mind's first legal officer, Larry Gostin – argued that law was necessary to protect patients' rights, to rebalance power relations between them and their doctors. They sought a new jurisdiction of 'medical law' to prise open the black box of clinical discretion by casting treatment without consent as a human rights issue, and arguing that clinical 'expertise' overreached itself into social, ethical and political affairs (Veitch, 2007). The MHA 1983 was a major victory for this 'new legalism', a partial reversal of the informality of the 1959 Act. It introduced new safeguards for 'treatment without consent' and re-established a supervisory body – the Mental Health Act Commission (MHAC) – to keep the Act's operations under review, investigate complaints, and visit and interview (in private) detained patients (s120–121). The 1983 Act's main ambit was the hospital, and it had little to say about 'informal' patients or those in the community. However, the legal netherworld they inhabited looked increasingly problematic in light of this new legalism. The MHAC (1985) began to express concern about the 'de facto detained'.

By the late 1970s, the Keynesian economic consensus was breaking down, and health and social care policy – alongside economic and welfare policy more generally – took a neoliberal turn (Jessop, 1997). This post-Keynesian phase was characterized by privatization and marketization across the economy, including health and social care. The new medical law jurisdiction contributed to this process by de-naturalizing the taken-for-granted dominance of professional discretion and public bodies (Harrington, 2017). As we saw in Chapter 4, social care policy from the 1980s onward wove together strands of post-carceral emancipatory rationalities – rights, choice and control, person-centred care – with the privatization and marketization of social care, into an overarching policy of 'personalization'. These changes were instrumental in the regrowth of the regulatory branch of the law of institutions, to supervise this new mixed economy of care, extending over both hospitals and the community (Challis, 1985; Peace, 2003; Davis et al, 2008; Prosser, 2010). A scandal in a local authority-run care home – Longcare – led to calls for a new national regulator to oversee both public and private sector care services in the community (Pring, 2011).

The Care Standards Act 2000 (CSA) established the National Care Standards Commission (NCSC), whose remit included private care homes and – for the first time – homecare services. Social care services were now inspected by a central body against a set of national standards, much as the Victorian lunacy regime that Percy had lambasted had operated. Within weeks of NCSC's creation, its successor was planned – the

CSCI – extending oversight to local authority-run services. Within a few short years a further merger was planned between the CSCI, the Healthcare Commission and the MHAC. The HSCA 2008 established a new super-regulator, the CQC, which since 2009 has been responsible for the registration and inspection of almost all health and social care services in England and for monitoring the rights of detained mental health patients. The Care and Social Services Inspectorate Wales (now Care Inspectorate Wales, CIW) was established in 2002, operating alongside the HIW which oversees hospitals and healthcare.

By the new millennium, post-carceral discourses of normalization, personalization, and promoting 'independence' and 'choice and control', were well embedded in health and social care policies, and in both branches of the law of institutions as they regrew. Yet the post-carceral era presented the law of institutions with an intractable dilemma. As carceral institutions no longer commanded the same social legitimacy, each branch of the law of institutions took on paradoxical functions of de-institutionalizing institutions, of de-carcerating the carceral. As we saw in Chapters 4 and 6, many new services in the community were established as 'homes' rather than 'institutions', yet replicated some of the dynamics of the institutions. This created particular problems for the regulatory branch of the law of institutions, which struggled to maintain a coherent distinction between institutions ('residential accommodation') and 'real homes' ('private dwellings'). I consider this regulatory branch of the law of institutions first, before turning to discuss the development of a capacity jurisdiction and social care detention. Social care detention itself initially pivoted on these troubled regulatory distinctions between 'homes' and 'institutions'. Furthermore, some have argued that social care detention is performing functions that are more appropriate for independent visiting commissions (Allen, 2015; Eldergill, 2019). Exploring the limits and dilemmas of regulatory supervision of community care arrangements can help expose the crevices and gaps from which social care detention sprang.[1]

---

[1] I focus here on the approach taken in England, rather than Wales, as its anti-institutional focus is more prominent. The regulations and guidance produced by Welsh Government (2019), guiding CIW's regulation of social care, places less emphasis on 'person-centred' care, choice and control than their English counterparts. Welsh Government (2018) has not adopted a specific policy to prevent registration of 'institutional' services, like the CQC's discussed here. This may reflect the Welsh Government's (2011: [3.16]) general antipathy toward personalization as a 'market-led model of consumer choice'. Tarrant (2019) describes how the Welsh Government's distinctive anti-market ethos can collide with the DPM's approach to independent living and its valuing of individual choice and control.

Regulating the community

Defining institutions

The CQC regulates any services providing 'personal care', which includes physical assistance with activities such as washing, dressing and eating, as well as 'prompting' and 'supervision' of those activities if a person 'is unable to make a decision for themselves' in regard to performing them (HSCA 2008 (Regulated Activities) Regulations 2014 SI 2014/2936 s2). By definition, this will include most services relied upon for care and support by people who 'lack capacity' to make decisions concerning everyday matters. However, the CQC and its forebears also distinguish homecare from residential services. While homecare services must be registered, care regulators cannot regulate the premises upon which homecare is delivered, because these are people's homes. The inspectorate's powers of entry only extend to 'regulated premises' and not premises where personal care might be delivered but which are 'used wholly or mainly as a private dwelling' (HSCA 2008 s62). Yet for services like supported living, where characteristics of home and institution can collide, drawing this regulatory distinction is not always straightforward.

A great deal hangs on which side of the imaginary regulatory boundary a service falls. If a location is registered as a 'care home' rather than a private dwelling then care recipient's benefits entitlements are substantially lower, local authorities can charge more for their care, and there are fewer revenue streams and less funding available to providers and public bodies commissioning care (Clements et al, 2019). On the other hand, if a setting is considered to be a private home rather than a care home, then there is minimal or no direct regulatory scrutiny of the care provided, and the CQC has no regulatory traction on the premises themselves. This has given rise to concerns about care provided 'behind closed doors', as home is a 'less easily regulated environment' (EHRC, 2011: 8; Joint Committee on Human Rights, 2012).

The regulatory boundary between regulated premises and private dwellings was tested in the *Alternative Futures* litigation. Alternative Futures was a small voluntary sector charity established in 1992 to provide care in the community for people with intellectual disabilities during the long-stay hospital closures. Alternative Futures applied to the NCSC to cancel the registration of 11 of its care homes and to re-register itself as a homecare provider of 'supported living' services. The residents, all adults with intellectual disabilities, would remain living in the same homes with the same staff, but the locations would become 'private dwellings' and therefore outside the scope of registration and inspection. The NCSC refused this request for deregistration on the grounds that the services would still meet the regulatory definition of a 'care home' within s3 CSA: 'an establishment is a care home if it provides accommodation, together with nursing or personal care'. The litigation turned on whether the providers would continue to be 'an establishment' providing 'accommodation together with personal care', or whether they would become – as they maintained – two legally distinct operations: a housing provider, and a homecare provider.

Alternative Futures appealed against NCSC's refusal to deregister the care homes to the Care Standards Tribunal (*Alternative Futures Ltd v National Care Standards Commission* [2002] EWCST 111(NC)). The tribunal approached the question *de novo*. The provider's case was that the accommodation was no longer provided 'together with' support: the accommodation provider (Alternative Homes) was a legally separate entity to the care provider (Alternative Futures), the residents had been provided with tenancies, and consistent with the new status of the residents' accommodation as a *home* they had 'privacy locks' on their bedroom doors. They stressed the financial advantages to the service users of the new arrangements, national policies encouraging supported living, and contended that NCSC's refusal to register the care homes amounted to interference with service users' article 8 ECHR rights to home and the providers' rights to property under article 1 Protocol 1 ECHR.

In response, the NCSC contended that these were not real tenancies: they questioned whether the residents had the mental capacity to enter into a tenancy agreement, whether the relatives and advocates signing tenancies on their behalf had the legal authority to do so, and whether the residents enjoyed 'exclusive possession' of the property. NCSC also queried whether service users had any real choice over entering into these 'tenancies' or receiving support from Alternative Futures as opposed to another provider. As discussed in Chapters 4 and 6, the right to choose your own support was a key tenet of early supported living, but is particularly problematic for providers, whose economic viability rests on coupling accommodation to support.

The tribunal panel held that the existence of a tenancy (whether valid or not) was not conclusive ([56]–[58]), what mattered was whether the service users enjoyed a 'real', 'significant' and 'genuine' *choice* ([56]–[60], [80]–[84]). Although the service users and their families had been 'consulted' about the changes, they had not been presented with a real choice over whether they accepted the tenancies and what support they received. Realistically, they could not opt to receive care from a different provider. Thus, even proceeding on the working assumption the tenancies might be valid, the services were still operating as care homes within the meaning of s3 CSA.

In an unusual litigation twist, Alternative Futures did not appeal this decision but some residents of the disputed services sought a judicial review of the tribunal's decision (*R (Moore) v Care Standards Tribunal* [2004] EWHC 2481 (Admin)). The service users were represented by the same barrister and solicitors as the provider, and it is unclear whether they instructed them directly or others did as litigation friends on their behalf. The residents' voices are altogether absent from the judgments, so we do not know whether the case was argued from their perspective or other parties (perhaps their families) seeking to preserve their existing living arrangements.

The High Court upheld the NCSC's decision, but for different reasons to the tribunal: an enquiry into whether or not the service users enjoyed 'genuine choice' was unnecessary [34], the matter turned on whether Alternative Homes and Alternative Futures were in fact operating in tandem as a single 'establishment' in the meaning of s3 CSA. The tenancy agreements themselves indicated that, in reality, both services were provided by Alternative Housing. The same conclusion and analysis were reached on appeal (R (Moore) v Care Standards Tribunal [2005] EWCA Civ 627).

Supported living providers complained that Alternative Futures impacted on their economic viability by leaving them unable to link care services to locations (Voluntary Organisations Disability Group and Anthony Collins Solicitors, 2011). Subsequently, the HSCA 2008 replaced the s3 CSA term 'care home' with the clumsier terminology of 'accommodation for persons who require nursing or personal care', and a fresh definition: 'The provision of residential accommodation together with nursing or personal care' (HSCA 2008 (Regulated Activities) Regulations 2014 SI 2014/2936 Sch 1 s2). Oddly, this new definition did not refer to an 'establishment' – a key concept in the Alternative Futures appeals. The stated intention behind this legislative change was to refocus attention on the nature of the service being delivered rather than the nature of the provider itself (Department of Health, 2010: [23]). To date, this new definition has not been tested in further litigation. However, it is doubtful this definition is rigorously policed by the CQC; the sector is awash with examples of 'supported living' style services that explicitly market themselves as providing both support and residential accommodation.

New guidance from the CQC (2015a) explains whether providers must register as 'accommodation together with care' (a care home) or personal care services (homecare). The guidance notes that some 'supported living' providers may need to register as accommodation together with care; approximately 10 per cent of services describing themselves as 'supported living' providers are registered as care homes.[2] The guidance offers an insight into the troubled and confusing regulatory distinction between 'institutional' and 'domestic' care arrangements. Some aspects echo the appellate rulings in Alternative Futures, stressing the importance of a clear legal separation between providers of accommodation and personal care. However, other aspects

---

[2]   Based on the proportion of providers with 'supported living' in their name registered as
      care homes on CQC's (2020a) care directory.

echo the ethos of early supported living. The guidance emphasizes the legal status and terms of occupancy agreements (tenancies or licences), referring providers to the 'Real Tenancy Test' produced by the National Development Team for Inclusion (2015). The Real Tenancy Test is influenced by the Reach Standards. It has five standards, including whether tenants have control over where they live, who they live with, who supports them and what happens in their home. The CQC also states that it will take account of whether or not service users enjoy 'exclusive possession' of at least part of their accommodation, whether they have 'control over "their own front door"', whether they can choose not to 'allow the care provider or the housing provider access' without this affecting their occupancy or accommodation agreement and whether providers keep any office equipment in any part of service users' homes (pp8, 10).

The guidance therefore stresses many aspects of 'home as territory' explored in Chapter 6, which can run into trouble in the context of care. It re-centres the emphasis on 'genuine choice' endorsed by the tribunal but rejected by the higher courts in *Alternative Futures*. Yet in this context, as Carr and Hunter (2012: 87–8) argue in their critique of the tribunal's decision in *Alternative Futures*, choice runs into the complications of 'mental incapacity'. As Mansell and others have acknowledged, many residents in supported living simply do not exercise the choices over where they live, who they live with, who provides care and how they are supported, implied by The Reach Standards, the True Tenancy Test or this guidance. They may not enjoy exclusive possession in the sense conventionally understood within housing law.

In a Court of Protection case concerning deprivation of liberty in a supported living service, lawyers argued that because care staff enjoyed unfettered access to the residence, E did not enjoy exclusive possession of the property and the service was thereby operating as an illegal unregistered care home, and the placement was 'tainted by illegality' (*G v E, A Local Authority & F* [2010] EWHC 621 (Fam), [110]). The Court of Protection sidestepped this argument, but the underlying question remains: how can we make sense of fundamental housing law concepts like 'exclusive possession' when they are so closely intertwined with presumptions around capacity, choice and control that are often complicated in the context of care and 'incapacity'? A significant proportion of tenancies for supported living services are putatively entered into by persons lacking the 'mental capacity' to contract and not by a person with formal authority to contract on their behalf. In English law, this means the contracts are technically voidable, but not usually void (Law Commission, 2015: 51–5). The complications of 'incapacity' mean that supported living is based on unstable legal foundations; yet the formalization of authority for substitute decision making runs counter to supported living's foundational ideologies. Meanwhile, the CQC guidance – in seeking to maintain post-carceral commitment to 'home as territory' in the face of the realities of caregiving and legal incapacity – produces an inherently unstable and contestable regulatory frontier. It seems that supported living itself requires a universal legal capacity paradigm to resolve these internal legal inconsistencies.

Taming institutions

The regulatory branch of the law of institutions aims to both curb the worst excesses of institutions and to steer them within dominant rationalities of care and confinement. In the 19th century this encoded therapeutic and non-restraint rationalities, and in the early 20th century it incorporated eugenic mentalities. In the new millennium, the law of institutions took on the paradoxical function of taming those everyday features of institutional life considered problematic under post-carceral ideology: 'institutionalization', depersonalization, loss of autonomy and privacy.

The CQC has several regulatory strategies it can call upon to this end. All registered services are assessed against the same regulatory standards (HSCA 2008 (Regulated Activities) Regulations 2014 SI 2014/2936), which encode central elements of post-carceral ideology. Regulation 9 requires services to deliver 'person-centred care'. Care and treatment must be appropriate to, meet the needs of, and reflect the preferences of service users. Assessments must be 'collaborative', service users enabled and supported to understand care and treatment choices, and to 'participate' in making decisions to the maximum extent possible. Regulation 10 requires service users to be treated with 'dignity and respect', 'ensuring' their privacy, supporting their 'autonomy, independence and involvement in the community of the service user'. Regulation 11 requires care and treatment to be provided on the basis of informed consent (subject to the provisions of the MCA and the MHA). Other regulations go to more traditional aspects of institutional regulation – safe care and treatment (regulation 12), safeguarding service users from abuse and improper treatment (regulation 13), meeting nutritional and hydration needs (regulation 14), appropriate 'premises and equipment' (regulation 15) and so on. Strikingly, these traditional regulatory foci are listed *after* regulations concerned with post-carceral imperatives.

The CQC and other care regulators face a dilemma, however, in securing those 'personalized' elements of post-carceral ideology: ultimately, they regulate and inspect at the level of the institution itself, not the individual. Crucially, the CQC cannot consider in any detail macro-questions of where a particular person is placed or consider other possible alternatives. Its focus is necessarily on the micro, the everyday and routine aspects of care within a service.

Many of the key senses in which care is 'personalized' are difficult to penetrate through regulatory scrutiny. Green's (2020) study of the CQC inspection reports and interviews with inspectors identifies certain 'exemplary issues' that the regulator focuses on. For example, inspection reports typically discussed whether residents had choice and control over decoration and furniture in their own bedrooms. Bedroom décor offers a visible shorthand for personalization practices, but may not interrogate whether a person is merely surrounded by personal possessions or supported in homemaking 'practices, routines and interactions' (Lovatt, 2018: 367, 372). The focus on *bedrooms* also reinforces the tightly circumscribed locus of control of care service residents discussed in Chapter 6.

Green found that the CQC considered whether care staff respected service users' private space, for example by knocking on bedroom doors or fitting privacy locks. Control over the threshold is a central element of 'home' that can be eroded by institutional life, but care service users' control over private spaces is highly conditioned by reliance on others for care. Less frequently addressed is whether they can exercise choice and control over *who* provides care and thereby enters their private spaces and touches their bodies. It is doubtful that care homes, and many homecare providers, can offer the level of choice and control over who provides support, when and how envisaged by the model of 'personal assistance' embedded within the concept of independent living (discussed in Chapter 4).

Care institutions may well offer some everyday choices – for example, a menu of food options, or activities – but within the constraints of the institution, perhaps akin to a hotel, and not necessarily the degree of choice individuals could exercise in their own homes. The CQC (2020b, 2021) is increasingly attentive to 'blanket restrictions' on residents, which are not necessarily the 'least restrictive' option for particular individuals. However, it relies upon providers to produce individualized justifications for restrictions rather than investigate alternatives for that person itself. Green found that the CQC also looked for documented evidence of care service users making informed choices about care, or capacity assessments and best interests decisions under the MCA. However, this focus on documentation may not dig into fundamental questions of how a particular individual's capacity was supported and assessed, nor how best interests decisions were made, competing risks and rights balanced, nor how they felt about the outcome. The CQC has no powers to re-assess capacity, nor to overrule assessments or best interests decisions, nor undertake its own risk assessments; its focus is on institution-level processes, not reviewing substantive outcomes for particular individuals.

A recent review of the CQC's inspection methodology in the wake of the abuse scandal at Whorlton Hall concluded that the CQC's own inspectors did not always have the necessary skills to communicate with residents or patients with limited or alternative communication methods. Unlike visits to those detained under the MHA, patients and residents might be interviewed in the presence of staff (not in private) and so be unwilling to voice concerns or express dissatisfaction (Murphy, 2020). Even if they were, the CQC has no powers to investigate complaints, only to ensure a complaints process is available.

Ultimately, the CQC's main inspection model accepts some restrictions on autonomy, privacy and independence as inevitable in congregate care settings, albeit tempered with elements of 'personalization', choice and control. Its focus is on carving out certain pockets of decision spaces, and ensuring the formalization and individualization of choices offered and denied, the adoption of appropriate policies, training and procedures. Its assessment is of the service as a whole against key standards, ensuring procedural compliance not a substantive assessment of whether a service or specific restrictions are right for the particular individual, leaving the very core of institutional jurisdiction over the micro unquestioned.

However, a new registration policy adopted by the CQC (2016, 2017b) in the wake of the Winterbourne View scandal, *Registering the Right Support* (RTRS), seeks more radical changes to the landscape of care. Its answer to the problem of 'institutional' services is the mirror of the closure policies of the post-carceral era: prevent them from being registered in the first place.

RTRS reflects a new national policy for people with intellectual disabilities and autism, *Transforming Care*, which emphasizes 'the norm' that people should 'live in their own homes' with the support they need for 'independent living', emphasizing 'community-based housing', 'independence, inclusion and choice' (Department of Health, 2012: [3.7]). RTRS is statutory guidance (s23 HSCA 2008) setting out the CQC's parameters for registering new services for people with autism or learning disabilities, or varying existing service registration conditions.

RTRS aims to prevent the registration of 'congregate' and 'campus'-based services, and to tackle some specific concerns raised in the post-Winterbourne policy response, including 'out-of-area' care placements at long distances from a person's family and home community. 'Campus' settings are defined as 'group homes clustered together on the same site and usually sharing staff and some facilities', and 'congregate' settings as 'separate from communities and without access to the options, choices, dignity and independence that most people take for granted in their lives' (CQC, 2017b: 12, 13). Controversially, the CQC also adopted a 'presumption of small services "usually accommodating six or less"' (p13), in line with statements of 'best practice' in the national post-Winterbourne policy *Building the Right Support* (NHS England et al, 2015). The 'six or less' approach is based on empirical findings that services for people with intellectual disabilities with more than six people tended to have worse outcomes for support and quality of life (Emerson, 2012; Bould et al, 2019; Bigby et al, 2020).

RTRS has been heavily criticized by care providers and regulatory lawyers in consultation responses, blogs, seminars and articles. They are especially exercised by the so-called 'six-person rule' discouraging larger congregate settings (for example, Cannon, 2018), complaining that this threatens the economic viability of services. They emphasize that commissioners favour larger and cheaper services, and that some larger services have been rated 'good' or 'outstanding' by the CQC whereas small size does not guarantee good quality care (OPM Group, 2017). RTRS also emphasizes that services should be located *within* communities (not out-of-town developments), that they should enjoy good transport links, and that there should be clear evidence of local demand for services not reliance on out-of-area placements. Providers complain that this does not take account of the higher cost of land and staffing in some areas (OPM Group, 2017).

RTRS is a potent (and controversial) policy because it inserts friction into the economic drivers of institutionalization within a privatized and marketized landscape of care. Providers complain that the care regulator has no business 'shaping the market' (OPM Group, 2017: 42), reflecting a minimalist vision of regulation that contrasts with the much broader 'regulatory enterprise' the CQC now embodies (Prosser, 2010). However, the policy has found support among care service users, their families, NHS and local authority professionals, and organizations directly representing disabled people (OPM Group, 2017; Pring, 2019).

Although a relatively young policy, RTRS has been extensively litigated. Several providers have challenged the CQC's refusal to register new services (hospitals or care homes) or to vary existing registrations by increasing the number of 'beds'. In all but one case (*Centurion Health Care Limited v CQC* [2018] UKFTT 615 (HESC)), the tribunal has upheld the CQC's decision (*Oakview Estates Ltd v CQC* [2017] UKFTT 513 (HESC); *Care Management Group Ltd v CQC* [2018] UKFTT 0434 (HESC); *Lifeways Community Care Ltd v CQC* [2019] UKFTT 0464 (HESC); *Action for Care Ltd v CQC* [2019] UKFTT 532 (HESC); *Bleak House Limited v CQC* [2020] UKFTT 171 (HESC)). Unsurprisingly, a significant focus of the litigation was the size of the service, whether it amounted to a 'congregate' setting, and whether it was a 'campus' environment. The proposed new size of the settings ranged from eight 'beds' (*Action for Care*) to 24 (*Bleak House*). In *Oakview* the proposed location was part of a hospital campus, and in the other cases new or extended registrations were refused on sites of existing care homes or supported living accommodation.

In all cases except *Centurion* the tribunal panels visited the sites of care. They approached the question of whether to register *de novo*, basing their decisions on their own perceptions of whether the services were 'institutional' or otherwise. Several of the judgments referenced the physical and aesthetic dimensions of homes/institutions discussed in Chapter 6, for example noting bare appearances, and 'inappropriate' artwork such as large murals (*Lifeways*), external signs and high surrounding fences (*Care Management Group*), the external appearance and 'proportions' of the building in comparison with its near neighbours (*Bleak House*). The tribunal members considered how freely and easily residents could move around within the services and whether some areas (such as kitchens) remained under the control of staff (for example, *Action for Care*). They considered how practically feasible it would be for residents to access the 'community' from the location (for example, *Care Management Group*), and how the service and its residents were viewed by neighbouring residents (for example, *Bleak House*, *Care Management Group*). Perceptively, the tribunal panels distinguished between *access to* the community and *integration into* the local community (*Bleak House*; *Care Management Group*).

The litigation also considered the overarching rationales for 'institutional' vs 'domestic' care environments. The providers argued that some people with intellectual disabilities or autism required 'transitional' settings between hospital care and homes of their own. They also stressed that commissioners sought cheaper services necessitating economies of scale. They highlighted that under the CQC's existing regulatory model many similar services had been rated 'good' or 'outstanding'. They argued that the CQC was stymying 'choice' to live in these settings and worsening existing problems in securing an adequate supply of 'community placements'.

In response, the CQC's experts and *Transforming Care* commissioners contended that 'transitional' services were unnecessary and inappropriate – the goal should be to support people to move directly into their own homes, to 'do it once and do it right' (*Action for Care*, [132]; *Lifeways* [51]). They highlighted that the providers had no clear plans for service users to transition into their own homes. They argued that what the providers had characterized as an 'inflexible' and unrealistic policy was in fact national policy based on empirical research into good care. Logically the more 'beds' in a service the harder it was for providers to guarantee privacy, choice and control over their living arrangements. They argued that the policy goal was to provide disabled people with the same rights to *home* as anybody else.

In terms of litigation outcomes, RTRS can be viewed as a resounding success for the post-carceral regulatory regime. The tribunal upheld the CQC's refusal to register new services or vary a registration in all but one case, *Centurion*, where the CQC did not enlist its star cast of expert witnesses and *Transforming Care* policymakers and nor did the tribunal panel personally visit the services. In the other cases the tribunal endorsed not only the policy itself but the CQC's market-shaping role. The CQC (2020d) recently revised the guidance (now 'Right Support, Right Care, Right Culture') but maintained the emphasis on smaller scale inclusive care settings, rather than congregate campus settings. That the CQC has not backed down in the face of these legal challenges and has (so far) refused to dilute the policy, which is especially admirable in the face of this coordinated assault from powerful provider interests and regulatory lawyers.

However, RTRS only applies to a relatively small proportion of service users – people with intellectual disabilities and/or autism – and excludes the vast majority of care service users, particularly older adults for whom larger congregate and campus-style services remain an accepted norm. Nor can RTRS be applied retrospectively to de-register already-registered services. Nevertheless, it demonstrates a novel regulatory approach to tackling structural and economic elements of institutionalization that evade the individual-level operations of mental capacity law and social care detention.

Yet it is unclear how big an impact RTRS is having on the ground. It only applies to an estimated 40 new registrations per year (CQC, 2017a). The average number of 'beds' in newly registered care homes for people with learning disabilities has increased from seven to around ten since 2017 (CQC, 2020a). The reality is that the policy only enables the CQC to refuse registration, it cannot compel the market to produce the kinds of non-institutional services and supports that are needed. As we saw in previous chapters, in a marketized and austerity stricken landscape of care, there are few incentives for providers to offer the kinds of highly personalized services representing genuine 'homes' if local authority commissioners cannot (or will not) pay the additional costs. This may mean that the CQC feels compelled to accept registrations from services that are not compliant with the RTRS model where there is high demand but few alternatives.

Meanwhile, care providers who have been refused registration of a new care home on the basis of the RTRS policy could, in theory, seek to operate the service as 'supported living' instead. The CQC would have very few regulatory levers to tackle this, even if they operated in practice as congregate or campus settings, since they could not regulate the premises themselves. Paradoxically, the option to register as a 'non-institutional' service weakens the anti-institutional grip of the law of institutions.

Care and capacity law

Let us now pick up the thread of how the liberty safeguards axis of the law of institutions regrew to extend supervision over the care and treatment of those who are, today, termed 'lacking mental capacity'.

The target populations of social care detention – primarily people with developmental disabilities or dementia – posed a particular problem for psychiatry as a modern, curative and non-custodial branch of medicine, since they were both likely to have a lengthy stay in hospital (as 'chronics' and 'incurables') yet were considered unable to seek 'voluntary' admission. It was put to a *Royal Commission on Lunacy and Mental Disorder* in 1926 that there should be three classes of patients – 'voluntary' (capable of making a written application for admission and treatment); 'non-volitional but passive'; and 'resistant' – with less onerous admission procedures for voluntary and non-volitional patients. The Royal Commission accepted this for 'voluntary' patients but not the 'non-volitional', commenting that the proposal did 'not adequately recognize that the liberty of the individual, even though there is no volition, is none the less infringed if he is removed and detained under treatment' (Macmillan, 1926: [105]). The 'non-volitional' continued to chafe against psychiatry's modernizing ambitions. Following the Mental Treatment Act 1930, 70 per cent of hospital admissions overall were 'voluntary', yet 70 per cent of hospital inpatients were 'certified' because 'non-volitional' patients tended to remain in hospital for much longer (Unsworth, 1987: 243).

The issue was revisited by Lord Percy (1957). There were conflicting views over whether people with intellectual disabilities (by then termed 'mentally subnormal') and 'elderly senile dements' should be subject to entirely separate legal codes, or no compulsory powers at all. Percy considered people with intellectual disabilities to be 'childlike and prepared to accept whatever arrangements are made for them', although compulsory powers might be needed to overcome family resistance [289]. 'Formal' procedures were both unnecessary and undesirable for these 'non-volitional' patients. He was persuaded that it was preferable to have a single legal framework, but so long as 'non-volitional' patients (and their families) were not resisting treatment or confinement, there was no more need for powers to detain them in hospital 'than in their own homes or any other place which they have no wish to leave' [289]. They were not to be subject to separate powers, but rather their care and treatment was de-juridified altogether.

The MHA 1959 embraced 'informal' admission (s5). By 1961 the revolution was complete: 92 per cent of 'mentally ill' patients in hospital were 'informal patients' (Jones, 1972: 360). For the formally detained, the 'safeguard' of a magistrate's order upon admission was replaced by a new right of appeal to a specially constituted mental health tribunal. No equivalent mechanism was available for 'informal' patients because *ex hypothesi* they were not objecting.

The 'non-volitional'

Let us pause for a moment to consider the logics of this new medico-legal category – the 'non-volitional'. The term did not enter into official use until the 1920s; it does not appear, for example, in the Select Committee on Lunacy Law's (1877) discussion of 'voluntary' patients nor any of the reports of the Lunacy Commission. But the concept of impaired 'volition' was in use among psychiatrists by the mid-19th century. Bucknill (1857: 141) distinguished 'acute mania' from those with 'chronic mania' whose symptoms were of a 'more tranquil and permanent kind', and 'incomplete mania', where 'defective powers of volition' were a prominent symptom. Robertson (1888: 47) compared the condition of patients with 'melancholia' and 'secondary dementia' to the reflex actions of amoeba or the severed limb of a cuttlefish; volition and intelligence were damaged as the 'intellectual fabric' gradually decayed 'from the top downward'. In 1923 Henry Maudsley opened a hospital which only accepted 'curable' patients, and on a voluntary basis. The 'non-volitional' designation was used by Mapother (1924) to distinguish this population from those with 'Maudsley conditions' for whom voluntarism was better accepted.

The term 'non-volitional' derives from the Latin, *volo*, meaning 'I wish'. To be *non*-volitional is to have no 'will', no 'wishes' or desires; to be akin to a severed cuttlefish limb, a bundle of meaningless reflexes. Carceral-era legalism was based upon the presumption that one could be 'non-volitional' (in the eyes of psychiatry) and yet require safeguards for individual liberty. However, Enlightenment philosophers – particularly David Hume – believed one must possess 'will' to possess 'liberty' (Hume et al, 2000). The logic that flows through informalism is that the 'non-volitional' did not possess a 'will' and therefore could not be deprived of their 'liberty', so safeguards were unnecessary for them. By this logic, the law of institutions is fundamentally recast – no longer as safeguards for individual liberty, but as a 'compulsory power' to overcome resistance by those deemed volitional.

The legacy of the 'non-volitional' can still be seen today. It is present in the sense discussed in Chapter 2, that detention under the MHA is somehow a more serious affair than detention under the MCA because it involves 'overcoming the will', and in the argument that using the MHA to detain 'incapacitated' patients in hospital instead of the MCA is an undesirable extension of 'the reach of compulsory powers' because formal 'compulsion' is not necessary for those without a will (Wessely et al, 2018b: 122). It is present in the forms and orders of the Court of Protection, which record the putative 'best interests' of the individual but only rarely their 'wishes and feelings', meaning it was impossible for us to discern in our study of Court of Protection files whether litigation outcomes generally reflected the wishes and feelings of the person or not (Series et al, 2017b). Similarly Ruck Keene and Friedman (2021: 32) were only able to identify 43 out of 281 Court of Protection judgments 'from which it is possible to glean some substantive idea of the person's wishes and feelings' for their more recent analysis. The legacy of the non-volitional is also discernible in the Law Commission's (1991: [4.23]) rationale for recommending a best interests standard for substitute decision making, as substituted judgement was 'difficult to apply in the case of someone who has never had capacity', as most decisions in their life 'will invariably have been taken by others' and choices will have been restricted, making it 'difficult to draw meaningful conclusions about the views or values he would have had if of full capacity'. The Commission expressed concern about the influence of the values of the decision makers in their interpretation. We will encounter the logics of the non-volitional again in the arguments over the meaning of deprivation of liberty surrounding *Cheshire West*.

For now, I will merely contrast the logic of 'the non-volitional' with the logic of article 12(4) CRPD, which maintains that all measures relating to legal capacity must possess safeguards that 'respect the rights, will and preferences of the person'. The CRPD's universal legal capacity formulation is a strident rejection of underlying logics of the 'non-volitional' category – implicitly asserting that *all* people, regardless of their disability, possess 'rights, *will* and preferences', mandating that others must discern this as best they can. The question is not *whether* a person possesses will, but rather how can we best come to understand, interpret or know what it is.

The 1983 Act changed little for 'informal' patients, preserving 'informal' admission (s131), and granting the newly established MHAC (1985, 2003) no powers to visit or report upon their situation. The distinction between 'objecting' or 'resisting' patients, who must be formally detained, and those who could be admitted 'informally' was explained in the new Code of Practice in terms echoing the old 'non-volitional' category. An 'informal' patient should not be allowed to 'wander' out of a ward, lest they come to harm (although use of locks was permissible). 'Informal' patients were to be formally detained if they 'persistently and/or purposely' attempted to leave (Department of Health and Welsh Office, 1999: [19.27]). To qualify for formal detention, one must be considered *purposeful* in attempting to exit a ward or expressing discontent, not merely 'wandering', distressed or agitated, nor institutionalized, sedated cowed or acquiescing.

The new capacity jurisdiction

The 1983 Act inadvertently created what would later be described as a 'lacuna' in the law for the care and treatment of 'incapacitated' people (as they were by now known) by limiting the authority of statutory guardians to a few 'essential' powers, which (deliberately) did not include powers to consent to treatment on a person's behalf (Department of Health and Social Security et al, 1981: 45). The 1959 Act had earlier removed an alternative source of authority to consent to treatment on a person's behalf, the possibility of establishing a 'committee of the person' through the lunacy inquisition procedure. This procedure was rarely used in the 20th century (Weston, 2020) and Lord Percy (1957) considered it undesirable that the courts and Lord Chancellor should exercise powers over a person's care or treatment.

The 1959 Act put management of the property and affairs of 'Patients' on a statutory footing, overseen by the (old) Court of Protection. The royal warrant which had conferred the courts' power over the 'person' since medieval times was revoked (Hoggett, 1988). By these two changes, as the Law Commission (1991: [3.5]) would later lament, '[t]here was no longer any machinery for assuming responsibility for every aspect of a completely incapacitated person's life.'

This 'lacuna' would only appear in hindsight; there was no deliberate policy intention to remove any lawful basis for care or treatment without (capable) consent or powers of substitute decision making. This was not an abolitionist reform. Rather, the 'informality' revolution of the mid-20th century was so thoroughgoing that it seems scarcely to have occurred to anyone that formal powers were necessary to treat the 'non-volitional'. The 1959 Act did not even explicitly confer powers to treat detained patients without consent, because 'consent was not part of the prevailing world view' (Bean, 1986: 129). For those who cared to ask what authority doctors had to treat patients without (capable) consent outside of the MHA, the prevailing view was that the patient's 'next of kin' could consent on their behalf, although medical lawyers warned there was no legal basis for this (Hoggett, 1976; Grubb, 1989b).

The story of how English law came to lose any formal legal authority for care and treatment of people considered 'incapable' of giving a valid consent, and why – by the mid-1980s – this became increasingly problematic, is complex and multidimensional, requiring a separate book. However, by the late 1980s the question of who could consent to treatment on behalf of an 'incapacitated' adult was increasingly discussed by medical lawyers, commentators, and doctors worried about possible liability (Hirsch and Harris, 1988; Grubb, 1989a; Fennell, 1996). Gostin (1986/2000) and Hoggett (1988) suggested the doctrine of necessity might be available for emergency treatments.

Things came to a head when the mother of an 'informal' hospital patient with intellectual disabilities – known as 'F' – asked doctors for her to be sterilized, as F had begun a sexual relationship with another patient and her mother was concerned that pregnancy would be 'disastrous' for her daughter. Owing to recent controversies concerning the sterilization of disabled children (Fennell, 1996), the doctors were hesitant to proceed without a clear legal basis, and so F's mother (acting as her litigation friend) sought a 'declaration' from the courts that the procedure would be lawful, it being in her 'best interests'. In *Re F (Mental Patient: Sterilisation)* [1990] 2 AC 1; [1991] UKHL 1, the House of Lords confirmed that there was no longer any formal authority under English law to consent to treatment on behalf of 'incapacitated' adults; neither F's family, nor the courts, nor any guardian could do so. To sterilize F without her (capable) consent could well amount to an assault or battery. Lord Goff noted that in theory any care or treatment that involved touching a person – from major surgery to simply helping them wash or get dressed – could be tortious. The 'lacuna' – which had been scarcely noticed only a decade earlier – had assumed unthinkable dimensions, extending even into everyday care.

The House of Lords held, however, that caregivers (medical or otherwise) had a defence against liability under the common law doctrine of necessity for acts of care or treatment in the 'best interests' of incapacitated adults. A person's 'best interests' were to be determined in accordance with the *Bolam* standard, acting 'in accordance with a responsible and competent body of relevant professional opinion'. The judgment reflected the logics of informality and the non-volitional. If F's own wishes were discussed in court, they are certainly not recorded. Meanwhile, the House of Lords held that while it might be 'good practice' for doctors to seek a judicial declaration from the court for a controversial procedure such as involuntary sterilization, it was 'not strictly necessary as a matter of law' (5).[3] While Gostin and Hoggett had considered the doctrine of necessity might extend to emergency treatments, *Re F* converted this limited defence into a broad quasi-authority to treat without consent, based entirely on the views of the treating professionals, encompassing even one of the most controversial treatments of the day.

As further cases concerning capacity and consent came before the courts, the principles of 'capacity' and 'best interests' were refined and elaborated (Bartlett, 2008; Fennell, 2010a). In parallel, the Law Commission (1991, 1995) undertook a programme of law reform concerning *Mentally Incapacitated Adults*. Lady Hale (then, Professor Brenda Hoggett) initially chaired the project before departing to become a judge (although she would later comment that it remained 'very much my project'; Hale, 2021: 117). As discussed in Chapter 4, many concepts and principles of the MCA can be linked to parallel developments in post-carceral ideology, which fed into the Law Commission's considerations. Although the Law Commission never used this term to describe it, the framework they proposed would come to be described as 'empowering' for disabled adults (Department for Constitutional Affairs, 2003: 52, 55, 56; 2007: Foreword; Joint Committee on Draft Mental Incapacity Bill, 2002–3: 71, 82).

The Law Commission (1993a), proposed codifying the common law defence for care and treatment in the best interests of 'incapacitated' adults, preferring 'informality' wherever possible to avoid large numbers of people requiring formal guardianship. This, they argued, reflected the principles of

---

[3] Contrary to what would later be said about the judgment in the Code of Practice (Department for Constitutional Affairs, 2007: [6.18], [8.18]).

'normalization' and 'least restriction'. The Law Commission (1993b, 1993c, 1995) did, however, propose formal procedural safeguards – including a second opinion scheme for serious medical treatment, a statutory duty to seek a court order for very serious treatments, and a public law scheme for adult safeguarding. For reasons the government chose to leave unexplained, the Commission's proposals for procedural safeguards on medical treatment and public law procedures for adult safeguarding were not taken forward (Lord Chancellor's Office, 1999). All that remained of the Commission's proposals for care and treatment without consent was the defence.

This defence is now encoded in section 5 MCA. It provides that so long as a person 'takes reasonable steps' to establish whether 'P' has capacity in relation to a matter, and 'reasonably believes' that P lacks capacity and the act will be in their best interests, then they have the same defence against potential liability that would have been available to them if P had consented. As I argued in Chapter 2, this confers a similar legal disability upon the person considered to lack capacity and the same immunity from liability upon those treating the person as a compulsory power like the MHA, differing only in terms of its context, specificity and procedures for use.

There is a great deal more that could be said about the development of MCA and its principles, but regrettably that must await another book. However, for the purposes of this genealogy of social care detention, I wish to highlight a relatively unusual feature of the post-carceral Anglo-Welsh capacity jurisdiction, which diverges from most comparable guardianship and substitute decision making legislation. The emphasis on 'informality' that was baked into the MCA first in *Re F* and then by the Law Commission means that the vast majority of substitute decisions concerning welfare, care and treatment are not made by formally appointed guardians or the courts, but via the 'general defence'. It is very rare for the courts to appoint named 'deputies' for health and welfare matters (*Lawson, Mottram and Hopton, Re (appointment of personal welfare deputies)* [2019] EWCOP 22 (25 June 2019)), and only a few hundred decisions are made each year by the Court of Protection itself (Ministry of Justice, 2020).

One outcome of this legacy of 'informality' is that such limits as exist on the general defence are ill defined. Section 6 of the MCA imposes an additional substantive threshold for acts involving restraint – they must be 'necessary' and a 'proportionate' response to the likelihood and seriousness of P suffering harm if it were not done. However, the only statutory limit imposed on acts taken in the 'best interests' of incapacitated adults under this defence was that it could not amount to a 'deprivation of liberty' (MCA s6(5)), a restriction inserted following the ECtHR ruling in *HL v UK*. The Code suggested that certain serious treatments – including sterilization – required judicial authorization, but the legal basis for this was always doubtful (Series et al, 2017a), recently confirmed by the Supreme Court in *An NHS Trust and Ors v Y and Anor* [2018] UKSC 46. In practice, when combined with the ability of public bodies to provide care or treatment free of charge, the defence can operate as a broad de facto power to administer non-consensual medical treatment or effect 'welfare'-related interventions without (capable) consent (Ruck Keene, 2016), with minimal independent oversight or procedural safeguards.

The second outcome of relying on a defence rather than a formal power or authority is that it is often unclear who should be making 'best interests' decisions on a person's behalf, leading to confusion over who is ultimately responsible for the decision (Ruck Keene et al, 2019a). Countries relying on formal systems of guardianship avoid this problem by having a clearly designated decision maker. In situations where no decision maker has been appointed but a decision must be made, many fall back on a statutory list of substitute decision makers, known as *ex lege* representation (Ward, 2017). Most such systems give priority to a person's close friends and family. For example, the Medical Treatment Planning and Decisions Act 2016 (Victoria, Australia), which otherwise incorporates similar concepts and principles to the MCA, specifies that if a person lacks capacity to make a decision for themselves, and there is no formal decision maker appointed for them, then the first person on a hierarchical statutory list of friends and family 'who is in a close and continuing relationship with the person' is their 'medical treatment decision maker' (s55).

This reliance on friends and family to make substitute decisions concerning the care and treatment of 'incapacitated' adults is found in most jurisdictions in the USA (Pope, 2016), Canada (Wahl et al, 2014) and Europe (Tibullo et al, 2018). By these lights, the Anglo-Welsh approach appears to remove a vital safeguard against conflicts of interest for health and care professionals – the need for 'consent' from a third party. Wahl, Dykeman and Gray (2014: 141), writing for the Ontario Law Commission, observe that whereas health practitioners in Ontario 'should not be asked to decide the value of their services to the patient, England seems quite comfortable with leaving these decisions with health practitioners'. A similar logic applies in Anglo-Welsh law concerning children: treating professionals require a valid consent from a (*Gillick* competent) child, or a parent, or the court, to ensure that '[n]o one can dictate the treatment to be given to the child' (*Re J (A Minor) (Wardship: Medical Treatment)* [1991] Fam 33, 41). However, the professional-centric approach to substitute decision making embedded within the MCA has barely attracted comment among most contemporary legal scholars, who instead focus their attention not on *who* decides, but on how courts and professionals should apply the Act's principles (although see Grubb, 1993). Perhaps decades of informality have normalized this state of affairs to the point it seems natural, even unquestionable, that health and care professionals have de facto authority to make health and care substitute decisions whilst family substitute decision making is regarded with suspicion.

Reliance on a defence short-circuits systems of checks and balances built into other jurisdictions. A person's family must be 'consulted' by professionals proposing care and treatment (MCA s4(7)), but families possess no powers to overrule or prevent proposed acts of care or treatment should they (or the person) object (as they would, for example, under the MHA). This likely comes as a surprise to most families when disabled children come of age or loved ones 'lose capacity', as most British people still believe – incorrectly – that 'next of kin' possess authority to make substitute decisions for their relatives (Office of the Public Guardian, 2019). In theory, both people who lack capacity and their relatives can challenge care and treatment substitute decisions made by professionals in the Court of Protection, but the reality is that this litigation is costly and inaccessible to most (Series et al, 2017b). The problem is perhaps exacerbated because in England and Wales all NHS care, and about half of social care, is provided without charge. While in itself a welcome state of affairs, this means there is rarely any intercession of 'formalities' – such as payment, or insurance schemes – which might provide a more formal requirement for 'consent' (although see *Aster Healthcare Ltd v Shafi (Estate of)* [2014] EWHC 77 (QB)).

This is not – I stress – an argument in favour of family substitute decision making, still less a critique of the welfare state itself, but rather an explanation of how it has come to pass that families often report being overridden by professionals making care and treatment substitute decisions (House of Lords Select Committee on the Mental Capacity Act 2005, 2014; Local Government Ombudsman, 2017). The lack of oversight and effective brakes on the Anglo-Welsh welfare–incapacity assemblage for disabled people and their families is, I will argue, one of the critical preconditions for the emergence of social care detention on the scale it has developed here. It is this situation that paved the way for the *Bournewood* case as the 'deprivation of liberty' jurisdiction became one of very few sources of external scrutiny for substitute decisions or avenues for disabled people or their families to exercise resistance.

Bournewood: the challenge to informality

The limits of healthcare professionals' de facto powers within the new incapacity jurisdiction came before the courts in the *Bournewood* case. HL was an autistic man who had lived in Bournewood Hospital for over 30 years, until he was discharged in a community resettlement scheme in 1994. HL lived with his carers, Mr and Mrs E, in their own home; an arrangement resembling 'shared lives' care services. One day in 1997 HL became agitated and distressed at his day centre; a local doctor sedated him and with a social worker arranged for him to be taken to hospital. HL was re-admitted to Bournewood Hospital on an 'informal' basis without the procedures of the MHA because, being sedated and not communicating verbally, he was not considered actively resisting admission or objecting. Healthcare professionals at Bournewood Hospital would not allow Mr and Mrs E to visit in case HL tried to leave with them, refusing their requests to discharge HL back into their care.

Because HL had not been formally detained under the MHA, the main levers for objecting to his admission, discharging him or appealing to a tribunal were unavailable. Nor would it have helped to challenge the doctors' assertion that informal admission was in HL's 'best interests' since in that era of *Bolam* the courts considered psychiatrists to be in a 'superior position' to his carers regarding his treatment (Fennell, 1998: 341, citing Lord Goff in *Bournewood*). His carers, therefore, sought a writ of habeas corpus, judicial review of the decision to admit him, and argued that he was falsely imprisoned.

The Court of Appeal concurred that HL was detained and held that the hospital should have used the formal procedures of the MHA (*R. v Bournewood Community and Mental Health NHS Trust Ex p. L* [1997] EWCA Civ 2879). HL was thereafter formally detained under the MHA, and discharged shortly after an independent psychiatric report secured for a tribunal hearing concluded he should not be in hospital. However, the case held wider significance – if HL was 'detained' then so, the MHAC argued, were as many as 50,000 other people 'informally' admitted to hospitals each year and a further 48,000 people in nursing homes, many of whom had intellectual disabilities or dementia. This provoked widespread consternation among healthcare and residential care providers, and the case was appealed. In *R. v Bournewood Community and Mental Health NHS Trust Ex p. L* [1998] UKHL 24, the House of Lords held, by a majority of three to two, that HL had not been 'detained' because he had not actually attempted to leave the hospital and been prevented. Lord Steyn, however, dissented, describing the suggestion that HL was 'free to go' as 'a fairy tale'. However, their Lordships held unanimously that even if HL was detained, the professionals had a defence against liability under the common law doctrine of necessity established in *Re F*. Lord Steyn regretted that this left patients like HL without the safeguards available to patients detained under the MHA.

As discussed in Chapter 5, HL's carers pursued the case to the ECtHR, which concluded that he was unlawfully deprived of his liberty in the meaning of article 5 ECHR, and there were insufficient safeguards available under the common law doctrine of necessity (*HL v UK* [2004] ECHR 720). Since the UK had passed the HRA 1998, public bodies were now potentially liable for unlawfully detaining patients like HL, and the domestic courts could entertain questions of liberty under article 5.

The Deprivation of Liberty Safeguards

Following the judgment, the government consulted on options to address what became known as the 'Bournewood gap' – the absence of safeguards required by article 5 ECHR for 'informal' patients like HL (Department of Health, 2005a, 2006b). The majority of consultation respondents opposed extending the MHA for patients like HL, citing the stigma attached to it, and the principle of 'least restriction'. A new framework of 'Deprivation of Liberty Safeguards' (DoLS) was therefore developed and inserted into the MCA during the passage of the MHA 2007. Owing to other controversial elements of the MHA 2007 such as CTOs (discussed by Fanning, 2018), the DoLS schedules received minimal parliamentary scrutiny and debate.

A complete description of the DoLS lies well beyond the scope of this book (see: Bowen, 2007; Bartlett, 2008; Jones and Piffaretti, 2018), and at the time of writing they are scheduled for replacement by the LPS in 2022 or later. However, a basic knowledge of their procedures is useful for understanding the litigation that ensued over the meaning of deprivation of liberty, discussed in the next chapter.

The DoLS provide administrative procedures for authorizing deprivation of liberty in hospitals and in care homes. As discussed in Chapter 2, they do have some narrow application to mental health detention – a legacy of *Bournewood* and opposition to use of the MHA for traditionally 'informal' patients. DoLS can also authorize detention in acute hospital settings where patients are being treated for physical conditions, however they are most frequently used to authorize deprivation of liberty in care homes.

The DoLS schedules rely on the definition of 'care homes' contained in s3 CSA (MCA Sch A1 s178(a)), discussed above, meaning the DoLS cannot authorize detention in other settings, such as supported living services. Several respondents to the consultation – including CSCI and the British Psychological Society[4] – raised concerns that supported living services could also operate in restrictive ways, citing the recent example of abuse in Cornish supported living services, where residents had been 'unlawfully detained'. However, the government chose not to include supported living within the DoLS administrative procedures 'because it considered it less likely that severe restrictions would be placed on people in supported living arrangements, who would tend to lead more independent lives'.[5]

The DoLS work by requiring the care home or hospital to identify that a person is deprived of their liberty and apply to a 'supervisory body'

---

[4] Consultation responses on file with author.

[5] Response to a freedom of information request by the author, discussed in Series (2013: 320).

153

(usually a local authority)[6] for authorization. The supervisory body must send out a BIA and Mental Health Assessor to assess whether the six qualifying requirements for authorizing the detention are met. Among these qualifying requirements are age (the person must be over 18), capacity (the person must lack the mental capacity to decide 'whether or not he should be accommodated in the relevant hospital or care home for the purpose of being given the relevant care or treatment', MCA Sch A1 s15), mental health, eligibility, and 'best interests'; these assessments, assessors, and their significance, are discussed in Chapter 2. The 'mental capacity' and 'best interests' assessments are generally regarded as the most vital for considering the wishes and interests of the person and substantive human rights matters.

If all six qualifying requirements are met, the supervisory body must 'authorize' the deprivation of liberty, for a period of up to one year, but reviewable before then. The supervisory body must appoint an RPR to represent and support the person in matters connected with the DoLS. Typically, this is a friend or relative of the person. In some circumstances an IMCA must be appointed to support the person and/or their RPR. The detained person and their RPR must be informed of their rights to ask the Court of Protection to review the authorization under s21A MCA – a right of 'appeal' in the sense required by article 5(4) ECHR – and the RPR and the detained person are entitled to non-means tested legal aid for this purpose.

The DoLS administrative procedures, therefore, overlay care arrangements made on behalf of people considered to 'lack capacity' with layers of independent scrutiny – chiefly through the formalized independent assessments based on the principles of the MCA and ('old paradigm') human rights law. They also provide a means for the detained person or their relatives to challenge the care arrangements in court. However, in reality, DoLS challenges are rare – as few as 1–2 per cent of all authorizations result in the Court of Protection application (Department of Health and Social Care, 2019a; Care Inspectorate Wales and Healthcare Inspectorate Wales, 2020). This is partly because many people subject to DoLS may not be seen as 'objecting' to their care arrangements – discussed in the next chapter – but, even where they are, there are serious problems in ensuring those representing and supporting the person are both willing and able to assist them in exercising rights of appeal (Series et al, 2017a, 2017b). Nevertheless, *HL v UK* and the DoLS procedures inserted the first clear substantive limits

---

[6] In England, local authorities are the supervisory body for both hospitals and care homes; in Wales local authorities are the supervisory body for care homes and Local Health Boards for hospitals.

and procedural safeguards over the welfare–incapacity jurisdiction, framed as safeguards for individual liberty.

The ruling of the ECtHR in *HL v UK* brought to an end half a century of 'informality', resurrecting a sense of the law of institutions as a *safeguard* for individual liberty. Although HL's voice – and the voices of many of those subject to this jurisdiction – is largely written out of history, his case positioned those previously considered 'non-volitional' as possessing rights, including a right to liberty. However, *Bournewood* posed questions of who else was therefore deprived of their liberty, where else, and what safeguards were required. These questions would preoccupy the courts for the years to come.

8

The Acid Test

The *Bournewood* case posed a new question of vast numbers of people in hospitals, residential care and other 'community' settings: is this person deprived of their liberty? If so, the DoLS or some other formal authority was needed to regulate the situation. Yet this question did not come naturally to the inhabitants of the post-carceral landscape of care, its very meaning imbued with liberation from the legal and institutional structures of the carceral era. Suggestions that people might be 'deprived of their liberty' by community care arrangements were outliers, curios for legal enthusiasts (Brearley et al, 1980/2001: 68). For most, this was a 'hitherto unknown question' (Allen, 2009: 19), a new game without written rules or clear traditions of practice, to secure or repel the law of institutions in the community through persuasion and other tactics.

Bournewood triggered extensive litigation on the meaning of 'deprivation of liberty' for a wide variety of post-carceral living arrangements. Space precludes a detailed survey of the mess of complex and contradictory case law preceding the Supreme Court's judgment in *Cheshire West* (see: Allen, 2012; Ruck Keene, 2013). Its heterogeneity was mirrored in highly variable rates of DoLS applications, as different hospitals, care homes and supervisory bodies adopted their own working definitions (Series, 2013). I do not offer here a doctrinal analysis of the legal rules for determining deprivation of liberty prior to the Supreme Court decision – I doubt any clear analysis is possible. Rather I am interested in attending to the rhetorical (Harrington et al, 2019) and discursive tactics of key players in the deprivation of liberty game, as they sought to fix the boundaries of the law of institutions in new terrain beset with controversy, ambiguity and paradox.

The key players in this litigation include the public bodies responsible for arranging care and securing appropriate safeguards for any care arrangements amounting to a deprivation of liberty; primarily local authorities but also some NHS bodies. Families and friends of older and disabled people made their own arguments, as custodians or liberators of the person, as to whether

156

they were deprived of their liberty or not. Disability and human rights organizations weighed in as interveners, arguing mainly for a more expansive interpretation of deprivation of liberty. Care recipients themselves played a less directly instrumental role in the litigation. Most were represented by the Official Solicitor (OS), a public official based in the Ministry of Justice who acts as litigation friend of last resort for people considered to lack the capacity to litigate. This 'hidden law maker' (Montgomery et al, 2014) represents the perceived 'best interests' of his clients, not necessarily the arguments they might wish him to make (Ruck Keene et al, 2016). Throughout this period of litigation, the office of OS was held by Alastair Pitblado until his death in 2018. For reasons I shall explain in the next chapter, he argued that MIG, MEG and P – among others – were deprived of their liberty, despite the significant repercussions this would have for his own office.

The judiciary themselves were divided in their approach. The courts were not neutral observers in this litigation; a lot hung on whether MIG, MEG or P were deprived of their liberty. Each lived in settings outside of the recognized ambit of social care detention at that time: P in a supported living style service and MIG with her foster carer. A broader definition of deprivation of liberty, encompassing more people in settings not subject to DoLS administrative procedures, would have a significant impact on the courts and public bodies, since these entailed costly judicial authorization at least annually (*Salford City Council v BJ* [2009] EWHC 3310 (Fam)). And while MEG was in a more 'institutional' setting she was also under 18, raising uncomfortable questions of whether minors could also be deprived of their liberty by their care arrangements, and the potential impact on the family court. These resource implications were noted in MIG, MEG and P's appeals, although the judges stressed that 'to have an eye' to this in determining the ambit of article 5 would be to 'raise it to the wrong end of the telescope' (*Cheshire West and Chester Council v P* [2011] EWCA Civ 1333; *P & Q* [5]).

MIG, MEG and P

The High Court and Court of Appeal judgments concerning MIG, MEG and P occupied nodal positions within this web of cases prior to their being conjoined and decided by the Supreme Court in 2014 in *Cheshire West*. A short description and brief chronology contextualizes the wider litigation.

MIG and MEG: reported facts

MIG and MEG were sisters, each with intellectual disabilities, who had been removed from their parents' care in public law child protection proceedings. Their case came before the Court of Protection when they reached 18 and 17, respectively, as they were considered to lack the mental capacity to make decisions about their care. At that time, MIG was still living with her foster mother, but MEG's foster care had broken down and she was moved into 'an NHS facility, not a care home, for learning disabled adolescents with complex needs' (*Cheshire West*, UKSC, [14]).

'Continuous supervision and control' were exercised over MIG and MEG by their caregivers. In MIG's case this was said to be because she had little awareness of danger, for example of road safety. In MEG's case this was partly connected with 'challenging behaviour' and 'outbursts' directed toward other residents. MEG was sometimes physically restrained by caregivers; MIG was not (*Surrey County Council v MEG & MIG v Anor* [2010] EWHC 785 (Fam), [210], [215]). MEG was prescribed Risperidone, a sedating antipsychotic drug of a kind considered overprescribed and harmful for people with intellectual disabilities and dementia (Banerjee, 2009; Harding and Peel, 2013; NHS England, 2017). Neither MIG nor MEG chose their placements, nor were they free to leave at will if they tried to do so (although neither had). Both attended a college, and MEG was said to have a more active social life than her sister. Their contact with family was restricted by court order.

In litigation concerning their care arrangements, the OS queried whether they were deprived of their liberty. At trial, Mrs Justice Parker ruled that neither was (*Surrey County Council v MEG & MIG v Anor* [2010] EWHC 785 (Fam)). The OS appealed and, in *P & Q v Surrey County Council* [2011] EWCA Civ 190, the Court of Appeal upheld Parker J's decision.[1]

P: reported facts

P had intellectual disabilities and cerebral palsy and had been living with his mother. When her health deteriorated the local authority concluded she was no longer able to care for him and sought a judicial declaration that it was in his best interests to live in a 'care setting', known as 'Z House'. The judgments do not explain why the local authority sought this declaration; usually an application of this nature is made because somebody (often a relative) objects to the proposals.

P lived in a 'spacious bungalow' with four other residents. He received continuous support from two members of staff, with additional staff for outings, such as to a day centre, hydrotherapy pool, a club, the pub and shops. He saw his mother regularly. P used a wheelchair for longer distances. He was doubly incontinent. His mother had 'allowed' him to be naked (*Cheshire West and Chester Council v P & Anor* [2011] EWHC 1330 (Fam),

---

[1] MIG and MEG were referred to as P and Q, respectively, by the Court of Appeal, but to avoid confusion with P in the *Cheshire West* case I refer to them as MIG and MEG throughout.

[8]). However, in Z House he wore incontinence pads, but he would pull at these, shred them, and sometimes put them in his mouth. On occasions that included faecal matter, and it presented a risk of choking that had once required a hospital admission. To manage this risk, staff would physically restrain P (although they referred to this as 'first aid' and they had no restraint training or policy), sweep his mouth to remove the contents, and clean and change him. P would 'attempt to fight against staff during these interventions' (*Cheshire West*, EWHC, [9]). A court-appointed independent social worker recommended that P wear a body suit with a zip at the back to prevent him accessing the pads. P was also described as having a 'long history of challenging behaviour', including being 'uncooperative', throwing things, self-injury, and on occasion assaulting others (*Cheshire West*, EWHC, [11]).

The OS represented P and argued that he was deprived of his liberty. At trial, Mr Justice Baker agreed that he was (*Cheshire West and Chester Council v P & Anor*, EWHC). The council appealed and Lord Justice Munby ruled that P was not deprived of his liberty (*Cheshire West and Chester Council v P* [2011] EWCA Civ 1333). P's case was then conjoined with MIG and MEG's in the appeals to the Supreme Court in *P v Cheshire West and Chester Council and another; P and Q v Surrey County Council* [2014] UKSC 19.

The contours of liberty before *Cheshire West*

Like HL, neither MIG, MEG nor P were said to be 'objecting' to their care arrangements, although like HL, this claim requires careful unpicking. If they were deprived of their liberty then many thousands more people, including many outside the DoLS administrative procedures, were likely to be as well. The system simply could not cope with this volume of DoLS or court applications – as the next chapter will relate in more detail. Meanwhile, the symbolism of finding detention in supported living, in a private family home (albeit foster care) and of a minor, jarred against post-carceral ideologies, the legacies of informality and the logics of the 'non-volitional'. The early case law reflects struggles between those calling attention to the carceral dynamics of residential and domestic care arrangements, and those seeking to preserve the traditional legal boundary line distinguishing 'institutions' – understood as large-scale hospital accommodation – and spaces representing home and community.

Deprivation of liberty as removal from the family and home

An early and consistent theme in the litigation equated deprivation of liberty to removal from home and family. 'Family' was construed broadly, encompassing Mr and Mrs E – HL's (paid) carers in the community – and foster parents (*G v E, A Local Authority & F* [2010] EWHC 621 (Fam)).

The first post-*Bournewood* domestic case on the meaning of deprivation of liberty concerned DE, an older man with dementia and physical and sensory impairments, who had been cared for by his wife, JE (*JE v DE & Ors* [2006] EWHC 3459 (Fam)). Unable to cope, JE had placed DE in a chair on the pavement outside their home and called the police. Surrey County Council had placed DE in a care home and prevented him from returning home, as both DE and JE later wanted. Paul Bowen, the barrister who had acted for HL and the Rampton smokers, represented JE and argued that DE was deprived of his liberty. The OS, representing DE, concurred. The council, however, argued that DE was in an ordinary care home, not subject to the 'controls' and restrictions HL had been. He went on outings and had 'as much choice as possible about his day-to-day life within the constraints of his disabilities' [105]. JE and DE's complaint, however, was not with his everyday care, but his desire to return home, describing him as a 'prisoner' [90], [91], [95]. Mr Justice Munby concluded that the critical question was less whether DE's freedom or liberty was 'curtailed *within* the institutional setting', than whether he was 'deprived of his liberty to leave the X home' – not for a trip or an outing, but 'removing himself permanently in order to live where and with whom he chooses', and specifically with JE [115].

The first rule of the 'deprivation of liberty' game, therefore, was that it concerned the macro-question of whether a person could return to an already existing home, not the micro-details of restrictions or institutional life. During the passage of the DoLS the Parliamentary Joint Committee on Human Rights (JCHR) (2007: [89]) had proposed a statutory definition of deprivation of liberty, as a person being 'taken from their home to a place where they will be prevented from leaving, and complete and effective control will be exercised over their movements'. This definition made sense of how HL could be deprived of his liberty in hospital, yet not while living with Mr and Mrs E where – his legal team noted – he would still be subject to 'continuous supervision and control' to keep him safe (Robinson and Scott-Moncrieff, 2005: 23). The government, however, preferred to remit the thorny question of the meaning of deprivation of liberty to the courts instead of adopting a statutory definition.

The deprivation of liberty jurisdiction provided formal procedures for disputes between families, care recipients and public bodies over where a person should live. This framing positioned the jurisdiction as 'safeguards' against the formidable welfare–incapacity complex, tools for resistance by families, leaning heavily on discourses of human rights and legalism. This perspective on the jurisdiction is embodied by the widely reported case of *London Borough of Hillingdon v Neary* [2011] EWHC 1377 (COP). Steven Neary was a young autistic man who had been living with his father, Mark Neary, who employed personal assistants to support Steven's activities and interests. Steven had been temporarily admitted to respite care in January

2010 while his father recovered from flu. However, the council refused to allow Steven to return home when his father recovered, asserting that his behaviour was 'challenging' and required input from a specialist 'behaviour support unit' run by Hillingdon Borough Council. Steven became increasingly distressed in the unit (a care home), and four months into his stay he escaped. After he was brought back his outside activities were cancelled, new locks and alarms were fitted to the building, and the unit applied for a DoLS authorization.

A BIA assessed it to be in Steven's best interests to remain there but did not consider his distress nor whether it would be 'less restrictive' or in his best interests to return home. Mark, meanwhile, continued to ask for Steven to return home. Hillingdon deliberately misled Steven's father that they were planning for this, while making plans for a permanent move elsewhere. The council also threatened to review Steven's direct payments if he returned home, leaving his father scared of 'rocking the boat' [146]. It was only after an IMCA was appointed almost a year later and raised concerns that the council applied to the Court of Protection. On 23 December, Mr Justice Mostyn ordered that Steven should return home by Christmas. Mr Justice Peter Jackson then reviewed Hillingdon's actions under s21A MCA (the review provision of the DoLS) and the HRA. He concluded that Steven had been unlawfully deprived of his liberty. Yet, for Peter Jackson J the 'nub of the matter' was not the deprivation of liberty 'to which [Steven] is to some degree or other necessarily subject wherever he lives', but rather his article 8 rights to family life [151], recasting the DoLS as a tool for adjudicating on rights to home and family life rather than restrictions and restraints.

The court's jurisdiction to review DoLS authorizations under s21A MCA also facilitated legal challenges to 'safeguarding' decisions removing people from their homes and families on the basis of concerns about abuse, neglect or risks of living alone. Sir James Munby (2011), the (now retired) President of the Family Court and the Court of Protection, compared their complexity to 'a heavy child care case', sometimes requiring extensive fact finding hearings about allegations, with added disputes about capacity and deprivation of liberty. Yet, unlike the formalized public law procedures for child protection, these hearings often took place *after* removal, with post-hoc safeguards on decisions made informally, guided by the MCA's overarching rationality of managing vulnerability. In several cases the courts concluded the evidence for the safeguarding intervention was poor and the person's human rights were violated, making orders to facilitate a person's return home and sometimes awarding damages (for example, *Somerset v MK (Deprivation of Liberty: Best Interests Decisions: Conduct of a Local Authority)* [2014] EWCOP B25; *Milton Keynes Council v RR & Ors* [2014] EWCOP B19; *Essex County Council v RF & Ors (Deprivation of Liberty and damage)* [2015] EWCOP 1; *Westminster City Council v Sykes* [2014] EWHC B9 (COP)).

Yet the history of the law of institutions tells us that 'safeguards' are also the cutting edge of power; that law's tools for resistance and liberation can also normalize and legitimate disciplinary power. Another cluster of cases, under the MCA's 'empowerment' rationality, concern public bodies seeking judicial authorization to remove people (typically younger adults with intellectual disabilities or autism) from family care, to promote their 'independence' or 'autonomy'. In some instances, this enabled the person to say they wanted to leave home (for example, *LBX v K, L, M* [2013] EWHC 3230 (Fam); *ZK (Landau-Kleffner Syndrome: Best Interests)* [2021] EWCOP 12); the judgments do not record this as a deprivation of liberty. However, in others the person's expressed preference to remain living at home is regarded as the product of 'undue influence' or simply not in their best interests. The Court of Protection has authorized deprivation of liberty in 'independent living' or other arrangements to enable the person 'to develop a social and emotional independence' freed from 'smothering' relationships (*A Primary Care Trust v P* [2009] EW Misc 10 (EWCOP) [64]), to learn 'skills and tools for everyday living' (*A Local Authority v WMA & Ors* [2013] EWHC 2580 (COP) [15]), 'to have a voice' (*A Local Authority v M & Ors* [2014] EWCOP 33 [60]). These cases reflect the paradoxical entanglements of social care detention as 'empowerment'.

The deprivation of liberty jurisdiction also manifests as a power to manage problematized sexuality, a major rationality for the use of guardianship and institutionalization in the early 20th century. Where a public body has reason to believe that a person lacks the mental capacity to make decisions around sexual activity (to consent to sex, to initiate sex, to commit sexual offences, or have 'contact' with potential sexual partners) the courts have held that they 'must undertake the very closest supervision of that individual to ensure, to such extent as is possible, that the opportunity for sexual relations is removed' (*IM v LM* [2014] EWCA Civ 37, [1]). Such measures aim to prevent what the law characterizes as an unlawful (and potentially criminal) sexual act, even where the person concerned might not consider this sexual activity exploitative; indeed they may actively want it (Series, 2015b). Within the judgments, it is generally accepted that this entails a deprivation of liberty. There are parallels between the sex cases and those concerning removal from home and family, since the outcome of a finding that a person lacks capacity regarding sex may be that they are removed from their existing home (for example, *D Borough Council v AB* [2011] EWHC 101 (COP)), or contact may be significantly restricted between people who are in longstanding relationships or even married (for example, *CH v A Metropolitan Council* [2017] EWCOP 12). These cases often result in orders that a person's 'capacity' to make decisions about sex must be enhanced, through programmes of 'education and empowerment' (*A Local Authority v TZ (No. 2)* [2014] EWHC 973 [59] (COP)) until such time as the person attains 'capacity' in relation to sexual matters.

But if deprivation of liberty means removal from one's homes or family, then what of those people without family or a home to return to? What of men and women, like HL before he lived with Mr and Mrs E, who had spent most of their life in institutional environments, or older adults whose tenancies may have been given up or their homes may have been sold to pay for their care? The suggestion in some cases is that without an alternative home, one cannot be deprived of liberty.

In his Court of Appeal ruling in *Cheshire West*, Munby LJ offered a very restrictive analysis of deprivation of liberty, considered shortly, but citing *Bournewood*, *JE v DE* and *Neary* created the following exemption: 'Matters are, of course, very different where a person has somewhere else to go and wants to live there but is prevented from doing so by a coercive exercise of public authority' (*Cheshire West*, EWCA, [58]). Citing this passage in *C v Blackburn and Darwen Borough Council* [2011] EWHC 3321 (COP), Peter Jackson J ruled that a man with a brain injury who had actively tried to leave his care home, to the point where the police had to be called after he had broken down a door trying to escape, was *not* deprived of his liberty because he had nowhere else to go. A crucial discursive move in concluding that MIG and MEG were not deprived of their liberty was defining their current living environment as their 'home' and excluding alternative living arrangements from consideration: 'there is no alternative home save that of their mother where neither wishes to live' (*MIG and MEG*, EWHC, [225], [230]).

Within this logic, then, deprivation of liberty is counterposed to home, and particularly to the family home reflecting the pictorial landscape underpinning the classical understanding of the law of institutions explored in Chapter 3. The jurisdiction concerns macro-questions of where a person lives. The restrictions, the micro-dynamics of care and control which I argued in Chapter 6 are integral to understanding institutionalization and its harms, are obscured from view. On this reading, for those without claim to another place or person, liberty has no meaning.

Family life as freedom

The corollary of deprivation of liberty as deprivation of home and family must be that life within the family home represents freedom. Shortly after Parker J's High Court ruling in *MIG and MEG*, a local authority applied to the Court of Protection seeking guidance on whether two unrelated people, A (a child) and C (an adult) were deprived of their liberty while living with their parents, and the obligations of public bodies if they were (*A Local Authority v A (A Child) & Anor* [2010] EWHC 978 (Fam)).

Questions of 'deprivation of liberty' within family homes are taboo; the suggestion that the law of institutions should regulate this is social care detention at its most transgressive. Even researchers identifying custodial or carceral care within family homes are hesitant to liken this to institutional care (Redfern et al, 2002; Askham et al, 2007; Ben-Moshe et al, 2014). Counsel for the local authority presented the case that A and C were deprived of their liberty as 'devil's advocate', distancing himself and the local authority from their own argument [50].

Both A and C had Smith Magenis Syndrome. The court was told that people with Smith Magenis Syndrome experience difficulties controlling emotions, leading to 'temper tantrums and outbursts, **aggression**,[2] anxiety, impulsiveness and difficulty paying attention' as well as 'self-injurious behaviours' and 'severe sleep disturbance' [8]. To cope and to prevent injury, the families maintained constant supervision, locking external doors and hiding the keys, and locked them in their bedrooms at night. Experts agreed that there were few alternatives to this; overnight carers would be overstimulating and unlocked doors presented serious risks of injury. Nobody suggested the measures were inappropriate; but did they amount to a deprivation of liberty?

Preserving the boundary between the law of institutions and the private domestic sphere of the family home entailed decoupling the restrictions imposed on A and C by their families from the meaning of deprivation of liberty. In his judgment, Munby LJ adopted three rhetorical tactics to repel the encroachment of the 'deprivation of liberty' jurisdiction into the family home. He first stressed the loving and caring quality of the relationship between the parents and their daughters, and the benevolence of the arrangements:

> In neither home does the regime involve a deprivation of liberty. And in saying this I should make clear that I do not see this as being a borderline case or a case which falls to be decided on a fine balance. In my judgment, the loving, caring, regime in each of these family homes – a reasonable, proportionate and entirely appropriate regime implemented by devoted parents in the context of a loving family relationship and with the single view to the welfare, happiness and best interests of A and C respectively – falls significantly short of anything that would engage Article 5. [115]

In theory, Munby LJ agreed, it was possible for a person to be deprived of their liberty by their family – thinking of 'Mrs Rochester' type cases [131] – but this would be rare in the domestic setting, especially in the context of 'care of children or vulnerable adults by their parents in the family home'

---

[2] Emphasis in judgment.

[131]. We will consider 'benevolence' as a strategy to repel 'deprivation of liberty' labels shortly.

Second, Munby LJ distinguished 'private' exercises of power by families from the role and powers of public bodies. The local authority had argued that if A and C were deprived of their liberty then it was not merely 'involved' but exercised 'complete and effective control' via its care plans and assessments, endorsing the arrangements [50]–[51]. The EHRC, intervening and represented by Paul Bowen, argued that if they were deprived of their liberty then the state was responsible as it was involved in providing care services for A and C, and had positive obligations toward them under human rights law. The EHRC expressed concern 'about the potential for abuse where there is no external scrutiny of the treatment of vulnerable adults within private homes' [44].

Munby LJ linked this approach to a 'mindset' or 'culture' encountered too frequently in cases where local authorities removed 'incapacitated' adults from family care into residential accommodation 'without the sanction of the court and, therefore, without any legal authority' [54]–[55]. He interpreted the law as providing local authorities with powers to provide community care services, establishing safeguarding duties, but conferring no powers 'to regulate, control, compel, restrain, confine or coerce' [66]. The local authority's role was 'the provision of services and support' [66], it was 'the servant of those in need of its support and assistance, not their master' [52]. This analysis was later cited by Peter Jackson J in holding that Hillingdon Council had violated Steven Neary's human rights. It is questionable whether Munby LJ's analysis that local authority removals without prior judicial sanction are straightforwardly *ultra vires*; he did not consider whether they were protected against liability by the MCA's general defence or authorizable under the DoLS (Ruck Keene, 2016; Series et al, 2017a: 64–75). However, viewed rhetorically, his polemic reinforced the idea that the purpose of the law of institutions is to protect the sacred domain of the family against officious intrusion, not to invite further intrusion. Reinforcing this logic, Munby LJ stressed that there was a 'common sense' distinction between a placement at home with family and a 'residential establishment' [134]; the plausibility of this distinction resting on accepting the traditional (yet increasingly troubled) regulatory boundary between homes and 'institutions'.

The third rhetorical strategy to decouple restrictions, supervision and control from 'deprivation of liberty' was to infantilize disabled adults, thereby naturalizing, normalizing and de-legalizing the control exercised over disabled people (including adults) by analogy to parental control over young children. As we saw in earlier chapters, people with intellectual disabilities have long been painted as 'childlike' innocents (Wolfensberger et al, 1972; Wright, 1996), a form of othering distinguishing them from the 'dangerous' deviance associated with mental health detention (Ben-Moshe, 2020). Goffman (1961) and Foucault (2001/1961) connected the 'minority' status of institutional inmates with the loss of their civil rights, Goffman arguing that staff needed to view inmates as 'not-fully-adults' so as not to 'feel a loss of self-respect by coercing deference from their charges' (p115). As we saw in the previous chapter, Lord Percy (1957: [289]) described people with intellectual disabilities as 'childlike' in constructing the category of the 'non-volitional', laying the groundwork for 'informality'. Unsurprisingly, disabled writers and activists connect infantilization to oppression of disabled people within society, and paternalistic and controlling forms of care (Oliver, 1990; Shakespeare, 2000). Meanwhile, the *adulthood* of people with intellectual disabilities is an important theme in the post-carceral ideology of normalization (Wolfensberger et al, 1972).

Nevertheless, infantilizing themes and discourses are prominent in decisions throughout the deprivation of liberty litigation, and across judgments of the Court of Protection more generally. There is no significant analysis of whether C's situation (as an adult) differed from A's (a child's) in *A Local Authority v A (A Child) & Anor* [3]. In *Cheshire West*, Munby LJ contrasted the 'illuminating examples' [41] of locking counsel for P (Robert Gordon QC) in a police cell for three hours where he 'would indubitably be deprived of his liberty' with placing a one-year-old child for three hours in a playpen, behind bars: 'The idea that Article 5 could be engaged, the idea that the child is being deprived of her liberty, is preposterous' [42]. Infantilizing tropes recur throughout the judgments. MIG was characterized by Parker J as loving her 'Mummy' [209], P's bodysuit likened by Munby LJ to a 'babygrow', his being strapped into a wheelchair as like a child in a buggy (*Cheshire West*, EWCA, [114]). Many judgments in the Court of Protection describe 'P' – an adult alleged to lack capacity – in terms of their 'mental age', a controversial metric derived from IQ scores which the British Psychological Society (2000) advises against using for adults. For example, Parker J prefaces her judgment in *MIG and MEG* by asserting that MIG has the 'cognitive ability of a child aged about two and a half' and MEG 'of a four to five year old child' (*MIG and MEG*, EWHC, [7]).

In a public seminar held shortly after Munby LJ's judgment in *Cheshire West* (One Crown Office Row, 2012), the philosopher A. C. Grayling weighed into the debate on the meaning of 'liberty' for 'incapacitated' adults:

> the term 'deprivation of liberty' is not quite the right term since I don't imagine that this very unfortunate individual ever had it before. There is an implication that 'deprivation' is removal of something that they've enjoyed and was of value to them ... I think it's more denial of liberty than deprivation of liberty. ... We wouldn't for a minute think about

having this kind of anxiety about a four-year-old ... or even for that matter a fourteen-year-old.[3]

His intervention as a philosopher of liberty connected this image of the child with the historical category of the non-volitional, the individual constructed by Enlightenment thought as without a will, and therefore without liberty to lose. From the audience, the OS, Alastair Pitblado, retorted 'one can be flippant about little children if one wants, but these aren't children, they're adults'.

'Normality' and the comparator

Players on all sides of the deprivation of liberty game appealed to the 'normality' or otherwise of a person's living arrangements to make their case. As I showed in Chapter 4, 'normalization' was central to the deinstitutionalization of people with intellectual disabilities, based on the idea that both a person's living arrangements, and the person themselves, should be made as 'normal' as possible (Wolfensberger et al, 1972). The normalization literature conceived of a continuum of 'normality' in living arrangements, with large hospitals and institutions at one end of the spectrum, small 'homes' and family homes at the other, and a variety of 'step down' or 'halfway' facilities between. Yet, as I have argued throughout, it is entirely possible for a person to be living in a space designated a 'normal home', in ways that violate the socio-cultural and legal norms of home explored in Chapter 6. Within Western cultures, 'home' signals a rich decision space where a person's identity can be expressed and flourish through a range of macro- and micro-decisions. 'Institutions' (whatever their size) are radically constrained decision spaces which seek to 'correct' (or 'normalize') a person's lifestyle and identity. A person can live an 'institutional' life in a space that others describe as their home. In Chapter 7, I showed how these liminal spaces tied the regulatory axis of the law of institutions in knots; in this section I show how discourses of normality entangled questions of liberty.

In several cases, including MIG and MEG's, it was held that a person was not deprived of their liberty because they were living in an 'ordinary care home' or an 'ordinary domestic environment' (for example, *MIG and MEG*, EWHC, [209], [233]; *LLBC v TG* [2007] EWHC 2640 (Fam), [105]; *CC v KK and STCC* [2012] EWHC 2136 (COP), [101]). On appeal in MIG

---

[3]   An online recording of the seminar, organized by One Crown Office Row (2012), has been taken down, but A. C. Grayling has kindly given permission for reproducing his remarks.

and MEG's case, Wilson LJ described a 'spectrum' of normality, featuring family life as the 'most normal life possible', and hospitals 'designed for compulsory detentions like Bournewood' at the other end, with small children's homes and nursing homes in between the two (*P & Q*, EWCA, [28]). The 'enquiry into normality' also considered community activities, such as attending school, college, day centres or other occupations, and any restrictions on social contact [29].

The difficulty with an 'enquiry into normality' is in selecting a comparator. Within the normalization literature, 'normal' meant the life enjoyed by non-disabled people, law's hypothetical ordinary and reasonable 'man on the Clapham omnibus'. It clearly did not mean what was 'normal' for most people with intellectual disabilities at the time, which was confinement in large institutions. This was an (ab)normality that normalization was trying to eradicate.

The judgments describe MIG, MEG and P's living arrangements as their 'homes'. However, this positioning glosses over the micro and the subjective; they did not enjoy the 'normal' home life of the man on the Clapham omnibus. Aside from MIG – who is explicitly described as regarding her foster placement as her 'home' (*MIG and MEG*, EWHC, [209]) – it is not clear that either MEG or P perceived their living arrangements as 'home' in the sense explored in Chapter 6. Although, as the courts were keen to emphasize, they enjoyed outings and activities that might be 'normal' for a person of a similar age, the level of supervision and control that each were subject to, and in MEG and P's cases the level of physical and chemical restraint, were anything but normal. They did not enjoy 'normal' decision spaces. Macro-choices over where they lived were made by the courts and social services, and the judgments do not explore who offered or made the micro-choices in their everyday lives.

The unstable foundation of appealing to 'normality' was exposed by Baker J, who at trial in *Cheshire West* applied Wilson LJ's 'relative normality' test and concluded that although features of P's care helped give his life 'a strong degree of normality' (attending a day centre, regular contact with family, regular outings in the community):

> On the other hand, his life is completely under the control of members of staff at Z House. He cannot go anywhere or do anything without their support and assistance. More specifically, his occasionally aggressive behaviour, and his worrying habit of touching and eating his continence pads, require a range of measures, including at times physical restraint, and, when necessary, the intrusive procedure of inserting fingers into his mouth whilst he is being restrained. (*Cheshire West*, EWHC, [59])

168

Overturning Baker J's analysis on appeal, Munby LJ found that he had erred by not comparing P's situation 'with the kind of life P would have been leading *as someone with his disabilities and difficulties* in what for such a person would be a normal family setting' [110].[4] When considering how 'normal' a life a person was living for the purposes of determining whether they are deprived of their liberty, the relevant 'comparator' is 'the normality of the life of someone with the relevant condition, *not* the normality of the life of the able-bodied man or woman on the Clapham omnibus' [87].

Munby LJ's comparator implicitly presumes that a disabled person's life situation is mainly determined by their impairment and not the responses of their caregivers or their environment; an inversion of the social model of disability. Clough (2015: 2, 8) describes this as a 'stark illustration' of a deeply embedded medicalization of disability permeating judicial discourse, ignoring 'the institutional and situational factors which can hinder or undermine liberty' and further perpetuating 'the illusion that the state and society play no role in the lived experience of those with cognitive impairment'. Both Munby LJ and Parker J relied upon a rhetorical manoeuvre also observed in disability litigation in the USA, depicting disability as a 'prison within', deflecting attention from disabling or restrictive features of a carceral environmental (Ben-Moshe, 2020: 263). Munby LJ stressed that 'some people are inherently restricted by their circumstances' [87] and Parker J describe MIG and MEG as lacking 'freedom and autonomy dictated by their own disability, rather than because it is imposed on them by their carers' [233].

The legal outcome of the 'relative normality' test was that disabled people, particularly those with more significant impairments, could be subject to substantially greater restrictions than the general population before qualifying for liberty safeguards (Troke, 2012). The number of DoLS applications received by supervisory bodies, already significantly lower than government projections, fell for the first time after the Court of Appeal judgments in *Cheshire West* and *P & Q* (NHS Information Centre for Health and Social Care, 2011; Health and Social Care Information Centre, 2013). In a nod to Wilson LJ's spectrum of normality, however, the courts did generally continue to find most people in psychiatric hospitals, or subject to non-consensual medical treatments for physical disorders such as forced feeding or forced interventions during childbirth, to be deprived of their liberty (for example, *Re LDV* [2013] EWHC 272 (Fam); *AM v South London & Maudsley NHS Foundation Trust and The Secretary of State for Health* [2013] UKUT 0365 (AAC); *A NHS Trust v Dr. A* [2013] EWHC 2442 (COP); *Great Western Hospitals NHS Foundation Trust v AA & Ors (Rev 1)* [2014]

---

4   Emphasis in judgment.

EWHC 132 (Fam)). The boundaries of the law of institutions were firmly retrenched; social care detention was in retreat.

Benevolence: reasons, motivation, purpose

A third rhetorical strategy in repelling the law of institutions stressed the benevolence of the care arrangements, and their necessity, reasonableness or proportionality in keeping someone safe. It implicitly appealed to deprivation of liberty's penal associations, and a sense that only 'bad', excessively restrictive care, or malintent, is a deprivation of liberty.

The Department of Health (2007: [82]) seemed to take this view, reducing estimates for the number of people requiring DoLS safeguards from 98,000 (the figure floated in the *Bournewood* litigation by the MHAC) to 21,000, asserting that only 'excessive limitations on freedom of movement' or 'unreasonable controls' on visits or outings would be a deprivation of liberty. In *MIG and MEG*, Parker J contrasted their situations with the paradigm example of the prisoner, emphasizing that the 'reasons' for the restrictions were to benefit MIG and MEG [164]–[166], [230]. Although on appeal Wilson LJ distanced himself from this approach (*P & Q*, EWCA, [27]), in *Cheshire West* (EWCA), Munby LJ returned to the theme. His analysis distinguished 'reason', 'purpose', 'motive' and 'intention'. While good intentions could not 'render innocuous' what would otherwise be a deprivation of liberty, an improper motive or intention could convert a situation into a deprivation of liberty which otherwise would not be [71]. Munby LJ agreed with Parker J that it was legitimate to have regard to the 'objective' reason or purpose for restrictions [75]–[76]. He applied this analysis to a hypothetical example of a man caring for a wife with dementia, whose (objective) purpose was to safeguard and protect her, with no malign motive that would convert this into a deprivation of liberty [77].

Legally speaking, this rhetorical strategy made no sense. It was undisputed by the ECtHR that the professionals in *Bournewood* acted in good faith in what they considered HL's best interests (*HL v UK*, [99]). Deprivation of liberty is only lawful under the MCA if it is assessed as being in the person's best interests, and is necessary and proportionate.[5] If this meant that a person was not deprived of their liberty it was hard to see when a DoLS authorization could ever be issued (Troke, 2012). As Munby J himself observed in *JE v DE*, 'The argument, if taken to its logical conclusion, would seem to lead to the absurd conclusion that a lunatic locked up indefinitely

---

5   Currently this is explicitly the case under the DoLS and judicial authorizations under s16 MCA, however the 'best interests' criterion has been removed from the LPS, creating some potential complications (Series, 2019).

for his own good is not being deprived of his liberty' [47]. The fact this logical and legal incoherence could be overlooked by the government and courts pursuing this rhetorical strategy reflects the strength of their desire to repel the law of institutions from settings where it is at its most socially and culturally transgressive.

'Objections' and ambiguity

The last critical frontier in the deprivation of liberty litigation that I wish to highlight is the ambivalent approach of the courts to the person's subjective experience of their living arrangements. In the previous chapter I showed how the carceral era's extensive frameworks for regulating deprivation of liberty were dismantled for the majority of people with intellectual disabilities and dementia by constructing a new legal category: the 'non-volitional'. The logic of this category was that this population had no 'will', no 'wishes', and therefore no need for liberty safeguards. If they were not actually passive – if their behaviour did suggest unhappiness, if they did try to leave places where they were confined – then unless this behaviour was 'purposeful' and 'persistent', it was mere 'wandering', meaningless 'challenging behaviours' reflecting illness and requiring treatment, not resistance or an 'objection' attracting legal protection. I contend that the logics of 'the non-volitional' are evident throughout the deprivation of liberty litigation, and that this lies at the root of some of *Cheshire West*'s most paradoxical outcomes.

The litigation discussed here concerned the 'objective' element of whether a person was deprived of their liberty, not the 'subjective' question of whether they had given a valid consent (see *Storck v Germany*, discussed in Chapter 5). It was undisputed that a 'valid consent' could never be given by somebody who, like HL, 'lacks the capacity to consent or object to medical treatment' (*HL v UK*, [9]). The policy of the ECtHR's judgment is that even a person who does not 'object' is entitled to safeguards; and this entailed paying little attention to HL's subjective experience.

Next to nothing is recorded in *HL v UK* about his subjective experience of this ordeal. Hospital notes cited by the courts recorded HL as 'calm' and 'compliant' [13], although Lord Steyn had found he was regularly sedated to remain tractable [46]. Other sources, however, recount how his carers found him 'in a dreadful state emotionally and physically' when they were finally able to visit. A care manager described HL as 'increasingly distressed' by his admission, and a charge nurse as 'disturbed for most of his stay' (Health Service Ombudsman, 2001: 24–7). Elsewhere, his carers described how HL had been frequently restrained by staff standing on his feet, so that he had no toenails when he left hospital (EHRC, undated). HL may not have verbally objected to his confinement, or tried to leave, but these accounts surely suggest profound unhappiness and distress at his situation. Yet for his clinicians, the question was not whether HL was deeply unhappy and distressed by his admission, but whether his behaviour reflected 'a psychiatric condition or a behavioural problem' (Health Service Ombudsman, 2001: 26). The non-volitional category is closely tied to the pathologization of behaviours, overlooking its meanings and potential communication.

More recent versions of the MHA Code of Practice require professionals to consider 'the patient's behaviour, wishes, feelings, views, beliefs and values, both present and past, so far as they can be ascertained', and to treat patients as objecting 'if there is reason to think that a patient would object, if able to do so' (Department of Health, 2008: [4.19]; 2015b: [13.15]). Ironically, HL would now likely be considered 'objecting' to his admission, meaning the MHA should be used rather than the DoLS (Allen, 2010). Even so, there is an important difference between 'not objecting' – even on this broader test – and a positive desire for a particular living arrangement.

Although the litigation proceeded on the basis that a person who 'lacked capacity' could not give a valid consent, both Parker J and Wilson LJ placed great emphasis on MIG and MEG's apparent happiness with their living arrangements in concluding they were not deprived of their liberty. Parker J went so far as to suggest that '[i]n a non legal sense they have the capacity to consent to their placements' and could not imagine any visitor gaining 'any sense of confinement of detention' [234], despite not having met them herself. In the Court of Appeal, Wilson LJ held that whether the person '**objects** to the confinement which is imposed on her'[6] is central to the analysis of whether they are deprived of their liberty. If objecting, 'the consequence will be conflict', at the very least 'arguments' and 'the stress of having her objections overruled' and potentially 'tussles and physical restraints', or even a forcible return. This 'level of conflict' was 'highly relevant to the objective element', while an absence of conflict was relevant in the opposite direction [25]. Wilson LJ also observed that 'antipsychotic drugs and other tranquilisers' were 'always a pointer towards the existence of the objective element: for it suppresses her liberty to express herself as she would otherwise wish', and particularly if administered by force or had the effect of 'suppressing' objections [26].

On this analysis there were indicators that MIG was not deprived of her liberty; she was 'devoted to her foster mother', considered it her home, and showed no wish to leave [14]. The courts' approach to MEG is puzzling, however. MEG was 'medicated' with a sedating antipsychotic. She was restrained because of 'tussles' with other residents. Interestingly, neither

---

[6] Emphasis in judgment.

Parker J nor Wilson LJ recorded – as the Supreme Court judgment did – that MEG 'mourned the loss of [her relationship with her foster carer] and wished she was still living with her' (*Cheshire West*, UKSC, [14]). Parker J's conclusion that MEG was 'consenting' in a 'non legal sense' seems quite a stretch given these details.

The irrelevance of the feelings and wishes of the 'non-volitional' was highlighted in *C v Blackburn with Darwen*. C told the court that he wanted to leave the care home. He had even broken down the front door attempting to escape. Yet, despite his powerful objections, and Wilson LJ's ruling in *P and Q*, he was not considered deprived of his liberty by Peter Jackson J because he had nowhere else to go. In *CC v KK*, Mrs KK gave such articulate direct evidence to the court explaining why she did not want to live in a care home that Baker J concluded she had the capacity to make that decision, yet there was not sufficient conflict to render her circumstances a deprivation of liberty [99].

These cases indicate a serious problem with judicial engagement with the subjective experiences of adults considered 'incapacitated' within the deprivation of liberty jurisdiction. HL's case demonstrates there is considerable scope for professionals and carers to disagree about whether a person is distressed by their circumstances. MEG's case shows that judges and others can exploit ambiguity over a person's wishes and feelings to arrive at the interpretation that suits their argument. C and Mrs KK's cases tell us that even judges whose cases are celebrated for their close and careful engagement with the wishes and feelings of the person (Series, 2016) can put aside a person's clear objections and conclude they are not deprived of their liberty. If neither MEG, C nor Mrs KK could meet Wilson LJ's threshold for 'objections' then it is extremely difficult to see how a disabled person who did not communicate verbally, or a polite, institutionalized, sedated or simply overawed person, could trigger the machinery of article 5 to attract scrutiny or challenge of their predicament.

Cheshire West in the Supreme Court

Given the far-reaching consequences of the Supreme Court's decision, considered in the next chapter, it is important to remind ourselves of this background of extraordinary, and often inconsistent, illogical and unjust, judgments, all but eliminating the functioning of the DoLS in social care settings.

Following the Court of Appeal rulings in *Cheshire West* and *P & Q*, the ECtHR handed down its landmark ruling in *Stanev v Bulgaria*, and further judgments finding people to be deprived of their liberty in 'social care' settings, repeating the same formula it had used in *HL v UK* that they were subject to continuous supervision and control, not free to leave, and deprived of their liberty (see Chapter 5). The OS indicated his willingness to take the matter to the ECtHR if necessary.

Reflecting the significance of the issue and the potential for divergent opinions, seven Supreme Court justices heard the case, including Lord Neuberger the court's president and Lady Hale, its deputy president. The Supreme Court granted the EHRC, the National Autistic Society and Mind (jointly) and the AIRE Centre permission to intervene. No fewer than 20 leading barristers represented the parties and intervenors. The courtroom benches were full of spectators consisting of academics (including myself), civil servants, lawyers, health and social care professionals, NGOs and others from the small and interconnected world of DoLS enthusiasts. The courtroom felt very far removed from the lives of MIG, MEG and P, who did not attend.

Lady Hale gave the leading judgment, and – perhaps surprisingly in view of the outcome – Lord Sumption agreed with her. Lady Hale's career began as a respected academic authority on mental health and family law, an authority she performed in the courtroom when occasionally correcting counsel for misunderstandings of the law.[7] She became a Law Commissioner, working on proposals for the MCA (Chapter 6), the Children Act 1989 and other areas of family law. As a judge she decided several landmark cases concerning capacity, including a case extending the capacity jurisdiction into non-medical-welfare matters (*Re S (Hospital Patient: Court's Jurisdiction)* [1995] Fam. 26) and a celebrated judgment on the importance of 'wishes and feelings' in best interests decision making (*Aintree University Hospitals NHS Foundation Trust v DJ*). She did not mind ruffling the feathers of her brother judges (for example, *R (McDonald) v Royal Borough of Kensington and Chelsea* [2011] UKSC 33) or the government (for example, *R (Miller) v The Prime Minister* [2019] UKSC 41). A celebrated feminist judge (Hunter and Rackley, 2020), she drew the ire of the *Daily Mail* for the Children Act proposals for removing 'the ultimate rights of parents over the care of children' and placing them 'firmly in the hands of the state', and for those on the MCA (Oddie and Torode, 1995). An analysis of her Supreme Court judgments found that the dominant value was 'universalism' and that '[w]hen *universalism* was opposed to *power*, Lady Hale supported *universalism* in all cases' (Cahill-O'Callaghan, 2020: 148).

---

[7]   In one notable courtroom intervention, she interrupted counsel for the AIRE Centre, who had argued that the phrase 'merely' should be read into article 14 CRPD, so that it would read that a person should not be deprived of their liberty 'merely' because of their disability, demonstrating her awareness of the considerable debates on this point in the negotiations of the CRPD.

The acid test

Lady Hale sought to identify a straightforward acid test for deprivation of liberty; metaphorics evoking a simple scientific test distinguishing two fundamentally opposing substances. Noting that this was a consistent feature in ECtHR jurisprudence since *HL v UK*, Hale found that the 'key' was whether the person 'was under continuous supervision and control' and 'not free to leave' [49]. The main part of her judgment, and that of Lord Kerr and Lord Neuberger, was given over to rebutting the arguments and discursive strategies of the lower courts and the dissenting justices – Lords Carnwath, Hodge and Clarke – and highlighting the policy imperative of providing safeguards. I pick up questions of policy in Chapter 10.

Benevolence

Lady Hale underscored the obvious logical flaw in arguing that restrictions were not a deprivation of liberty if they were necessary and benevolent, describing this as setting the 'cart before the horse'; the very purpose of article 5 was to 'secure that the legal justifications for the constraints' on a person is 'made out' [56] (see also Lord Kerr at [84]). To see things otherwise was to let the 'comparative benevolence' of a person's living arrangements 'blind us to their essential character' [56]. Drawing a striking contrast with infantilizing play pen imagery, she commented that '[a] gilded cage is still a cage' [46].

Objections

The dissenting justices stressed that neither MIG, MEG nor P 'evinced dissatisfaction with or objection to' their placements [90], describing them as 'people living happily in a domestic setting' [99], [109]. For the reasons outlined above, we might doubt the accuracy of this description. Both Lord Neuberger and Lady Hale countered this by framing the appellants as persons who lacked the (de facto) 'capacity to object' [55], [67]. Lord Neuberger noted that if objections were necessary, people without the capacity to object could therefore never be found deprived of their liberty, no matter how confining the circumstances, a proposition that 'cannot possibly be right' [67]. Lord Kerr asserted that deprivation of liberty was an 'objective state', not dependent 'on one's disposition to exploit one's freedom' [76]. In tacit reference to the historical policy of 'informality' for the 'non-volitional', Lady Hale commented that 'it might once have been suggested that a person cannot be deprived of his liberty if he lacks the capacity to understand and object to his situation', but this approach was rejected in *HL v UK* [33]. Like the ECtHR in *Bournewood*, *Cheshire West* rejected 'informality' yet tacitly accepted the existence of a 'non-volitional' category of persons.

The reverse-comparator: universal human rights

In court, no advocate – including the councils who argued the appellants were not deprived of their liberty – defended Munby LJ's 'comparator' approach. Even the dissenting justices agreed with some of the criticisms made ([77], [79], [88], [99]). Lady Hale adopted a rhetorically potent strategy to reject this appeal to the 'relative normality' of a disabled person's living arrangements, drawing from post-carceral discourses of human rights universalism and equality. She framed the overarching question to be determined by the Supreme Court as whether article 5 'is the same for everyone, regardless of whether or not they are mentally or physically disabled'[33], implicitly challenging her audiences to counter powerful post-carceral and liberal norms in arguing that liberty is 'different' for disabled than non-disabled people.

Lady Hale stressed, '[t]he whole point about human rights is their universal character', the ECHR guarantees these rights to 'everyone', and the same philosophy underpins the CRPD [36]. It is 'axiomatic that people with disabilities, both mental and physical, have the same human rights as the rest of the human race' [45]. Yet her reading of these rights was reformist, not abolitionist: these rights might sometimes have to be limited or restricted 'because of their disabilities', but the 'starting point' was the same for everyone [45]. Tacitly positioning those restricting the scope of article 5 as 'denying' disabled people their rights, she argued that such differences as existed instead required the state to 'make reasonable accommodation' for their 'special needs' [45]. Here 'accommodation' could be read as potentially even including restrictions themselves, but certainly including safeguards. The logic is that detention safeguards, and possibly restrictions on liberty themselves, bring benefits that promote rather than inhibit the human rights of disabled people.

Expressing the universalist ethos noted by Cahill-O'Callaghan she stated that 'what it means to be deprived of liberty must be the same for everyone, whether or not they have physical or mental disabilities' [46]. Bringing the matter into sharp focus she went on to say:

> If it would be a deprivation of my liberty to be obliged to live in a particular place, subject to constant monitoring and control, only allowed out with close supervision, and unable to move away without permission even if such an opportunity became available, then it must also be a deprivation of the liberty of a disabled person. [46]

By substituting herself – one of the foremost lawyers of her age – for the appellants, Lady Hale inserted the archetypal 'rational legal subject' (Naffine, 2003) into the place of those whose legal status had been clouded by decades of informality, infantilization and 'non-volitional' status, crystallizing and solidifying them as legal persons.

Dissolving the home/institution boundary

The most divisive and controversial outcome, I suggest, of the Supreme Court's ruling in *Cheshire West* is that it extended a legal machinery for regulating the threat of institutionalized carceral care into the private and domestic sphere. Echoing Wilson LJ in *P and Q*, and Munby LJ in *A Local Authority v A (A Child) & Anor*, the dissenting justices argued that 'nobody using ordinary language' would describe 'people living happily in a domestic setting' as deprived of their liberty, labouring to keep deprivation of liberty within its 'ordinary meaning' ([99], [108]).

This rhetorical strategy, frequently employed by those criticizing the judgment, appeals to a 'common sense' connecting deprivation of liberty to the large institutions of the late carceral era. Yet this common sense is based on a fictional construction of the past. As I showed in Chapter 3, there are historical precedents for domestic deprivation of liberty: 'madhouses' began as domestic settings where 'lunatics' might be 'kept' for profit; 'single houses' where a person might live with a doctor or paid attendants required 'certification' and visitation for most of the 19th century; and by the late carceral era the Lunacy Commission was empowered to visit and require medical reports concerning those 'detained or treated as a lunatic or alleged lunatic' even within private families. The Victorians might well have considered MIG, MEG and P to be detained. The boundary line underpinning the law of institutions has always been contested, unstable and deeply political. However, post-carceral care arrangements presented particular dilemmas since they were ideologically bound up with alternatives to institutional and carceral modes of care.

The acid test dissolved this unstable boundary delimiting the law of institutions. Lady Hale accepted that MIG and MEG might enjoy 'comparative normality in the sense of their "home-like" quality' but asserted this did not answer whether they were deprived of their liberty [47]. She went on to remark that if they lived 'under the same constraints' in the kind of 'institution' Rusi Stanev was confined in 'we would have no difficulty' deciding they were deprived of their liberty: 'In the end, it is the constraints that matter' [56]. Although MIG lived in an 'ordinary family home' with her foster mother, the 'reality' was the same as MEG's: her foster mother and others 'exercised complete control over every aspect of her life', and she was not allowed to go out, see people or do things 'which they did not wish her to do' [53]. Conceding as a 'fair point' that the ECtHR had never considered a deprivation of liberty concerning an ordinary domestic home, Lord Neuberger commented, 'I cannot see any good reason why the fact that a person is confined to a domestic home, as opposed to a hospital or other institution, should prevent her from contending that she has been deprived of her liberty' [71].

Lady Hale's reasoning resonated with an older 'battlefield' over children and families (Hoggett, 1994: 8), asserting the rights of people subject to the power of caregivers in private settings and the onus on the state to provide safeguards and protections even if that encroached upon the 'rights', authority or privacy of families.[8] Yet it raised thorny questions – highlighted by the dissenting justices – about whether this would now mean that a person like HL would be deprived of his liberty when living with his carers in the community [100]. *Cheshire West* reframed deprivation of liberty as a relation of control, irrespective of who exercised control, where, or for what reasons. The policy imperative at stake was securing an 'independent check' on care arrangements satisfying the acid test – I discuss this further in Chapter 10.

Responses and backlash

The Supreme Court's judgment sent shockwaves through adult social care and the courts. The *Cheshire West* earthquake was – as Butler and Drakeford (2005: 5) wrote of scandals – 'a powerful signal that change is occurring', that 'pressure for change has reached unsustainable levels', after which 'we have to reconstruct the world we inhabit'. The inconsistencies and paradoxes of the post-carceral era, of people 'liberated' from legal and 'institutional' structures yet remaining under constraint in the community, could no longer be contained. New questions of consent, capacity, legal personality and human rights unsettled a realm of legal ghosts. *Cheshire West* rejected the founding principle of post-carceral legal thought – informality – with a new kind of legalism. 'In a sense', Lady Hale observed, 'the wheel has turned full circle' [2].

I will revisit the legal and administrative aftermath of the judgment in the next chapter, including new legislation – the Mental Capacity (Amendment) Act 2019 – establishing LPS to replace the DoLS. Here, I turn to immediate reactions to the judgment from different audiences. Many welcomed the ruling. Civil society groups and social care professionals found it plausible to describe the appellants as detained and felt the universalist ethos of this new legalism expressed their own professional values. Others sounded doubts as to whether this particular form of legalism would resolve the (acknowledged) problems of the post-carceral era, highlighting the sheer scale of what must now be regulated. Meanwhile, some rejected the judgment,

---

[8]   I am grateful to Professor Rosemary Hunter for her help in thinking through this point.

its rationale and implications wholesale, invoking old discourses of the 'non-volitional', informality and the 'prison within'. Others critiqued the judgment by reference to a libertarian populist narrative, rejecting human rights themselves.

A victory for human rights?

Mind (2014) praised *Cheshire West* as a 'landmark' judgment 'for the protection of vulnerable people'. Disability Rights UK (2014) endorsed it, remarking that residential care placements without any option to leave 'should not "just happen"'. Counsel for the National Autistic Society and Mind, intervenors in the case, described it as recognizing that depriving a person of their liberty 'is such a profoundly invasive step to take that it must be independently justified' (Wise and Spurrier, 2014). Richard Gordon (2014) – counsel for the appellants – felt it addressed the 'profound fallacy' that liberty was different for a person without capacity, and the subtext that they should 'thank their lucky stars for having a nice care home'.

Despite bearing the brunt of the judgment's administrative effects, many social workers voiced support for the outcome. Dawn Whitaker (2014: 1), the independent social worker for P in *Cheshire West*, described it as 'social justice', 'a wake-up call to all those involved in safeguarding adults at risk', providing 'essential and necessary protections for many thousands of adults, subject to high levels of restrictive practice, supervision and control'. Blair McPherson (2014) contrasted the ruling with past practices of routinely admitting older people to residential care without involving them in the decision, then responding to their distress by locking the doors, sedating residents and restricting their movements. Ian Burgess (2014) welcomed the judgment as enshrining 'social work values in law', describing the take-away message for social workers as 'that human rights are for everyone' and 'there is no sliding scale of rights'. James, Mitchell and Morgan (2019: 60–1), authors of a popular social work book, described it as 'a wake-up call to adult social work', reminding the profession 'of its roots' in promoting empowerment and 'liberation of people', social justice and human rights. The government observed that 'the judgment has been welcomed by many stakeholders and professionals' and that 'handled appropriately' it 'could have a significant positive effect' in raising awareness of DoLS, 'empowering individuals and protecting their rights' (HM Government, 2014: [7.15]).

Others were sceptical of the judgment's implicit claims that the law of institutions would help solve problems in community care, sounding a cautious note over the operational challenges of securing safeguards on this scale with insufficient resources (McNicholl, 2014; McPherson, 2014). The CQC (2015c: 6) welcomed 'the clarity' the judgment provided 'and the increase in applications' but recognized the 'challenges' facing providers and supervisory bodies. Sir James Munby (2018) (by then retired) commented that the proper resourcing of the system to replace DoLS would be 'more significant and important than its structure'. Jones and Piffaretti (2018: v), a former director of adult social services turned specialist mental health and capacity law solicitor, described the judgment as coming 'at great cost to the public purse' diverting resources from service provision to regulation, and categorizing thousands of people 'who are being cared for appropriately and without complaint' as detained.

Others – while acknowledging the need for an 'independent check' – doubted that deprivation of liberty safeguards were the best way to secure this. Echoing Foucauldian scholarship on regulatory paradoxes, Neil Allen (2015: 46) (counsel for Cheshire West and Chester Council and Surrey County Council) argued that basing safeguards on the paradigm of a 'prison cell' risks 'cementing the care relationship to a prison paradigm ... in the perception and consequence of the law', and further 'institutionalising' those living in the community, 'legitimising rather than preventing the problem'. District Judge Anselm Eldergill commented that where interferences with liberty may have been 'occasional, guilty, tentative or furtive' they may become 'confidently asserted against a person incapable of resisting' (Law Society, 2020).

Gordon Ashton (2017: 103), a retired Court of Protection judge who was the father of a man with intellectual disabilities who died in a care service after choking while being inadequately supervised while eating, doubted whether the DoLS would have given his son more freedom or saved his life. DoLS might have enabled the family to 'ventilate our concerns', but the 'reality was that no other options were then available and the courts could not oblige the authorities to fund something better'. He would have 'found it laughable' if anyone had suggested his son was deprived of his liberty when being cared for at home by family, and expressed sympathy for Munby P's attempts to 'head off the looming disaster'.

Judicial resistance

The reception from Court of Protection judges was lukewarm at best, re-enacting the same discursive strategies and skirmishes that had characterized the litigation throughout. Several came perilously close to simply refusing to apply the acid test. In the next chapter I look at some of the satellite litigation prompted by the decision, where questions of liberty and appropriate safeguards continued to be raised and resisted in other contexts.

When faced with applying the acid test to people living in their own homes, Mostyn J and Bodey J made originalist arguments that *Cheshire West* took article 5 ECHR beyond the intentions of its drafters as a safeguard against the 'mischief of state interference' (Bodey J in *W City Council v Mrs*

L, [27]), the 'midnight knock on the door; the sudden disappearance; the prolonged detention' (Mostyn J in *The London Borough of Tower Hamlets v TB & Anor*, [58]). The purpose of article 5 ECHR was against the 'lawless abuses' of Nazi Germany and totalitarian states (*Rochdale Metropolitan Borough Council v KW & Ors*, [10], [11]). For the reasons given in Chapter 5, I doubt this originalist reading of article 5 is correct.

Mostyn J resurrected old tropes of infantilization and the non-volitional, arguing that J. S. Mill could not have conceived of KW as deprived of her liberty since his doctrine of liberty applied only to humans 'in the maturity of their faculties' not 'still in a state' requiring care from others, asserting that liberty required 'a positive and reasoned intellectual function which is hard to ascribe to a person of unsound mind' (*Rochdale Metropolitan Borough Council v KW & Ors*, [14]). KW was 'ambulant', walking with a frame, but appealing to the logic of the 'prison within' Mostyn J 'stress tested' her situation by asserting that a man in a coma with no relations 'demanding to take him away' was 'surely not' deprived of his liberty, so therefore since KW could not 'realistically leave' it must follow that the 'freedom to leave' element of the acid test was not satisfied [22]. His repeated refusal to apply the acid test in KW's case saw him criticized twice by the Court of Appeal, who eventually removed him from the case (*KW & Ors v Rochdale Metropolitan Borough Council* [2015] EWCA Civ 1054).

Libertarian backlash

Cheshire West provoked a libertarian backlash from critics of human rights and the 'juridification of everyday life' (Holbrook, 2017), sceptical of law regulating care or protecting 'vulnerable' persons in the private sphere ('Fancy having a judge in your living room?' asked Hewson (2012)). Jon Holbrook, a lawyer and critic of human rights law (Holbrook and Allan, 2017), argues that *Cheshire West* reflects its 'distorting influence' (Holbrook, 2014b). The litigation had posed the 'wrong question' – whether the care arrangements amount to a deprivation of liberty, rather than how living arrangements could be improved – and had therefore resulted in the 'wrong answer' (Holbrook, 2014a). The outcome, Holbrook conceded, might be desirable if 'those lacking capacity were routinely deprived of adequate care', but 'this is not the case'. The judgment was emblematic of 'bloody lawyers' taking leave of common sense.

This view was echoed by barrister Barbara Hewson (2013) writing in the libertarian online magazine *Spiked*. The judgment was motivated by 'a lack of trust in public services' exacerbated by scandals such as Winterbourne View, but the 'bureaucracy of detention regulation' would not ameliorate this bad care, merely provide false reassurances as lawyers and judges 'micromanage the conditions in which a disabled person lives'. It is not a proper function of law, she argued, to 'shine a light into dark places' – dismissing a key narrative motif championing the law of institutions (for example, CQC, 2014: 3; HM Government, 2014: 29).

For both Holbrook and Hewson, *Cheshire West* either constructs a fictitious problem (a claim I contest in Chapter 10) or else poses the wrong question and presents the wrong solution (claims I have more time for). Their rhetoric invoked the old motifs of informality and the non-volitional: 'Keep the law out of disabled care', as Hewson (2013) expressed it. However, their specific complaints resemble Lord Sumption's (2019: 10, 13) more nuanced critique of human rights and 'law's expanding empire', penetrating 'every corner of human life', regulating areas of clinical discretion and family life 'that once belonged exclusively to the domain of personal judgement'.

Given the historical regulation of 'lunacy' and domestic psychiatry, we can query whether the juridification of the private sphere is as new as these critiques suggest. Caregiving arrangements– familial and clinical – have not been 'private in the sense of outside public regulation' for several centuries (Rose, 1987: 65); the critical question is what form regulation takes. Sumption's suggestion that the law should retreat from these arenas does not answer questions of *whose* personal judgement should prevail when disabled people, their families and public bodies are in conflict. However, in the context of a global libertarian populist backlash against human rights (Alston, 2017), against 'regulation' more generally, we must pay close attention to these critiques and engage with them. *Cheshire West* could spell significant trouble for human rights and capacity law as it potentially inserts into family life a form of law geared toward regulating institutional spaces.

A statutory definition?

Some of those objecting to *Cheshire West* hoped that Parliament would adopt a statutory definition reversing or limiting the acid test. The Law Commission (2017b: [5.37]) viewed this as 'misguided', since the HRA still required courts to apply a test derived from article 5 ECHR. The JCHR (2018a, 2018b: 16–17), concerned about domestic deprivation of liberty, considered statutory definitions to 'clarify' the Supreme Court's judgment. They rejected as discriminatory a 'causative' approach whereby if a person's physical condition prevented them from leaving they were not deprived of their liberty (the 'prison within' strategy). However, they endorsed an approach suggested by English barrister and mental capacity law academic Alex Ruck Keene (2017a) based on 'valid consent'.

This approach would not alter the acid test approach to the 'objective' limb of article 5 (see *Storck v Germany* in Chapter 5), but instead considered whether a person 'validly consented' to the arrangements. It was influenced by the CRPD's universal legal capacity paradigm, and the logic that even people assessed to 'lack mental capacity' have a 'will' that can be given legal effect through supported decision making or an act of interpretation. The JCHR's (2018a: 12–13) proposed model required that a person was 'capable of expressing their wishes and feelings (verbally or otherwise)', and had 'expressed their persistent contentment with their care and treatment arrangements', there was 'no coercion involved' in their care, and this was confirmed in writing by two professionals, one of whom was independent of the person's care arrangements.

A variant of this approach was also proposed by District Judge Anselm Eldergill (2019), who – expressing particular concern about MIG's case – proposed a 'but for' test establishing what the individual can and wishes to do ('wills') 'but for' interferences with their freedom. Some abolitionist proponents of the universal legal capacity paradigm have also argued that people who 'lack mental capacity' may still give valid consent if others appropriately interpret their 'will' (Centre for Disability Law and Policy, in Department of Health (Ireland), 2019: [1.111]). This model symbolizes a wholesale rejection of the logics of the 'non-volitional', requiring much closer judicial engagement with a person's subjective experience than any of the existing deprivation of liberty litigation, and could address some of the more paradoxical outcomes of the acid test (Series, 2020). I revisit this possibility in the final chapter.

Lord Woolf tabled the JCHR's 'valid consent' proposals as an amendment to the 2018 Bill. However, the government rejected it on the basis that these cases would thereby be excluded from the LPS scheme and hence require direct authorization in court (HL Deb 21 November 2018 vol 794 col 253–4). The implication was that whatever one put in the legislation, a person who 'lacked capacity' simply could not be regarded as giving a valid consent under the ECHR or English law; their will either did not exist or did not matter, but certainly could not form the basis of a legally valid consent.

Influenced by concerns 'about the state involving itself unnecessarily in family and private life' (HL Deb 5 September 2018 vol 792 col 1848) the government adopted its own statutory definition, significantly limiting the circumstances where the acid test would apply. The Lords rejected this amendment and proposed their own. Eventually the government dropped the attempt at crafting a statutory definition, and a revised Code of Practice will offer detailed guidance on case law on the evolving meaning of 'deprivation of liberty'.

Tremors

The *Cheshire West* acid test is binding on all four UK jurisdictions. This includes Northern Ireland, which has recently adopted DoLS-like legislation (Mental Capacity Act (Northern Ireland) 2016 SI 2016/18), and Scotland, which is consulting on proposals (Scottish Law Commission, 2014: [1.1]; Scottish Government, 2016: [5]). While acknowledging the need for safeguards, however, the Scottish Government (2018a: [12]) felt that 'deprivation of liberty' was 'not a particularly helpful term', preferring a graded guardianship scheme that could satisfy the requirements of article 5 without explicitly coupling the safeguards to the concept of detention.

Tremors from *Cheshire West* spread beyond the UK. Legislation establishing DoLS-like safeguards in Jersey and Gibraltar – who were not bound by the Supreme Court's interpretation of article 5 in *Cheshire West*[9] – adopted definitions and thresholds modelled on the acid test, yet chose to forgo the term 'deprivation of liberty' preferring 'significant restrictions on liberty' (Capacity and Self-Determination (Jersey) Law 2016; Lasting Power of Attorney and Capacity Act 2018 (Gibraltar)). The safeguards applied only in regulated settings, however, avoiding 'domestic deprivation of liberty' situations. Guernsey,[10] meanwhile, preferred the term 'significant restriction of a person's personal rights' yet coupled its definition to article 5 ECHR, and explicitly included 'private dwellings' within its scope (Capacity (Bailiwick of Guernsey) Law, 2020). In the Republic of Ireland, government proposals for DoLS-like legislation spoke of 'admission decisions' rather than deprivation of liberty, yet employed the acid test's as threshold criteria. The Centre for Disability Law and Policy argued this 'euphemism' masked the individual's right to liberty (Department of Health (Ireland), 2017; 2019: [1.5]).

The approaches adopted by these jurisdictions suggest the judgment's plausibility lies in arguing for the need for safeguards – both to protect 'vulnerable' persons considered to lack capacity, and to forestall litigation before the ECtHR. However, the symbolism of 'deprivation of liberty' remains controversial in connection with 'incapacity' and social care. As I discussed in Chapters 1 and 5, lawyers, activists and some public officials in other jurisdictions – including Canada, Australia, the USA and France – continue to argue that disabled people are deprived of their liberty by care arrangements in the community and require deprivation of liberty safeguards, but the symbolism of social care detention is currently resisted by their governments.

---

[9] Jersey is a Crown Dependency and Gibraltar is a British Overseas Territory. They are closely related but distinct from the UK legal system. They have their own human rights legislation, and their highest court of appeal is the Judicial Committee of the Privy Council. Supreme Court justices sit on this committee, but UK Supreme Court rulings are not directly binding on Crown Dependencies or British Overseas Territories.

[10] Guernsey is also a Crown Dependency.

9

Aftermath

A week before the Supreme Court handed down its ruling in *Cheshire West*, the House of Lords Select Committee on the MCA (2014) reported on its post-legislative scrutiny of the Act. It concluded that while the MCA's principles were 'visionary' for their time, its 'empowering ethos has not been delivered' owing to poor awareness and understanding, and cultures of paternalism and risk aversion in health and social care. The Committee concluded the DoLS were poorly drafted, overly complex, tens of thousands of people were unlawfully detained, and 'far from being used to protect individuals and their rights, they are sometimes used to oppress individuals, and to force upon them decisions made by others without reference to the wishes and feelings of the person concerned'. The Committee recommended that the government 'start again' (pp6–7).

Without the Supreme Court's ruling, the government may have ignored this invitation to replace the legislation. In the words of one critic of the DoLS, *Cheshire West* 'placed a gun' to the government's head;[1] there was now no denying the system was broken. Administrative and judicial systems for authorizing deprivation of liberty could not cope with the sheer volume of cases after the ruling. Lady Hale anticipated the need for revised legislation, commenting that DoLS could be 'simplified' and extended to other settings [57].

Meanwhile, *Cheshire West* did not put to bed arguments about the meaning of liberty. Further litigation probed the recesses and paradoxes of the acid test: did it really mean that a person living happily in their own home was deprived of their liberty? Might children in care also be deprived of their liberty? What about a baby? Or a person in a coma? Deprivation of

---

[1] Comment of expert lawyer Richard Jones, a critic of DoLS and the Supreme Court's judgment, at: www.mentalcapacitylawandpolicy.org.uk/cheshire-west-the-supreme-courts-right-hook/#comment-13

liberty tactics were deployed by those wanting to extend safeguards to other vulnerable groups – especially children in care – or embroiled in disputes over medical treatment and deaths in care. Their efforts were increasingly rebuffed by the lower courts, which began to reign in the acid test.

A broken system

The volume of applications to authorize deprivation of liberty after *Cheshire West* overwhelmed the systems' administrative and judicial safeguards. The DoLS were designed to process relatively few applications; the Department of Health (2007) had estimated 21,000 in the first year, falling to 5,000 annually. In fact, applications started around 7,000 annually but rose slowly, reaching 14,346 in 2013–14 (Health and Social Care Information Centre, 2014; Care and Social Services Inspectorate Wales and Health Inspectorate Wales, 2015). After the Supreme Court's ruling, this increased tenfold to 148,221 (Health and Social Care Information Centre, 2015b; Care and Social Services Inspectorate Wales and Healthcare Inspectorate Wales, 2016) and continued to rise, reaching 255,836 applications in 2018–19 (NHS Digital, 2019b; Care Inspectorate Wales and Healthcare Inspectorate Wales, 2020). Factoring in deprivation of liberty outside the DoLS scheme, the government estimated a new scheme might need to process 304,132 applications annually (Department of Health and Social Care, 2019a). To put this in perspective, the annual number of detentions under the MHA is estimated to be around 50,000 (NHS Digital, 2019c).

Supervisory bodies were completely overwhelmed. The Association of Directors of Adult Social Services (ADASS, 2016) produced a 'screening tool' to help them work out, in the words of the JCHR (2018b: 3), 'how best to break the law'. Social workers were pulled from casework to help clear assessment backlogs (McNicholl, 2014) but, by 2018–19, 131,350 applications remained unprocessed (NHS Digital, 2019b). ADASS and the Local Government Association (2014) estimated it would cost £88m to clear this backlog; money that local authorities did not have. Four local authorities unsuccessfully sought judicial review of what they characterized as the government's failure to adequately fund the DoLS; the court suggested they defund other activities, such as libraries (*R (Liverpool City Council) v Secretary of State for Health* [2017] EWHC 986 (Admin)). Meanwhile, the Local Government Ombudsman (2019: 6) investigated a local authority adopting higher thresholds than the ADASS screening tool for processing DoLS authorizations. Although the Local Government Ombudsman received no complaints, those affected were 'likely to be vulnerable' and unable to complain. It examined a representative sample of 57 unprocessed applications from one week in 2017, finding among them a case raising such significant concerns it was escalated to the Court of Protection. The

CQC (2015c) took enforcement action against some care providers for non-compliance with the MCA DoLS.

The Court of Protection set about developing a less resource-intensive process for an anticipated tidal-wave of applications for judicial authorization of deprivation of liberty outside of care homes and hospitals. Munby P's initial efforts to do this via a collective 'hearing' and written judgments (*X & Ors (Deprivation of Liberty)* [2014] EWCOP 25; *Re X and others (Deprivation of Liberty) (Number 2)* [2014] EWCOP 37) were rebuffed by the Court of Appeal, chiefly on the basis that this was a procedural matter not a 'judgment' in a specific case (*Re X (Court of Protection Practice)* [2015] EWCA Civ 599). The Court of Appeal also expressed concern that the proposed process entailed authorizing deprivation of liberty without any independent representation of 'P'. They doubted this was compliant with article 5 ECHR, observing that 'no other example could be found' of court-sanctioned detention where the person to be detained was not a party to the proceedings [106]. The Court of Protection Rules were subsequently adapted to accommodate a new 'streamlined' procedure, in which P could be 'represented' by a lay person (now known as a Rule 1.2 representative) without being joined as a party to the proceedings, since this would require costly legal representation (Ashton et al, 2019). The number of cases the Court of Protection hears concerning deprivation of liberty has steadily increased since *Cheshire West*, including s21A DoLS 'appeals', 'streamlined' deprivation of liberty authorizations and welfare cases involving a deprivation of liberty. However, the overall number received (5,219 in 2019, Ministry of Justice, 2020) is still an order of magnitude lower than the estimated number of people deprived of their liberty outside the DoLS procedures, suggesting tens of thousands remain illegally detained.

In view of these difficulties, and the House of Lords Committee's criticisms, the government asked the Law Commission (2015, 2017b) to review the DoLS and make recommendations for their replacement. The Law Commission undertook what was reputed to be the largest stakeholder consultation exercise in its history, publishing its proposals for the LPS in 2017. In 2018, the government introduced a Bill into the House of Lords containing an 'adjusted' version of the LPS, which it had not consulted on. Stakeholders raised concerns that the Bill was ill thought through, unworkable and offered inadequate safeguards. It was substantially amended in Parliament. The Mental Capacity (Amendment) Act 2019 will replace the DoLS with a version of the LPS that differs from the Law Commission's proposals in several important respects. Implementation has been delayed by the COVID-19 pandemic; at the time of writing it is anticipated that the LPS scheme will begin to replace the DoLS in April 2022. I have published an extended analysis and critique of the LPS elsewhere, comparing them with the DoLS and the requirements of article 5 ECHR (Series, 2019). In this chapter, I provide an overview of the LPS, highlighting some of the tensions, concerns, themes and possibilities in this new scheme for regulating social care detention; the points I raise are explained at greater length in my review article.

The Liberty Protection Safeguards

Those designing the successor to DoLS faced a fundamental difficulty: securing the safeguards required by article 5 ECHR, on the scale required by *Cheshire West*. The Law Commission (2017b) estimated that properly implementing existing administrative and judicial authorization schemes would cost £2.2bn per year. In contrast, the Department of Health and Social Care (2019a: 4) estimated the 'adjusted' LPS would cost £204.44m annually. Although a marked reduction in cost, to put this in perspective, the annual operating expenditure of the CQC (2019a) – which regulates *all* health and social care services across England – is £227.7m, most of which comes from providers' fees. Securing even minimally compliant individual safeguards on this scale comes with a considerable price tag, explaining many of the unsatisfactory outcomes and compromises reached in the LPS.

Reconceptualizing 'deprivation of liberty' safeguards?

Social care detention is part of a family of 'non-paradigmatic' carceral practices, which are mobile, dispersed and extend beyond the traditional confines of 'institutions'. Whereas the DoLS scheme understood 'deprivation of liberty' as being 'accommodated' within the institutional spaces of a care home or hospital (for example, MCA Sch A1 s15; MCA Sch A1 s20(1)), the LPS adopts the more fluid formulation of 'arrangements' that 'give rise to' a deprivation of liberty, *wherever* these take place and *whosoever* is responsible for them (MCA Sch AA1 s2). This has the advantage, post-*Cheshire West*, of encompassing care arrangements in any kind of environment (including private homes), and spanning multiple settings (for example, day care, colleges, 'community' activities).

This, in turn, poses new questions about the purpose of the safeguards. Paradigmatic deprivation of liberty safeguards sort populations between institutional carceral spaces and spaces representing freedom. The acid test and the LPS do not tie deprivation of liberty to a specific kind of space, they are concerned with what Lady Hale called 'the constraints'. By authorizing (or not) specific 'arrangements', the LPS aim to go beyond 'the "binary" question of whether a person should be deprived of their liberty or not' and direct attention to the 'ways in which a person may justifiably be deprived of liberty' (Law Commission, 2017b: [7.12]).

This method potentially confers flexible control over the 'constraints' a person may be subject to, but much still hangs on what is meant by 'deprivation of liberty'. In guidance published shortly after *Cheshire West*, the Law Society (2015: [3.17]) found it was still not 'absolutely clear' whether the 'freedom to leave' element of the acid test included the 'micro' sense of freedom to come and go temporarily, or only the 'macro' sense of freedom to leave on a permanent basis (as Munby J had held in *JE v DE*, [115]).

This difference is important. If 'deprivation of liberty' is understood only in the 'macro' sense, then many 'constraints' slip through the net. A person might be subject to significant restrictions for a specific purpose – for example, to restrict contact with others, to prevent sex, to stop them harming themselves or others, to administer a treatment, to manage everyday risks such as road traffic – yet since these constraints are not about preventing the person from leaving a place *permanently* (and may well follow them if they did) then on this macro reading they would not constitute 'arrangements giving rise to a deprivation of liberty' that are regulated via the LPS. The person may very well *also* be deprived of their liberty, because they could not simply 'pack their bags and go' if somebody arrived at the door to take them away[2] – doubtless capacity assessments, best interests decisions and risk assessments would intercede. However, the critical point is that if we adopt a macro reading of deprivation of liberty the LPS can only regulate those constraints that prevent a person from leaving *permanently*, not other constraints that they might be subject to.

Many of the 'constraints' that would potentially slip out of the grip of the LPS are connected with experiences of home as a territory, as a centre for self-identity and as a social and cultural unit (discussed in Chapter 6). Some will be protected by article 8 ECHR, and in theory could be litigated through the Court of Protection's general 'welfare' jurisdiction. However, although article 8 ECHR does confer some procedural protection, particularly when coupled to formal restrictions on legal capacity or involuntary medical treatment (for example, *Shtukaturov v Russia* [2008] ECHR 223; *X v Finland* [2012] ECHR 1371), the procedural safeguards are notably weaker than those secured by article 5. There are, for example, no automatic duties to inform a person of their rights, to secure representation for them when their rights are restricted, or to actively facilitate rights of challenge if the person objects. Non-means tested legal aid is not available for 'welfare' litigation in the Court of Protection, unlike DoLS/LPS reviews by a court, and cases can cost tens or hundreds of thousands of pounds (Series et al, 2017b).

The Law Commission (2015, 2017b) had proposed additional safeguards for article 8 rights, but the government preferred to address 'culture' rather

---

[2]   A test helpfully suggested by Alex Ruck Keene.

than legislate for this (Department of Health, 2015a: 3). Lady Hale appears to have intended these micro-issues to be included within the *Cheshire West* acid test of deprivation of liberty. Applying the test to MIG and MEG, she observed that their carers exercised 'control over every aspect' of their lives, they were not 'allowed out without supervision, or to see anyone whom [their caregivers] did not wish [them] to see, or to do things which they did not wish [them] to do' [52], [53]. She also considered that restrictions on HL's carers from visiting him in hospital were 'relied upon in concluding that the hospital had deprived HL of his liberty' [53]. Yet – as I will shortly explain – the lower courts and government prefer a 'macro' interpretation.

Three core assessments

Assessments are both the gateway to the system and intended as safeguards in themselves, ensuring ECHR and other substantive thresholds for detention are met. The LPS adopt three core conditions for authorization:

1. the person must lack the mental capacity 'to consent to the arrangements';
2. they must have a qualifying 'mental disorder' (discussed in Chapter 2); and
3. the arrangements must be 'necessary to prevent harm to the cared-for person and proportionate in relation to the likelihood and seriousness of harm to the cared-for person'. (MCA Sch AA1 s13)

Both the mental capacity and 'necessary and proportionate' conditions reflect the shift in emphasis from deprivation of liberty as a matter of 'accommodation' to a matter of 'arrangements'. However, this also brings added complexity.

The Law Commission (2017b: [10.14]) drew a 'bright-line distinction between a decision to deprive someone of their liberty and a decision about treatment'. This mirrors important distinctions within mental health law, whereby powers of detention do not automatically authorize involuntary treatment, and separate treatment safeguards are needed. The Department of Health and Social Care (2019b: [35]) interpreted this to mean that the LPS apply to 'arrangements enabling care or treatment' not the 'direct delivery of the care and treatment', which continues to be 'governed' by s5 MCA's general defence.

The Law Commission seems to have intended to convey that an LPS authorization does not confer unfettered power to treat or impose care-related interventions without some further process. This message is important where 'authorization' is understood as a compulsory power. However, in the context of the DoLS and LPS, the authorization process is widely understood as inserting *safeguards*, or an 'independent check', on substitute decisions concerning a person's living arrangements (*Cheshire West*, UKSC, [1], [32], [57]). If the 'arrangements' are separate from underlying substitute decisions determining where a person should live and any specific care, treatments or welfare matters, the distinction implies the LPS cannot serve as an 'independent check' on substitute decisions; they are simply a check on the arrangements 'enabling' them.

In trying to make sense of this to frame the capacity and necessary and proportionate assessments one enters a hall of mirrors. Does 'capacity to consent to the arrangements' thereby imply something different to the capacity to make decisions about whatever care and treatment matters the arrangements are intended to 'enable'? When determining whether the 'arrangements to enable' care and treatment are necessary and proportionate, is the starting point that the underlying substitute decisions about care and treatment were correct, and the safeguards merely look to how they are being implemented?

For example, let us say that clinicians assess a person as unable to make decisions about a particular medical treatment, and they conclude it is in their best interests to have this treatment. The clinicians propose arrangements to bring and retain the person in hospital while they have the treatment, and – recognizing that these give rise to a deprivation of liberty – they seek authorization under the LPS. Should LPS assessments review whether the person has capacity to make decisions about their treatment, or just about the measures the hospital put in place to prevent them leaving? How can these matters be disentangled? Can one determine whether arrangements to enable the treatment are necessary and proportionate without considering the merits of the treatment itself, or is the starting point that the treatment is – as the clinicians believe – in the person's best interests, and the safeguards merely review *how* they intend to retain the person in hospital to deliver it?

Turning to a social care example, suppose a person is assessed to lack the mental capacity to consent to sex, and a local authority therefore imposes a placement and restrictions to prevent them from having sex. Recognizing these arrangements give rise to a deprivation of liberty they seek an LPS authorization. Should the LPS assessors, or courts reviewing an authorization, also determine whether the person has capacity to consent to sex? Similarly, supposing a person is deprived of their liberty in a care home and their contact with family is restricted pursuant to safeguarding allegations, should LPS assessors accept these allegations at face value or consider their veracity and whether the intervention itself is merited? Everything of substance hangs on these question, yet it would appear that a 'macro' reading of deprivation of liberty in combination with the 'bright-line' distinction between the intervention itself (preventing sex, 'safeguarding') and the 'arrangements' to secure this, implies that these substantive welfare matters do not fall to be considered within the deprivation of liberty jurisdiction. We are left wondering what is the purpose of the safeguards if this is the case, and what assessors are supposed to be assessing?

Matters are complicated yet further by the LPS eschewing the 'best interests' assessment described as the 'cornerstone' of the DoLS. The Law Commission (2015: [7.101]; 2017b: [9.23], [9.27]) concluded that the test 'added nothing' to the more fundamental and human rights oriented question of whether the 'arrangements' were necessary and proportionate to the risk of harm that might befall the person otherwise. The Commission observed that the language of 'best interests' implied a choice between different arrangements, when the reality was that public bodies were often only willing to fund one option, which families or professionals might not consider 'best' for that person. The Law Commission, and the Wessely (2018a) review of the MHA, also hoped that by removing 'best interests' the LPS scheme could authorize deprivation of liberty on the basis of *risk to others*, including some instances of mental health detention. However, the House of Lords voted down this proposal as it would have taken this scheme into untested waters and created numerous legal complications as the basis for detention under the MCA collided with its core principles (Series, 2019). The Department of Health and Social Care and Ministry of Justice (2021b) have chosen not to pursue this for now. At present, therefore, the 'necessary and proportionate' test could be understood as imposing a higher substantive threshold on interventions purporting to be in the 'best interests' of the person, but only those aspects of the interventions relating to 'deprivation of liberty' and not necessarily the substantive welfare matters at stake.

Rationing safeguards

The Law Commission and the government tried to reduce the administrative functions overwhelming supervisory bodies in three ways:

1. Dispersing the LPS administrative functions across a broader range of 'responsible bodies', which would now include NHS bodies such as hospitals and clinical commissioning groups (CCGs), and giving responsible bodies discretion to delegate some responsibilities to care home managers (known as the 'care home arrangements').
2. 'Streamlining' the core assessments and processes into ordinary care planning by local authorities, NHS bodies and care providers as far as possible.
3. Adopting a more flexible and 'proportionate' approach to procedural safeguards, intended to ensure that resources were directed to areas of greatest risk and need.

They hoped that dispersing responsibilities for authorizing deprivation of liberty across those directly responsible for providing or arranging care and treatment, and streamlining core assessments into ordinary care planning processes, would better embed the principles and values of the MCA and human rights into ordinary care planning. However, the same professionals and organizations making decisions about care and treatment giving rise to a deprivation of liberty then become responsible for key assessments and safeguards under the LPS; the counterweight to the welfare–incapacity jurisdiction required by the ECHR is diluted.

The independent professional scrutiny offered by BIAs was one of the most valued elements of the DoLS, but it was resource intensive. Following *Cheshire West* there were simply not enough assessors to keep up with the volume of applications. Instead, the LPS require somebody who is independent of the day-to-day care of the person to undertake a desktop review of recorded assessments and determine whether the authorization should be granted. However, where certain criteria are met this review must be undertaken by an AMCP – the successor to BIAs.

AMCPs have powers and duties to consult directly with the individual and others concerned with their care and welfare, and to 'take any other action' that appears to the AMCP to be appropriate and practicable, before deciding whether to authorize the arrangements. AMCPs could, for example, refuse to authorize a particular set of arrangements unless certain modifications were made. This potentially affords considerable power to shape the 'constraints' a person is subject to, although much hinges on how deprivation of liberty is interpreted. This is an important difference between the role of AMCPs under the LPS and their counterparts AMHPs – under the MHA, who consider only the more general question of whether a person meets threshold criteria to be detained in hospital (Stone et al, 2021), not whether a person should be deprived of their liberty in this specific place, in this specific way. These more flexible powers of AMCPs stem directly from the non-paradigmatic nature of social care detention.

The LPS scheme requires an AMCP review where there is reason to believe that the person does not wish to reside in a particular place, or to receive care or treatment there, or if the person is detained in an independent hospital. Responsible bodies also have discretionary powers to refer cases to AMCPs. The Law Commission (2017a) estimated that 25 per cent of all LPS applications will require an AMCP review, based on an ADASS estimate that 30 per cent of DoLS applications would meet these criteria. This estimate depends on how one characterizes 'objections'. Some might put this higher; a recent study of hospital care of people with dementia found that 'every patient living with dementia we observed, resisted care to some extent' (Featherstone et al, 2019: 55).

The LPS scheme targets one of its most potent safeguards toward people who appear to be objecting in some way to the arrangements, echoing the longstanding post-carceral distinction between those 'resisting' care and treatment and the compliant 'non-volitional'. It remains to be seen how the revised Code of Practice will define these referral criteria, and whether it reflects the more expansive approach to 'objections' of the revised MHA Code of Practice. The danger, as we saw in the cases of HL and MEG, is that there can be very different interpretations of whether a person's behaviour indicates they do not wish to reside in a particular place or receive care or treatment there. 'Challenging behaviour' could be taken to indicate distress about a particular environment, treatment or restrictions, but could also be explained away as a symptom of 'mental disorder'. Meanwhile difficulties may arise for those who are sedated, institutionalized, resigned, unaware of other options, or scared of upsetting those they rely upon for care and treatment. It will be incumbent upon those providing care and treatment to consult with the person about their views (MCA Sch AA1 s23, ss 18–20), creating conflicts of interest in interpreting potentially quite ambiguous signs of (dis)contentment.

A second tier of safeguards establish 'rights of challenge', including the right to request a court review of the authorization. The House of Lords Select Committee on the MCA (2014) and the Law Commission (2015, 2017b) identified serious problems exercising rights of challenge under the DoLS. Unlike the MHA, where patients are automatically referred for a tribunal if they do not exercise rights of appeal after six months, the DoLS scheme relies entirely on the detained person or their representatives applying to the Court of Protection, or the supervisory body referring the case on their behalf.

For most people subject to DoLS, exercising rights of challenge requires external assistance. Even friends or family members acting as 'liberators' can find this very difficult, and sometimes the person may be objecting to care arranged by (or with agreement from) their own families. The Law Commission proposed that most (75 per cent) people should benefit from independent advocacy, to compensate for limited independent scrutiny within the scheme and difficulties exercising rights of challenge. However, the government expressed concerns about the 'imposition of advocacy', feeling 'support from family and friends may be more appropriate' for some (Law Commission, 2017c: [8.7]). The 'adjusted' LPS are expected to provide independent advocates in only 25 per cent of cases, and the legislation is framed so that whoever is appointed as an 'appropriate person' to represent the person exercises control over their access to independent advocacy (I explain the mechanism in Series, 2019). This means where families – as custodians – occupy this role, the person may struggle to challenge their care arrangements.

Perhaps unsurprisingly then, the government anticipates court reviews of deprivation of liberty authorizations will fall from 1 per cent under the DoLS to 0.5 per cent under the LPS (Department of Health and Social Care, 2019a). The LPS scheme also reduces the frequency of reviews and permits authorizations to be renewed without necessarily undertaking a fresh battery of assessments. The overall sense is of a still-costly scheme inserting many layers of what Percy (Lord Percy 1957) dismissively referred to as 'formalities', treading carefully around professional substitute decision making and families as custodians of the person.

Aftershocks

The *Cheshire West* acid test was supposed to provide a clear definition of 'deprivation of liberty', replacing the mess of case law preceding it and the heterogeneous tests and thresholds employed by those administering the DoLS. Yet even this supposedly clear test proved surprisingly difficult to apply in practice. Since much still hung on 'cliff edge' questions of liberty for different groups, it continued to be litigated, giving the courts opportunities to include or exclude swathes of issues and populations from the ambit of article 5 ECHR. This litigation would test some of the most paradoxical outcomes and questions posed by the acid test.

'Domestic' deprivation of liberty

In dissolving the imaginary boundary separating the 'institution' from homes and community, the acid test brings the legal machinery of deprivation of liberty regulation into the private domestic sphere. This is perhaps the most socially and politically divisive aspect of *Cheshire West*, exercising the dissenting justices and inspiring Mostyn J's rebellion. MIG's case came closest to an 'ordinary' family home, although even so her foster mother was paid to care for her, the care was arranged by the local authority, and the courts had ordered restrictions on contact with family. How far would the ruling extend to other families, caring for relatives at home?

The case inciting Mostyn J to rebellion, *Rochdale MBC v KW* [2014] EWCOP 45, concerned a woman – 'Katherine' – who lived in her own home with 24-hour support provided by the local authority and CCG following a road traffic accident. She had previously been unlawfully detained in hospital and a care home, for which she had successfully sought damages. As I discussed in Chapter 8, Mostyn J concluded that she was not deprived of her liberty, relying on an originalist reading of article 5 and the legally tenuous argument that in his view J. S. Mill would have found this an 'utterly impossible' idea. Yet he also stressed the domestic context, finding it 'impossible to conceive that the best interests arrangement for

Katherine, <u>in her own home</u>,[3] provided by an independent contractor, but devised and paid for by Rochdale and CCG, amounts to a deprivation of liberty within Article 5' [7].

In a later case, concerning a young woman in supported living accommodation, Mostyn J did conclude that she was deprived of her liberty because – unlike Katherine – she was not cared for in a place that 'she understands to be her home', and because TB had 'motor functions to achieve a departure in a meaningful sense' (*London Borough of Tower Hamlets v TB & Anor* [2014] EWCOP 53, [59]).

Contradicting this reasoning, however, Mostyn J subsequently concluded that a man who was objecting to his placement was not deprived of his liberty, arguing that 'almost all people would share my difficulty' in seeing how people needing 'intensive support and care' could be deprived of their liberty (*Bournemouth Borough Council v BS* [2015] EWCOP 39, [26]). The facts concerned a young man with intellectual disabilities living in a two-bedroom bungalow with 24-hour waking support staff. He had been removed from his family by a care order. He wanted to return to an earlier institutional placement or to live with his mother, and did not consider the placement to be his home. His everyday life was timetabled, staff controlled his movements within the bungalow (although they left him alone in his bedroom if he wished to masturbate). He was closely supervised outside the home to prevent inappropriate sexual activity. Door sensors would detect him attempting to leave, and staff planned to ask police to use s136 MHA powers to remove him to a place of safety if he ever did so. Mostyn J held that BS was not deprived of his liberty since he was (technically) free to leave unless and until apprehended by the police. Perhaps cognisant of contradicting the reasoning in previous cases, Mostyn J described himself as applying ' "I know it when I see it" legal technique' to the acid test [29]. His approach echoes Lord Clarke's dissenting judgment that deprivation of liberty was 'essentially a jury question' for the trial judge, a 'question of fact and degree' not amenable to precise definition (*Cheshire West*, UKSC, [106]).

Mostyn J's aim in *Rochdale*, and perhaps in these later cases, was to trigger a 'leapfrog' appeal to the Supreme Court, where they could 'reconsider' the acid test (*Rochdale Metropolitan Borough Council v KW & Ors*, [27]). His efforts were rebuffed by the parties and the Court of Appeal, which directed the case be retried by a different judge (*KW & Ors v Rochdale Metropolitan Borough Council* [2015] EWCA Civ 1054).

Litigation tested how far privately arranged care was 'imputable to the state' in the sense required by article 5 ECHR (*Storck v Germany*). The

---

[3]   Underscore emphasis in judgment.

Court of Protection confirmed even if a person's parents consented to the care arrangements as court-appointed deputies, any deprivation of liberty was still imputable to the state (*Re R* [2016] EWCOP 33). In a subsequent case where a professional deputy had secured private care arrangements in a specially adapted private home, purchased via a damages award, the Secretary of State for Justice intervened to argue that this was not 'imputable to the state' and therefore did not engage article 5 ECHR (*Staffordshire CC v SRK & Ors* [2016] EWCOP 27). With 'real reluctance' Mr Justice Charles held that article 5 was engaged wherever the state 'knows or ought to know' that a person is deprived of their liberty. Here, the state was involved because the courts had awarded the damages and appointed the deputy. Although in this case it was not obvious what value an 'independent check' would achieve, in other cases a deputy might act differently. The Secretary of State appealed, arguing that a private domestic deprivation of liberty was not imputable to the state unless there was some reason to suspect abuse. The Court of Appeal rejected this argument, observing that public bodies would only intervene in cases of suspected abuse if someone drew their attention to the matter (*SSJ v Staffordshire CC & Ors* [2016] EWCA Civ 1317). Absent the periodic assessment guaranteed by a Court of Protection welfare order, 'there are insufficient procedural safeguards against arbitrary detention in a purely private care regime' [76].

Following *Cheshire West*, local authorities began to ask the Court of Protection to authorize 'deprivation of liberty' by family carers in private homes. The first case – heard by Bodey J shortly before the appeals in *Rochdale* – concerned Mrs L, a 93-year-old woman with Alzheimer's who lived in her home of 39 years. Her care was arranged by her daughters and the local authority (*W City Council v Mrs L* [2015] EWCOP 20. The local authority argued she was deprived of her liberty, but her daughter (acting as L's litigation friend) argued she was not. Mrs L lived alone with three visits a day from a specialist dementia home care service provided by the local authority. She could open the front door to access her garden, which she frequently did by day, but at night a sensor system would alert her daughters or the emergency services if she left the building. Following an incident when she had left the house unsuitably dressed and been brought back by the police, gates and a fence were fitted to the property which Mrs L could not open by herself. The local authority argued that she was not free to leave and that 'in effect' was subject to complete supervision and control by the arrangements [14]. Her daughter contended that she was not deprived of her liberty, being 'happy and contented' where she was, 'oriented within the property', with 'a strong sense of belonging in her current home' and a 'fierce sense of independence' [7]. She 'positively and actively wants to live' at home [18]. This was not a 'placement' and she was not 'obliged' to live there; she was 'an old lady who wishes to remain in her own home' [19].

In response, the local authority argued that Mrs L's happiness was 'irrelevant' and the fact this was her own home 'a red herring'; these confused deprivation of liberty with her 'best interests' and embarked on 'a dangerous path' [15]. The arrangements were fundamentally 'imputable' to the local authority, working closely with the family, and the court should be slow to say otherwise lest Mrs L 'lose the important protection of Article 5' [16]. Bodey J agreed the case was finely balanced. Without providing detailed reasoning, he concluded that her contentment and clear expression of her wishes and feelings and choice of what she does within the property 'must be relevant' [24]. He distinguished her situation from 'one involving institutional accommodation ... where that person, or someone on his or her behalf, is challenging the need for such confinement' [25]. This was not a deprivation of liberty and the 'mischief of state interference at which Article 5 was and is directed' did not sufficiently exist in such circumstances [27].

In *SCCG v MSA & Anor* [2017] EWCOP 18, the Court of Protection publicly affirmed for the first time that deprivation of liberty could occur in wholly private care arrangements in the family home. The judgment considered whether a man's mother could act as a lay representative for him in proceedings to authorize deprivation of liberty, given her role in the arrangements. The man concerned was 'unable to communicate or mobilise independently', was 'frequently strapped into his wheelchair', and he was kept for some of his time 'in a padded room at his home with a closed door that he cannot open'. His mother used physical restraint to administer personal care, to which he was resistant. There were no 'external carers' in the family home [13]. This was considered to be a 'particularly high degree' of restrictions on his physical liberty [16].

In *Re AEL* [2021] EWCOP 9, a parent carer 'vigorously' objected to the idea he was depriving his 31-year-old daughter of her liberty [11], describing this as 'palpably nonsense', and the proceedings as 'a complete waste of everyone's time' and public money [21]. He refused to participate in the proceedings until this matter was resolved. AEL had 'significant learning disabilities' and physical and sensory disabilities. She lived with her parents, receiving 24-hour support from them and two private carers employed using direct payments. She was supervised at all times because of concerns about road safety, her inability to 'alert others to her needs' and 'manage her own nourishment or hygiene', but she was not restrained or sedated [28]. AEL's father asserted that she was 'not the subject of "continuous control"' as his daughter's care was founded on 'the principle' that 'AEL decides what she wants to do and when she wants to do it excepting if her safety could be compromised' [21]. As an example, he described taking AEL out at night to an all-night McDonalds or café because she was unable to sleep and wished to go out [22]. He asserted that where her care plan was 'more restrictive than it should be' this reflected limited financial support [25]. The case took place against a backdrop of longstanding disputes between the family and the council. Senior Judge Hilder concluded that AEL was deprived of her liberty, 'rhetorically' inviting her father 'to consider how he would categorise AEL's living arrangements and "the principle" if they were applied to him', strongly suspecting that 'he, and ordinary members of the public, would consider such arrangements to deprive them of their liberty' [49].

The cases of L and AEL reveal how divisive the 'deprivation of liberty' jurisdiction can be when applied to care provided or arranged by families within private homes. We should carefully consider the utility of deprivation of liberty safeguards in this context, where the ordinary 'institutional' interfaces and levers that the law of institutions engages with are absent. We should take seriously the possibility that in situations where there are already tensions between local authority social services and a family, labelling – and regulating – care as a deprivation of liberty could make relations worse. Liberty safeguards are not the only way to investigate whether a person being cared for by their family is happy with the arrangements, nor to intervene if they are not. If there are substantive concerns about a person's care, the LPS confer no power upon responsible bodies to require families to change the way they provide care, although families may not be aware of this. Where there are concerns about restrictive practices or the person being unhappy with their living arrangements, the answer remains – as it was before – to explore this by offering the person or their family assessments, support and services under community care legislation (including the option for the person concerned to live elsewhere if they wish to), to investigate concerns via safeguarding procedures, and if there are still serious concerns or disputes to remit the matter to the Court of Protection to address. It is not obvious what regulating this as a 'deprivation of liberty' adds, since public bodies already have tools at their disposal to address concerns about family care.

The new LPS scheme can authorize 'domestic deprivation of liberty' and will potentially affect significant numbers of people being cared for by families. The JCHR (2018b) opened an inquiry into the 'The Right to Freedom and Safety' and the future of the DoLS. Among those giving oral evidence was Mark Neary, father of Steven Neary, and Graham Enderby, HL's carer.[4] Steven was now living in his own flat, supported by a team of personal assistants employed by his father using direct payments. Mark Neary told the Committee that following *Cheshire West*, the local authority who almost a decade earlier had unlawfully detained his son in a 'positive behaviour unit' were now asserting that Steven was deprived of his liberty in his own home. Steven was, he stressed, 'very much king of his castle in

---

[4] Full disclosure: I also gave evidence in this session. I had a wonderful chat with Mark Neary and 'Mr E' in the Westminster café beforehand.

his own place' [38]. He required 24-hour support, and the carers would accompany him when he goes out. Mark Neary stated, 'I find it very difficult to square that one', contrasting Steven going about his everyday life with his support workers with being kept away from his own home, secluded, medicated and sometimes physically restrained: 'None of that exists now in his own home, but we have come down such a crazy road in the last eight years that we cannot tell the difference between deprivation of liberty in an institutionalised unit and in someone's own home' [38].

In his blog, Mark Neary (2018) described how assessments of Steven's capacity triggered by the deprivation of liberty authorization process caused him distress. Giving evidence in the same JCHR session, Graham Enderby concurred: '[w]e have gone so overboard after this judgment, it is ridiculous' [39]. The JCHR noted other cases where families and carers objected to care arrangements being described as a deprivation of liberty, and called upon Parliament to legislate for a new, article 5 compliant, statutory definition of deprivation of liberty, which – as we saw in Chapter 8 – it did not do.

Children

The DoLS scheme only applied to people aged over 18. MEG, being 17, was outside its scope. After *Cheshire West*, questions of liberty were put to the court concerning children and young people in hospitals or local authority accommodation. Sometimes public bodies sought judicial authorization of a putative deprivation of liberty; other times the issue was raised by the Official Solicitor (OS). What 'objective' test of deprivation of liberty would the courts apply for children and young people?

Recognizing that '[a]ll children are (or should be) subject to some level of restraint' [78], Lord Kerr had proposed a test comparing the extent of a child's freedom with 'a person of similar age and full capacity' (*Cheshire West*, UKSC [77]). However, treading carefully around the sensitive terrain of domestic deprivation of liberty, Lord Neuberger suggested that what might otherwise be a deprivation of liberty of children living at home would not normally engage article 5 because it was not imposed by the state but via an exercise of 'parental authority' (*Cheshire West*, UKSC, [72], citing *Neilsen v Denmark* (1988) 11 EHRR 175). But how did one go about comparing the life of a child in state care with another child? And could someone with parental responsibility also consent to a deprivation of liberty there?

Applying the acid test to the circumstances of a 15-year-old in a psychiatric hospital in *Re D (A Child: deprivation of liberty)* [2015] EWHC 922 (Fam), Mr Justice Keehan concluded that the 'objective' element of deprivation of liberty was satisfied, but as his parents consented the 'subjective' element of deprivation of liberty was not met – a matter I pick up below. A ten-year-old child in a specialist children's home was found to be deprived of his liberty

(*Re Daniel X* [2016] EWFC B31), as was a 17-year-old with complex health needs living with his parents and subject to higher levels of supervision and control at home and in education than a child of a similar age (*A London Borough v X (Wardship: Parental Responsibility; Deprivation of Liberty)* [2019] EWHC B16 (Fam)). In *Re A-F (Children)* [2018] EWHC 138 (Fam), the President of the Family Division and the Court of Protection, Lord Justice Munby, adopted a rough 'rule of thumb' that a child aged under ten was unlikely to be objectively deprived of their liberty 'even if under pretty constant supervision', whereas a child aged 11 might be but 'the court should be astute to avoid coming too readily to such a conclusion'; once over 12, 'the court will more readily come to that conclusion' [43].

In other cases, judges were more reluctant to conclude that young people were deprived of their liberty. In *Re RD (Deprivation or Restriction of Liberty)* [2018] EWFC 47, Mr Justice Cobb held that a 14-year-old girl was not deprived of her liberty in a rural children's home, describing its regime as 'boundaried, yet supportive' and distinguishing between 1:1 'supervision' and 1:1 support and 'attention' which RD was said to 'crave' [38]. In *Hertfordshire CC v K (Deprivation of Liberty)* [2020] EWHC 139 (Fam), Mr Justice Macdonald held that a 16-year-old was not deprived of his liberty despite being subject to 2:1 supervision and checks every 15 minutes, since he was 'not satisfied that the level of supervision and control' differed sufficiently 'from a child of AK's age and station' to satisfy the adapted acid test [33].

The limits of 'parental authority' to consent to a deprivation of liberty in formal care arrangements were considered by the courts. In *Re D (A Child: deprivation of liberty)*, Keehan J characterized any suggestion that D's parents could not consent to his detention in a psychiatric hospital as 'wholly disproportionate', flying 'in the face of common sense' [64] and as state interference in D's life and that of his family [63]. In a subsequent judgment, however, he held that this parental authority did not survive a child's 16th birthday, and after this point formal authorization for deprivation of liberty would be required. The local authority appealed against this and in *D (A Child)* [2017] EWCA Civ 1695, Munby P held that there was no 'bright-line' distinction between under and over 16s in the scope for parental consent to a deprivation of liberty. The issue was whether the child was *Gillick* competent; if they were not, then the parents could consent to the deprivation of liberty. In his judgment in *D (A Child)*, Munby P also took the opportunity to assert that the 'freedom to leave' element of the acid test should be interpreted along the lines he had proposed in *JE v DE*, as about removing oneself 'permanently in order to live where and with whom' one chooses [22].

D's case aroused considerable interest and concern. By extending parental authority to consent to deprivation of liberty, the family courts closed the floodgates against deprivation of liberty applications currently threatening its sister Court of Protection. The rulings reflected judicial disquiet about the potential for this new and rapidly expanding deprivation of liberty jurisdiction to 'interfere' with family life. However, numerous sources expressed concern about *Re D*, comparing it to Munby P's 'comparator' (39 Essex Chambers, 2015). Parker (2016) argued it 'renders disabled children's rights in this area almost non-existent', while the Children's Commissioner (2019), the JCHR (2019) and the independent review of the MHA (Wessely et al, 2018b: 170) expressed concern about the lack of safeguards for children 'informally' admitted to hospital with parental consent. Ruck Keene and Xu (2020) characterized the fundamental issues at stake as how to balance the child's right to liberty with the 'rights of parents' under article 8 ECHR and the common law.

The OS, acting on behalf of D, appealed to the Supreme Court, and the EHRC once again intervened. Lady Hale, once again, gave the leading judgment in *Re D (A Child)* [2019] UKSC 42, with whom Lady Black and Lady Arden agreed. Lord Carnwath (with whom Lord Lloyd-Jones agreed) once again dissented. Echoing her earlier judgment in *Cheshire West*, Lady Hale observed that 'quite clearly' the degree of supervision and control that D was subject to in both placements 'was not normal for a child of 16 or 17 years old', and would have amounted to a deprivation of liberty for any child not lacking capacity, so 'the question' then was 'what difference, if any, does D's mental disability make?' [39]. Reiterating the principles of universality and non-discrimination that animated *Cheshire West*, Lady Hale held it would be a 'startling proposition' that parents could 'license the state to violate the most fundamental human rights of a child' [48]. The Supreme Court therefore held, by a split majority, that it was not within the scope of parental responsibility to consent to a placement depriving their child of their liberty, despite having their best interests at heart. Echoing the policy rationale in *Cheshire West* and *Bournewood*; article 5 requires safeguards because without them 'there is no way of ensuring that those with parental responsibility exercise it in the best interests of the child' [49].

Re D may have significant implications for local authorities with responsibilities toward 'looked after children' and young people in need of care and support. Prior to the ruling the courts received roughly 200 applications a year to authorize deprivation of liberty of young people (Children's Commissioner, 2019: 33–4), but the Law Commission estimated this could increase to several thousand following the ruling.[5] Anticipating this potential outcome in *Re D*, the LPS scheme applies to 16- and 17-year-olds (MCA Schedule AA1 s2(2)(a); Law Commission, 2017b). For younger children, a more onerous court application will still be required, under s25

---

[5]   The Law Commission kindly provided a memo of their estimated working under the Freedom of Information Act 2000 (received 10 May 2019).

Children Act 1989 for 'secure accommodation' or under the High Court's inherent jurisdiction.

The Supreme Court did not explicitly consider whether care provided directly by families could engage article 5 ECHR, although Lady Hale did stress that the state has positive obligations to protect against deprivation of liberty by 'private persons' [47]. Ruck Keene and Xu (2020: 8) conclude that '[p]ublic authorities will also need to be alert to situations where "private" confinements may be under way in relation to 16/17-year olds in their own homes'.

Medical treatment

The *Cheshire West* decision considered when 'living arrangements' in community settings amounted to a deprivation of liberty (*Cheshire West*, UKSC, [1]). The Supreme Court did not consider medical treatment in hospital, however the acid test had potentially significant implications here. Did it, for example, apply to patients in Intensive Care Units (ICU) (Crews et al, 2014: 322). Dykes and Wheeler (2015: 80) questioned what 'moral risk' the safeguards addressed in medical treatment, concerned that clinicians could become 'desensitised and disillusioned' by 'irrelevant' complex bureaucracy. Baharlo, Bryden and Brett (2018) worried DoLS could harm relationships between clinicians and the patient's family. However, Ashby, Griffin and Agrawal (2015: 361) argued *Cheshire West* reflected a general shift away from medical paternalism, posing questions 'that were probably never asked before' about the 'immense power' exercised over some patients, ensuring that 'independent checks' existed and means of challenging it.

In the immediate aftermath of *Cheshire West* some people in minimally conscious states were considered deprived of their liberty, authorized under the DoLS. This entitled patients and their relatives (as RPRs) to access independent advocacy and non-means tested legal aid to challenge authorizations under s21A MCA. Families used these entitlements to bring to court disputes over the medical treatment, arguing their relatives would not wish to be kept alive in these circumstances. The courts were initially willing to stretch the purpose of s21A reviews of DoLS authorizations to include disputes over medical treatment itself (for example, *Briggs v Briggs* [2016] EWCOP 48). Cowley (2017), an IMCA, describes the DoLS in these cases as 'giving voice to people with minimal consciousness'. Unfortunately for families, this strategy for funding costly medical treatment disputes was shut down when the Court of Appeal distinguished 'deprivation of liberty' appeals from underlying disputes over medical treatments (*Director of Legal Aid Casework & Ors v Briggs* [2017] EWCA Civ 1169).

Another strand in the bundle of rights conferred by article 5 is an inquest into the death of a person in 'state detention' (Coroners and Justice Act

2009 s 4(2)(b)). Following *Cheshire West*, coroners' courts were inundated with thousands of requests for inquests into 'deaths in state detention' (Ministry of Justice and Office for National Statistics, 2017). The vast majority concerned deaths by natural causes,[6] often of older people who had died in care homes. However, some families of people with developmental disabilities who had died preventable deaths in hospitals, care homes and supported living had successfully relied upon *Cheshire West* to secure jury inquests.[7]

In *R (Ferreira) v HM Senior Coroner for Inner South London* [2017] EWCA Civ 31, the sister of a woman with Down Syndrome who had died in an ICU argued that she had died in state detention and therefore was entitled to a jury inquest. Maria Ferreira was sedated and intubated due to breathing difficulties yet had managed to pull her tube out. The Court of Appeal examined how the acid test applied in an acute medical treatment context. Lady Justice Arden concluded she was not deprived of her liberty because:

> she was being treated for a physical illness and her treatment was that which it appeared to all intents would have been administered to a person who did not have her mental impairment. She was physically restricted in her movements by her physical infirmities and by the treatment she received (which for example included sedation) but the root cause of any loss of liberty was her physical condition, not any restrictions imposed by the hospital. [10]

Arden LJ also held that in general, life-saving medical treatment would not give rise to a deprivation of liberty.

The policy underlying the decision was welcomed, perhaps unsurprisingly, by intensivists and clinicians (Stevenson, 2017; Baharlo et al, 2018), although they queried how straightforward it would be to apply in practice. The JCHR (2018b: [42]) described it as 'backtracking' from the acid test and potentially discriminatory because it attributed loss of liberty to a person's physical condition. Nevertheless, *Ferreira* was tacitly endorsed by the Supreme Court in *Re D (A Child)*, when Lady Arden (now elevated to the Supreme Court) reiterated this distinction [120]. Meanwhile, the government amended the statutory definition of 'state detention' for coronial inquests, removing from scope anyone deprived of their liberty under the MCA (s178 Policing and Crime Act 2017).

Subsequently, some families embroiled in disputes over medical treatment of very ill young children argued that medical interventions

---

[6] Freedom of information response from the Ministry of Justice, January 2019.

[7] For example, the inquests into the deaths of Connor Sparrowhawk and Nico Reed.

and court orders preventing them from seeking alternative treatments in other hospitals deprived their children of their liberty. In *Gard and Others v UK* [2017] ECHR 605, the ECtHR declined to address whether article 5 was engaged by the high-profile case of Charlie Gard, a very ill baby whose family was prevented from seeking an experimental treatment by a court ruling that this was not in his best interests. Subsequently, the parents of Alfie Evans – a toddler being treated in Alder Hey hospital in Liverpool – sought a writ of habeas corpus for what they characterized as Alfie's unlawful detention, preventing his parents from taking him to Italy for treatment there. The Court of Appeal considered this application 'misconceived' and, relying on *Ferreira*, concluded that Evans was not deprived of his liberty (*Evans & Anor v Alder Hey Children's NHS Foundation Trust & Ors* [2018] EWCA Civ 805, [56]). The argument was put forward once again by the family of Tafida Raqeeb, who also sought treatment in Italy. Citing *Evans*, the court rejected this argument (*Barts NHS Foundation Trust v Raqeeb & Ors* [2019] EWHC 2530 (Fam). The hospital later characterized deprivation of liberty arguments as an 'attack' on the Trust and its doctors; the court considered them 'always bound to fail' (*Raqeeb v Barts Health NHS Trust (Costs)* [2019] EWHC 3320 (Admin) [15], [47]).

For families embroiled in disputes with healthcare professionals, 'deprivation of liberty' may hold intuitive rhetorical appeal, evoking the sense of 'deprivation of family life' discussed in Chapter 8. As in *Bournewood* and other early DoLS cases, deprivation of liberty is invoked by families challenging professional power. However, the domestic courts have conclusively put to bed deprivation of liberty tactics in relation to medical treatment disputes, reaffirming connections between the *Cheshire West* acid test and regulation of 'living arrangements' rather than medical interventions themselves.

★★★

The practical consequences of *Cheshire West* have been undeniably challenging. Lady Hale's explicit policy rationale was to insert an 'independent check' on 'living arrangements' for 'vulnerable' people receiving care. I consider the nature of this 'vulnerability' in the next chapter. However, the judgment collapsed systems responsible for securing these checks. The LPS are intended to alleviate the administrative burdens imposed by the DoLS but do so by further diluting the safeguards. There is a high risk of 'regulatory paradox' in this scenario, when 'safeguards' can authorize and legitimate restrictive and coercive practices yet offer limited independent scrutiny and weak rights of challenge. *Cheshire West* overstretched legalism until the DoLS' rigid elastic snapped. The LPS are made of such weak elastic they cover rather than contain, and at critical moments may leave people exposed.

Hitching safeguards to an unstable definition of 'deprivation of liberty' means we are still unclear about what these are safeguards against. The courts and government increasingly cleave toward a macro interpretation of deprivation of liberty, meaning significant constraints and interferences in people's lives may slip through the net. For example, during the pandemic, care home residents were required to spend 14 days isolating in their bedrooms after any outings or hospital visits. Government lawyers told their families they were not deprived of their liberty by this 'enforced isolation' because they were always, in theory, free to leave – they just cannot 'come back unless they are prepared to quarantine for 14 days' (John's Campaign, 2021: 38). The government also advised care providers that 'freedom to leave' should be interpreted in line with Munby P's *obiter* remark in *Re D* that freedom to leave means 'not free to leave the accommodation permanently' (Department of Health and Social Care, 2020b) limiting the application of the deprivation of liberty jurisdiction to the social isolation imposed on care home residents. It seems likely the new MCA Code of Practice will be based on this 'macro' interpretation of deprivation of liberty. Taken together with the bright-line distinction between the 'arrangements' and underlying care and treatment decisions, it is unclear what benefits the LPS will bring to anybody who is in dispute over restrictive rules, regimes and interventions rather than where they live.

Litigation following *Cheshire West* has confirmed that the acid test applies in wholly private domestic care arrangements, including care provided by families themselves. Some authorities have begun seeking judicial authorization for this, and many more families may be affected when the LPS come into force enabling local authorities to 'authorize' deprivation of liberty administratively. It is not hard to imagine this having toxic consequences for relations between individual families and local authority social services, and doing considerable reputational damage to the safeguards and human rights law more generally as families' stories increasingly reach the public domain.

Some of these living arrangements are undeniably very restrictive – for example, family carers using seclusion and physical restraint. In others, by families' own accounts at least, the living arrangements map closely onto the person's expressed wishes and preferences. We might certainly want to be reassured by an 'independent check' that these accounts are accurate; that a person really is happy with their living arrangements and not coerced in any way. However, if these descriptions are accurate, then surely this is precisely the goal any system of safeguards should be seeking: living arrangements reflecting how a person wishes to live their life, affording them an expansive decision space and a subjective experience of home, with the support and safety measures they need to achieve this.

By defining someone who is positively happy with their support and living arrangements as 'deprived of their liberty' simply because they cannot satisfy legal tests of 'mental capacity', we risk losing sight of positive goals and alienating support for the safeguards themselves. It is striking how rarely, across this morass of extensive (and expensive) litigation, we get any real sense of what the people at the heart of this litigation want, feel and experience. They may now be possessed of an abstract right to liberty, but the law still presents them as non-volitional. Adopting a 'valid consent' model similar to that proposed by the JCHR would both secure an 'independent check' on whether a person is happy with their living arrangements, and de-paradoxify these most troubling outcomes of the acid test.

My argument is not that a person cannot be deprived of their liberty by their families or in 'private' homes. Rather, it is that if a person is positively happy with their living arrangements and free of coercion, then we should not describe this as a deprivation of liberty *wherever* they live. Furthermore family living arrangements are not the kind of problem the law of institutions is designed to solve. It is engineered to interlock with regulatory and other administrative and legal levers to secure compliance, none of which families have. In circumstances where we have cause for concern about family-based care, the ordinary tools of local authority care assessment, care planning and – if necessary – safeguarding and the involvement of the courts are the appropriate response; there is no obvious benefit in regulating this as a question of detention.

Cheshire West and its aftermath demonstrate that when we become mired in technical legal arguments about the meaning of deprivation of liberty, we lose sight of the social problems we are trying to solve. What is needed is deep and careful thought about the kinds of problems we want to address in the contemporary landscape of care and what positive goals we are aiming for. This is a conversation requiring input from those receiving care or support, those providing it, and the 'empowerment entrepreneurs', reformers and abolitionists waging daily battles against carceral practices. These matters are too important to cede to arenas where only specialist lawyers can join in, displacing the critical issues and losing essential voices.

10

'Protecting the Vulnerable'

The critical question posed by *Cheshire West* and its aftermath is *why* are we invoking this classical carceral-era legal machinery at the height of the post-carceral era, and in places far beyond the reaches of the 'institution'? What 'problem-space' (Scott, 2004) shaped the litigation strategies that led to DoLS and its later expansion? Why were problems framed in terms of 'deprivation of liberty', and not some other form, inviting an alternative regulatory response? Why, indeed, turn to law at all?

Vulnerability and domination

Lady Hale spelled out the underlying policy rationale for her judgment in *Cheshire West* in the first paragraph: if 'a mentally incapacitated person' was found to be deprived of their liberty then it must be authorized by a court or the DoLS; if they were not, then 'no independent check is made on whether those arrangements are in the best interests of the mentally incapacitated person' (*Cheshire West*, UKSC, [1], see also [33]). This was 'no criticism' of the social care bodies arranging the placements, who 'do so in the hope and belief that they are the best which can practicably be devised' [1]. But '[b]ecause of the extreme vulnerability of people like P, MIG and MEG ... we should err on the side of caution in deciding what constitutes a deprivation of liberty' [57]. Even the dissenting justices in *Cheshire West*, and the judgment's critics, such as Allen (2015), concurred that MIG, MEG and P were 'vulnerable' and in need of 'a policy of periodic supervision of arrangements made under' the MCA (*Cheshire West*, UKSC, [89]); they merely doubted whether deprivation of liberty safeguards were the most appropriate vehicle for achieving this.

Vulnerability is a potent discourse in contemporary health and social care policy and the (in)capacity jurisdiction, grounding many protective interventions responding to concerns about abuse, exploitation, self-neglect, or everyday risks and hazards that the person may not understand.

Yet *Cheshire West* was not about whether MIG, MEG and P required 'protective' arrangements, but whether such arrangements required a periodic 'independent check'. The implication is that protective interventions themselves create vulnerability, in addition to the vulnerability invoked to justify them. During the public seminar discussed in Chapter 8, the OS, Alastair Pitblado, put it like this: 'Quite often people need protection, but not by the state assuming control without any regulation of that control' (One Crown Office Row, 2012). The motivation behind his litigation strategy and Lady Hale's judgment was reformist, not abolitionist; to invoke the law of institutions to regulate the welfare–incapacity complex.

In *Bournewood*, HL was characterized by Lord Steyn and the ECtHR as 'vulnerable' and needing protection against 'misjudgments and professional lapses', the 'wide discretionary power' of professionals notwithstanding that they will 'almost invariably act in what they consider to be the best interests of the patient' and in 'good faith' (*HL v UK*, [49], [113], [131]). However well-meaning caregivers are, when they impose protection measures they might get it wrong and cause other harms, and the person on the receiving end is not in a position to protect themselves from this. Procedural safeguards, periodic independent checks, are required to protect people against the vulnerability that protective measures themselves create.

Concern about human vulnerability to the interferences of others infuses the right to liberty and the wider human rights canon. The architecture of Article 5 is designed as safeguards against arbitrary detention (*Lawless v Ireland (No 3)* (App 332/57) [1961] ECHR 2, [14]). The aim is not to prevent detention altogether, but to ensure that it tracks clearly established norms. Mental health and social care detention do so through 'fixed procedural rules' at admission (*HL v UK*, [120]), reviews of whether detention criteria continue to be met at 'reasonable intervals' (*Winterwerp v UK*, [55]), and rights to information (article 5(2)) and appeal (article 5(4)). This is closely tied to the ideals of the rule of law, as protection against arbitrary, capricious or simply misguided decision making by those in positions of power. Where discretion is unavoidable – as is almost always the case in the domain of care – it must be subject to external rules and standards, and some means of challenge (Bingham, 2010).

This understanding of liberty is associated with civic republicanism (Pettit, 1997a; Lovett, 2010). Republican liberty differs from the negative liberty doctrine of J. S. Mill, invoked by *Cheshire West*'s critics. It is not about freedom from actual interferences or external constraints, but rather freedom from the ability of others to arbitrarily interfere or impose constraints. Republican liberty is structural and conditional, sensitive not only to what *is* happening but what *could* happen without appropriate checks and balances over power. To a republican, it is no argument that a person in a position of power acts in good faith, in a person's best interests, or with love and devotion or skill and expertise; the question is what checks and balances there are on their power. To put this in terms familiar to vulnerability theorists, republican liberty is concerned with the *resilience* of non-interference.

More recent formulations of republican liberty describe it as 'the absence of alien or alienating control' by other persons, and in particular 'control over choice', regardless of whether there are *actual* interferences (Pettit, 2008: 102–3): 'Alien control without interference materializes when the controller or associates invigilate the choices of the controlled agent, being ready to interfere should the controlled agent not conform to a desired pattern or should the controller have a change of mind.' The *Cheshire West* acid test is a useful red flag that a person's choices are 'invigilated' to such an extent – through 'continuous supervision and control' – that we should be alert to a potentially significant loss of republican liberty.

Civic republicans view the rule of law as an important means to constrain arbitrary power. However, republicanism is also concerned with domination within the private sphere – which the rule of law may not (traditionally) penetrate (Pettit, 1997b; Lovett, 2010). Civic republicans emphasize the role of the state in securing resilient protection of liberty, 'carving out the areas' where people enjoy 'personal sovereignty' and securing 'basic liberties' such as healthcare, education and social security (Pettit, 2015: 1059). This echoes capabilities accounts of freedom, however Sen (2010: 306) distinguishes 'pure' capabilities approaches from republican approaches by contrasting the situation of a disabled person who depends on the goodwill of volunteers to get out of her house with someone who has 'well-remunerated servants' who obey her 'commands'; both have the 'capability' to go out, but only the second has 'republican liberty' to do so. Republican liberty resonates with the disability rights ideal of 'independent living' and 'personal assistance' as opposed to 'care'.

Civic republicans have a name for vulnerability arising from exposure to the arbitrary power of others: domination. This term (much like 'deprivation of liberty') is unlikely to find much favour in the context of care. 'Vulnerability', in contrast, is usefully ambiguous; it appears to be a quality of the care recipient and not a description of power relations with caregivers or others. However, republican perspectives can usefully analyse the legal and institutional power encountered by people with mental disabilities (O'Shea, 2018b). The welfare–incapacity jurisdiction presents considerable risks of domination, owing to its highly discretionary character with limited external checks and balances (Series, 2013; Arstein-Kerslake and Flynn, 2017; O'Shea, 2018a).

O'Shea (2018b) and Lazar (2021: 1) call attention to the potential for 'micro-domination', in which 'a series of dominated choices are individually inconsequential for a person's freedom but collectively consequential'.

O'Shea provides examples from psychiatric and residential care, of being at the 'whim' of staff moods or attitudes over mundane and routine matters; matters which were important to patients yet individually were 'too minor to be contested in a court or a tribunal' (p136). However, Lazar (2019: 682) rejects purely procedural accounts of domination, arguing that 'highly rule-bound, tightly controlled areas of life', such as total institutions, may have 'elaborate rulebooks' constraining behaviour, but 'can produce the same bundle of psychological effects' – anxiety and fear – connected with domination. The difficulty is what one does about this micro-domination. It presents a threshold problem for republican strategies of 'creating arenas for contestation' relied upon by the rule of law (Lazar, 2021: 1). O'Shea argues that republicans should attend to 'sub-legal power', and 'turn away from proceduralist accounts that privilege the rule of law', calling for 'a participatory republican politics of self-emancipation' (p145).

Social care as a landscape of domination

What problems of 'domination' might we be concerned about in the contemporary landscape of social care? Employing the distinction made throughout this book, it is helpful to distinguish 'macro'-questions of *where* a person lives from 'micro'-questions of the constraints, limited choices or interferences they might experience within their living arrangements.

Neary and *Bournewood* are paradigmatic examples of 'macro-domination', as are removals from home or family based on poorly investigated safeguarding concerns and unfair procedures. Macro-domination does not, however, require that a person has 'somewhere else to go'; republican liberty may also be imperilled by dependence on the goodwill of others to secure 'basic liberties'. 'Micro-domination' within a setting is not less important than macro-domination, and can occur in tandem with it (as, for example, the constraints Steven Neary and HL lived under during their detentions). A person's 'liberty' in a republican sense may be imperilled by potential physical or chemical interventions, rules and regulations, and the 'invigilation of choices' by others that permeates their living arrangements. Although individually these may be too minor to contest in court (even assuming a person could initiate litigation), cumulatively these can erode the sense of 'home of territory', constraining the decision space, and producing the harms associated with institutionalization.

Both macro- and micro-domination have a complex aetiology. Not all the reasons can be connected with 'incapacity' or regulated via social care detention, but are linked to the wider context of social care.

This landscape is a source of growing national anxiety (Bunting, 2020). Even before the COVID-19 pandemic, following decades of privatization and underfunding, exacerbated by the 2008 financial crash, social care was widely said to be 'in crisis'.[1] Indicators include fewer older people getting support from local authority social services and a real-terms fall in public spending on social care despite a growing population in need of services and increases in the cost of care (Bottery et al, 2019). Restricted eligibility and funding for social care have impaired independent living for disabled people (Joint Committee on Human Rights, 2012). Privatization worsened working conditions for front line care workers (Hayes, 2017), leading to recruitment problems and high staff turnover (Skills for Care, 2020). Yet some private equity-backed providers continued to generate substantial profits (Centre for Health and the Public Interest, 2016). The CQC (2017c, 2018, 2019d) highlights people's difficulties accessing services, deteriorating standards in mental health and learning disability services, and 'fragile' social care markets with some providers close to collapse. Finding a 'solution' to the funding and structural provision of social care has been a recurring policy concern for decades, with successive governments commissioning reports then ignoring their recommendations (The King's Fund, 2019).

The COVID-19 crisis added considerable stresses to this system, lending weight to calls for radical solutions. Socialist politicians and former Conservative ministers alike call for the re-nationalization of social care (Altmann, 2020; McDonnell, 2020). Others call for the merger of the NHS and local authority social care or the creation of a centralized 'National Care Service'. As the pandemic ravages care home populations, some call for a move away from congregate models of care altogether. Another government commissions another report on what to do.

This economic context matters because – as I argued in Chapters 4 and 6 – it produces tendencies toward more 'institutional' models of care. It is cheaper for those purchasing care, and more profitable for those providing it, to do so using congregate models of care that facilitate economies of scale. This, in turn, creates a context ripe for 'macro-domination' since it does not deliver the kinds of support needed to enable people to enjoy the 'basic liberty' of remaining in one's own home or being supported to live in 'ordinary homes, on ordinary streets'. Economies of scale also reduce individual choice and control over *who* supports a person and how, rendering service users reliant on adequate funding and institutional goodwill to send them preferred carers and to be supported in their preferred ways according to their own daily rhythms and activities.

---

[1]   A Google search in August 2020 turns up descriptions of care 'in crisis' by Age UK, the Multiple Sclerosis Society, the Voluntary Organisations Disability Group, the Care and Support Alliance (representing 80 charities), Unison and the Trades Union Congress. See also Bunting (2020).

Social care detention safeguards cannot fix these problems. It cannot penetrate what Clements (2020) calls 'clustered injustice', situations where people experience 'multiple and synchronous legal problems', including the allocation of (scarce) community care resources. 'Safeguards' on liberty will not re-fund or re-nationalize care provision, reshape the care market, nor determine whose and which care needs are met. Neither the DoLS, nor the LPS, nor even the Court of Protection, can require local authority social services to fund or provide particular care services. The MCA requires decision makers to choose among the *actually existing options*, however limited or unpalatable these are (*N v ACCG and others* [2017] UKSC 22, [1]). This has resulted in cases where the courts have been obliged to describe care arrangements as being in a person's 'best interests' where professionals advise they do not provide dignity and comfort and they may even cause physical or emotional harm (for example, *North Yorkshire CC v MAG & Anor* [2016] EWCOP 5).

This limits the courts' ability to rectify macro-domination. For example, the Court of Protection ruled that Milton Keynes Council had violated RR's human rights by removing her from her home and placing her in a care home following ill-founded safeguarding allegations against her son. However, the court was unable to order her return home because the council refused to restore her direct payments and only offered to fund a care home placement (*Milton Keynes Council v RR & Ors* [2014] EWCOP B19; *RR (Costs Judgement)* [2014] EWCOP 34). RR was exposed to the arbitrary power of local authority social services to decide what support it will fund; she had no enforceable right to be supported to live in her own home (EHRC, 2021). Her only legal recourse against the funding decision was judicial review, a route that is rarely effective and which she was unlikely to be able to initiate herself (Clements, 2020). The MCA and the DoLS require the courts to stand 'in the person's shoes' and choose between the options available to them; too often these choices are undesirable or unacceptable, and substitute decision makers stand in ragged, pinching, shoes.

There is also growing anxiety about certain kinds of 'micro-domination' within community services. At the most extreme, there are widespread concerns about abuse of 'vulnerable' adults in both health and social care settings. As Allen (2015) commented, *Cheshire West* was decided under the long shadow of the Winterbourne View scandal, although he and others note that the article 5 machinery of the MHA did not prevent it (Green, 2013). There are also growing concerns about neglect and preventable deaths in formal care, particularly of people with intellectual disabilities (Heslop et al, 2014, 2019).

Less extreme, but nevertheless important, are the everyday restrictions and interventions a person might experience within a setting, often referred to as 'restrictive practices'. Many older people with dementia and people with intellectual disabilities or autism living in the community are prescribed antipsychotic medications, which are often harmful and unnecessary, instead of addressing the underlying causes of their distress and 'challenging behaviour' (Banerjee, 2009; NHS England, 2017). There are longstanding concerns about the use of physical restraint, seclusion and restrictive practices in the care of people with intellectual disabilities, autism and dementia, in both hospital and community settings (Commission for Social Care Inspection, 2007; CQC, 2019b, 2020b; Joint Committee on Human Rights, 2019; Featherstone and Northcott, 2021). The CQC (2020b) and its predecessors have long voiced concerns about 'blanket restrictions' imposed on everyone within a ward or service, although a recent study of care for people with intellectual disabilities found these were more prevalent for people in hospital than community settings. Researchers are more likely than regulators to raise concerns about the kinds of rules and regimes people may experience in community services (discussed in Chapter 6), suggesting they may pass under regulatory radars.

The MCA can only partially penetrate concerns about restrictive practices; it depends on the actually existing options within a particular context. To give an example from my own experience, a person might live in an environment where there are multiple triggers for 'challenging behaviour' – for example, sensory stimuli, other residents they do not like, staff members they have poor relationships with. Or the physical environment might present risks, for example, an insecure garden near a road, or dangerous stairs. In such an environment, a person might regularly be physically restrained, restricted or sedated to manage genuine risks instead of addressing the context. Fox (2018) describes other examples of environmentally triggered 'challenging behaviour'. The MCA can prompt caregivers to look for less restrictive ways to minimize risks – for example, to secure the stairs and the garden not the person. However, where there are significant resource or institutional constraints – for example, if the problem is regular use of agency staff because employment terms or working conditions are poor, or living with other residents that the person does not get on with, or the lighting throughout the building is causing sensory overload – the MCA itself cannot overcome these obstacles. The MCA is, in this sense, also vulnerable to the 'arbitrary power' of those providing the actually existing options and alternatives to restrictions.

Occasionally, the MCA has been used in combination with public law mechanisms to review care arrangements. In *C v A Local Authority* [2011] EWHC 1539 (Admin), a young person with autism was frequently secluded in a padded blue room because he 'refused' to wear clothes. This was a behaviourist intervention intended to teach C 'appropriate' behaviour and ensure his 'dignity'. A court-appointed expert identified that tactile sensitivity meant wearing clothes caused him pain. The court, exercising public law powers of judicial review, directed the local authority to secure alternative care arrangements where C could live alone, and without clothing if he preferred. This outcome is highly unusual but demonstrates that the MCA may need to be coupled to public law mechanisms to address context-driven problems. Even there, the courts are generally reluctant to interfere with resource allocation decisions. The fundamental problems around resourcing and reliance on care markets to deliver the kinds of services needed are political in character and turning to law can only get us so far.

Care-professional legalism

I have identified two broad categories of problem within the landscape of social care that people might turn to law to address – 'macro'-domination concerning *where* a person lives, and 'micro'-domination concerning the constraints and 'invigilation of choices' within their living arrangements. I have already highlighted some jurisdictional limits on the MCA's ability to tackle 'clustered injustice' (Clements, 2020). Nevertheless, for the 'empowerment entrepreneurs' and 'street level human rights lawyers' championing the MCA and the DoLS (Chapter 2), social care detention still contains useful tools that can potentially reduce macro- and micro-domination, carving out larger decision spaces for a person even within these significant constraints. These tools are connected to the bundle of rights secured by article 5 ECHR (Chapter 5): independent assessments and reviews, advocacy and representation, and rights of challenge.

Lorraine Currie (2016: 184–5), a social worker and leading DoLS professional, describes the DoLS assessments of best interests and mental capacity as safeguards 'against arbitrary decision making' by scrutinizing how residential care admission decisions were made, what options were considered (or not), and how the person's views were taken into account. DoLS assessors 'put the person at the centre of the process' by creating 'a pen picture of a real human being', to listen and take into account the person's wishes, feelings and values. They can challenge 'risk-averse decision making' as 'informed by their trained eye, [the BIA will often] see less restrictive ways of delivering care/ treatment'. They protect against 'discriminatory approaches' and ensure 'that unwise decisions are not confused with incapacitated decisions'. Hubbard and Stone (2020: 10) echo the belief that BIAs 'observe, scrutinise and offer fresh perspectives on a known situation'. The logic – whether delivered in reality or not – is that there is something about the BIA's experience, training and role that enables them to bring a counter-carceral lens, a human rights gaze, to a person's living arrangements, seeing ways that others might have missed to expand decision spaces.

In practice, however, it is rare for assessors to conclude the DoLS criteria are not met. Out of 216,005 'completed' assessments in 2018–19, 99,065 (46 per cent) were not granted. The main reasons for this were that a person's circumstances had changed (for example, they had been discharged or returned home), or they had died (in one third of cases). There were only 7,570 cases where the DoLS criteria were found not to be met, of which 3,890 concerned the mental capacity assessment and only 245 the best interests assessment (NHS Digital, 2019b). So, out of 216,005 'completed' DoLS assessments, 0.1 per cent were refused on 'best interests' grounds, and 1.8 per cent on mental capacity grounds. It is vanishingly rare for a BIA to obstruct a DoLS authorization on substantive grounds. Part of the difficulty may be that BIAs feel they are forced to describe living arrangements as in a person's 'best interests' even where they have significant concerns, because they are the only available option other than destitution (Law Commission, 2017b: [9.25]).

Clements (2020: 58) does not hold back in his critique of a 'tortuously complex' system that incurs 'staggering' economic costs and bureaucracy, yet the initial problem 'of individuals being incarcerated unnecessarily and without adequate protection' still remains. The problem, he argues, is that legal processes to regularize detention approach 'complex "messes"' in overly simplistic terms. Costly legal 'process' rights proliferate, while the real problem is cuts to the substance of social care support.

No doubt Clements is right to suggest DoLS are partly a response to increasingly parched social care provision; precisely the problem they cannot tackle. Yet even if social care were adequately funded, the welfare–incapacity complex would still exercise considerable power over disabled and older people and their families to characterize their 'needs', capacity and best interests, with considerable power to intervene under its rationalities of vulnerability and empowerment. Restrictions on contact with family or the management of sexuality, for example, are not usually linked to insufficient resources. We should also not forget that some of the most restrictive services most associated with abuse – ATUs – are also among the most expensive. Care economics and austerity drive many forms of macro- and micro-domination, but not all.

The DoLS statistics do not tell the complete story of what BIAs and others do with the tools of social care detention. BIAs may not often (formally) find that care arrangements are not in a person's best interests, but they may informally negotiate with those arranging or providing support to do so in alternative or less restrictive ways before making their final assessment. Similarly, IMCAs may prefer to raise concerns 'informally' rather than initiate formal challenges (Series, 2013). BIAs can recommend the supervisory body attach 'conditions' to an authorization (MCA Sch A1 s43); if these are not complied with then the detention is unlawful. They can also authorize for only a short period of time, pending the rectification of an issue of concern. Under the LPS, AMCPs could adopt a similar strategy, defining the specific 'arrangements' that they are willing to authorize and those they are not. Prior to *Cheshire West* there were accounts of BIAs making creative use of conditions to champion a person's rights to live at home, to see their family or access the community, or clever tweaks to care plans to increase happiness, or reduce distress or restrictions in their care (Series, 2013; Jepson et al, 2014). The extent to which BIAs and other DoLS professionals are still able to make such changes given the volume problem after *Cheshire West* is unclear, although similar anecdotes continued to feature in the CQC's (2014, 2015b) reports on the DoLS and in the Law Commission's consultation (see also Currie, 2016).

Many interventions reported by BIAs and IMCA concern 'micro'-constraints, those (potentially) engaging article 8 rather than 'deprivation of liberty'. The ability of BIAs, AMCPs and IMCAs to bring a 'human rights gaze' to care arrangements, to see alternative ways of tackling problems and expanding decision spaces inch by inch, provides an interesting strategy for tackling the kinds of 'sub-legal' concerns giving rise to threshold problems of when formal rights of challenge should be activated. However, these strategies are imperilled by 'macro' readings of deprivation of liberty, which imply that BIAs and their successors, AMCPs, may only consider the kinds of constraints directly linked to 'freedom to leave' on a permanent basis. As we have seen, this may leave even significant constraints and issues around contact untouched.

A further tool in the social care detention armoury is the possibility of asking a court to review the authorization under the DoLS (s21A MCA) or LPS (s21ZA MCA). Where this tool is successful it can be very powerful. Celebrated landmark judgments like *Neary*, or other cases where the court has restored a person to live in their home or with family, show that the DoLS can potentially be a potent weapon for challenging macro-domination (for example, *Westminster City Council v Sykes* [2014] EWHC B9 (COP); *Essex County Council v RF & Ors (Deprivation of Liberty and damage)* [2015] EWCOP 1). In our study of Court of Protection cases we found that s21A reviews often end with a judicial declaration that a person has capacity in relation to some contested matter or ordering alternative arrangements in the person's best interests (Series et al, 2017b). However, there are significant obstacles in getting to court. Both DoLS and LPS interpose a series of discretionary decisions between the detained person and assistance in exercising rights of challenge: whether the supervisory/responsible body will appoint somebody who is both willing and able to assist them in exercising rights of challenge, whether referrals for independent advocacy are secured, whether those representing or advocating from them consider the person to be 'objecting' and are willing to initiate costly and stressful litigation on their behalf. In short, there is considerable potential for 'domination' within frameworks for challenging domination itself. The statistics speak for themselves: although it was (conservatively) estimated that 30 per cent of people subject to DoLS are 'objecting', fewer than 1 per cent of DoLS authorizations (not even applications) result in an 'appeal' to the Court of Protection and appeal rates are projected to halve with the introduction of LPS. In our study, 8 per cent of people died before their appeals were resolved (Series et al, 2017b). In contrast, there were 28,493 tribunal applications appealing against detention under the MHA in 2018–19 from roughly 49,500 new detentions that year (CQC, 2019c).

Given these facts, are the DoLS 'a hugely positive tool that shines a light on the circumstances of an individual's care' (HM Government, 2014: [7.14]) or, as their critics contend, a 'bureaucratic procedure' whereby 'lots of forms are signed and boxes ticked' but 'in practice, nothing changes as a result' (Baroness Elaine Murphy, HL Deb 6 July 2018 vol 792 col 1097)? What kind of legalism does social care detention embody?

Unsworth (1987: 341) characterized the 'old legalism' of the Lunacy Act 1890 as 'rooted in the logic of repression', of protecting the public against inappropriate incarceration while ensuring those who 'should' be incarcerated were. The MHA 1959 is recognized as a victory for 'medicalism' or anti-legalism (Fennell, 1986). Unsworth (1987: 342) characterized the 'new legalism' of the MHA 1983 as imbued by a 'logic of resistance', inviting critical assessment of psychiatric coercion in more than purely medical terms. Rose (1985b) queried whether this reduced social control exercised over patients, or simply transferred control to other professionals – social workers or lawyers. Responding, Fennell (1986: 59) argued this could still require 'professionals to reflect on, explain and justify what they are doing', asking what 'other mechanisms' were available.

Social care detention's legalism, as embodied by the DoLS and LPS, does not embody a logic of resistance – it is still extremely hard for disabled and older people, or their families, to challenge professional decisions within the welfare–incapacity jurisdiction. Securing stronger rights of challenge on the scale required after *Cheshire West* would require an entirely different judicial mechanism, not the resource-intensive procedures of the Court of Protection. Inadequate rights of challenge are also, I suggest, coupled to a lingering sense that these are not really proper matters for the law, that objections and resistance by care recipients are not, properly speaking, *legal* matters, but problems to be delegated to the jurisdiction of their caregivers.

Rather, I suggest, social care detention embodies care-professional legalism. It has produced a new elite of specially trained care professionals – mainly social workers, but also psychologists and others concerned with non-medical aspects of care. Many are trained as BIAs (or as AMCPs), IMCAs, or else profess specialist expertise in the MCA and human rights. Although social workers have been criticized for a lack of legal literacy (Braye et al, 2011, 2015), this new care-professional elite are highly knowledgeable about the law. They use it to tell compelling human rights stories of liberation, deploying judicial catchphrases to bolster emancipatory practices ('the local authority is the servant not the master' (*A Local Authority v A (A Child) & Anor*, [52]), 'what good is it making someone safer if it merely makes them miserable' (*Re MM (An Adult)* [2007] EWHC 2003 (Fam) [120])). They revel in knowledge of the arcane technicalities of MCA case law and the convoluted DoLS and LPS schedules. Social care detention elevates the status of care professionals, and social workers in particular (Hubbard, 2018). They have considerable discretionary power at their disposal, interpreting the flexible principles of the MCA. It offers them new weapons in an ongoing intra-professional culture war against medical paternalism (for example, 'homes not hospitals' (British Association of Social Workers, 2021)) and restrictive or depersonalizing practices within social care.

Certainly, these professionals consider their work very important: 'The social worker is the Safeguard', assert James, Mitchell and Morgan (2019: 60–1), 'protecting the person's right to experience dignity, equality and liberty'. Ascertaining their efficacy requires empirical research that is sorely lacking, and forms of monitoring the CQC as yet has rarely undertaken. Most conspicuously absent from our knowledge is how these 'safeguards' are experienced by those whose liberty is imperilled. After over a decade of DoLS, their voices have been barely heard within either research or regulatory monitoring and inspection. We have spent an exorbitant amount protecting the rights of people in vulnerable situations, without asking about their own experiences or what difference these safeguards makes to their care or wider outcomes.

Alternative regulatory strategies

Social care detention layers a particular regulatory framing – safeguards for individual liberty – over 'macro'-questions of where a person lives, and potentially also 'micro'-questions of restrictive practices and the 'invigilation' of choices within a person's living arrangements. For the reasons outlined above, we might doubt whether safeguards for individual liberty really are the most effective way to tackle some of these problems. Abolitionists seek the eradication of all carceral and restrictive practices, however many countries pursue reform, securing an 'independent check' on some of these problems in other ways than liberty safeguards. Here, I briefly consider some alternative regulatory framings for related problems.

'Substituted consent', guardianship and adult protection laws

Several countries frame 'macro'-questions of placement in terms of 'consent' to admission to residential care, modelled on medical treatment decisions rather than questions of liberty. The Canadian provinces of British Columbia, Yukon and Ontario have legislation that states that if an adult is 'incapable' of consenting to placement in residential care, then consent must be sought from a substitute decision maker (Health Care (Consent) and Care Facility (Admission) Act 1996 (British Columbia); Care Consent Act 2003 (Yukon); Long-Term Care Homes Act 2007 (Ontario)). Like the Australian medical treatment legislation I discussed in Chapter 7, they employ a hierarchical list of those empowered to give substituted consent to residential placements, giving priority to formal decision makers (for example, guardians) and then to family members. This private law model confers substantial power to families as 'custodians' of the person, remitting problems of domination to the private sphere.

Canadian substituted consent frameworks operate alongside adult protection and guardianship laws, conferring 'public law' powers to intervene where there are concerns about abuse or neglect by family or self-neglect. These mechanisms potentially override family authority (as either liberators or custodians), displacing them as substitute decision makers by appointing another person as a guardian. Such disputes are questions of 'who decides' rather than substantive questions of a person's living arrangements.

Several provinces also have public law adult protection frameworks of the kind the Law Commission (1993c) had proposed but which the government did not adopt. These allow public bodies to investigate allegations of abuse, restrict contact with alleged abusers, offer support and assistance, and seek a court order if an 'incapable' adult refuses 'assistance' (for example, Adult Guardianship Act 1996 (British Columbia); Adult Protection Act 1989 (Nova Scotia)). Problematic though these systems are (Harbison, 2016), their public law character arguably provides greater procedural protection against some forms of macro-domination by public bodies than the DoLS, requiring investigative processes and judicial safeguards prior to interventions rather than challenging it after the fact.

Second opinion schemes

The Law Commission (1993b) had also proposed procedural safeguards for medical treatment decisions. For very serious decisions – for example, sterilization – there would be a statutory duty to seek a court order. A second tier of medical decisions would require an independent second opinion, similar to that required under Part IV of the MHA 1983 for treatment for mental disorder that a patient does not consent to. Again, this proposal was not adopted by the government. However, it could potentially be used to examine treatment decisions in the community – for example, to monitor the use of psychoactive medication.

Regulating 'restrictive practices'

In England, new laws will eventually regulate restraint in psychiatric services (Mental Health Units (Use of Force) Act 2018, known as 'Seni's law'), but this does not extend to 'community' settings although restraint is used there as well. Mostyn J has held that article 8 may require more structured oversight of restrictive practices than the MCA currently provides (*J Council v GU & Ors (Rev 1)* [2012] EWHC 3531 (COP)). Some jurisdictions, especially in Australia (Chandler, 2019), have adopted systems for regulating 'restrictive practices' in community care.

For example, in Victoria any use of restrictive practices (seclusion, chemical, physical or mechanical restraint) by National Disability Insurance Scheme providers is overseen by the 'Senior Practitioner', who is responsible for ensuring people's 'rights' are protected and 'appropriate standards' are complied with (s23(2) Disability Act 2006). They are empowered to issue prohibitions and directions governing the use of restrictive practices. Each provider must also appoint an 'Authorised Program Officer' (APO), who reports to the Senior Practitioner. APOs must develop individual support plans for service users, review and monitor these, and ensure than an independent person explains to the person why the measure is included in their support plan, and their right to request a review of the inclusion of restraint or seclusion in their support plan from the Victorian Administrative Appeals Tribunal. The independent person may also report any concerns to the Senior Practitioner or the Public Advocate. By 2014, however, no independent persons had formally raised concerns nor had the tribunal been asked to review any restrictive practices, and there were concerns about whether these procedural safeguards were operating effectively (Dearn, 2014).

These frameworks purport to regulate the most obviously coercive examples of micro-domination, but do not necessarily penetrate 'macro'-questions of 'placement' and whether the person's wider living situation is a cause of the problems. One possible advantage of DoLS-like frameworks could be the ability to consider both macro- and micro-issues in tandem, asking whether a different environment might offer fewer micro-restrictions.

Visiting commissions and inspectorates

Several critics of the *Cheshire West* decision have argued that the 'independent check' needed was more appropriately secured via the second branch of the law of institutions – regulatory or visiting commissions (Allen, 2015; Eldergill, 2019). In Chapter 3, we saw that historically the Lunacy Commission both regulated 'micro' matters such as the use of restraint, daily activities, even prescribing matters such as inmates' diet, and had powers to address 'macro'-questions by discharging patients (which it rarely did) or moving them between different carceral spaces. Today's care regulators are, by comparison, far less interventionist, with far weaker powers to address these concerns.

As discussed in Chapter 7, almost all community care services are regulated by the CQC or the CIW. However, the CQC in particular is widely viewed as poorly equipped to tackle concerns about even the most significant abuses within the care sector. Its troubles are too extensive to elaborate here, but are connected with its early origins as a 'better regulation' inspectorate whose key aims included reducing administrative 'burdens' on providers (Hampton, 2005; Prosser, 2010). Since its creation, the frequency of care home inspections plummeted, as Figure 10.1 shows.

As explored in Chapter 6, the CQC has very limited regulatory powers outside of the 'institutional' settings of care homes and hospitals; it has no powers to inspect supported living services or directly regulate their premises. The outcome in *Cheshire West* may have been influenced by a sense that the kinds of post-carceral services that P and others lived in, falling outside the scope of the CQC's powers of inspection and the DoLS system, lacked any other reliable source of independent scrutiny. Meanwhile, public faith in the CQC to detect and prevent even the most serious abuses has been seriously damaged by scandals such as the Mid Staffordshire NHS Trust, where several hundred patients – mainly elderly – died in appalling conditions. The CQC's response to Mid Staffordshire and Winterbourne View, and its 'risk based' approach to regulation, were heavily criticized in a public inquiry (Francis, 2013). The CQC's failure to detect or respond to abuse of adults with intellectual disabilities was criticized more recently by an independent review into its actions surrounding Whorlton Hall (Noble, 2020). The JCHR (2019: [157]) recently concluded that '[a] regulator which gets it wrong is worse than no regulator at all' and called for 'substantive reform of [the CQC's] approach and processes'.

One suggested answer may be to better fund the CQC, increase the frequency of inspections and expand its remit to include supported living style services (Allen, 2015). However, tackling this regulatory 'gap' would require powers for inspectors to enter what are nominally private dwellings. This may potentially be required by OPCAT, although as we saw in Chapter 5 very few states yet include 'supported housing' style services. Here, too, there is a risk that imposing an 'institutional' model over private dwellings may further 'institutionalize'. As I explained in Chapter 7, the CQC's regulatory model is concerned with the overall operation of services, not the care of specific individuals. The CQC can check whether MCA processes are documented, and may sometimes scrutinize the apparent quality of assessments, but it cannot conduct its own substantive reviews or assessments of individual circumstances, nor receive or address individual complaints. It cannot address 'macro'-questions of alternative living arrangements, nor whether specific

Figure 10.1: Inspections of registered social care locations (care homes) under the CQC and its predecessors[2]

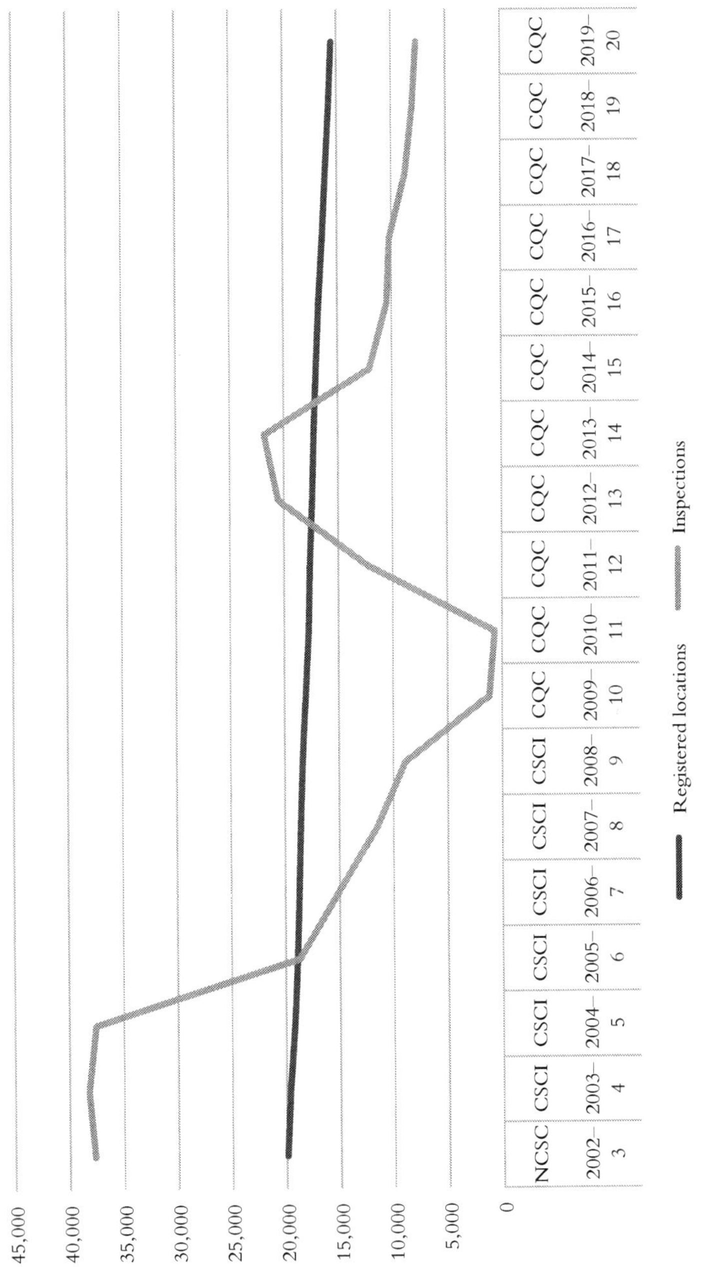

	NCSC	CSCI	CSCI	CSCI	CSCI	CSCI	CSCI	CSCI	CQC	CQC	CQC	CQC	CQC	CQC	CQC	CQC	CQC	CQC
	2002–	2003–	2004–	2005–	2006–	2007–	2008–	2009–	2010–	2011–	2012–	2013–	2014–	2015–	2016–	2017–	2018–	2019–
	3	4	5	6	7	8	9	10	11	12	13	14	15	16	17	18	19	20

— Registered locations   — Inspections

---

2   Data for this chart were provided by the CQC under the Freedom of Information Act 2000, and are available from the author on request.

micro-restrictions are appropriate for that individual. As currently construed, the CQC and CIW cannot answer questions of whether somebody like MIG, MEG or P are in living arrangements that are right for them.

District Judge Eldergill (2019: 529) proposes that what is needed is a legally led Mental Health Law and Welfare Commission, perhaps something akin to the former MHAC or else the Mental Welfare Commission for Scotland (MWCS). The MWCS monitors the implementation of Scottish mental health and capacity legislation. It is empowered to investigate complaints made about any intervention under the Adults with Incapacity (Scotland) Act 2000, and to visit people subject to these Acts wherever they are – hospital, care home or their own home. The MWCS produces thematic reports on specific issues it encounters, as well as visits to specific services. The Commission describes itself as protecting and promoting 'human rights',[3] and advocates for more progressive capacity and mental health legislation that is closer to the 'new paradigm' of the CRPD (McKay and Stavert, 2017).

In some jurisdictions, similar functions might be undertaken by the equivalent of the Office of the Public Guardian. For example, the Assisted Decision-Making (Capacity) Act 2015 (Republic of Ireland) will establish a 'decision support service', whose director must promote awareness of the Act and the CRPD, supervise the compliance of formal supporters and substitute decision makers with the legislation, provide information and assistance, investigate complaints and make recommendations for changes in practice.

It is possible that such commissions could tackle some of the macro- and micro-issues of concern. A model based on visiting individuals, monitoring and investigating the use of specific legal frameworks rather than regulating services, surmounts the limits of the CQC's role in examining an individual's circumstances. A 'capacity' based commission can also circumvent the thorny question of what a 'regulator' is doing visiting a person in a private home, and supervise care arrangements within family settings without labelling those arrangements a 'deprivation of liberty'. The House of Lords Committee on the MCA (2014) recommended such a body be created in England and Wales. However, the government instead elected to establish a 'National Mental Capacity Forum',[4] closer to a forum for discussion of issues and dissemination of some information, with minimal budget and without powers to supervise, monitor, visit or investigate complaints.

'New paradigm' safeguards?

Each of the above models is resolutely 'reformist' not abolitionist, reflecting 'old' not 'new' models of human rights (albeit Scottish and Irish models

---

[3]   See website: www.mwcscot.org.uk/

[4]   www.scie.org.uk/mca/directory/forum

increasingly exhort 'new paradigm' values). Article 12(4) CRPD could provide a basis for an alternative model for regulating concerns about legal capacity, through systems of safeguards on supporting or 'facilitating' decisions. Within the CRPD's 'new paradigm' the focus of these models would be on ensuring that people's 'will and preferences' are supported and expressed, addressing concerns about 'undue influence' and 'conflicts of interest', and resolving disputes over support and the 'interpretation' of a person's 'will and preferences'. It might, for example, operate as an 'independent check' on whether a person really has given a 'valid consent' to living arrangements that could otherwise amount to a deprivation of liberty.

Frameworks based on supported or substitute decision making are, however, restricted in their ability to address the limited 'choices' available within the field of social care. If the choices are between 'institutional' living arrangements or destitution, or different kinds of 'institutional' arrangement, then no amount of supported decision making will enable a person to enjoy the expansive decision spaces associated with home.

In Chapter 7, I argued there were potentially interesting levers for regulators to shape social care provision to reflect the values of independent living, of *homes* not institutions. These could be expanded to include all services providing 'living arrangements', not only those targeting people with intellectual disabilities and autism. I suggested earlier that it may be important for courts resolving disputes to exercise 'public law' powers to *require* public bodies to provide certain kinds of services. The recent review of the MHA has suggested that mental health tribunals could be given powers to direct services in the community (Wessely et al, 2018b) and the government has not rejected this out of hand (Department of Health and Social Care and Ministry of Justice, 2021b). This approach could also usefully be adopted by any future care and capacity jurisdiction, to tackle the 'clustered' injustices outlined in this chapter.

However, even these powers to refuse registration or direct certain care arrangements cannot create the kinds of services we want to see. That requires major political reforms of the economic fabric of social care. In advocating for this, a framing of enabling everyone to live 'in the place we call home with the people and things that we love, in communities where we look out for one another, doing the things that matter to us and that we're good at' (Crowther, 2019b) may help address the recurrent problem of 'independence' being conflated with reduced support or coercive corrective interventions. Nevertheless, *Cheshire West* poses challenging questions for those pursuing total abolition of all carceral and restrictive practices, which even this revolutionary new paradigm of capacity and support may struggle to resolve.

11

Out of the Shadows
of the Institution?

Social care detention is transgressive. The *Cheshire West* acid test collapsed the imaginary boundary line bisecting the landscape of the law of institutions, extending regulatory structures developed to manage the threat of institutionalized carceral care into the spheres of home, family and 'community'. This signals trouble for post-carceral ideology, which identifies homes and community as sites of freedom. Whatever liberty is now, its locus cannot be neatly drawn on a map, but rather requires a careful unpicking of relational-spatial micro-dynamics of power across diverse and dispersed care arrangements.

Cheshire West is a powerful sign of a system in crisis, of unsustainable pressures and tensions within the post-carceral landscape of care. On one reading, *Cheshire West* is a victorious story of human rights, finally recognizing the legal personhood of populations too long consigned to a legal netherworld of 'informality'. Another telling of *Cheshire West* is a tale of tragedy, of a lost future horizon free of the carceral institution, of a journey back into our carceral past. There are now more people deprived of their liberty in Britain's care homes than its prisons, or any other paradigmatic carceral site (Series, 2019).

These are non-paradigmatic detentions to be sure, but the association of community care with detention jars against its brochure imagery, as Alastair Pitblado witheringly put it of 'nice care homes' with 'red roses around the front door' (Samuel, 2012). We are heavily culturally invested in the idea that the community care services that many of us, our friends and family rely upon are caring, benevolent places, certainly not sites of 'detention'. As growing numbers of people encounter social care detention in arranging, providing or receiving care we should expect a backlash against its logics and values, especially as it transgresses into that most sacred space of care: the family home.

Yet *Cheshire West* also embodies growing cultural recognition of the potential carcerality of modern community care, expressed in literary tales and films depicting fantastical escapes by older people consigned to care homes (for example, Mitchell, 2004; Carrington, 2005; Jonasson, 2009; Walliams, 2015; Nell, 2020). The fantastical quality of these escapes tells us something else: that we cannot imagine how *in reality* individuals, let alone our society, can liberate ourselves from carceral care. Our cultural fascination with these stories of carceral care speaks to an awareness that while these 'gilded cages' are not prison cells, most of us would not want to live in them. Most of us want 'to live in the place we call home with the people and things that we love, in communities where we look out for one another, doing the things that matter to us', and we have no good reason to believe that older or disabled people want anything different (Crowther, 2019b).

The crisis is that although we 'closed' the large Victorian institutions – the asylums, 'mental deficiency colonies', workhouses and long-stay hospitals – we continue to discover 'institutional' living arrangements in the community. The aetiology of this crisis is complex: the institutional treadmill is powered by both state-driven logics of care and the 'free market'; by historically accumulating problematizations of people with long-term cognitive impairments which we now seek to manage in the community; by the fusing of historic rationalities of correction and managing 'burdensome' populations with post-carceral rationalities of 'normalization', promoting independence, 'empowerment' and managing 'vulnerability'; by culturally entrenched discourses of deviance, incapacity, infantilization, of care itself. Scott's (2004: 21) writings on postcolonial narratives as tragedy offer a useful way to reconceptualize deinstitutionalization, not as a failed programme of closures but rather as grappling with a 'permanent legacy that has set the conditions in which we make of ourselves what we make and which therefore demands constant renegotiation and readjustment'. The answer is not to despair but rather to bring our careful attention to the complex and varied forms of power that drive the institutional treadmill today, some of which are legal/regulatory but many are not. To reflect carefully on the particular problem-space we find ourselves in today and the journey we took here.

The problem-spaces of social care detention

Social care detention began as a particular regulatory framing – safeguards for individual liberty – imposed over an underlying material reality of 'institutional', restrictive, supervisory and sometimes coercive practices in community care settings. This framing was invited by those strategically posing questions of liberty at critical moments, narrating systems in crisis, modes of care in need of reform, inviting legal-regulatory responses via courts and commissions, bringing often reluctant governments along. Liberty tactics are intimately connected to the history and development of the law of institutions, from the early habeas cases highlighting 'wrongful confinement' in the 18th century and contributing to the intensifying legalism of the 19th century, to the mid-20th-century habeas litigation highlighting the conflicts of interest and systemic apathy of late carceral-era 'safeguards'.

Bournewood resurrected questions of liberty to contest 'informal' arrangements for those historically categorized as 'non-volitional'. The early development of DoLS was mainly characterized by families in conflict with health and social care professionals over placements of their relatives in hospitals and care homes. Rusi Stanev's pivotal case enabled a narration of social care provision and laws governing legal capacity as themselves problems of liberty.

For some families and care recipients, liberty tactics have proven transformative, restoring rights to home, family and something we once called liberty. Yet within this historical sweep *Cheshire West* stands apart: none of the appellants themselves, nor their families (so far as we are told) claimed they were deprived of their liberty; the claim was made by others on their behalf, hoping to extend the regulatory machinery of the law of institutions to address other kinds of problems in the landscape of social care, not so much *where* a person was confined, but the everyday constraints and restrictions they lived under, and might live under wherever they were.

Social care detention in the 21st century began as a civic republican project, an attempt to layer legal controls over institutional, professional and (increasingly) familial forms of power by repurposing the law of institutions to address certain forms of domination in contemporary social care arrangements. These include 'macro'-domination, the arbitrary power to place someone in a particular living arrangement, and 'micro'-domination, the ability to arbitrarily impose constraints, exercise control and invigilate a person's choices in their everyday life. This civic republican project was, I suggest, a response to a powerful welfare–incapacity complex, a historical legacy of the de-juridification of the early post-carceral era, eradicating legal emblems of our carceral past. In some respects, the law of institutions is a natural choice for this project, since these problems of domination are so similar to those found in the 'total institutions' of the past, and many people still live in places that are regulated as caregiving institutions. Yet in other spaces, where the logics of 'home' and 'institution' collide and regulators and courts can no longer draw easy, clear or plausible distinctions between them, the law of institutions can lose traction and we may be less clear about what problems we are trying to solve.

Social care detention embodies a breathtakingly ambitious form of legalism. It is non-paradigmatic, taking no institutional centre, and its spatio-temporal scale is vast: stretched across large populations, diverse loci and often very long timescales in comparison with other detention regulation frameworks.

Social care detention – at least as construed under the DoLS and the LPS – is not based on a logic of resistance; unlike its counterpart – mental health detention – it is often extremely difficult for care recipients or others on their behalf to exercise formal rights of challenge. This is partly because it is difficult to configure a legal system that could cope with the volume of challenges on this scale, and at the level of granularity the decision-specific capacity jurisdiction invites.

Instead, social care detention expresses a new care-professional legalism, tasking a new elite of legally literate social care professionals with ensuring care arrangements in community (and other) services adhere to new post-carceral norms embedded within capacity and human rights law. Social care detention elevates the status, expertise and authority of social care professionals over other caregivers (including care providers, medical professionals and, increasingly, families) in much the same way that lunacy law elevated doctors over other contenders and competitors on the management of the mad. The MCA and its frameworks for regulating detention provide these 'empowerment entrepreneurs' with new weapons in a long-running intra-professional culture war to de-carcerate, deinstitutionalize and emancipate those subject to medical, care and familial paternalism, echoing the work of 19th-century lunacy reformers intent upon eradicating mechanical restraint.

These professionals – by their own accounts – can bring a new gaze to care practices and a person's living arrangements, informed by human rights norms and post-carceral ideologies of person-centred care, choice and control. They may explore 'less restrictive' alternatives – either in alternative locations, or less restrictive ways of caring for a person in a particular place. 'Liberation' may often mean simply reducing certain constraints for the individual, even if they remain in the same place. Successful outcomes for care-legalism are harder to define than paradigmatic forms of liberty, and therefore harder to count for the purposes of official statistics. Following *Cheshire West* many people will be deprived of their liberty wherever they live, under varying constraints. However, their subjective experience of different constraints might radically differ – as, for example, the experience of Steven Neary when detained in a 'positive behaviour unit' or as 'king of his castle' living at home. Some people might remain in the same place but specific restrictions – for example, on 'contact' with specific persons – might be lifted, transforming their life situation.

Care-professional legalism may well deliver important benefits, although without more effective regulatory scrutiny of the DoLS (and LPS), better data collection on outcomes, and empirical research on the experiences of those subject to social care detention it is difficult to be sure. However, this legalism also operates within important constraints. Following *Cheshire West* the most obvious constraint is resources – the DoLS system virtually collapsed following the ruling, and we do not yet know whether demand for AMCPs, IMCAs and court reviews following the implementation of the LPS will be met by the necessary resources.

These 'empowerment entrepreneurs' also operate within steadily encroaching legal limits. Although many (including, I suggest, Lady Hale) believed a key function of the 'safeguards' was to tackle micro-domination, the 'macro' reading of the acid test by the Court of Appeal and, it seems, the government, casts doubt on whether AMCPs and others tasked with administering or adjudicating on the LPS can scrutinize and address micro-domination. The distinction between care, treatment and welfare substitute decisions, and the 'arrangements' to secure these, may also limit the ability of AMCPs and others to penetrate the substantive matters of concern or under dispute giving rise to the 'deprivation of liberty'. The MCA's principles are highly flexible – arguably they confer potential for arbitrary decision making even within this safeguard against arbitrary power. However, like anyone making substitute decisions or adjudicating within the capacity jurisdiction, AMCPs and others are faced with an increasingly limited and unattractive range of alternatives to choose between, with no powers to require that better alternatives be made available. The extent to which they can improve a person's living situation may be extremely limited.

It is possible to imagine reforms that could improve upon this legalism. Such a system would explicitly establish safeguards on 'micro' matters and constraints, perhaps by explicitly including 'article 8' matters within its remit. It would explicitly enable these 'empowerment entrepreneurs' to dig into the substantive care and treatment decisions that are the underlying reason a person is deprived of their liberty in the first place (or a source of concern or distress to the person), instead of drawing legalistic distinctions between these substantive decisions and the 'arrangements' to secure them. It would impose explicit – democratically debated – constraints on what could be done through this system of administrative safeguards, which matters required judicial authorization prior to acting, and clearer thresholds for acting under rationalities of 'empowerment' and managing 'vulnerability'.

This system might configure AMCPs as care navigators, explicitly tasked with helping the person explore alternative care arrangements that could be secured from the local authority, NHS or through their own resources, perhaps even empowered to recommend certain resources or services be secured for them. A court or tribunal overseeing this system might even be empowered to *require* that those services or supports be provided, much as it has recently been suggested mental health tribunals should be (Wessely et al, 2018b). Ultimately, however, even this much-improved system would still be operating within an impoverished landscape with often limited choices. All individuals within this tragic landscape – even judges – are faced with the 'mighty conundrums and divisions' of the age (Scott, 2004: 12), of there often simply being few options expressing post-carceral values, because they are not funded, commissioned or readily available within the 'markets' of care.

In this context, as I have argued, there are serious risks of some degree of 'regulatory paradox' – of a system of safeguards that authorizes, legitimates and normalizes some of the very practices and living arrangements we would hope to eradicate. In some cases this will be reluctantly done, and courts and other empowerment entrepreneurs might use their professional and legal platforms to voice discontent and alarm about the choices it faces when stepping into another person's shoes.

However, history also shows us that safeguards for the liberty of the subject are also the cutting edge of new forms of power. We have seen examples of the new deprivation of liberty jurisdiction being used to expand interventionist and sometimes highly coercive rationalities of 'empowerment' and management of vulnerability, and extending new forms of surveillance and control over family caregivers. What was once done hesitantly, cautiously, may now be done more boldly and confidently. New forms of authority may be asserted under the deprivation of liberty jurisdiction. Liberty safeguards and compulsory powers are two sides of the same coin. Their legal fundamentals are often the same; what differs between them are the contexts and populations they target, and the stories we tell.

Beyond the gilded cage?

In the introduction to this book I explained that it was necessary to put social care detention and *Cheshire West* in a historical context, using the tools of critical genealogy to loosen the hold of present-day ways of conceptualizing our problems of liberty in order to clear a space for alternative ways of conceptualizing them, to examine the historically conditioned terms of present-day debates that shape our problem-spaces, to recognize – perhaps exorcise – the ghosts of our past (Rose, 1999; Scott, 2004; Garland, 2014). This is quite some promise to make good on.

The first lesson from our past is to be strategic about where, when and why we pose questions of liberty; to clarify what problems we are trying to resolve and be sure that liberty tactics are the best available means for this – sometimes they are, often they are not. Before posing questions of whether a particular population is or is not deprived of their liberty we should – as Scott (2004: 12) comments – always seek to clarify whether this is a 'question worth having answers to'. Sometimes it might be better not to frame a criticism within the 'conventions of the language-game we find ourselves participants in' or to strategically evade a response.

When we frame problems by posing questions of liberty, we invite the law of institutions as a legal response. This response is based on certain presuppositions that may not hold good, especially for non-paradigmatic forms of 'liberty'. The law of institutions may not necessarily have traction on the ultimate source of our concerns, and we reinforce the underlying logics of this system: that *some people should be confined somewhere at least some of the time*. I have suggested that although family-based care can sometimes operate in 'carceral' and restrictive ways, it is not strategically useful to frame this as a 'deprivation of liberty', because the law of institutions adds nothing helpful to our existing toolkit of responses, bringing only administrative-legal problems and socio-cultural resistance. Furthermore, it may toxify relations with the very people we need to help to secure improvements and quite possibly alienate others from seeking help.

There are other living situations where the 'deprivation of liberty' label presents particular problems and paradoxes. These are care arrangements that involve some degree of 'supervision and control' but where the person concerned is positively happy with their living arrangements. By this I do not mean that they are 'not objecting' in the sense used in mental health law – a person may be 'not objecting' because they are surrounded by people who cannot understand their attempts at communication (perhaps because they interpret signs of 'resistance' as pathology or 'challenging behaviour' to be managed), or because they are unwell, drugged, scared, institutionalized or simply exhausted. By 'positively happy' I mean people like Mrs L, living where she 'positively and actively' wants to live, 'happy and contented', 'oriented' within her home, which provides the fundamental scaffolding for her self. Or like Steven Neary, supported by a team of personal assistants to live as the 'king of his castle' within his own home.

By categorizing people who are *positively happy* with their living arrangements and who are not actively being coerced as deprived of their liberty we lose sight of our positive goals and what problems we should be trying to solve. We collapse together the kinds of situations we would like to limit or abolish entirely – HL in Bournewood Hospital, Steven Neary in a 'positive behaviour unit', Mr C hammering on the door of his care home, MEG – restrained, sedated and yearning for her foster placement – with those that represent our best understanding of what liberty can and should mean for people with cognitive impairments. We do this because we have carried forward the logics of the non-volitional into the capacity jurisdiction, which imposes a threshold test – 'mental capacity' – upon a person's ability to perform legally valid acts. The 'universal legal capacity' paradigm of the CRPD invites us to reject the logics of the non-volitional, the idea that some people do not really have a 'will', or that it is somehow more tenuous or less important than those attaining this mental capacity threshold. It offers us new tools to radically reconceptualize what it means to offer a 'valid consent' to one's living arrangements, in a way that does not sacrifice our desire to secure an 'independent check' to ensure that this really is a person's positive wish.

The *Cheshire West* acid test can still serve as an important red flag that a person's living arrangements involve a measure of supervision and control, of *potential* interferences and invigilation of choices, requiring investigation. We can secure republican liberty where we adopt independent checks to ensure that this control and invigilation of choices reflects what AEL's father called 'the principle' – that it reflects our best understanding of the person's own wishes and feelings. It is undeniably true that in some cases this may involve a difficult (and sometimes contested) exercise in interpretation, to which those doing the interpreting will bring their own values; but this is no less true for 'best interests' substitute decisions, and no less important for it.

The closure of carceral-era institutions invites us to reconceptualize the kinds of problems we are trying to solve, and the positive goals we seek. Closure of long-stay hospitals and other 'institutions' and the relocation of populations into the community is necessary but not sufficient, because 'institutional' phenomena can follow an individual even into homes and 'private dwellings', and the most progressive and aspirational services in the community. Instead, I suggest we reconceptualize these problems and our goals in terms of 'decision spaces'.

The harms of 'institutions' did not lie in the buildings (as those living in new apartments in old asylum buildings can attest), but in radically constrained decision spaces, through logics of surveillance and control, invigilation of choices, and the imposition of other people's goals and agendas to 'correct' perceived problems in a person's identity. The harms of these constrained decision spaces are well documented: depersonalization, 'institutionalization', 'mortification of the self'. Meanwhile the benefits of 'home' lie not in its location or legal status as a private dwelling, but in affording a more expansive decision space, which gives expression to a person's identity, securing a space for self to develop and flourish, essential scaffolding as a person grows and ages. The idea of an expansive decision space is also closely linked to the logics of 'independent living' encoded in article 19 CRPD, yet as I have argued, the language of 'independence' is too readily imbued with historical corrective discourses of self-reliance and normalization. 'Independence' is a powerful counter-narrative against master-narratives of burden and deficit, yet it is also framed within the same overall logics (Tarrant, 2019).

By reconceptualizing our positive goals as expansive decision spaces, and systems of supports that enable a person to express their will and live accordingly, we can now make sense of how Steven Neary, AEL, Mrs L and others can be said to enjoy 'liberty', in a fuller sense than mere non-confinement, perhaps something closer to the 'pursuit of happiness'. We can envisage an abolitionist future horizon where we remain vigilant against the turning of the institutional treadmill, secured through many and varied policies, better resourcing and experiments with living arrangements that can harness our goals and guard against the logics of institutional care.

And yet, within this abolitionist future there is a shadow on the horizon: figures like P in *Cheshire West* for whom some measure of *actual* control – quite possibly even physical intervention on occasion – may always be necessary to ensure safety. As I have argued, many 'challenging behaviours' and risky behaviours are environmental, contextual, historical in aetiology, yet some will remain even if we strive to ensure the best possible environment that most closely maps onto our best interpretation of how a person wishes to live. These are not, I suggest, the kinds of chosen risks captured by 'dignity of risk' or equalities arguments in the context of mental health detention, but very serious imminent risks that permeate everyday environments that some people are unable to navigate alone. From the distance of legal academic scholarship undertaken at a desk, it is rarely possible to say what measures or changes could address particular risks for particular individuals. However, risks there truly are: in P's case, of choking on items he puts in his mouth; in MIG and MEG's case concerns about road safety. As scholars operating at this distance, we must be cautious about airily referring to the need for more 'support' without recognizing that sometimes part of the function of this 'support' is a measure of (in the words of the acid test) 'continuous supervision and control'.

However, the 'decision space' conceptualization of our goals helps us to be more specific here. To be clear about *which* choices are invigilated, *why* supervision is entailed, *by whom*, and under what limited circumstances 'control' or intervention might be exercised. The 'cliff edge' logics of liberty imply that 'continuous supervision and control' might mean control over anything and everything; yet it is also possible to frame this in much more specific ways. To say that P is 'deprived of his liberty' because somebody is always with him to stop him from choking or hurting himself or walking in front of a car tells us next to nothing about whether he *likes* the people who support him (or might prefer somebody else), whether they have a good rapport with him and are skilled in assisting him with expressing his preferences and interpreting his responses, whether he likes where he lives and who he lives with, whether he finds meaning in his daily activities or they are somebody else's 'normalizing' agenda, whether he lives according to his own rhythms or an 'institutional clock', enjoys some measure of privacy and a 'locus of control', and establishes and sustains meaningful relationships with others, and experiences belonging within a wider community. Whether, in short, he truly enjoys his living arrangements as a home.

Doubtless we shall continue to pose questions of liberty and invite the courts and others to answer them. Liberty tactics have brought the inherent tensions and contradictions of the post-carceral era out of the shadows and placed them under an often uncomfortable spotlight. They have forced governments to act when it is unlikely they would have done otherwise without liberty's powerful rallying cry. They have established new tools to tackle some of the problems we face, although it is doubtful this regulatory machinery can resolve all of the problems that have been unearthed. I have suggested alternative ways that we might more productively frame and approach these problems. Questions of liberty are posed by the ghosts of our carceral past, but they may also represent a critical first step toward new horizons.

References

General comments

CRPD Committee (Committee on the Rights of Persons with Disabilities) 2014a. General comment No. 1 (2014) Article 12: Equal recognition before the law. 19 May 2014, *CRPD/C/GC/1*. Geneva.

CRPD Committee 2014b. Statement on article 14 of the Convention on the Rights of Persons with Disabilities. *12th Session of the Committee, 15 September–3 October 2014.* Geneva.

CRPD Committee 2017. General comment No. 5 on article 19: Living independently and being included in the community. *29 August 2017, UN Doc CRPD/C/18/1.*

United Nations Treaties and human rights instruments

United Nations 1948. Universal Declaration of Human Rights. *UDHR.* 10 December 1948.

United Nations 1966. International Covenant on Civil and Political Rights. *ICCPR.* New York: 6 December 1966.

United Nations 1971. Declaration on the Rights of Mentally Retarded Persons. *Proclaimed by General Assembly resolution 2856 (XXVI) of 20 December 1971.*

United Nations 1975. Declaration on the Rights of Disabled Persons. *Proclaimed by General Assembly resolution 3447 (XXX) of 9 December 1975.*

United Nations 1991. The Protection of Persons with Mental Illness and the Improvement of Mental Health Care. *MI Principles.* 75th plenary meeting of the United Nations General Assembly: 17 December 1991.

United Nations 2006a. Convention on the Rights of Persons with Disabilities *CRPD.* New York: 13 December 2006.

United Nations 2006b. Optional Protocol to the Convention against Torture and other Cruel, Inhuman or Degrading Treatment or Punishment. *OPCAT.* New York: 18 December 2002.

United Nations 2006c. Optional Protocol to the Convention on the Rights of Persons with Disabilities. *OPCRPD.* New York: 13 December 2006.

United Nations Human Rights Committee 2014. General comment No. 35: Article 9: Liberty and security of person. *CCPR/C/GC/35*. Adopted at the 112th session of the Committee, 7–31 October 2014, Geneva.

WGAD (Working Group on Arbitrary Detention) 2012. Deliberation No. 9 concerning the definition and scope of arbitrary deprivation of liberty under customary international law. *Report of the Working Group on Arbitrary Detention, A/HRC/22/44, 24 December 2012.*

WGAD 2017. Report of the Working Group on Arbitrary Detention. *UN Doc A/HRC/36/37.*

Council of Europe Treaties and declarations

Council of Europe 1950. Convention for the Protection of Human Rights and Fundamental Freedoms. *ECHR*. Rome: 4 November 1950.

Council of Europe 2002. European Convention for the Prevention of Torture and Inhuman or Degrading Treatment or Punishment. 26 November 1987.

Council of Europe Committee of Ministers 1999. Recommendation (99) 4 on principles concerning the legal protection of incapable adults. Adopted by the Committee of Ministers on 23 February 1999.

Council of Europe Committee of Ministers 2004. Recommendation No Rec (2004)10 of the Committee of Ministers to member states concerning the protection of the human rights and dignity of persons with mental disorder and its Explanatory Memorandum. Adopted 22 September 2004 at the 896th meeting of the Ministers' Deputies.

Council of Europe Committee of Ministers 2009. Recommendation CM/Rec (2009)3 of the Committee of Ministers to member states on monitoring the protection of human rights and dignity of persons with mental disorder. 20 May 2009.

Statutes (UK)

Adults with Incapacity (Scotland) Act 2000
Assisted Decision-Making (Capacity) Act 2015
Care Act 2014
Care Standards Act 2000
Community Care (Direct Payments) Act 1996
Coroners and Justice Act 2009
County Asylums Act 1845 (8 & 9 Vict. c.126)
Health and Social Care Act 2008
Human Rights Act 1998
Idiots Act 1886 (49 & 50 Vict. c.16)
Lunacy Act 1845 (8 & 9 Vict. c.100)
Lunacy Act 1890 (53 & 53 Vict. c.5)

Lunacy Acts Amendment Act 1862 (25 & 26 Vict. c.111)
Lunacy Amendment Act 1853 (16 & 17 Vict. c.96)
Madhouses Act 1774 (14 Geo. III, c.49)
Madhouses Act 1828 (9 Geo. IV., c.40)
Mental Capacity Act 2005
Mental Capacity Act (Northern Ireland) 2016 (SI 2016/18)
Mental Capacity (Amendment) Act 2019
Mental Deficiency Act 1913
Mental Deficiency Act 1927
Mental Health Units (Use of Force) Act 2018
Mental Treatment Act 1930 (20 & 21 Geo. V, c.23)
National Assistance Act 1948
Policing and Crime Act 2017
Poor Law Amendment Act 1834 (4 & 5 Will. IV, c.76)
Poor Law Amendment Act 1867 (30 & 31 Vict., c.106)
Social Services and Well-being (Wales) Act 2014

Statutes (non–UK)

Adult Guardianship Act 1996 (British Columbia)
Adult Protection Act 1989 (Nova Scotia)
Capacity (Bailiwick of Guernsey) Law 2020
Capacity and Self-Determination (Jersey) Law 2016
Care Consent Act 2003 (Yukon)
Disability Act 2006 (Victoria, Australia)
Health Care Consent Act 1996, S.O. 1996, c. 2 (Ontario, Canada)
Health Care (Consent) and Care Facility (Admission) Act [RSBC 1996]
  Chapter 181 (British Columbia)
Lasting Power of Attorney and Capacity Act 2018 (Gibraltar)
Long-Term Care Homes Act 2007 (Ontario)
Medical Treatment Planning and Decisions Act 2016 (Victoria, Australia)

Secondary legislation (UK)

Health and Social Care Act 2008 (Regulated Activities) Regulations 2014
  SI 2014/2936
The Care and Support and After-care (Choice of Accommodation)
  Regulations 2014 SI 2014/2670
The Mental Capacity (Deprivation of Liberty: Standard Authorisations,
  Assessments and Ordinary Residence) Regulations 2008 SI 2008/1858

Cases (European Court of Human Rights)

D.D. v Lithuania [2012] ECHR 254

Gard and Others v UK Decision [2017] ECHR 605

Guzzardi v Italy [1980] 3 EHRR 333

Hiller v Austria [2016] ECHR 1028

HL v UK [2004] ECHR 720

HM v Switzerland (2002) 38 EHRR 314

IN v Ukraine [2016] ECHR 565

Kędzior v Poland [2012] ECHR 1809

MH v UK [2013] ECHR 1008

Mihailovs v Latvia [2013] ECHR 65

MS v Croatia (No 2) [2015] ECHR 196

Neilsen v Denmark (1988) 11 EHRR 175

Shtukaturov v Russia [2008] ECHR 223

Stanev v Bulgaria [2012] ECHR 46

Storck v Germany [2005] ECHR 406

Van Der Leer v The Netherlands [1981] ECHR 6

Winterwerp v the Netherlands [1979] ECHR 4

X v Finland [2012] ECHR 1371

ZH v Hungary [2012] ECHR 1891

Cases (UK)

A Local Authority v A (A Child) & Anor [2010] EWHC 978 (Fam)

A Local Authority v ED & Ors [2013] EWCOP 3069

A Local Authority v M & Ors [2014] EWCOP 33

A Local Authority v TZ (No. 2) [2014] EWHC 973 (COP)

A Local Authority v WMA & Ors [2013] EWHC 2580 (COP)

A London Borough v X (Wardship: Parental Responsibility; Deprivation of Liberty) [2019] EWHC B16 (Fam)

A NHS Trust v Dr. A [2013] EWHC 2442 (COP)

A Primary Care Trust v P [2009] EW Misc 10 (EWCOP); [2009] CoPLR Con Vol 956

Action for Care Ltd v Care Quality Commission [2019] UKFTT 532 (HESC)

Aintree University Hospitals NHS Foundation Trust v James [2013] UKSC 67

AJ v A Local Authority [2015] EWCOP 5

Alternative Futures Ltd v National Care Standards Commission [2002] EWCST 111(NC)

An NHS Trust & Ors v Y & Anor [2018] UKSC 46

AM v South London & Maudsley NHS Foundation Trust and The Secretary of State for Health [2013] UKUT 0365 (AAC)

Aster Healthcare Ltd v Shafi (Estate of) [2014] EWHC 77 (QB)

Barts NHS Foundation Trust v Raqeeb & Ors [2019] EWHC 2530 (Fam)

Bleak House Limited v CQC [2020] UKFTT 171 (HESC)

Bolam v Friern Hospital Management Committee [1957] 1 WLR 583

Bournemouth Borough Council v BS [2015] EWCOP 39

Briggs v Briggs [2016] EWCOP 48

Care Management Group Ltd v Care Quality Commission [2018] UKFTT 0434 (HESC)

CC v KK and STCC [2012] EWHC 2136 (COP)

Centurion Health Care Limited v CQC [2018] UKFTT 615 (HESC)

CH v A Metropolitan Council [2017] EWCOP 12

Cheshire West and Chester Council v P & Anor [2011] EWHC 1330 (Fam)

Cheshire West and Chester Council v P [2011] EWCA Civ 1333

D (A Child) [2017] EWCA Civ 1695

D Borough Council v AB [2011] EWHC 101 (COP)

Director of Legal Aid Casework & Ors v Briggs [2017] EWCA Civ 1169

Essex County Council v RF & Ors (Deprivation of Liberty and damage) [2015] EWCOP 1

Evans & Anor v Alder Hey Children's NHS Foundation Trust & Ors [2018] EWCA Civ 805 (16 April 2018)

G v E, A Local Authority & F [2010] EWHC 621 (Fam)

Great Western Hospitals NHS Foundation Trust v AA & Ors (Rev 1) [2014] EWHC 132 (Fam)

Hertfordshire CC v K (Deprivation of Liberty) [2020] EWHC 139 (Fam)

IH (Observance of Muslim Practice) [2017] EWCOP 9

IM v LM [2014] EWCA Civ 37

J Council v GU & Ors (Rev 1) [2012] EWHC 3531 (COP)

JE v DE & Ors [2006] EWHC 3459 (Fam); (2007) 10 CCL Rep 149

K v LBX [2012] EWCA Civ 79

KW & Ors v Rochdale Metropolitan Borough Council [2015] EWCA Civ 1054

Lawson, Mottram and Hopton, Re (appointment of personal welfare deputies) [2019] EWCOP 22 (25 June 2019)

LBX v K, L, M [2013] EWHC 3230 (Fam)

Lifeways Community Care Ltd v Care Quality Commission [2019] UKFTT 0464 (HESC)

LLBC v TG [2007] EWHC 2640 (Fam)

London Borough of Hillingdon v Neary [2011] EWHC 1377 (COP)

Lyons v Board of the State Hospital [2011] ScotCS CSOH_21

Mazhar v Birmingham Community Healthcare Foundation NHS Trust & Ors (Rev 1) [2020] EWCA Civ 1377

Mazhar v The Lord Chancellor [2017] EWFC 65

Milton Keynes Council v RR & Ors [2014] EWCOP B19

N v ACCG and others [2017] UKSC 22

North Yorkshire CC v MAG & Anor [2016] EWCOP 5

Northamptonshire Healthcare NHS Foundation Trust v ML (Rev 1) [2014] EWCOP 2

Nottinghamshire Healthcare NHS Trust v RC [2014] EWHCOP 1317

Oakview Estates Ltd v CQC [2017] UKFTT 513 (HESC) (26 June 2017)

P & Q v Surrey County Council [2011] EWCA Civ 190

P v Cheshire West and Chester Council and another; P and Q v Surrey County Council [2014] UKSC 19

PC & Anor and City of York Council [2013] EWCA Civ 478

R (D) v Worcestershire County Council [2013] EWHC 2490 (Admin)

R (Davey) v Oxfordshire County Council & Ors [2017] EWCA Civ 1308

R (Davey) v Oxfordshire County Council [2017] EWHC 354 (Admin)

R (E) v Nottinghamshire Healthcare NHS Trust [2009] EWCA Civ 795

R (Ferreira) v HM Senior Coroner for Inner South London [2017] EWCA Civ 31

R (G) v Nottinghamshire Healthcare NHS Trust [2008] EWHC 1096 (Admin)

R (Liverpool City Council) v Secretary of State for Health [2017] EWHC 986 (Admin); [2017] WLR (D) 314; [2017] COPL 295

R (McDonald) v Royal Borough of Kensington and Chelsea [2011] UKSC 33

R (Miller) v The Prime Minister [2019] UKSC 41).

R (Moore) v Care Standards Tribunal [2004] EWHC 2481 (Admin)

R (Moore) v Care Standards Tribunal [2005] EWCA Civ 627

R. v Bournewood Community and Mental Health NHS Trust Ex p. L [1997] EWCA Civ 2879

R. v Bournewood Community and Mental Health NHS Trust Ex p. L [1998] UKHL 24

Raqeeb v Barts Health NHS Trust (Costs) [2019] EWHC 3320 (Admin) (03 December 2019)

RB v Brighton and Hove City Council [2014] EWCA 561

Re A (Capacity: Social Media and Internet Use: Best Interests) [2019] EWCOP 2

Re A (Male Sterilisation) [2000] 1 FLR 549

Re AEL [2021] EWCOP 9

Re A-F (Children) [2018] EWHC 138 (Fam)

Re C (Adult: Refusal of Medical Treatment) [1994] 1 W.L.R. 290

Re C; C v A Local Authority [2011] EWHC 1539 (Admin)

Re C; C v Blackburn and Darwen Borough Council [2011] EWHC 3321 (COP)

Re D (A Child) [2019] UKSC 42

Re D (A Child: deprivation of liberty) [2015] EWHC 922 (Fam)

Re Daniel X [2016] EWFC B31

Re F (Mental Patient: Sterilisation) [1990] 2 AC 1; [1991] UKHL 1

Re GC [2008] EWHC 3402 (Fam)

Re J (A Minor) (Wardship: Medical treatment) [1991] Fam 33

Re LDV [2013] EWHC 272 (Fam)

Re MM (An Adult) [2007] EWHC 2003 (Fam)

Re MM [2018] UKSC 60

Re PB [2014] EWCOP 14
Re R [2016] EWCOP 33
Re RD (Deprivation or Restriction of Liberty) [2018] EWFC 47
Re S (Hospital Patient: Court's Jurisdiction) [1995] Fam. 26
Re X (Court of Protection Practice) [2015] EWCA Civ 599
Re X and others (Deprivation of Liberty) (Number 2) [2014] EWCOP 37
Rex v Turlington (1761) 97 ER 741
Rex v William Clarke (1762) 97 ER 875
Rochdale Metropolitan Borough Council v KW & Ors [2014] EWCOP 45
RR (Costs Judgement) [2014] EWCOP 34
Salford City Council v BJ [2009] EWHC 3310 (Fam)
SCCG v MSA & Anor [2017] EWCOP 18
Secretary of State for Justice v Staffordshire CC [2016] EWCA Civ 1317.
Semayne's Case (January 1st, 1604) 5 Coke Rep. 9
Somerset v MK (Deprivation of Liberty: Best Interests Decisions: Conduct of a Local Authority) [2014] EWCOP B25
Southend-On-Sea Borough Council v Meyers [2019] EWHC 399 (Fam) (20 February 2019)
Staffordshire County Council v SRK & Ors [2016] EWCOP 27
Street v Mountford [1985] AC 809 (House of Lords)
Surrey County Council v MEG & MIG v Anor [2010] EWHC 785 (Fam)
The London Borough of Tower Hamlets v TB & Anor [2014] EWCOP 53
W City Council v Mrs L [2015] EWCOP 20
Welsh Ministers v PJ [2018] UKSC 66
Westminster City Council v Sykes [2014] EWHC B9 (COP)
Wye Valley NHS Trust v Mr B [2015] EWHC 60 (COP)
X & Ors (Deprivation of Liberty) [2014] EWCOP 25
ZK (Landau-Kleffner Syndrome: Best Interests) [2021] EWCOP 12

Cases (non-UK)

AC v Patricia Hickey General Solicitor and Ors & AC v Fitzpatrick and Ors [2019] IESC 73 (Republic of Ireland)
Conseil d'État, Juge des référés No 439822 8 avril 2020 (France)
José Antonio Guillén Tejada TRIBUNAL CONSTITUCIONAL. 2019. Sentencia recaída en el Exp. 0019–2014-PHC/TC (Peru)
Sarah White v Local Health Authority & Anor [2015] NSWSC 417 (Australia)
Skyllas v Retirement Care Australia (Preston) Pty Ltd [2006] VSC 409 (Australia)

Complaints (CRPD Committee)

DR v Australia (14/2003) 19 May 2017, CRPD/C/17/D/14/2013
HM v Sweden (3/2011) 21 May 2012 CRPD/C/7/D/3/2011

Kendall v Australia (15/2013) 29 April 2019 CRPD/C/21/D/15/2013

MR v Australia (16/2013) 5 July 2018 CRPD/C/18/D/16/2013

Simon Bacher v Austria (26/2014) 6 April 2018 CRPD/C/19/D/26/2014

Y v Tanzania (23/2014) 30 October 2018 CRPD/C/20/D/23/2014

Works Cited

39 Essex Chambers. 2015. *D (A Child) (Deprivation of Liberty)*. COP Cases [Online]. Available from: www.39essex.com/cop_cases/d-a-child-deprivation-of-liberty/.

Allen, N. 2009. Restricting movement or depriving liberty? *Journal of Mental Health Law*, 18, 19–32.

Allen, N. 2010. The Bournewood gap (as amended?). *Medical Law Review*, 18, 78–85.

Allen, N. 2012. Restricting movement or depriving liberty? *Court of Protection Note*, London: 39 Essex Chambers.

Allen, N. 2015. The (not so) great confinement. *Elder Law Journal*, 5, 45.

Alston, P. 2017. The populist challenge to human rights. *Journal of Human Rights Practice*, 9, 1–15.

Altermark, N. 2017. The post-institutional era: visions of history in research on intellectual disability. *Disability & Society*, 32, 1315–1332.

Altmann, R. 2020. The lesson of the Covid-19 care homes tragedy: renationalising is no longer taboo. *The Guardian*, 6 July 2020.

Andrews, E. 2014. *Senility before Alzheimer: old age in British psychiatry, c. 1835–1912*. PhD, University of Warwick.

Andrews, E.S. 2017. Institutionalising senile dementia in 19th-century Britain. *Sociology of Health & Illness*, 39, 244–257.

Angus, J., Kontos, P., Dyck, I., Mckeever, P. & Poland, B. 2005. The personal significance of home: habitus and the experience of receiving long-term home care. *Sociology of Health & Illness*, 27, 161–187.

Antaki, C., Finlay, W., Walton, C. & Pate, L. 2008. Offering choices to people with intellectual disabilities: an interactional study. *Journal of Intellectual Disability Research*, 52, 1165–1175.

Antaki, C., Finlay, W.M.L. & Walton, C. 2009. Choices for people with intellectual disabilities: official discourse and everyday practice. *Journal of Policy and Practice in Intellectual Disabilities*, 6, 260–266.

Arstein-Kerslake, A. & Flynn, E. 2017. The right to legal agency: domination, disability and the protections of Article 12 of the Convention on the Rights of Persons with Disabilities. *International Journal of Law in Context*, 13, 22–38.

Ashby, G.A., Griffin, C. & Agrawal, N. 2015. Brain injury and deprivation of liberty on neurosciences wards: 'a gilded cage is still a cage'. *Practical Neurology*, 15, 361–368.

Ashton, G. 2017. DoLS or Quality Care? *International Journal of Mental Health and Capacity Law*, 22, http://journals.northumbria.ac.uk/index.php/IJMH MCL/article/view/483.

Ashton, G.R., Rt Hon Lord Justice Baker, District Judge Marc Marin, Beck, J., Lee, A., Van Overdijk, C., Ruck Keene, A., et al. (eds) 2019. *Court of Protection Practice 2019*, London: LexisNexis.

Askham, J., Briggs, K., Norman, I. a. N. & Redfern, S. 2007. Care at home for people with dementia: as in a total institution? *Ageing and Society*, 27, 3–24.

Association for the Prevention of Torture 2010. *Optional Protocol to the UN Convention against Torture: Implementation Manual*. Revised edition. Geneva, Switzerland.

Association of Directors of Adult Social Services 2016. *ADASS TASK FORCE: A Screening tool to prioritise the allocation of requests to authorise a deprivation of liberty*. London.

Association of Directors of Adult Social Services & Local Government Association 2014. *LGA and ADASS warn changes to safeguarding rules could take £88 million from care budgets*. London.

Astin, D. 2018. *Housing Law Handbook*. London: Legal Action Group.

Autistic Self Advocacy Network, Self-Advocates Becoming Empowered & National Youth Leadership Network 2011. *Keeping the promise: self-advocates defining the meaning of community*. Available from: www.autisticadvocacy. org/.

Avni, N. 1991. Battered wives: the home as a total institution. *Violence and Victims*, 6, 137–149.

Bach, M. & Kerzner, L. 2010. *A new paradigm for protecting autonomy and the right to legal capacity*, Toronto: Law Commission of Ontario.

Baggs, A. 2012. What makes institutions bad? *Ballast Existenz* [Online]. Available from: https://ballastexistenz.wordpress.com/2012/01/23/what-makes-institutions-bad/ [Accessed 23 January 2012].

Baharlo, B., Bryden, D. & Brett, S. J. 2018. Deprivation of liberty and intensive care: an update post Ferreira. *Journal of the Intensive Care Society*, 19, 35–42.

Banerjee, S. 2009. *The use of antipsychotic medication for people with dementia: time for action*. A report for the Minister of State for Care Services, London: Department of Health.

Bank-Mikkelsen, N. 1969. Programs for the Mentally Retarded of Denmark. *Keynote speech presented at a meeting sponsored by the Southern Regional Education Board*. Atlanta, Georgia.

Bantekas, I., Stein, M.A. & Anastasiou, D. (eds) 2019. *The UN Convention on the Rights of Persons with Disabilities*, Oxford: Oxford University Press.

Barnes, C. (ed.) 1992. *Making Our Own Choices: independent living, personal assistance and disabled people*, British Council of Disabled People. London.

Barros, D.B. 2004. Home as a legal concept. *Santa Clara Law Review*, 46, 255.

Bartlett, P. 1998. The asylum, the workhouse, and the voice of the insane poor in 19th-century England. *International Journal of Law and Psychiatry*, 21, 421–432.

Bartlett, P. 1999a. *The Poor Law of Lunacy*, Leicester: Leicester University Press.

Bartlett, P. 1999b. *The Poor Law of Lunacy: the administration of pauper lunatics in mid-nineteenth century England*, Leicester: Leicester University Press.

Bartlett, P. 2008. *Blackstone's Guide to The Mental Capacity Act 2005*, Oxford: Oxford University Press.

Bartlett, P. 2009. The United Nations Convention on the Rights of Persons with Disabilities and the future of mental health law. *Psychiatry*, 8, 496–498.

Bartlett, P. & Wright, D. 1999. Community care and its antecedents. *In:* Bartlett, P. & Wright, D. (eds) *Outside the Walls of the Asylum: the history of care in the community, 1750–2000*, London and New Brunswick, NJ: Athlone Press.

Bartlett, P., Lewis, O. & Thorold, O. 2007. *Mental disability and the European Convention on Human Rights*, Leiden, the Netherlands: Martinus Nijhoff Publishers.

Beamer, S. & Brookes, M. 2001. *Making Decisions: best practice and new ideas for supporting people with high support needs to make decisions*, London: Values into Action.

Bean, P. 1986. *Mental Disorder and Legal Control*, Cambridge: Cambridge University Press.

Becker, H.S. 1963/2018. *Outsiders: studies in sociology of deviance*, New York: Simon & Schuster.

Ben-Moshe, L. 2013. Disabling incarceration: connecting disability to divergent confinements in the USA. *Critical Sociology*, 39, 385–403.

Ben-Moshe, L. 2020. *Decarcerating Disability: deinstitutionalization and prison abolition*, Minneapolis: University of Minnesota Press.

Ben-Moshe, L., Chapman, C. & Carey, A.C. (eds) 2014. *Disability Incarcerated: imprisonment and disability in the United States and Canada*, New York: Palgrave Macmillan.

Beresford, P. 2014. *Personalisation*, Bristol: Policy Press.

Beveridge, W. 1942. *Social Insurance and Allied Services*. Cmd. 6404.

Bigby, C., Bould, E. & Beadle-Brown, J. 2017. Conundrums of supported living: the experiences of people with intellectual disability. *Journal of Intellectual & Developmental Disability*, 42, 309–319.

Bigby, C., Bould, E. & Beadle-Brown, J. 2018. Comparing costs and outcomes of supported living with group homes in Australia. *Journal of Intellectual & Developmental Disability*, 43, 295–307.

Bigby, C., Bould, E., Iacono, T., Kavanagh, S. & Beadle-Brown, J. 2020. Factors that predict good Active Support in services for people with intellectual disabilities: a multilevel model. *Journal of Applied Research in Intellectual Disabilities*, 33, 334–344.

Bingham, T. 2010. *The Rule of Law*, London: Allen Lane.

Bitner, G.A. 2019. *The 'home'/'homelessness' continuum in residential aged care.* PhD, Queensland University of Technology.

Blackstone, W. 2016. *The Oxford Edition of Blackstone's: Commentaries on the Laws of England: Book IV: Of Public Wrongs*, Oxford: Oxford University Press.

Boente, W. 2017. Some continental European perspectives on safeguards in the case of deprivation of liberty in health and social care settings. *International Journal of Mental Health and Capacity Law*, 23, http://dx.doi.org/10.19164/ijmhcl.v2017i23.632.

Borg, M., Sells, D., Topor, A., Mezzina, R., Marin, I. & Davidson, L. 2005. What makes a house a home: the role of material resources in recovery from severe mental illness. *American Journal of Psychiatric Rehabilitation*, 8, 243–256.

Bottery, S., Ward, D. & Fenney, D. 2019. *Social care 360*, London: The King's Fund.

Bould, E., Bigby, C., Iacono, T. & Beadle-Brown, J. 2019. Factors associated with increases over time in the quality of Active Support in supported accommodation services for people with intellectual disabilities: a multi-level model. *Research in Developmental Disabilities*, 94, 103477.

Bowen, P. 2007. *Blackstone's Guide to The Mental Health Act 2007*, Oxford: Oxford University Press.

Bowers, H., Lockwood, S., Eley, A., Catley, A., Runnicles, D., Mordey, M., Barker, S., Thomas, N., Jones, C. & Dalziel, S. 2013. *Widening Choices for Older People with High Support Needs*. York: Joseph Rowntree Foundation and the National Development Team for Inclusion.

Boyer, G. 2016. 'Work for their prime, the workhouse for their age': old age pauperism in Victorian England. *Social Science History*, 40, 3–32.

Branfield, F. & Beresford, P. 2010. *A Better Life: alternative approaches from a service user perspective*, York: Joseph Rowntree Foundation.

Braye, S., Preston-Shoot, M. & Wigley, V. 2011. Deciding to use the law in social work practice. *Journal of Social Work*, 13, 75–95.

Braye, S., Orr, D. & Preston-Shoot, M. 2015. Learning lessons about self-neglect? An analysis of serious case reviews. *Journal of Adult Protection*, 17, 3–18.

Brearley, P., Hall, F., Gutridge, P., Jones, G. & Roberts, G. (eds) 1980/2001. *Admission to Residential Care*, Oxon: Routledge.

Brend, M. 2008. *First and Last: closing learning disabilities hospitals*, London: Choice Press.

British Association of Social Workers 2021. *Homes not hospitals: The role of the social worker and legal literacy*. London.

British Psychological Society 2000. *Learning Disability: definitions and contexts*. Leicester.

Brown, H. 2014. *Executive Summary from the Safeguarding Adults Review into failures in the care and abuse of residents at a care home in Peterborough*. SAR for Peterborough Safeguarding Adults Board.

Brown, K. 2011. 'Vulnerability': handle with care. *Ethics and Social Welfare*, 5, 313–321.

Brydall, J. 1700. *Non compos mentis: or, the law relating to natural fools, mad-folks, and lunatick persons, inquisted, and explained, for common benefit*, London: Assigns of R. & E. Atkins, for I. Cleave (via Wellcome Collection).

Bucknill, J.C. 1857. The diagnosis of insanity. *The Asylum Journal of Mental Science*, 3, 141–185.

Bunting, M. 2020. *Labours of Love: the crisis of care*, London: Granta.

Burgess, I. 2014. We should welcome this Supreme Court ruling – it enshrines social work values in law. *Community Care*, 12 September 2014.

Buse, C., Martin, D. and Nettleton, S. 2018. Conceptualising 'materialities of care': making visible mundane material culture in health and social care contexts. *Sociology of Health & Illness*, 40, 243.

Butler, I. & Drakeford, M. 2005. *Social Policy, Social Welfare and Scandal: how British public policy is made*, London: Palgrave Macmillan.

Cadwallader, J.R., Spivakovsky, C., Steele, L. & Wadiwel, D.J. 2018. Institutional violence against people with disability: recent legal and political developments. *Current Issues in Criminal Justice*, 29, 259.

Cahill-O'Callaghan, R. 2020. *Values in the Supreme Court: Decisions, Division and Diversity*, Oxford: Hart.

Callaghan, S. & Ryan, C. 2016. An evolving revolution: evaluating Australia's compliance with the 'Convention on the Rights of Persons with Disabilities' in mental health law. *UNSW Law Journal*, 39, 596–624.

Campbell, D. & Thomas, P. (eds) 2016. *Fundamental Legal Conceptions as Applied in Judicial Reasoning By Wesley Newcomb Hohfeld*, London and New York: Routledge.

Campbell, J. 2008. *Fighting for a slice, or for a bigger cake?* The 6th Annual Disability Lecture, St John's College, University of Cambridge.

Campbell, J. & Oliver, M. 1996. *Disability Politics: understanding our past, changing our future*, Abingdon: Routledge.

Campbell, P. 2005. From little acorns: the mental health service user movement. *In:* Bell, A. & Lindley, P. (eds) *Beyond the Water Towers: the unfinished revolution in mental health services 1985–2005*, London: Sainsbury Centre for Mental Health.

Campbell, T. & Heginbotham, C. 1991. *Mental Illness: prejudice, discrimination and the law*, Aldershot: Dartmouth Publishing Company Ltd.

Canadian Centre for Elder Law 2019. *Conversations about care: the law and practice of health care consent for people living with dementia in British Columbia.* CCEL Report 10.

Cannon, A. 2018. *Registering the right support: challenging the six person rule.* LaingBuisson Events.

Carboni, J. 1990. Homelessness among the institutionalized elderly. *Journal of Gerontological Nursing,* 16, 32–37.

Care and Social Services Inspectorate Wales & Health Inspectorate Wales 2015. Deprivation of Liberty Safeguards: annual monitoring report for health and social care 2013–14. London.

Care and Social Services Inspectorate Wales & Healthcare Inspectorate Wales 2016. Deprivation of Liberty Safeguards: annual monitoring report for health and social care 2014–15. Cardiff.

Care Inspectorate Wales & Healthcare Inspectorate Wales 2020. Deprivation of Liberty Safeguards: annual monitoring report for health and social care 2018–19. Cardiff.

Carpenter, P.K. 2000. The Bath Idiot and Imbecile Institution. *History of Psychiatry,* 11, 163–188.

Carr, H. & Hunter, C. 2012. Are judicial approaches to adult social care at a dead-end? *Social & Legal Studies,* 21, 73–92.

Carr, H., Edgeworth, B. & Hunter, C. (eds) 2018. *Law and the Precarious Home: socio-legal perspectives on the home in insecure times,* Oxford: Hart.

Carrington, L. 2005. *The Hearing Trumpet,* London: Penguin Classics.

Carvalho, S.R. & Lima, E.M.F.A. 2016. Powers of freedom, governmentality and the psy knowledges: dialogues with Nikolas Rose (Part 2). *Interface – Comunicação, Saúde, Educação,* 20, 797–808.

Case, P. 2016. Dangerous liaisons? Psychiatry and law in the Court of Protection: expert discourses of 'insight' (and 'compliance'). *Medical Law Review,* 24, 360–378.

Castel, R. 1988. *The Regulation of Madness: the origins of incarceration in France,* Cambridge: Polity.

Centre for Health and the Public Interest 2016. The failure of uthorizat adult social care in England: what is to be done? London: CHPI.

Challis, L. 1985. Controlling for care: private and voluntary homes registration and inspection—a forgotten area of social work. *The British Journal of Social Work,* 15, 43–56.

Chandler, K. 2019. *The uthorization of restrictive practices used on people with intellectual and cognitive impairments: a rights-based approach.* PhD, Queensland University of Technology.

Chandler, K., White, B. & Wilmott, L. 2016. The doctrine of necessity and the detention and restraint of people with intellectual impairment: is there any justification? *Psychiatry, Psychology and Law,* 23, 361–387.

Chandler, K., White, B. & Willmott, L. 2018a. Safeguarding rights to liberty and security where people with disability are subject to detention and restraint: a practical approach to the adjudication, interpretation and making of law (Part Two). *Psychiatry, Psychology and Law*, 25, 550–577.

Chandler, K., White, B. & Willmott, L. 2018b. Safeguarding rights to liberty and security where people with disability are subject to detention and restraint: a rights-based approach (Part One). *Psychiatry, Psychology and Law*, 25, 465–484.

Changing Our Lives 2014. Quality of life: standards and toolkit. Hagley: West Midlands.

Chapman, T. & Hockey, J. (eds) 2002. *Ideal Homes? Social change and domestic life*, London and New York: Routledge.

Chappell, A.L. 1992. Towards a sociological critique of the Normalisation Principle. *Disability, Handicap & Society*, 7, 35–51.

Children's Commissioner 2019. Who are they? Where are they? Children locked up. London.

Clarke, C.L., Keady, J., Wilkinson, H., Gibb, C.E., Luce, A., Cook, A. & Williams, L. 2010. Dementia and risk: contested territories of everyday life. *Journal of Nursing and Healthcare of Chronic Illness*, 2, 102–112.

Clement, T. & Bigby, C. 2010. *Group Homes for People with Intellectual Disabilities Encouraging Inclusion and Participation*, London and Philadelphia: Jessica Kingsley Publishers.

Clements, L. 2011. Disability, dignity and the cri de coeur. *European Human Rights Law Review*, 6, 675–685.

Clements, L. 2020. *Clustered Injustice and the Level Green*, London: Legal Action Group.

Clements, L. & Aiello, A.L. 2021. *Institutionalising parent carer blame*, Leeds: Cerebra and University of Leeds.

Clements, L., Ashton, K., Garlick, S., Goodall, C., Mitchell, E. & Pickup, A. 2019. *Community Care and the Law*, London: Legal Action Group.

Clough, B. 2015. 'People like that': realising the social model in mental capacity jurisprudence. *Medical Law Review*, 23, 53–80.

Clough, B. 2017. Disability and vulnerability: challenging the capacity/incapacity binary. *Social Policy and Society*, 16, 469–481.

Clough, R., Leamy, M., Miller, V. & Bright, L. 2005. *Housing Decisions in Later Life*, London: Palgrave Macmillan.

Coggon, J. 2008. Best interests, public interest, and the power of the medical profession. *Health Care Analysis*, 16, 219–232.

Coggon, J. & Kong, C. 2021. From best interests to better interests? Values, unwisdom and objectivity in mental capacity law. *The Cambridge Law Journal*, 80, 245–273.

Cojocariu, I.B. & Kokic, N. 2018. Briefing on the use of EU funds for independent living. European Network on Independent Living.

Collingbourne, T. 2014. The Care Act 2014: a missed opportunity? *Web Journal of Current Legal Issues,* 20. Available from: http://webjcli.org/arti cle/view/365/464. Brussels.

Collins, J. 1993. *The Resettlement Game: policy and procrastination in the closure of mental handicap hospitals,* London: Values into Action.

Collins, J. 2003. Bill of no rights. *Community Care,* 28 August 2003, 32–33.

Commission for Social Care Inspection & Healthcare Commission 2006. Joint investigation into the provision of services for people with learning disabilities at Cornwall Partnership NHS Trust. London.

Commission for Social Care Inspection 2007. Rights, risks and restraints: an exploration into the use of restraint in the care of older people. London.

Commissioner for the Administration and Protection of Human Rights (Cyprus) 2019. Review on the action of the National Preventive Mechanism for the years 2018 and 2019.

Commissioners in Lunacy 1847. Further report of the Commissioners in Lunacy, to the Lord Chancellor. *CP 858.*

Commissioners in Lunacy 1850. Fourth annual report of the Commissioners in Lunacy, to the Lord Chancellor, 1849. *HC 291.*

Commissioners in Lunacy 1858. Thirteenth report of the Commissioners in Lunacy to the Lord Chancellor. *House of Commons Papers 204.*

Commissioners in Lunacy 1883. Thirty-seventh annual report to Lord Chancellor. *HC 262.*

Commissioners in Lunacy 1899. Fifty-third report to the Lord Chancellor. *HC 255.*

Committee on Madhouses 1815. Select Committee on provisions for better regulation of madhouses in England: first report.

Committee on Madhouses 1816. Select Committee on provisions for better regulation of madhouses in England: second report.

Contrôleur Général des Lieux de Privation de Liberté 2012. Annual Report 2012.

Contrôleur Général des Lieux de Privation de Liberté 2014. Annual Report 2014.

Cowley, J. 2017. How the DoLS can give voice to people with minimal consciousness. *Community Care* [Online]. Available from: www. communitycare.co.uk/2017/01/27/dols-can-give-voice-people-minimal-consciousness/.

CQC (Care Quality Commission) 2012. Learning Disability Services Inspection Programme: national overview. London.

CQC 2014. Monitoring the use of the Mental Capacity Act Deprivation of Liberty Safeguards in 2012/13. London.

CQC 2015a. Housing with care: guidance on regulated activities for providers of supported living and extra care housing. London.

CQC 2015b. Monitoring the Deprivation of Liberty Safeguards in 2014–15. London.

CQC 2015c. Monitoring the use of the Mental Capacity Act Deprivation of Liberty Safeguards in 2013–14. London.

CQC 2016. Registering the right support: CQC's policy on registration and variations to registration for providers supporting people with learning disabilities. February 2016. London.

CQC 2017a. Changes to our policy on registration of services for people with a learning disability and/or autism CQC's view on the likely impact on providers and people who use services. London.

CQC 2017b. Services for people with learning disabilities: registering the right support. London.

CQC 2017c. The state of health care and adult social care in England 2016/17. London.

CQC 2018. The state of health care and adult social care in England 2017/18. London.

CQC 2019a. Annual report and accounts: 2018/19. London.

CQC 2019b. Interim Report: Review of restraint, prolonged seclusion and segregation for people with a mental health problem, a learning disability or autism. London.

CQC 2019c. Monitoring the Mental Health Act in 2017/18. London.

CQC 2019d. The state of health care and adult social care in England 2018/19. London.

CQC 2020a. CQC care directory – with filters. 1 June 2020. London.

CQC 2020b. Out of sight – who cares? A review of restraint, seclusion and segregation for autistic people, and people with a learning disability and/or mental health condition. London.

CQC 2020c. Promoting sexual safety through empowerment. London.

CQC 2020d. Right support, right care, right culture. October 2020. London.

CQC 2021. How CQC identifies and responds to closed cultures [Online]. Available from: www.cqc.org.uk/guidance-providers/all-services/how-cqc-identifies-responds-closed-cultures [Accessed 22 June 2021]. London.

Crews, M., Garry, D., Phillips, C., Wong, A., Troke, B., Keene, A. & Danbury, C. 2014. Deprivation of liberty in intensive care. *Journal of the Intensive Care Society*, 15, 320–324.

Crowther, N. 2019a. *The right to live independently and to be included in the community in European States: ANED synthesis report.* On behalf on the European network of academic experts in the field of disability (ANED).

Crowther, N. 2019b. Talking about a brighter social care future. #socialcarefuture.

Crowther, N., Quinn, G. & Hillen-Moore, A. 2017. *Opening up communities, closing down institutions: harnessing the European Structural and Investment Funds.* Report for Community Living for Europe: Structural Funds Watch.

Cruikshank, B. 1999. *The Will to Empower: democratic citizens and other subjects*, Ithaca, NY: Cornell University Press.

Currie, L. 2016. Deprivation of liberty safeguards: a personal overview of the safeguards post-Cheshire West. *Elder Law Journal*, 6, 181–186.

Curryer, B., Stancliffe, R.J., Dew, A. & Wiese, M.Y. 2018. Choice and control within family relationships: the lived experience of adults with intellectual disability. *Intellectual and Developmental Disabilities*, 56, 188–201.

Daes, E.-I. 1986. Principles, guidelines and guarantees for the protection of persons detained on grounds of mental ill-health or suffering from mental disorder. *Report of the Special Rapporteur of the Sub-Commission on Prevention of Discrimination and Protection of Minorities, UN Doc E/CN.4/Sub.2/1983/17.*

Davis, H., Raine, J., Martin, S., Bundred, S., Clarke, J., Downe, J., Grace, C., Johns, C., Lock, D. & Martin, J. (eds) 2008. *Public Services Inspection in the UK*, London: Jessica Kingsley Publishers.

Dawson, J. & Szmukler, G. 2006. Fusion of mental health and incapacity legislation. *The British Journal of Psychiatry*, 188, 504–509.

Dawson, M. 2004. The Misbehaviour of Behaviourists: ethical challenges to the Autism-ABA industry [Online]. Available from: www.sentex.ca/~nexus23/naa_aaba.html [Accessed 9 November 2021]. Montreal, QC.

Dearn, L. 2014. The effectiveness of the independent person as a procedural safeguard in the use of restrictive interventions as prescribed by the Disability Act 2006. Office of the Public Advocate, Victoria, Australia.

Deeley, S. 2002. Professional ideology and learning disability: an analysis of internal conflict. *Disability & Society*, 17, 19–33.

Defoe, D. 1728. *Augusta Triumphans. Or, the Way to Make London the Most Flourishing City in the Universe*. Oxford Text Archive, http://hdl.handle.net/20.500.12024/K059801.000.

Department for Constitutional Affairs 2003. Draft Mental Incapacity Bill. *Cm 5859*. London: TSO.

Department for Constitutional Affairs 2007. Mental Capacity Act Code of Practice. TSO.

Department of Health 1989. Caring for People: community care in the next decade and beyond. *Cm 849*. London: HMSO.

Department of Health 2001. Valuing People: a new strategy for learning disability for the 21st century. *Cm 5086*. London: TSO.

Department of Health 2005a. 'Bournewood' consultation: the approach to be taken in response to the judgment of the European Court of Human Rights in the Bournewood case. *Gateway Ref 267902*. London.

Department of Health 2005b. Independence, well-being and choice: our vision for the future of social care for adults in England. *Cm 6499*. London: TSO.

Department of Health 2005c. Valuing People: what do the numbers tell us? London.

Department of Health 2006a. Our Health, Our Care, Our Say: a new direction for community services. *Cm 6737*. London: TSO.

Department of Health 2006b. Protecting the vulnerable: the 'Bournewood' Consultation: summary of responses. *In:* Department of Health (ed.) *Gateway Ref 5834*, London.

Department of Health 2007. Mental Health Bill Regulatory Impact Assessment Revised Version June 2007. *Gateway Ref 8455*. London.

Department of Health 2008. Code of Practice: Mental Health Act 1983. London: TSO.

Department of Health 2010. Explanatory Notes: The Health and Social Care Act 2008 (Regulated Activities) Regulations 2010 SI 2010/781.

Department of Health 2012. Transforming Care: a national response to Winterbourne View Hospital. *Department of Health Review: Final Report*.

Department of Health 2015a. Department of Health response to the Law Commission's consultation on mental capacity and deprivation of liberty. London.

Department of Health 2015b. Mental Health Act 1983: Code of Practice. London: TSO.

Department of Health (Ireland) 2017. Deprivation of Liberty: safeguard proposals. Consultation Paper.

Department of Health (Ireland) 2019. The Deprivation of Liberty Safeguard Proposals: report on the public consultation.

Department of Health and Others 2007. Putting People First: A shared vision and commitment to the transformation of Adult Social Care.

Department of Health and Welsh Office 1999. *Code of Practice: Mental Health Act 1983*. Published March 1999, pursuant to Section 118 of the Act. London: TSO.

Department of Health and Social Care 2019a. Impact Assessment: Mental Capacity (Amendment) Bill. *Revised IA, dated 31/01/2019*.

Department of Health and Social Care 2019b. Mental Capacity (Amendment) Act 2019: Explanatory Notes.

Department of Health and Social Care 2020a. *Care and support statutory guidance* [Online]. Available from: www.gov.uk/government/publications/care-act-statutory-guidance/care-and-support-statutory-guidance [Accessed 9 November 2021].

Department of Health and Social Care 2020b. The Mental Capacity Act (2005) (MCA) and Deprivation of Liberty Safeguards (DoLS) during the coronavirus (COVID-19) pandemic: additional guidance. *Version of 15 October 2020*.

Department of Health and Social Care. 2021. *Guidance: COVID-19: guidance for supported living* (Updated 17 August 2021) [Online]. Available from: www.gov.uk/government/publications/supported-living-services-during-coronavirus-covid-19/covid-19-guidance-for-supported-living [Accessed 9 November 2021]

Department of Health and Social Care & Ministry of Justice 2021a. Reforming the Mental Health Act. *CP 355.*

Department of Health and Social Care & Ministry of Justice 2021b. Reforming the Mental Health Act: Government response to consultation. *CP 501.*

Department of Health and Social Security 1971. Better Services for the Mentally Handicapped. *Cmnd 4683.*

Department of Health and Social Security 1975. Better Services for the Mentally Ill. *Cmnd. 6233.*

Department of Health and Social Security 1981. *Growing Older.* London: HMSO.

Department of Health and Social Security, Home Office, Welsh Office & Lord Chancellor's Department 1981. Reform of Mental Health Legislation. *Cmnd. 8405.*

Despouy, L. 1991. Human Rights and Disabled Persons. *Report by the Special Rapporteur of the United Nations Sub-Commission on Prevention of Discrimination and Protection of Minorities, UN Doc E/CN.4/Sub.2/1991/31.*

Devandas Aguilar, C. 2019. Report of the Special Rapporteur on the rights of persons with disabilities. *Human Rights Council, Fortieth session, 25 February–22 March 2019,* A/HRC/40/54.

Devon and Cornwall Constabulary 2009. *Operation Apple.* Disclosed to Lucy Series under the Freedom of Information Act 2000 on 22 June 2010. Cornwall.

Dhanda, A. 2006–7. Legal capacity in the Disability Rights Convention: stranglehold of the past or lodestar for the future? *Syracuse Journal of International Law and Commerce,* 34, 429.

Digby, A. 1996. Contexts and perspectives. *In:* Wright, D. & Digby, A. (eds) *From Idiocy to Mental Deficiency: historical perspectives on people with learning disabilities,* London and New York: Routledge.

Dilnot, A., Warner, L.N. & Williams, D.J. 2011. Fairer Care Funding: The report of the Commission on Funding of Care and Support. London: The Stationery Office.

Disability Rights Commission 2002. Policy Statement on Social care and Independent Living. London: Disability Rights Commission.

Disability Rights UK. 2014. *Deprivation of Liberty Safeguards* [Online]. Available from: www.disabilityrightsuk.org/news/2014/october/deprivation-liberty-safeguards [Accessed 9 November 2021].

Downs, M. 2015. *Introduction to Dementia Care Mapping™ (DCM™)*, University of Bradford School of Dementia Studies.

Dowson, S. 1990. *Who Does What? The process of enabling people with learning difficulties to achieve what they need and want*, London: Values into Action.

Dowson, S. 2007. *Independent Support Brokers: the why, what, and how*. London: National Development Team for Inclusion.

Doyle Guilloud, S. 2019. The right to liberty of persons with psychosocial disabilities at the United Nations: a tale of two interpretations. *International Journal of Law and Psychiatry*, 66, 101497.

Drakeford, M. 2006. Ownership, regulation and the public interest: the case of residential care for older people. *Critical Social Policy*, 26, 932–944.

Drinkwater, C. 2005. Supported living and the production of individuals. *In:* Tremain, S. (ed.) *Foucault and the Government of Disability*, Ann Arbor, MI: University of Michigan Press.

Duffy, S. 2005. Individual budgets: transforming the allocation of resources for care. *Journal of Integrated Care*, 13, 8–16.

Duffy, S. 2012. A Fair Society and the Limits of Personalisation. *A discussion paper from the Centre for Welfare Reform, first presented at the Tizard Memorial Lecture*.

Dunn, M.C., Clare, I.C.H. & Holland, A.J. 2008. To empower or to protect: constructing the vulnerable adult in English law and public policy. *Legal Studies*, 28, 234–253.

Dupuis, D. & Thorns, D. 1996. Meanings of home for older home owners. *Housing Studies*, 11, 485–501.

Duyvendak, J.W. & Verplanke, L. 2016. Struggling to belong: social movements and the fight for feeling at home. *In:* Miller, B., Nicholls, W. & Beaumont, J. (eds) *Spaces of Contention: spatialities and social movements*, Farnham: Ashgate.

Dykes, B.J. & Wheeler, R.A. 2015. Deprivations of liberty safeguards: not fit for purpose. *Journal of the Intensive Care Society*, 16, 80.

Easthope, H. 2004. A place called home. *Housing, Theory and Society*, 21, 128–138.

Edge, J. 2001. Demonstrating control of decisions by adults with learning difficulties who have high support needs. *Research by Values into Action for the Joseph Rowntree Foundation*.

Edgerton, R.B. 1967. *The Cloak of Competence: stigma in the lives of the mentally retarded*, Berkeley, CA: University of California Press.

Editorial 1861. Medical Certificates of Insanity. *Journal of Mental Science*, 7, 139–144.

EHRC (Equality and Human Rights Commission) 2011. Close to Home: an inquiry into older people and human rights in home care. London: EHRC.

EHRC 2021. *Strengthening the right to independent living* [Online]. Available from: www.equalityhumanrights.com/en/publication-download/strengthening-right-independent-living [Accessed 9 November 2021].

EHRC undated. *Film: The Bournewood case* [Online]. Available from: www.equalityhumanrights.com/en/what-are-human-rights/human-rights-stories/bournewood-case [Accessed 10 April 2019].

Eldergill, A. 2019. Are all incapacitated people confined in a hospital, care home or their own home deprived of liberty? *ERA Forum,* 19, 511–535.

Emerson, E. 2012. *A Review of the Results of the 2011/12 Focused CQC Inspection of Services for People with Learning Disabilities.* Learning Disability Observatory, supported by the Department of Health.

European Committee for the Prevention of Torture and Inhuman or Degrading Treatment or Punishment 1998. Involuntary Placement in Psychiatric Establishments. *CPT/Inf(98)12-part.*

European Court of Human Rights undated. Travaux Préparatoires to the Convention [Online]. Available from: www.echr.coe.int/Documents/Library_TravPrep_Table_ENG.pdf [Accessed 9 November 2021].

European Expert Group on the Transition from Institutional to Community-Based Care 2012. Common European Guidelines on the Transition from Institutional to Community-based Care. Brussels.

European Union Agency for Fundamental Rights (FRA) 2012. *Choice and control: the right to independent living. Experiences of persons with intellectual disabilities and persons with mental health problems in nine EU Member States.* Vienna: FRA.

Evans, J. 2003. *The Independent Living Movement in the UK* [Online]. Available from: www.independentliving.org/docs6/evans2003.html#1 [Accessed 9 November 2021]. The Independent Living Institute.

Family Mosaic 2012. *No going back: Is institutionalisation being recreated in modern care and support settings?* Family Mosaic, 20 Queen Elizabeth Street, London.

Fanning, J. 2016. Continuities of risk in the era of the Mental Capacity Act. *Medical Law Review,* 24, 415–433.

Fanning, J. 2018. *New Medicalism and the Mental Health Act,* Oxford: Hart.

Fay, R. & Owen, C. 2012. 'Home' in the aged care institution: authentic or ersatz. *Procedia-Social and Behavioral Sciences,* 35, 33–43.

Featherstone, K. & Northcott, A. 2021. *Wandering the Wards: an ethnography of hospital care and its consequences for people living with dementia,* London and New York: Routledge.

Featherstone, K., Northcott, A. & Bridges, J. 2019. Routines of resistance: an ethnography of the care of people living with dementia in acute hospital wards and its consequences. *International Journal of Nursing Studies,* 96, 53–60.

Fennell, P. 1986. Law and psychiatry: the legal constitution of the psychiatric system. *Journal of Law and Society,* 13, 35.

Fennell, P. 1992. Balancing care and control: guardianship, Community Treatment Orders and patient safeguards. *International Journal of Law and Psychiatry*, 15, 205–235.

Fennell, P. 1996. *Treatment Without Consent: law, psychiatry and the treatment of mentally disordered people since 1845*, London: Routledge.

Fennell, P. 1998. Doctor knows best? Therapeutic detention under common law, the Mental Health Act, and the European Convention. *Medical Law Review*, 6, 322–353.

Fennell, P. 2010a. Chapter 4: Mental Capacity. *In:* Gostin, L.O., McHale, J., Fennell, P., McKay, D. & Bartlett, P. (eds) *Principles of Mental Health Law*, Oxford: Oxford University Press.

Fennell, P. 2010b. Institutionalising the community: the codification of clinical authority and the limits of rights-based approaches. *In:* McSherry, B. & Weller, P. (eds) *Rethinking Rights-Based Mental Health Laws*, Oxford and Portland, OR: Hart.

Fennell, P. & Khaliq, U. 2011. Conflicting or complementary obligations? The UN Disability Rights Convention, the European Convention on Human Rights and English law. *European Human Rights Law Review*, 6, 662–674.

Fineman, M.A. 2010. The Vulnerable Subject and the Responsive State. *Emory Public Law Research Paper No. 10–130*.

Finlay, W.M.L., Antaki, C. & Walton, C. 2008. Saying no to the staff: an analysis of refusals in a home for people with severe communication difficulties. *Sociology of Health and Illness*, 30, 55–75.

Flynn, E. 2013. Mental (in)capacity or legal capacity? A human rights analysis of the proposed fusion of mental health and mental capacity law in Northern Ireland. *Northern Ireland Legal Quarterly*, 64, 485–505.

Flynn, E. & Arstein-Kerslake, A. 2014. Legislating personhood: realising the right to support in exercising legal capacity. *International Journal of Law in Context*, 10, 81–104.

Flynn, E. & Arstein-Kerslake, A. 2017. State intervention in the lives of people with disabilities: the case for a disability neutral framework. *International Journal of Law in Context*, 13, 39–57.

Flynn, E. & Gómez-Carrillo, M. 2019. *Good Practices to Promote the Right to Liberty of Persons with Disabilities*. Centre for Disability Law and Policy, and Institute for Lifecourse and Society, NUI Galway.

Flynn, E., Arstein-Kerslake, A., De Bhailís, C. & Serra, M.L. 2018. *Global Perspectives on Legal Capacity Reform: Our Voices, Our Stories*, Oxon: Routledge.

Flynn, E., Pinilla-Rocancio, M. & Gómez-Carrillo De Castro, M. 2019. Disability-specific forms of deprivation of liberty: report on a two-year project. Centre for Disability Law and Policy, and Institute for Lifecourse and Society, NUI Galway.

Flynn, M. 2018. Safeguarding Adults Review: Mendip House. Somerset Safeguarding Adults Board.

Flynn, M. 2019. Safeguarding Adults Review: Atlas Care Homes. Devon Safeguarding Adults Partnership.

Forty, A. & Cameron, I. 1986. *Objects of Desire: design and society since 1750,* London: Thames and Hudson.

Foucault, M. 1977a. *Discipline and Punish: the birth of the prison,* London: Penguin Books.

Foucault, M. 1977b. Nietzsche, genealogy, history. *In:* Bouchard, D.F. (ed.) *Language, Counter-Memory, Practice: selected essays and interviews.* Ithaca, NY: Cornell University Press.

Foucault, M. 2001/1961. *Madness and Civilization,* London: Routledge Classics.

Foucault, M. 2003. *Abnormal: lectures at the Collège de France, 1974–1975,* New York: Picador.

Foucault, M. 2006. *Psychiatric Power: lectures at the Collège de France, 1973–1974,* London: Palgrave Macmillan.

Fox, A. 2018. *A New Health and Social Care System: escaping the invisible asylum,* Bristol: Policy Press.

Fox, L. 2002. The meaning of home: a chimerical concept or a legal challenge? *Journal of Law and Society,* 29, 580–610.

Fox, L. 2005. The idea of home in law. *Home Cultures,* 2, 25–49.

Fox O'Mahony, L. 2006. *Conceptualising Home: theories, laws and policies,* Oxford: Hart.

Fox O'Mahony, L. 2013. The meaning of home: from theory to practice. *International Journal of the Built Environment,* 5, 156–171.

Fox O'Mahony, L. & Sweeney, J.A. 2010. The exclusion of (failed) asylum seekers from housing and home: towards an oppositional discourse. *Journal of Law and Society,* 37, 285–314.

Francis, R. 2013. Report of the Mid Staffordshire NHS Foundation Trust Public Inquiry Volume 2: Analysis of evidence and lessons learned (part 2). *HC 898-II.*

Fraser, N. & Gordon, L. 1994. A genealogy of dependency: tracing a keyword of the U.S. welfare state. *Signs,* 19, 309–336.

Fyson, R., Tarleton, B. & War, L. 2007. *Support for living? The impact of the Supporting People programme on housing and support for adults with learning disabilities.* York: Joseph Rowntree Foundation.

Garland, D. 2014. What is a 'history of the present'? On Foucault's genealogies and their critical preconditions. *Punishment and Society,* 16, 365.

Georgiou, N. 2014. Orchid View: Serious Case Review. *Serious Case Review for West Sussex Safeguarding Adults Board.*

Gladstone, D. 1996. The changing dynamic of institutional care: The Western Counties Idiot Asylum 1864–1914. *In:* Wright, D. & Digby, A. (eds) *From Idiocy to Mental Deficiency: historical perspectives on people with learning disabilities.* London and New York: Routledge.

Glasby, J., Needham, C., Allen, K., Hall, K. & McKay, S. 2018. The Goldilocks question: what size is 'just right' for social care providers? *International Journal of Care and Caring,* 2, 65–87.

Goffman, E. 1961. *Asylums,* London: Pelican Books.

Golder, B. & Fitzpatrick, P. 2009. *Foucault's Law,* Abingdon, Oxon: Routledge.

Goodall, E. & Wilkins, P. 2015. The Deprivation of Liberty Safeguards: A Best Interest Assessor time study. Cornwall Council.

Gooding, P. 2015. Navigating the 'flashing amber lights' of the right to legal capacity in the United Nations Convention on the Rights of Persons with Disabilities: responding to major concerns. *Human Rights Law Review,* 15, 45–71.

Gooding, P. & Flynn, E. 2015. Querying the call to introduce mental capacity testing to mental health law: does the doctrine of necessity provide an alternative? *Laws,* 4, 245–271.

Gordon, R. 2014. Thoughts on *P v Cheshire West; P & Q v Surrey County Council.* Community Care Law Reports.

Gostin, L. 1986. *Mental Health Services, Law and Practice,* London: Shaw and Sons.

Gostin, L. 1986/2000. *Mental Health Services: law and practice,* Supplement no. 18, June 2000. London: Shaw and Sons.

Gostin, L.O. 2007. From a civil libertarian to a sanitarian. *Journal of Law and Society,* 34, 594–616.

Graham, M. & Cowley, J. 2015. *A Practical Guide to the Mental Capacity Act 2005: putting the principles of the Act into practice,* London: Jessica Kingsley Publishers.

Grant Thornton 2018. Care homes for the elderly: Where are we now? [Online]. Available from: www.grantthornton.co.uk/globalassets/1.-member-firms/united-kingdom/pdf/documents/care-homes-for-the-elderly-where-are-we-now.pdf [Accessed 9 November 2021].

Greek Ombudsman 2016. National Preventive Mechanism Against Torture and Ill-Treatment: Annual Report 2016.

Green, C. 2020. *The potential role of human rights and the right to privacy in the context of English care homes for older people: multiple perspectives.* PhD, King's College London.

Green, S.L. 2013. 'An unnoticing environment': deficiencies and remedies – services for adults with learning disabilities. *Journal of Adult Protection,* 15, 192–202.

Greig, R. 1995/2001. *Moving On: a workbook for managers and others involved in developing new services to replace the remaining mental handicap hospitals*, London: National Development Team.

Greig, R. and Other Signatories 2011. Letter to David Cameron: a national response to the abuse of people with learning disabilities. National Development Team for Inclusion.

Grenfell, L. 2019. Aged care, detention and OPCAT. *Australian Journal of Human Rights*, 25, 248–262.

Griffiths, R. 1988. *Community Care: agenda for action*, London: HMSO.

Groger, L. 1995. A nursing home can be a home. *Journal of Aging Studies*, 9, 137–153.

Grubb, A. 1989a. *Decision-Making and Problems of Incompetence*, London: John Wiley & Sons.

Grubb, A. 1989b. Introduction. *In:* Grubb, A. (ed.) *Decision-Making and Problems of Incompetence*, London: John Wiley & Sons.

Grubb, A. 1993. Treatment decisions: keeping it in the family. *In:* Grubb, A. (ed.) *Choices and Decisions in Health Care*, London: John Wiley and Sons.

Gurbai, S., Fitton, E. & Martin, W. 2020. Insight under scrutiny in the Court of Protection: a case law survey. *Frontiers in Psychiatry*, 11.

Hacking, I. 2004. Between Michel Foucault and Erving Goffman: between discourse in the abstract and face-to-face interaction. *Economy and Society*, 33, 277–302.

Haigh, A., Lee, D., Shaw, C., Hawthorne, M., Chamberlain, S., Newman, D.W., Clarke, Z. & Beail, N. 2013. What things make people with a learning disability happy and satisfied with their lives: an inclusive research project. *Journal of Applied Research in Intellectual Disabilities*, 26, 26–33.

Hale, B. 2011. *Mental Health Law*, London: Sweet & Maxwell.

Hale, B. 2014. Book review: Rethinking Rights-based Mental Health Laws. Edited by Bernadette McSherry and Penelope Weller, Oxford: Hart Publishing, 2010. *International Journal of Law in Context*, 10, 140–142.

Hale, B. 2021. *Spiderwoman: A life*, London and New York: Vintage.

Hampton, P. 2005. *Reducing Administrative Burdens: effective inspection and enforcement*, London: HM Treasury.

Harbison, J.R. 2016. *Constesting Elder Abuse and Neglect: ageism, risk and the rhetoric of rights in the mistreatment of older people*, Vancouver: University of British Columbia Press.

Harding, R. & Peel, E. 2013. 'He was like a zombie': off-label prescription of antipsychotic drugs in dementia. *Medical Law Review*, 21, 243–277.

Harrington, J. 2017. *Towards a Rhetoric of Medical Law: against ethics*, Abingdon: Routledge.

Harrington, J., Series, L. & Ruck Keene, A. 2019. Law and rhetoric: critical possibilities. *Journal of Law and Society*, 46, 302–327.

Hatton, C. 2020. People with Learning Disabilities in England. Public Health England.

Hayes, L. 2017. *Stories of Care: a labour of law*, London: Palgrave.

Hayes, L. 2020. Criminalizing care workers: a critique of prosecution for ill-treatment or neglect. *In:* Bogg, A., Collins, J., Freedland, M. & Herring, J. (eds) *Criminality at Work*. Oxford: Oxford University Press.

Haynes, S. 1870. Voluntary patients in asylums. *Journal of Mental Science,* 15, 563–575.

Hayward, D.G. 1975. Home as an environmental and psychological concept. *Landscape,* 20, 2–9.

Health and Social Care Information Centre 2013. Mental Capacity Act 2005, Deprivation of Liberty Safeguards Assessments, England – 2012–13, Annual report. London.

Health and Social Care Information Centre 2014. Mental Capacity Act 2005, Deprivation of Liberty Safeguards (England) Annual Report, 2013–14. London.

Health and Social Care Information Centre 2015a. Learning Disability Census Report. London.

Health and Social Care Information Centre 2015b. Mental Capacity Act (2005) Deprivation of Liberty Safeguards (England) Annual Report, 2014–15. London.

Health Service Ombudsman 2001. Health Service Ombudsman for England – Annual Report for 2001–2: Case No. E. 2280/98–99. London: HSO.

Herr, S.S. 1976. Rights into action: protecting human rights of the mentally handicapped. *Catholic University Law Review,* 26, [i].

Herring, J. 2016. *Vulnerable Adults and the Law*, Oxford: Oxford University Press.

Hervey, N. 1986. Advocacy or Folly: The Alleged Lunatics' Friend Society, 1845–6. *Medical Science,* 30, 245–275.

Hervey, N.B. 1987. *The Lunacy Commission 1845–60, with special reference to the implementation of policy in Kent and Surrey.* PhD, University of Bristol.

Heslop, P., Blair, P.S., Fleming, P., Hoghton, M., Marriott, A. & Russ, L. 2014. The Confidential Inquiry into premature deaths of people with intellectual disabilities in the UK: a population-based study. *The Lancet,* 383, 889–895.

Heslop, P., Calkin, R. & Huxor, A. 2019. *The Learning Disabilities Mortality Review (LeDeR) – Annual Report 2018.* Report by University of Bristol Norah Fry Centre for Disability Studies for the Healthcare Quality Improvement Partnership.

Hewson, B. 2012. Fancy having a judge in your living room? *Spiked* [Online]. Available from: www.spiked-online.com/newsite/article/12853#.W3KjbuhKg2w.

Hewson, B. 2013. Keep the law out of disabled care. *Spike* [Online], 23 October 2013.

Hillman, A., Donelly, M., Whitaker, L., Dew, A., Stancliffe, R.J., Knox, M., Shelley, K. & Parmenter, T.R. 2012. Experiencing rights within positive, person-centred support networks of people with intellectual disability in Australia. *Journal of Intellectual Disability Research*, 56, 1065–1075.

Hilton, C. 2019. A tale of two inquiries: sans everything and Ely. *Political Quarterly*, 90, 185–193.

Hirsch, S.R. & Harris, J. (eds) 1988. *Consent and the Incompetent Patient: ethics, law and medicine*, London: Royal College of Psychiatrists.

HM Government 2010. Valuing people now: the delivery plan 2010–2011'Making it happen for everyone'.

HM Government 2014. Valuing every voice, respecting every right: making the case for the Mental Capacity Act. The Government's response to the House of Lords Select Committee Report on the Mental Capacity Act 2005. *Cm 8884*. London.

Hoggett, B. 1976. *Mental Health*, London: Sweet and Maxwell.

Hoggett, B. 1988. The Royal Prerogative in relation to the mentally disordered: resurrection, resuscitation or rejection. *In:* Freeman, M.D.A. (ed.) *Medicine, Ethics and the Law: current legal problems.* London: Stevens & Sons.

Hoggett, B. 1994. Joint parenting systems: the English experiment. *Tolley's Journal of Child Law*, 6, 8.

Holbrook, J. 2014a. The big question. *New Law Journal* [Online]. Available from: www.newlawjournal.co.uk/nlj/content/big-question-0.

Holbrook, J. 2014b. A distorted view. *New Law Journal*, 07 May 2014.

Holbrook, J. 2017. Against the juridification of everyday life. *Spiked* [Online]. Available from: www.spiked-online.com/2017/01/24/against-the-juridification-of-everyday-life/ [Accessed 24 January 2017]

Holbrook, J. & Allan, J. 2017. *Global Governance: The challenge to the UK's liberal democracy*, London: Policy Exchange.

Hollins, S., Lodge, K.-M. & Lomax, P. 2019. The case for removing intellectual disability and autism from the Mental Health Act. *The British Journal of Psychiatry*, 1–3.

Holman, A. & Collins, J. 1997. *Funding Freedom: a guide to direct payments for people with learning difficulties*, London: Values into Action.

Horden, P. & Smith, R. (eds) 1998. *The Locus of Care: families, communities, institutions, and the provision of welfare since antiquity*, London: Routledge.

Horwitz, M.J. 1982. The history of the public/private distinction. *University of Pennsylvania Law Review*, 130, 1423–1428.

House of Commons Social Services Committee 1985. Community care with special reference to adult mentally ill and mentally handicapped people. Volume I. *HC 13*. London: HMSO.

House of Lords Select Committee on the Mental Capacity Act 2005 2014. Mental Capacity Act 2005: post-legislative scrutiny. *HL Paper 139*. London: TSO.

Howe, G. 1969. Report of the Committee of Inquiry into Allegations of Ill-Treatment of Patients and other irregularities at the Ely Hospital, Cardiff. *Cmnd. 3975*. London: HMSO.

Hubbard, R. 2018. Best Interests Assessor role: an opportunity or a 'dead end' for adult social workers? *Practice: Social Work in Action*, 30, 83–98.

Hubbard, R. & Stone, K. 2020. *The Best Interests Assessor Practice Handbook*, Bristol: Bristol University Press.

Human Rights Committee 1982. General comment No. 8: Article 9 (Right to liberty and security of persons). *UN Doc ICCPR/GEC/6628/E*.

Human Rights Implementation Centre 2011. 'Deprivation of liberty' as per Article 4 of OPCAT: the scope. Bristol: University of Bristol.

Human Rights Ombudsman of the Republic of Slovenia 2018. National Preventive Mechanisms Report 2017.

Hume, D. & Beauchamp, T. 2000. *An Enquiry Concerning Human Understanding: A Critical Edition*, Clarendon Press.

Hunter, R. & Rackley, E. 2020. Feminist judgments on the UK Supreme Court. *Canadian Journal of Women and the Law*, 32, 85–113.

Hurley, R. 2013. *Home, Materiality, Memory and Belonging: keeping culture*, London: Palgrave Macmillan.

Jackson, M. 1996. Institutional provision for the feeble-minded in Edwardian England: Sandlebridge and the scientific morality of permanent care. *In:* Wright, D. & Digby, A. (eds) *From Idiocy to Mental Deficiency: historical perspectives on people with learning disabilities*, London and New York: Routledge.

James, E., Mitchell, B. & Morgan, H. 2019. *Social work, Cats and Rocket Science: stories of making a difference in social work with adults*, London and Philadelphia: Jessica Kingsley Publishers.

Jarrett, S. 2015. The meaning of 'community' in the lives of people with intellectual disabilities: an historical perspective. *International Journal of Developmental Disabilities*, 61, 107–112.

Jarrett, S. 2020. *Those They Called Idiots: the idea of the disabled mind from 1700 to the present day*, London: Reaktion Books.

Jay, P. 1979. Report of the Committee of Enquiry into Mental Handicap Nursing and Care. *House of Commons Sessional Papers, Cmnd. 7468-I*.

Jepson, M., Langan, J., Carpenter, J., Lloyd, L., Patsios, D. & Ward, P.L. 2014. The Deprivation of Liberty Safeguards: their impact on care practice. University of Bristol and NIHR School for Social Care Research.

Jessop, B. 1997. Capitalism and its future: remarks on regulation, government and governance. *Review of International Political Economy*, 4, 561–581.

Jingree, T. 2014. Duty of care, safety, normalisation and the Mental Capacity Act: a discourse analysis of staff arguments about facilitating choices for people with learning disabilities in UK services. *Journal of Community & Applied Social Psychology,* 25.

Jingree, T. & Finlay, W.M.L. 2011. 'It's got so politically correct now': parents' talk about empowering individuals with learning disabilities. *Sociology of Health & Illness,* 1–17.

John's Campaign 2021. *The Holding Pen: 14 days enforced isolation for people living in care homes,* Chelmsford: Golden Duck.

Johnson, J., Rolph, S. & Smith, R. 2010. *Residential Care Transformed: revisiting 'The Last Refuge',* Basingstoke: Palgrave Macmillan.

Joint Committee on Draft Mental Incapacity Bill 2002–3. Draft Mental Incapacity Bill. *HL Paper 189 HC 1083.* London: HMSO.

Joint Committee on Human Rights 2007. Legislative scrutiny: Mental Health Bill. *HC 288, HL Paper 40.*

Joint Committee on Human Rights 2012. Implementation of the Right of Disabled People to Independent Living. *HC 1074, HL Paper 257.* London.

Joint Committee on Human Rights 2018a. Legislative scrutiny: Mental Capacity (Amendment) Bill. *Twelfth Report of Session 2017–19, HC 1662, HL Paper 208.*

Joint Committee on Human Rights 2018b. The right to freedom and safety: reform of the Deprivation of Liberty Safeguards. *HC 890, HL Paper 161.*

Joint Committee on Human Rights 2019. The detention of young people with learning disabilities and/or autism. *HC 121, HL Paper 10.*

Jonasson, J. 2009. *The Hundred-Year-Old Man Who Climbed Out of the Window and Disappeared,* London: Abacus.

Jones, K. 1972. *A History of the Mental Health Services,* London: Routledge & Kegan Paul.

Jones, K. 1980. The limitations of the legal approach to mental health. *International Journal of Law and Psychiatry,* 3, 1–15.

Jones, N. & Shattell, M. 2014. Beyond easy answers: facing the entanglements of violence and psychosis. *Issues in Mental Health Nursing,* 35, 809–811.

Jones, R. & Piffaretti, E. 2018. *Mental Capacity Act Manual,* London: Sweet & Maxwell.

Kanter, A. 2015. *The Development of Disability Rights Under International Law: from charity to human rights,* Abingdon: Routledge.

Kapp, M.B. 1998. The voluntary status of nursing facility admissions: legal, practical, and public policy implications. *New England Journal on Criminal and Civil Confinement,* 24, 1–36.

Kayess, R. & French, P. 2008. Out of darkness into light? Introducing the Convention on the Rights of Persons with Disabilities. *Human Rights Law Review,* 8, 1–34.

Kazin, C. 1989. Nowhere to go and chose to stay: using the tort of false imprisonment to redress involuntary confinement of the elderly in nursing homes and hospitals. *University of Pennsylvania Law Review,* 137, 903–928.

Keeling, A. 2018. Article 16: Freedom from violence, exploitation and abuse. *In:* Bantekas, I., Stein, M. & Anastasiou, D. (eds) *Commentary on UN Convention on the Rights of Persons with Disablities.* Oxford: Oxford University Press.

Kelly, C. 2016. *Disability Politics and Care: the challenge of direct funding,* Vancouver: University of British Columbia Press.

Killaspy, H. 2007. From the asylum to community care: learning from experience. *British Medical Bulletin,* 79–80, 245–258.

Kinsella, P. 1993. *Supported Living – A New Paradigm,* Manchester: National Development Team.

Kinsella, P. 2008. *Supported living – fact or fiction?* Available from: www.paradigm-uk.org.

Kitwood, T. 1997. *Dementia Reconsidered: the person comes first,* Maidenhead, UK: Open University Press.

Kitwood, T. & Booker, D. (eds) 2019. *Dementia Reconsidered: the person still comes first,* London: Open University Press.

Kong, C. 2017. *Mental Capacity in Relationship: decision-making, dialogue and autonomy,* Cambridge: Cambridge University Press.

Kong, C., Coggon, J., Dunn, M. & Keene, A.R. 2020. An aide memoire for a balancing act? Critiquing the 'balance sheet' approach to best interests decision-making. *Medical Law Review,* 28, 753–780.

Kritsotaki, D., Long, V. & Smith, M. 2016. *Deinstitutionalisation and After: Post-war psychiatry in the Western world,* Switzerland: Springer International Publishing.

Kulick, D. & Rydström, J. 2015. *Loneliness and Its Opposite,* Durham and London: Duke University Press.

Laing, W. 2018a. Care homes for older people: UK market report. London: LaingBuisson.

Laing, W. 2018b. Homecare and supported living: market report, 2nd edn. London: LaingBuisson.

LaingBuisson 2018. Mental health hospitals: UK market report. London: LaingBuisson.

LaingBuisson 2019. Mental health: UK market report, 4th edn. London: LaingBuisson.

Langer, E.J. & Rodin, J. 1976. The effects of choice and enhanced personal responsibility for the aged: a field experiment in an institutional setting. *Journal of Personality and Social Psychology,* 34, 191.

Lashewicz, B., Mitchell, J., Salami, E. & Cheuk, S. 2014. Understanding and addressing voices of adults with disabilities within their family caregiving contexts: implications for capacity, decision-making and guardianship. Commissioned by the Law Commission of Ontario.

Law Commission 1991. Mentally incapacitated adults and decision-making: an overview. *Law Com No 119, HMSO.* London: HMSO.

Law Commission 1993a. Mentally incapacitated adults and decision-making: a new jurisdiction. *Law Com No 128, HMSO.* London: HMSO.

Law Commission 1993b. Mentally incapacitated adults and decision-making: medical treatment and research. *Law Com no 129, HMSO.* London: HMSO.

Law Commission 1993c. Mentally incapacitated and other vulnerable adults: public law protection. *Law Com No 130, HMSO.* London: HMSO.

Law Commission 1995. Mentally incapacitated adults. *Law Com No 231, HMSO.* London: HMSO.

Law Commission 2015. Mental capacity and deprivation of liberty: a consultation paper. *Consultation Paper 222.* London: TSO.

Law Commission 2017a. Impact assessment: mental capacity and detention. *LAWCOM0055.*

Law Commission 2017b. Mental capacity and deprivation of liberty. *Law Com No 372.*

Law Commission 2017c. Mental capacity and deprivation of liberty – consultation analysis.

Law Commission of Ontario 2017. Legal capacity, decision-making and guardianship.

Law Society 2015. Identifying a deprivation of liberty: a practical guide.

Law Society 2020. 15 years of the Mental Capacity Act 2005. 7 October 2020 online conference.

Lawson, A. & Series, L. 2018. United Kingdom. *In:* Lawson, A. & Waddington, L. (eds) *The UN Convention on the Rights of Persons with Disabilities in Practice: a comparative analysis of the role of courts,* Oxford: Oxford University Press.

Lazar, O. 2019. A republic of rules: procedural arbitrariness and total institutions. *Critical Review of International Social and Political Philosophy,* 22, 681–702.

Lazar, O. 2021. Micro-domination. *European Journal of Political Theory* (published online 6 September 2021) doi.org/10.1177/14748851211020626.

Lea, M., Beaupert, F., Bevan, N., Celermajer, D., Gooding, P., Minty, R., Phillips, E., Spivakovsky, C., Steele, L., Wadiwel, D.J. & Weller, P.J. 2018. A disability aware approach to torture prevention? Australian OPCAT ratification and improved protections for people with disability. *Australian Journal of Human Rights,* 24, 70–96.

Leadbeater, C. 2004. *Personalisation through Participation: a new script for public services.* London: Demos.

Leadbeater, C., Bartlett, J. & Gallagher, N. 2008. *Making It Personal.* London: Demos.

Leece, J. & Bornat, J. 2006. *Developments in Direct Payments,* Bristol: Policy Press.

Leibing, A., Guberman, N. & Wiles, J. 2016. Liminal homes: older people, loss of capacities, and the present future of living spaces. *Journal of Aging Studies,* 37, 10–19.

Leith, K.H. 2006. 'Home is where the heart is ... or is it?': a phenomenological exploration of the meaning of home for older women in congregate housing. *Journal of Aging Studies,* 20, 317–333.

Levenson, R. & Joule, N. 2005. What older people say about care services: a literature review for The King's Fund Care Services Inquiry. The King's Fund.

Lewis, F., Karlsberg Schaffer, S., Sussex, J., O'Neill, P. & Cockcroft, L. 2014. The trajectory of dementia in the UK – making a difference. Office of Health Economics for Alzheimer's Research UK.

Lewis, O. 2011. Advancing legal capacity jurisprudence. *European Human Rights Law Review,* 700–714.

Lewis, O. 2012. Stanev v. Bulgaria: on the pathway to freedom. *Human Rights Brief,* 19, 1–6.

Lewis, O. 2018. Council of Europe. *In:* Lawson, A. & Waddington, L. (eds) *Interpreting and Domesticating the UN Convention on the Rights of Persons with Disabilities: a comparative analysis of the role of courts,* Oxford: Oxford University Press.

Lilly, M. 1984. *The National Council for Civil Liberties: the first fifty years,* London: Macmillan.

Lindemann, H. 2009. Holding one another (well, wrongly, clumsily) in a time of dementia. *Metaphilosophy,* 40, 416–424.

Lindsey, J. 2016. Developing vulnerability: a situational response to the abuse of women with mental disabilities. *Feminist Legal Studies,* 24, 295–314.

Lindsey, J. 2019. Competing professional knowledge claims about mental capacity in the court of protection. *Medical Law Review,* 28, 1–29.

Lipsky, M. 2010/1980. *Street Level Bureaucracy: dilemmas of the individual in public services,* New York: Russell Sage Foundation.

Local Government Ombudsman 2017. The right to decide: towards a greater understanding of mental capacity and deprivation of liberty.

Local Government Ombudsman 2019. Investigation into a complaint against Staffordshire County Council (reference number: 18 004 809).

Lord Chancellor's Office 1999. 'Making Decisions': the government's proposals for making decisions on behalf of mentally incapacitated adults. A Report issued in the light of responses to the consultation paper Who Decides? *Cm 4465.* London: HMSO.

Lord Percy 1957. Report of the Royal Commission on the Law Relating to Mental Illness and Mental Deficiency 1954–1957. *Cm 169.* HMSO: London.

Lord Renton 1980. Mental handicap legislation in the 1980s. *Law and the Mentally Retarded Citizen, Report of the Thirteenth Spring Conference on Mental Retardation, National Society for Mentally Handicapped Children and Adults (Mencap).* University of Exeter.

Lord, J. 2010. Shared understanding or consensus-masked disagreement: The Anti-Torture Framework in the Convention on the Rights of Persons with Disabilities. *Loyola of Los Angeles International & Comparative Law Review,* 33, 27.

Lovatt, M. 2018. Becoming at home in residential care for older people: a material culture perspective. *Sociology of Health & Illness,* 40, 366–378.

Lovett, F. 2010. *A General Theory of Domination and Justice,* Oxford: Oxford University Press.

Lowman, J., Menzies, R.J. & Palys, T.S. 1987. *Transcarceration: essays in the sociology of social control,* Aldershot: Gower.

Lundgren, E. 2000. Homelike housing for elderly people? Materialized ideology. *Housing, Theory and Society,* 17, 109–120.

Lushington, S.J. 1895. *Archibold's Lunacy,* London: Shaw & Sons.

Lyle O'Brien, C. & O'Brien, J. 2000. The origins of person-centered planning: a community of practice perspective. National Institute on Disability and Rehabilitation Research, Washington DC; Minneapolis Institute on Community Integration, Minnesota University and the New York Center on Human Policy, Syracuse University.

Lynch, K., Baker, J. & Lyons, M. 2009. *Affective Equality: love, care and injustice,* London: Palgrave.

Macmillan, P. 1926. Report of the Royal Commission on Lunacy and Mental Disorder. *Cmd. 2700.*

Mallers, M.H., Claver, M. & Lares, L.A. 2014. Perceived control in the lives of older adults: the influence of Langer and Rodin's Work on gerontological theory, policy, and practice. *The Gerontologist,* 54, 67–74.

Mallett, S. 2004. Understanding home: a critical review of the literature. *The Sociological Review,* 52, 62–89.

Malmedal, W. 2014. Norwegian nursing home: a care facility or a home? *Open Journal of Nursing,* 4, 6.

Mansell, J. 1993. Services for people with learning disabilities and challenging behaviour or mental health needs: report of a project group. HMSO.

Mansell, J. 2007. Services for people with learning disability and challenging behaviour or mental health needs. *In:* Department of Health (ed.) *The Mansell Report.* London.

Mansell, J. 2010. Raising our sights: services for adults with profound intellectual and multiple disabilities. *In:* Department of Health (ed.) *Valuing People Now.* London.

Mansell, J. 2011. Bristol care home: a failure on every level. *The Guardian,* 01 June 2011.

Mansell, J. & Beadle-Brown, J. 2010. Deinstitutionalisation and community living: position statement of the Comparative Policy and Practice Special Interest Research Group of the International Association for the Scientific Study of Intellectual Disabilities 1. *Journal of Intellectual Disability Research,* 54, 104–112.

Mapother, E. 1924. The treatment of mental disorder on a voluntary basis. *The Lancet,* 204, 897–902.

Marsden, J.P. 1999. Older persons' and family members' perceptions of homeyness in assisted living. *Environment and Behavior,* 31, 84–106.

Marshall, J. 2014. *Human Rights Law and Personal Identity,* London: Routledge.

Martin, W. & Gurbai, S. 2019. Surveying the Geneva impasse: coercive care and human rights. *International Journal of Law and Psychiatry,* 64, 117–128.

McDonnell, J. 2020. Care services must now be nationalised, says John McDonnell. *The Guardian,* 20 July 2020.

McKay, C. & Stavert, J. 2017. Scotland's Mental Health and Capacity Law: the case for reform. Centre for Mental Health and Capacity Law, Edinburgh Napier University and the Mental Welfare Commission for Scotland.

McNicholl, A. 2014. Deprivation of liberty: social workers, lawyers and carers on the impact of a landmark Supreme Court ruling. *Community Care,* 9 September 2014.

McPherson, B. 2014. 'All too often dementia in older age leads to professionals disregarding human rights'. *Community Care,* 28 April 2014.

Means, R. 2007. Safe as houses? Ageing in place and vulnerable older people in the UK. *Social Policy & Administration,* 41, 65–85.

Means, R. & Smith, R. 1983. From public assistance institutions to 'Sunshine Hotels': changing state perceptions about residential care for elderly people, 1939–48. *Ageing and Society,* 3, 157–181.

Means, R., Richards, S. & Smith, R. 2008. *Community Care: Policy and Practice,* Basingstoke: Palgrave Macmillan.

Mental Health Act Commission 1985. The First Biennial Report of the Mental Health Act Commission 1983–85.

Mental Health Act Commission 2003. Placed amongst strangers: twenty years of the Mental Health Act 1983 and future prospects for psychiatric compulsion. *Tenth Biennial Report 2001–2003.* London: Mental Health Act Commission.

Metropolitan Commissioners in Lunacy 1844. Metropolitan Commissioners in Lunacy: report to Lord Chancellor. *House of Commons Papers 001.*

Milligan, C. 2000. 'Bearing the burden': towards a restructured geography of caring. *Area,* 32, 49–58.

Milligan, C. 2009. *There's No Place Like Home: place and care in an ageing society,* London and New York: Routledge.

Mind 2014. *Mind welcomes landmark judgment for protection of vulnerable people* [Online]. Available from: www.mind.org.uk/news-campaigns/news/mind-welcomes-landmark-judgment-for-protection-of-vulnerable-people/#.XJ4rhpj7Q2w [Accessed 9 November 2021].

Ministry of Health 1963. Health & welfare: the development of community care plans for the health and welfare services of the local authorities in England and Wales. *Cmnd 1973.*

Ministry of Justice 2020. Family court statistics quarterly: October to December 2019.

Ministry of Justice & Office for National Statistics 2017. Coroner Statistics Annual 2017: England and Wales.

Minkowitz, T. 2006–7. The United Nations Convention on the Rights of Persons with Disabilities and the right to be free from nonconsensual psychiatric interventions. *Syracuse Journal of International Law and Commerce,* 34, 405.

Minkowitz, T. 2017. CRPD and transformative equality. *International Journal of Law in Context,* 13, 77–86.

Miola, J. 2007. *Medical Ethics and Medical Law: a symbiotic relationship,* Oxford: Hart.

Mitchell, D. 2004. *Cloud Atlas,* London: Sceptre.

Mladenov, T. & Petri, G. 2019. Critique of deinstitutionalisation in postsocialist Central and Eastern Europe. *Disability & Society,* 1–24.

Montgomery, J. 1989. Medicine, accountability, and professionalism. *Journal of Law and Society,* 319–339.

Montgomery, J., Jones, C. & Biggs, H. 2014. Hidden law-making in the province of medical jurisprudence. *The Modern Law Review,* 77, 343–378.

Moore, J. 2000. Placing home in context. *Journal of Environmental Psychology,* 20, 207–217.

Moran, D. 2014. Leaving behind the 'total institution'? Teeth, transcarceral spaces and (re)inscription of the formerly incarcerated body. *Gender, Place & Culture,* 21, 35–51.

Morris, P. 1969. *Put Away: a sociological study of institutions for the mentally retarded,* London: Routledge & Kegan Paul.

Morrison, L.J. 2005. *Talking Back to Psychiatry,* New York and Abingdon: Routledge.

Murphy, G. 2020. CQC inspections and regulation of Whorlton Hall 2015–2019: an independent review. CQC.

Murray, R., Steinerte, E., Evans, M. & Hallo De Wolf, A. 2011. *The Optional Protocol to the UN Convention Against Torture*, Oxford: Oxford University Press.

Naffine, N. 2003. Who are law's persons? From Cheshire cats to responsible subjects. *The Modern Law Review*, 66, 346–367.

National Council for Civil Liberties 1951. 50,000 outside the law: an examination of the treatment of those certified as mentally defective. London.

National Development Team for Inclusion 2011. Feeling Settled Project.

National Development Team for Inclusion 2015. The Real Tenancy Test: tenancy rights in supported accommodation. *Revised November 2015.*

National Health Service 1962. A hospital plan for England and Wales. *Cd 1604.*

National Society for Mentally Handicapped Children and Adults (Mencap) 1980. *Report of the Thirteenth Spring Conference on Mental Retardation. Law and the Mentally Retarded Citizen.* University of Exeter.

Naylor, A. & Magnusson, J. 2019. Data that cares. Future Care Capital.

Neary, M. 2015. A state of flux. *Love, Belief and Balls* [Online]. Available from: https://markneary1dotcom1.wordpress.com/2015/03/08/a-state-of-flux/ [Accessed 8 March 2015.]

Neary, M. 2018. Silly DoLS talking. *Love, Belief and Balls* [Online]. Available from: https://markneary1dotcom1.wordpress.com/2018/06/09/silly-dols-talking/ [Accessed 9 June 2018.]

Needham, C. & Glasby, J. (eds) 2014. *Debates in Personalisation*, Bristol: Policy Press.

Nell, J. 2020. *The Great Escape from Woodlands Nursing Home*, London: Hodder & Stoughton.

Nettleton, S., Buse, C. & Martin, D. 2018. 'Essentially it's just a lot of bedrooms': architectural design, prescribed personalisation and the construction of care homes for later life. *Sociology of Health & Illness*, 40, 1156–1171.

Neugebauer, R. 1996. Mental handicap in Medieval and Early Modern England: criteria, measurement and care. *In:* Wright, D. & Digby, A. (eds) *From Idiocy to Mental Deficiency: Historical Perspectives on People with Learning Disabilities.* London and New York: Routledge.

New Zealand Human Rights Commission 2018. Monitoring places of detention 2016/17: Annual report of activities under the Optional Protocol to the Convention Against Torture (OPCAT).

NHS Digital 2018. Mental Capacity Act 2005, Deprivation of Liberty Safeguards England, 2017–18.

NHS Digital 2019a. Adult social care activity and finance report, England, 2018–19 [PAS].

NHS Digital 2019b. Mental Capacity Act 2005, Deprivation of Liberty Safeguards England, 2018–19.

NHS Digital 2019c. Mental Health Act statistics, annual figures 2018–19.

NHS Digital 2019d. Supplementary information: DoLS activity by disability group during reporting period 2017–18.

NHS Digital 2020a. Adult social care activity and finance report, England, 2018–19 [PAS] Data Pack.

NHS Digital 2020b. Bed availability and occupancy data – overnight. *Version published 27 February 2020.*

NHS Digital 2021. Learning disability services monthly statistics AT: May 2021.

NHS England 2017. Stopping over-medication of people with a learning disability, autism or both (STOMP).

NHS England, Local Government Association & Association of Directors of Adult Social Services 2015. Building the right support.

NHS Information Centre for Health and Social Care 2011. Mental Capacity Act 2005, Deprivation of Liberty Safeguards assessments (England) – Second report on annual data, 2010/11: Appendix A – Annual DoLS Supporting Tables. London: NHS IC.

Nirje, B. 1969. The normalization principle and its human management implications. *SRV-VRS: The International Social Role Valorization Journal,* 1, 19.

Noble, D. 2020. Report to the Board of the Care Quality Commission ('CQC') on how CQC dealt with concerns raised by Barry Stanley-Wilkinson in relation to the regulation of Whorlton Hall Hospital and to make recommendations. Care Quality Commission.

Norwegian Parliamentary Ombudsman 2018. The Parliamentary Ombudsman's annual report for 2017 as National Preventive Mechanism against Torture and Other Cruel, Inhuman or Degrading Treatment or Punishment.

Nowak, M. 2007. Promotion and protection of all human rights, civil, political, economic, social and cultural rights, including the right to development. *Report of the Special Rapporteur on torture and other cruel, inhuman or degrading treatment or punishment, Manfred Nowak. 15 January 2008. UN Doc A/HRC/7/3.*

Nowak, M., Birk, M. & Monina, G. 2019. *The United Nations Convention Against Torture and its Optional Protocol: a commentary,* Oxford: Oxford University Press.

O'Brien, J. 1994. Down stairs that are never your own: supporting people with developmental disabilities in their own homes. *Mental Retardation,* 32, 1–6.

O'Brien, J. & Lovett, H. 1993. Finding a way toward everyday lives: the contribution of person centered planning. Office of Mental Retardation, Pennsylvania State Department of Public Welfare and New York Center on Human Policy at Syracuse University.

O'Cinneide, C. 2009. Extracting protection for the rights of persons with disabilities from human rights frameworks: Established limits and new possibilities. *In:* Arnardóttir, O.M. & Quinn, G. (eds) *The UN Convention on the Rights of Persons with Disabilities: European and Scandinavian perspectives.* Leiden: Martinus Nijhoff Publishers.

Oddie, W. & Torode, J. 1995. Legal commissars subverting family values: last week *The Mail* exposed moves to equate marriage with living together. Today we focus on the faceless lawyers behind these disturbing measures. *Daily Mail,* 1 November 1995.

Office for National Statistics 2020. Care home and non-care home populations used in the Deaths involving COVID-19 in the care sector article, England and Wales. *Released 8 September 2020, Reference number 12215.*

Office of the Public Guardian 2019. Lasting power of attorney: campaign leaflet.

Oliver, M. 1990. *The Politics of Disablement,* Basingstoke: Palgrave Macmillan.

Ombudsman of the Republic of Croatia 2017. Report on the Performance of Activities of the National Preventive Mechanism.

One Crown Office Row 2012. Dignity, death and deprivation of liberty: human rights in the Court of Protection. London: One Crown Office Row.

OPM Group 2017. CQC's next phase of regulation consultation: Summary analysis report.

O'Shea, T. 2018a. A civic republican analysis of mental capacity law. *Legal Studies,* 38, 147–163.

O'Shea, T. 2018b. Disability and domination: lessons from Republican political philosophy. *Journal of Applied Philosophy,* 35, 133–148.

Parker, C.H. 2016. *Trust A v X and Others:* The ghost of *Nielsen* returns? *Medical Law Review,* 24, 268–277.

Parliamentary Ombudsman of Finland 2018. Summary of the annual report 2018: National Preventive Mechanism against Torture.

Parry-Jones, W.L. 1972. *The Trade in Lunacy: a study of private madhouses in England in the eighteenth and nineteenth centuries,* London: Routledge and Kegan Paul.

Partington, J.S. 2003. H.G. Wells's eugenic thinking of the 1930s and 1940s. *Utopian Studies,* 14, 74–81.

Pathare, S. & Sagad, J. 2013. Mental health: a legislative framework to empower, protect and care: A review of mental health legislation in Commonwealth member states. *Commissioned by the Commonwealth Health Professions Alliance, prepared by Centre for Mental Health Law & Policy Indian Law Society, Pune, India.*

Peace, S. 2003. The development of residential and nursing care in the United Kingdom. *In:* Katz, J.S. & Peace, S.M. (eds) *End of Life in Care Homes: a Palliative Approach.* Oxford: Oxford University Press.

Peace, S. and Holland, C. 2001. Homely residential care: a contradiction in terms? *Journal of Social Policy*, 30, 393.

Pettit, P. 1997a. Republican political theory. *In:* Vincent, A. (ed.) *Political Theory: tradition and diversity.* Cambridge: Cambridge University Press.

Pettit, P. 1997b. *Republicanism: a theory of freedom and government,* Oxford: Oxford University Press.

Pettit, P. 2008. Republican freedom: three axioms, four theorems. *In:* Laborde, C. & Maynor, J. (eds) *Republicanism and Political Theory.* Oxford: Wiley-Blackwell.

Pettit, P. 2015. Freedom and the state: nanny or nightwatchman? *Public Health,* 129, 1055–1060.

Pirjola, J. & Raškauskas, V. 2015. Checklist for visits to social care institutions where persons may be deprived of their liberty. *European Committee for the Prevention of Torture and Inhuman or Degrading Treatment or Punishment, CPT/Inf (2015) 23.*

Polish Commissioner for Human Rights. 2018. *RPO w sprawie lepszej ochrony praw mieszkańców domów pomocy społecznej (RPO on better protection of the rights of residents of social welfare homes)* [Online]. Available from: www.rpo. gov.pl/pl/content/rpo-w-sprawie-lepszej-ochrony-praw-mieszkancow-domow-pomocy-spolecznej [Accessed 9 November 2021].

Poole, G. 2014. Solar Centre Serious Case Review Report. On behalf of Doncaster Safeguarding Adults Partnership Board.

Poor Law Commissioners 1834. Report from His Majesty's commissioners for inquiring into the administration and practical operation of the Poor Laws. *HC 44.*

Pope, T.M. 2016. Unbefriended and unrepresented: Better Medical Decision Making for Incapacitated Patients without Healthcare Surrogates Symposium: Exploring the Right to Die in the U.S. *Georgia State University Law Review,* 923–1020.

Porter, R. 1987. *Mind-forg'd Manacles: a history of madness in England from the Restoration to the Regency,* Cambridge, MA: Harvard University Press.

Porter, R. 1994. Rethinking institutions in late Georgian England. *Utilitas,* 6, 65–80.

Powell, E. 1961. 'Water Tower Speech'. *Annual Conference for the National Association for Mental Health.* London.

Prince, M., Knapp, M., Guerchet, M., Mccrone, P., Prina, M., Comas-Herrera, A., Wittenberg, R., Adelaja, B., Hu, B., King, D., Rehill, A. & Salimkumar, D. 2014. Dementia UK: update. *Report prepared for the Alzheimer's Society by King's College London and the London School of Economics.*

Pring, J. 2011. *Longcare Survivors: the biography of a care scandal,* London: Disability News Service.

Pring, J. 2019. Tribunal decision 'could deter companies from building more institutions'. Disability News Service.

Prosser, T. 2010. *The Regulatory Enterprise: government, regulation, and legitimacy*, Oxford: Oxford University Press.

Public Defender of Rights 2017. Protection against ill-treatment 2016: Report of the Public Defender of Rights as the National Preventive Mechanism.

Quinn, G. 2009. The United Nations Convention on the Rights of Persons with Disabilities: toward a new international politics of disability. *Texas Journal of Civil Liberties and Civil Rights,* 15, 33–52.

Quinn, G. 2013. 'Liberation, cloaking devices and the law.' Or a personal reflection on the law and theology of Article 12 of the UN CRPD. *Rights & Enforcement – The Next Steps. UN CRPD Article 12 standards and their implementation in legal frameworks. BCNL Conference.* Sofia.

Quinn, G. & Arstein-Kerslake, A. 2012. Restoring the 'human' in 'human rights': personhood and doctrinal innovation in the UN disability convention. *In:* Gearty, C. & Douzinas, C. (eds) *Cambridge Companion to Human Rights Law.* Cambridge: Cambridge University Press.

Redfern, S., Norman, I., Briggs, K. & Askham, J. 2002. Care at home for people with dementia: routines, control and care goals. *Quality in Ageing and Older Adults,* 3, 12.

Rees, N. 2010. The fusion proposal: a next step? *In:* McSherry, B. & Weller, P. (eds) *Rethinking Rights-Based Mental Health Law.* Oxford: Hart Publishing.

Richardson, G. 1999. Report of the Expert Committee: review of the Mental Health Act 1983. London.

Robb, B. 1967. *Sans Everything: a case to answer.* London: Nelson.

Roberts, A. 1981. *The Lunacy Commission* [Online]. Middlesex University Web. Available from: www.mdx.ac.uk/www/study/01.htm [Accessed 03 July 2012].

Roberts, E. 2012. *Legislating home: The impact of the regulation of small house settings for long term care residents in Nova Scotia, Canada.* PhD, University of Missouri.

Robertson, G.M. 1888. Reflex speech. *Journal of Mental Science,* 34, 43–51.

Robinson, R. & Scott-Moncrieff, L. 2005. Making sense of Bournewood. *Journal of Mental Health Law,* 17.

Rochester, C. 1989. Southwark consortium 1984–1987: organisation and action in the local development of services for people with learning difficulties. *Building Community Strategies Working Paper No. 2,* The King's Fund.

Rodin, J. & Langer, E.J. 1977. Long-term effects of a control-relevant intervention with the institutionalized aged. *Journal of Personality and Social Psychology,* 35, 897–902.

Rose, N. 1985a. *The Psychological Complex: psychology, politics and society in England, 1869–1939,* London: Routledge and Kegan Paul.

Rose, N. 1985b. Unreasonable rights: mental illness and the limits of the law. *Journal of Law and Society,* 12, 199–218.

Rose, N. 1987. Beyond the public/private division: law, power and the family. *Journal of Law and Society,* 14, 61–76.

Rose, N. 1998. The crisis of the social: beyond the social question. *In:* Hänninen, S. (ed.) *Displacement of Social Policies.* Jyväskylä, Finland: Publications of Social and Political Sciences and Philosophy, University of Jyväskylä.

Rose, N. 1999. *Powers of Freedom: reframing political thought,* Cambridge: Cambridge University Press.

Rose, N. 2018. *Our Psychiatric Future,* Cambridge: Polity Press.

Rose, N. & Miller, P. 1992. Political power beyond the state: problematics of government. *British Journal of Sociology,* 43, 172–205.

Rose, N. & Valverde, M. 1998. Governed by law? *Social & Legal Studies,* 7, 541–551.

Rosenthal, E. & Rubenstein, L.S. 1993. International human rights advocacy under the 'principles for the protection of persons with mental illness'. *International Journal of Law and Psychiatry,* 16, 257–300.

Rowntree, B.S. 1947/1980. *Old People: Report of a Survey Committee on the problems of ageing and the care of old people,* New York: reprinted by Arno Press.

Royal Commission into Aged Care Quality and Safety 2021. Final Report – Volume 1: Summary and Recommendations. Commonwealth of Australia.

Royal Commission into Violence, Abuse, Neglect and Exploitation of People with Disability, 2020. Issues Paper: Restrictive Practices. 26 May 2020.

Royal Commission on the Care and Control of the Feeble-Minded 1908. Report of the Royal Commission on the Care and Control of the Feeble-Minded. Volume VIII. *Cd. 4202.*

Ruck Keene, A. 2013. Tying ourselves into (Gordian) knots? Deprivation of liberty and the MCA 2005. London: 39 Essex Chambers.

Ruck Keene, A. 2016. Powers, defences and the 'need' for judicial sanction. *Elder Law Journal,* Autumn, 244.

Ruck Keene, A. 2017a. Discussion paper: deprivation of liberty, Cheshire West and the CRPD. London: 39 Essex Chambers.

Ruck Keene, A. 2017b. Is mental capacity in the eye of the beholder? *Advances in Mental Health and Intellectual Disabilities,* 11, 30–39.

Ruck Keene, A. & Xu, X. 2020. Case Comment: Re D (A Child) [2019] UKSC 42. *Medical Law Review.*

Ruck Keene, A. & Friedman, M. 2021. Best interests, wishes and feelings and the Court of Protection: 2015–2020. *Journal of Elder Law and Capacity,* 31–54.

Ruck Keene, A., Bartlett, P. & Allen, N. 2016. Litigation friends or foes? Representation of 'P' before the Court of Protection. *Medical Law Review,* 24, 333–359.

Ruck Keene, A., Butler-Cole, V., Allen, N., Lee, A., Kohn, N., Scott, K., Barnes, K., Edwards, S. & David, S. 2019a. A brief guide to carrying out best interests assessments. *39 Essex Chambers Guidance Note.*

Ruck Keene, A., Kane, N.B., Kim, S.Y.H. & Owen, G.S. 2019b. Taking capacity seriously? Ten years of mental capacity disputes before England's Court of Protection. *International Journal of Law and Psychiatry,* 62, 56–76.

Saaltink, R., Mackinnon, G., Owen, F. & Tardif-Williams, C. 2012. Protection, participation and protection through participation: young people with intellectual disabilities and decision making in the family context. *Journal of Intellectual Disability Research,* 56, 1076–1086.

Samuel, M. 2012. Many deprived of liberty without safeguards, warn experts. *Community Care* [Online]. Available from: www.communitycare.co.uk/2012/02/29/many-deprived-of-liberty-without-safeguards-warn-experts/ [Accessed 1 March 2012].

Sandbank, M., Bottema-Beutel, K., Crowley, S., Cassidy, M., Dunham, K., Feldman, J.I., Crank, J., Albarran, S.A., Raj, S., Mahbub, P. & Woynaroski, T.G. 2020. Project AIM: autism intervention meta-analysis for studies of young children. *Psychological Bulletin,* 146, 1–29.

Sandland, R. 2013. Concubitu prohibere vago: sex and the idiot girl, 1846–1913. *Feminist Legal Studies,* 21, 81–108.

Saunders, P. 1989. The meaning of 'home' in contemporary English culture. *Housing Studies,* 4, 177–192.

Scott, D. 2004. *Conscripts of Modernity: the tragedy of colonial enlightenment,* Durham and London: Duke University Press.

Scottish Government 2016. Scottish Government consultation on the Scottish Law Commission report on adults with incapacity: summary of responses to consultation.

Scottish Government 2018. Adults with Incapacity (Scotland) Act 2000 Proposals for Reform.

Scottish Law Commission 2014. Report on adults with incapacity. *Scot Law Com No 240.* Edinburgh.

Scull, A.T. 1993. *The Most Solitary of Afflictions: madness and society in Britain, 1700–1900,* New Haven, CT: Yale University Press.

Scully, J.L. 2014. Disability and vulnerability: on bodies, dependence, and power. *In:* Mackenzie, C., Rogers, W. & Dodds, S. (eds) *Vulnerability: new essays in ethics and feminist philosophy.* Oxford: Oxford University Press.

Select Committee on Lunacy Law 1877. Select Committee to inquire into Operations of Lunacy Law, as regards Security against Violations of Personal Liberty. *HC 373.* London.

Select Committee on Lunacy Law 1878. Select Committee to inquire into Operations of Lunacy Law, as regards Security against Violations of Personal Liberty. *HC 113.* London.

Select Committee on Lunatics 1860. Report from the Select Committee on Lunatics; together with the proceedings of the committee, minutes of evidence, and appendix. *HC 495.*

Sen, A. 2010. *The Idea of Justice,* Cambridge, MA: Harvard University Press.

Senate Standing Committee on Legal and Constitutional Affairs 2019. Supplementary budget estimates 2019–20: Attorney General's Department: LCC-SBE19–141 – OPCAT – National Preventive Mechanism. Canberra, Australia.

Series, L. 2013. *The Mental Capacity Act 2005 and the Institutional Domination of People with Learning Disabilities.* University of Exeter.

Series, L. 2015a. Relationships, autonomy and legal capacity: mental capacity and support paradigms. *International Journal of Law and Psychiatry,* 40, 80–91.

Series, L. 2015b. The use of legal capacity legislation to control the sexuality of people with intellectual disabilities. *In:* Shakespeare, T. (ed.) *Disability Research Today: international perspectives.* London and New York: Routledge.

Series, L. 2016. The place of wishes and feelings in best interests decisions: Wye Valley NHS Trust v Mr B. *The Modern Law Review,* 79, 1101–1115.

Series, L. 2019. On detaining 300,000 people: The Liberty Protection Safeguards. *International Journal of Mental Health and Capacity Law,* 25.

Series, L. 2020. Making sense of *Cheshire West. In:* Spivakovsky, C., Steele, L. & Weller, P. (eds) *The Legacies of Institutionalisation: disability, law and policy in the 'deinstitutionalised' community.* Oxford: Hart.

Series, L. & Clements, L. 2013. Putting the cart before the horse: resource allocation systems and community care. *Journal of Social Welfare and Family Law,* 35, 207–226.

Series, L. & Nilsson, A. 2018. Article 12: equal recognition before the law. *In:* Bantekas, I., Stein, M. & Anastasiou, D. (eds) *Commentary on UN Convention on the Rights of Persons with Disabilities.* Oxford: Oxford University Press.

Series, L., Fennell, P. & Doughty, J. 2017a. The participation of P in welfare cases in the Court of Protection. *Report for the Nuffield Foundation, Cardiff University.*

Series, L., Fennell, P. & Doughty, J. 2017b. Welfare cases in the Court of Protection: a statistical overview. *Report for the Nuffield Foundation, Cardiff University.*

Shakespeare, T. 2000. *Help,* Birmingham: Venture Press.

Shearer, A. 1972. Conference report. *Campaign for Mental Health Our Life Conference.* Castle Priory College, Berkshire.

Sheridan Rains, L., Zenina, T., Dias, M.C., Jones, R., Jeffreys, S., Branthonne-Foster, S., Lloyd-Evans, B. & Johnson, S. 2019. Variations in patterns of involuntary hospitalisation and in legal frameworks: an international comparative study. *The Lancet Psychiatry,* 6, 403–417.

Shin, J.-H. 2014. Making home in the age of globalization: a comparative analysis of elderly homes in the U.S. and Korea. *Journal of Environmental Psychology,* 37, 80–93.

Sines, D., Hogard, E. & Ellis, R. 2012. Evaluating quality of life in adults with profound learning difficulties resettled from hospital to supported living in the community. *Journal of Intellectual Disabilities,* 16, 247–263.

Sir James Munby 2011. Dignity, happiness and human rights. *Elder Law Journal,* 1, 32–38.

Sir James Munby 2018. Despatches from the front line: some current problems. *Legal Action Group Community Care Law Conference.*

Sixsmith, A. & Sixsmith, J. 2008. Ageing in place in the United Kingdom. *Ageing International,* 32, 219–235.

Sixsmith, J. 1986. The meaning of home: an exploratory study of environmental experience. *Journal of Environmental Psychology,* 6, 281–298.

Skeet, M. 1986. Home from hospital: providing continuing care for elderly people. *King's Fund Centre for Health Services Development (King Edward's Hospital Fund for London), Continuing Care Project.*

Skills for Care 2020. The state of the adult social care sector and workforce in England.

Skowron, P. 2019. Giving substance to 'the best interpretation of will and preferences'. *International Journal of Law and Psychiatry,* 62, 125.

Smith, S.G. 1994. The essential qualities of a home. *Journal of Environmental Psychology,* 14, 31–46.

Spandler, H. 2006. *Asylum to Action: Paddington Hospital, therapeutic communities and beyond,* London and Philadelphia: Jessica Kingsley Publishers.

Spandler, H. & Poursanidou, D. 2019. Who is included in the Mad Studies project? *Journal of Ethics in Mental Health,* 10.

Spandler, H., Anderson, J. & Sapey, B. 2015. *Madness, Distress and the Politics of Disablement,* Bristol: Policy Press.

Spivakovsky, C. 2014. Making risk and dangerousness intelligible in intellectual disability. *Griffith Law Review,* 23, 389–404.

Spivakovsky, C. 2017. Governing freedom through risk: locating the group home in the archipelago of confinement and control. *Punishment & Society,* 19, 366.

Spivakovsky, C. & Steele, L.R. 2021. Disability law in a pandemic: the temporal folds of medico-legal violence. *Social & Legal Studies,* published online 10 June 2021, https://doi.org/10.1177/09646639211022795.

Spivakovsky, C., Steele, L. & Weller, P. (eds) 2020. *The Legacies of Institutionalisation: disability, law and policy in the 'deinstitutionalised' community,* Oxford: Hart.

Stark, S.W. 2019. Deprivations of liberty: beyond the paradigm. *Public Law,* 380–401.

Steel, H. 1991. Report of the working group on the principles for the protection of persons with mental illness and for the improvement of mental health care. *Report prepared for the United Nations Human Rights Commission and the Economic and Social Council, UN Doc E/CN.4/1991/39.*

Steele, L. 2017. Temporality, disability and institutional violence: revisiting In re F. *Griffith Law Review*, 26, 378–400.

Stevenson, C. 2017. Deprivation of Liberty and Intensive Care Units: The Queen (on the Application of Ferreira) v HM Senior Coroner for Inner South London and Others [2017] EWCA Civ 31. *Elder Law Journal*, 2017, 141–146.

Stone, K., Vicary, S. & Spencer-Lane, T. 2021. *The Approved Mental Health Professional Practice Handbook*, Bristol: Bristol University Press.

Stones, D. & Gullifer, J. 2016. 'At home it's just so much easier to be yourself': older adults' perceptions of ageing in place. *Ageing and Society*, 36, 449–481.

Strnadová, I., Johnson, K. & Walmsley, J. 2018. '… but if you're afraid of things, how are you meant to belong?' What belonging means to people with intellectual disabilities? *Journal of Applied Research in Intellectual Disabilities*, 31, 1091–1102.

Sumption, J. 2019. *Trials of the State: law and the decline of politics*, London: Profile Books.

Suzuki, A. 2006. *Madness at Home: the psychiatrist, the patient and the family in England, 1820 – 1860*, Berkeley: University of California Press.

Svanelöv, E. 2019. An observation study of power practices and participation in group homes for people with intellectual disability. *Disability & Society*, 35(9), 1419–1440.

Szasz, T. 1961. *The Myth of Mental Illness: foundations of a theory of personal conduct*, New York: Hoeber-Harper.

Szasz, T. 1971. American Association for the Abolition of Involuntary Mental Hospitalization. *American Journal of Psychiatry*, 127, 1698.

Szmukler, G. & Rose, N. 2013. Risk assessment in mental health care: values and costs. *Behavioral Sciences & the Law*, 31, 125–140.

Tanner, B., Tilse, C. & De Jonge, D. 2008. Restoring and sustaining home: the impact of home modifications on the meaning of home for older people. *Journal of Housing for the Elderly*, 22, 195–215.

Tarrant, A. 2019. *When resistance meets law and policy: disabled people and the independent living counter-narrative in Wales*. PhD, Cardiff University.

Tarrant, A. 2020. Personal budgets in adult social care: the fact and the fiction of the Care Act 2014. *Journal of Social Welfare and Family Law*, 42, 281–298.

Taylor, S.J. 2005. The institutions are dying, but are not dead. *In:* Johnson, K. & Traustadóttir, R. (eds) *Deinstitutionalization and People with Intellectual Disabilities: in and out of institutions.* London and Philadelphia: Jessica Kingsley Publishers.

The British Psychological Society 2013. Response to the American Psychiatric Association: DSM-5 Development. London.

The King's Fund 1979. The Danish experience. *Report of a conference on 20 March 1979 at the King's Fund Centre.*

The King's Fund 1980 [reprinted 1982]. An ordinary life: comprehensive locally-based residential services for mentally handicapped people. London: King's Fund Center.

The King's Fund 1986. Living Well into Old Age: applying principles of good practice to services for people with dementia. London: King's Fund Centre.

The King's Fund 2019. A short history of social care funding reform in England: 1997 to 2019 [Online]. Available from: www.kingsfund. org.uk/audio-video/short-history-social-care-funding [Accessed 9 November 2012].

The King's Fund, Age Concern & Institute of Gerontology King's College London 1986. The mentally frail elderly: should we prescribe care? *Proceedings of a conference held at The King's Fund Centre, London, on 25 May 1986.*

The Silent Minority 1981. Directed by Evans, N.: Associated Television for ITV.

The Union of the Physically Impaired against Segregation & The Disability Alliance 1976. Fundamental principles of disability. Reproduced for Leeds University Disability Studies Group Archives.

Thein, N.W., D'Souza, G. & Sheehan, B. 2011. Expectations and experience of moving to a care home: perceptions of older people with dementia. *Dementia,* 10, 7–18.

Then, S.-N. 2013. Evolution and innovation in guardianship laws: assisted decision-making. *Sydney Law Review,* 35, 132.

Tibullo, L., Esquinas, A.M., Vargas, M., Fabbo, A., Micillo, F., Parisi, A. & Vargas, N. 2018. Who gets to decide for the older patient with a limited decision-making capacity: a review of surrogacy laws in the European Union. *European Geriatric Medicine,* 9, 759–769.

Tipper, B. 2003. *'Home-Making': negotiating the 'meaning of home' in a residential home for people with learning difficulties.* MA in Social Research, University of Leeds.

Townsend, P. 1962. *The last refuge: a survey of residential institutions and homes for the aged in England and Wales,* London: Routledge and Kegan Paul.

Townshend, T. 1763. A Report From The Committee, Appointed (Upon the 27th Day of January, 1763) To Enquire into The State Of The Private Madhouses In This Kingdom. With The Proceedings of the House thereupon. House of Commons Select Committee Report: London.

Trägårdh, L. 2014. Statist individualism: the Swedish theory of love and its Lutheran imprint. *In:* Halldorf, J., Wenell, F. & Hauerwas, S. (eds) *Between the State and the Eucharist: Free Church Theology in conversation with William T. Cavanaugh.* Eugene, OR: Pickwick Publications.

Troke, B. 2012. The death of deprivation of liberty safeguards (DoLS)? *Social Care and Neurodisability,* 3, 56.

Tuke, D.H. 1882. *Chapters in the History of the Insane in the British Isles*, London: K. Paul (made available via the Internet Archive).

Tuke, S. 1813. *Description of the Retreat*, Wellcome Archive RET/1/6/1/1.

Twigg, J. 1999. The spatial ordering of care: public and private in bathing support at home. *Sociology of Health & Illness*, 21, 381–400.

Twigg, J. 2000. *Bathing – the Body and Community Care*, London: Routledge.

Undercover Care: The Abuse Exposed, 2011. Directed by Kenyon, P. UK: BBC.

Undercover Hospital Abuse Scandal, 2019. Directed by Plomin, J.: BBC.

Unsworth, C. 1987. *The Politics of Mental Health Legislation*, Oxford: Clarendon Press.

Unsworth, C. 1991. Mental disorder and the tutelary relationship: from pre- to post-carceral legal order. *Journal of Law and Society*, 18, 254–278.

Unsworth, C. 1993. Law and lunacy in psychiatry's 'Golden Age'. *Oxford Journal of Legal Studies*, 13, 479–507.

Urban, S. 1763. A Case humbly offered to the Consideration of Parliament. *Gentleman's Magazine*.

Valuing People Now team to be disbanded. *Learning Disability Today*, 07 March 2011.

Van Der Horst, H. 2004. Living in a reception centre: the search for home in an institutional setting. *Housing, Theory and Society*, 21, 36–46.

Veitch, K. 2007. *The Jurisdiction of Medical Law*, Aldershot: Ashgate.

Vihma, S. 2012. Artification for well-being: institutional living as a special case. *Contemporary Aesthetics*, 4, 13.

Vihma, S. 2013. Homelike design in care residences for elderly people. *In:* Hujala, A., Rassenen, S. & Vihma, S. (eds) *Designing Wellbeing in Elderly Care Homes.* Helsinki: Aalto University, School of Art and Design.

Vincent, N. 2010. *Voluntary Madness*, London: Vintage.

Voluntary Organisations Disability Group & Anthony Collins Solicitors 2011. When is a care home not a care home? London.

Wahl, J., Dykeman, M.J. & Gray, B. 2014. Healthcare consent and advance care planning in Ontario: legal capacity, decision-making and guardianship. Commissioned by the Law Commission of Ontario.

Walliams, D. 2015. *Grandpa's Great Escape*, London: Harper Collins.

Ward F13 1968. Directed by Nairn, C.: Grenada Television.

Ward, A. 2017. Legal protection of adults – an international comparison. *Elder Law Journal*, 7, 147–159.

Ware, N.C., Desjarlais, R.R., Avruskin, T.L., Breslau, J., Good, B.J. & Goldfinger, S.M. 1992. Empowerment and the transition to housing for homeless mentally ill people: an anthropological perspective. *New England Journal of Public Policy*, 8, 26.

Warren, S. & Giles, J. 2019. A practical guide to The Reach Standards. London: Paradigm.

Weller, P. 2019. OPCAT monitoring and the Convention on the Rights of Persons with Disabilities. *Australian Journal of Human Rights*, 25, 130–149.

Welsh Government 2011. Sustainable social services for Wales: a framework for action.

Welsh Government 2018. Learning disability: improving lives programme.

Welsh Government 2019. Statutory guidance for service providers and responsible individuals on meeting service standard regulations for: care home services; domiciliary support services; secure accommodation services; and residential family centre services.

Welsh Local Government Association 2019. Guidance: commissioning accommodation and support for a good life for people with a learning disability.

Welshman, J. & Walmsley, J. (eds) 2006. *Community Care in Perspective: care, control and citizenship*, Basingstoke and New York: Palgrave.

Wessely, S., Gilbert, S., Hedley, M. & Neuberger, J. 2018a. The independent review of the Mental Health Act: Interim report.

Wessely, S., Gilbert, S., Hedley, M. & Neuberger, J. 2018b. Modernising the Mental Health Act: increasing choice, reducing compulsion. *Final report of the Independent Review of the Mental Health Act 1983*.

Weston, J. 2020. Managing mental incapacity in the 20th century: a history of the Court of Protection of England & Wales. *International Journal of Law and Psychiatry*, 68, 101524.

Whitaker, D. 2014. Social justice for safeguarded adults deprived of their liberty in the United Kingdom? *Disability & Society*, 1–5.

White, M. 2019. The role and scope of OPCAT in protecting those deprived of liberty: a critical analysis of the New Zealand experience. *Australian Journal of Human Rights*, 25, 44–65.

Williams, M., Chesterman, J. & Laufer, R. 2014. Consent versus scrutiny: restricting liberties in post-Bournewood Victoria. *Journal of Law and Medicine*, 21, 641–660.

Williams, P. & Salamon, A. 1979. Make us citizens and see us grow. London: Campaign for the Mentally Handicapped.

Williams, V. & Robinson, C. 2001. More than one wavelength: identifying, understanding and resolving conflicts of interest between people with intellectual disabilities and their family carers. *Journal of Applied Research in Intellectual Disabilities*, 14, 30–46.

Wilson, K.E. 2019. The abolition or reform of mental health law: how should the law recognise and respond to the vulnerability of persons with mental impairment? *Medical Law Review*, 28, 30–64.

Wise, I. & Spurrier, M. 2014. A gilded cage is still a cage. *New Law Journal*, 164(7607) 7.

Wise, S. 2012. *Inconvenient People*, London: Random House.

Wittgenstein, L. 2001. *Philosophical Investigations*, Oxford: Blackwell Publishing.

Wolfensberger, W. 1983. Social role valorisation: a proposed new term for the principle of normalization. *Mental Retardation*, 21, 234–239.

Wolfensberger, W., Nirje, B., Olhansky, S., Perske, R. & Roos, P. 1972. *The Principle of Normalization in Human Services*, Toronto: National Institute on Mental Retardation.

Wood, A. & Greig, R. 2010. Supported living – making the move: developing supported living options for people with learning disabilities. *NDTi Housing and Social Inclusion Project Discussion Paper One*. Bath: National Development Team for Inclusion.

Wood, A., Greig, R., Strong, S. & Hall, C. 2010. The Real Tenancy Test – tenancy rights in supported living. *NDTI Housing and Social Inclusion Project Discussion Paper Two*. Bath: National Development Team for Inclusion.

Wootton, B. 1963. *Crime and the Criminal Law*, London: Stevens & Sons.

Working Group on Congregated Settings, Health Service Executive, 2011. Time to move on from congregated settings: a strategy for community inclusion. Dublin.

World Health Organization 2017. Mental Health Atlas.

World Health Organization & World Bank 2011. World Report on Disability.

Wormald, J. & Wormald, S.T. 1914. *A Guide to the Mental Deficiency Act, 1913*. London: P.S. King and Son.

Wright, D. 1996. 'Childlike in his innocence': lay attitudes to 'idiots' and 'imbeciles' in Victorian England. *In:* Wright, D. & Digby, A. (eds) *From Idiocy to Mental Deficiency: historical perspectives on people with learning disabilities.* London and New York: Routledge.

Wright, D. 1997. Getting out of the asylum: understanding the confinement of the insane in the nineteenth century. *Social History of Medicine*, 10, 137–155.

Wright, D. 1998. Familial care of 'idiot' children in Victorian England. *In:* Horden, P. & Smith, R. (eds) *The Locus of Care: families, communities, institutions, and the provision of welfare since antiquity*, London: Routledge.

Wright, D. 2001. *Mental Disability in Victorian England: The Earlswood Asylum 1847–1901*, Oxford: Oxford University Press.

Wright, D. & Digby, A. (eds) 1996. *From Idiocy to Mental Deficiency: historical perspectives on people with learning disabilities*, London and New York: Routledge.

Wright, K., Haycox, A. & Leedham, I. 1994. *Evaluating Community Care*, Buckingham: Open University Press.

Wyatt, S., Aldridge, S., Callaghan, D., Dyke, A. & Moulin, L. 2019. Exploring mental health inpatient capacity across sustainability and transformation partnerships in England. The Strategy Unit, for the Royal College of Psychiatrists.

Yang, C. 2013. Being independent from whom? Analysing two interpretations in the paradigm of 'independent living'. *Disability & Society*, 29, 671–684.

Yates, S., Dyson, S. & Hiles, D. 2008. Beyond normalization and impairment: theorizing subjectivity in learning difficulties – theory and practice. *Disability & Society,* 23, 247.

Yeates, V. 2007. Ambivalence, contradiction, and symbiosis: carers' and mental health users' rights. *Law & Policy,* 29, 435–459.

Yeo, R. 2020. The regressive power of labels of vulnerability affecting disabled asylum seekers in the UK. *Disability & Society,* 35, 676–681.

Index

References to figures appear in *italic* type.